How to access the supplemental online student resource

We are pleased to provide access to an online student resource that supplements *Dimensions of Leisure for Life.* This resource offers chapter overviews, research assignments, response assignments, vocabulary lists, glossary definitions, and Web links. We are certain you will enjoy this unique online learning experience.

Accessing the online student resource is easy! Follow these steps if you purchased a new book:

1. Using your web browser, go to **www.HumanKinetics.com/ DimensionsOfLeisureForLife**.

2. Click on the **View Student Resources** button on the right side of the home page.

3. Click on the please register now link. You will create your personal profile and password at this time.

4. Write your e-mail and password down for future reference. Keep it in a safe place. You'll use this e-mail address and password to access your profile any subsequent time you visit the Human Kinetics Web site. Logging into this profile will grant you access to the online student resource.

5. Once you are registered, enter the key code exactly as it is printed at the right, including all hyphens. Click **Submit**

6. Once the key code has been submitted, you will see a welcome screen. Click the **Continue** button to open your online student resource.

7. After you enter the key code the first time, you will not need to use it again to access the online student resource. In the future, simply log in using your e-mail and the password you created.

How to access the online student resource if you purchased a used book:

You may purchase access to the online student resource by visiting **www.HumanKinetics.com/DimensionsOfLeisureForLife** or by calling 1-800-747-4457 in the U.S.; 1-800-465-7301 in Canada; +44 (0) 113 255 5665 in Europe; 08 8372 0999 in Australia; or 0800 222 062 in New Zealand.

For technical support, send an e-mail to:
support@hkusa.com . . . . U.S. and international customers
info@hkcanada.com . . . . Canadian customers
academic@hkeurope.com . . . . European customers
keycodesupport@hkaustralia.com . . . . Australian customers

HUMAN KINETICS
The Information Leader in Physical Activity & Health

D/A: 05–10

KT-195-849

Product: Dimensions of Leisure for Life online student resource

Key code: HKDIMLL-RN2X8QG2-9780736096188

Human Kinetics

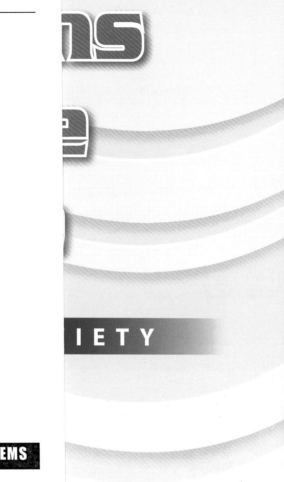

Library of Congress Cataloging-in-Publication Data

Dimensions of leisure for life : individuals and society / Human Kinetics, Inc.
  p. cm.
  Includes bibliographical references and index.
  1. Leisure. 2. Recreation.   I. Human Kinetics (Organization)
  GV14.D55 2010
  790.1--dc22

                                                        2010002430

ISBN-10: 0-7360-8288-3 (print)
ISBN-13: 978-0-7360-8288-4 (print)

The Web addresses cited in this text were current as of May 2010, unless otherwise noted.

Acquisitions Editor: Gayle Kassing, PhD; **Developmental Editors:** Bethany J. Bentley and Ray Vallese; **Assistant Editor:** Derek Campbell; **Copyeditor:** Julie Anderson; **Indexer:** Bobbi Swanson; **Permission Manager:** Dalene Reeder; **Graphic Designer:** Fred Starbird; **Graphic Artist:** Denise Lowry; **Cover Designer:** Bob Reuther; **Photo Asset Manager:** Laura Fitch; **Visual Production Assistant:** Joyce Brumfield; **Photo Production Manager:** Jason Allen; **Art Manager:** Kelly Hendren; **Associate Art Manager:** Alan L. Wilborn; **Illustrator:** Keri Evans; **Printer:** United Graphics

Printed in the United States of America   10 9 8 7 6 5 4 3 2 1

The paper in this book is certified under a sustainable forestry program.

Human Kinetics
Web site: www.HumanKinetics.com

United States: Human Kinetics, P.O. Box 5076, Champaign, IL 61825-5076
800-747-4457
e-mail: humank@hkusa.com

Canada: Human Kinetics, 475 Devonshire Road Unit 100, Windsor, ON N8Y 2L5
800-465-7301 (in Canada only)
e-mail: info@hkcanada.com

Europe: Human Kinetics, 107 Bradford Road, Stanningley, Leeds LS28 6AT, United Kingdom
+44 (0) 113 255 5665
e-mail: hk@hkeurope.com

Australia: Human Kinetics, 57A Price Avenue, Lower Mitcham, South Australia 5062
08 8372 0999
e-mail: info@hkaustralia.com

New Zealand: Human Kinetics, P.O. Box 80, Torrens Park, South Australia 5062
0800 222 062
e-mail: info@hknewzealand.com

E4448

Contents

Chapter **13** Leisure for All **271**

Chapter **14** Leisure and Geography **289**

Chapter **15** Leisure Through the Life Span **315**

Chapter **16** Charting Your Course. **335**

Preface

Leisure is everywhere in many forms. This book addresses the myriad of ways that leisure can be understood. Most people would rather "find" leisure than "define" it, but the more we understand the dimensions of leisure that contribute to our quality of life and that of our communities, the more likely we are to appreciate leisure.

Leisure is sometimes perceived as insignificant in the large scope of life. When you are asked to board an airplane "at your leisure," the suggestion is that it's mostly about relaxing. To some people, leisure means "doing nothing." On the other hand, leisure means doing a lot of things when we consider all the public, not-for-profit, commercial, and tourism industries around the world that provide many opportunities for leisure activities. Leisure can be serious and an integral part of our lives.

Several years ago a friend of mine was dying of cancer. She told me how fulfilling her life had been with her family and friends and the fun activities and vacations that had been shared. She never once mentioned that she wished she had worked harder or made more money. Assessing her life was about the many leisure connections that had existed. Therefore, although leisure is sometimes trivialized, it offers many opportunities for personal development, as you will see in this book.

This book is aimed toward young people—primarily college students who are taking a general elective class that focuses on an academic examination of leisure. Most of you have had a good deal of experience with leisure in your lives, from the time you were children, when daily "work" was playing, through adolescence, when you participated in structured activities like sports and music or informal opportunities such as interacting with the Internet and listening to music. Often leisure focuses on spending time with friends doing activities or just "hanging out." We all have a context for leisure. We know what we like and don't like and learn what we enjoy and do not enjoy. Sometimes people take leisure for granted, and that is not a negative thing. However, as people move beyond formal schooling, leisure sometimes becomes more elusive when full-time paid work and personal relationships take great amounts of time. Therefore, understanding more about the value of leisure and its many opportunities may be useful throughout people's lives.

Some people have described 18- to 24-year-olds as *emerging adults*. Many of you probably fit that age category. You have the opportunity to hang on to your youth while preparing for adulthood. Different cohorts of people go through this period of development in varying ways. Clearly your lives are different than those of your parents and certainly much different from the lives of your grandparents, when the instantaneous world of communication that you know did not exist. In some ways, the psychosocial elements of the benefits of play, recreation, and leisure remain the same, and yet as emerging adults you will find that many more opportunities are available. Although this book examines leisure through an academic approach, you can link the concepts presented here to your lives if you consider the personal as well as societal aspects of each concept.

The title of this book is *Dimensions of Leisure for Life: Individuals and Society*. Dimensions refer to the scope and importance of leisure for individuals as well as society. You can relate fairly easily to your personal take on leisure. However, the social impact of leisure, related to economics, health, and the environment, for example, is not as often considered.

The authors of this book explore many of these dimensions. A unique aspect of the notion of leisure is that it emanates from scholarly disciplines, as you will note in the chapters about geography, history, politics, health, economics, and the natural environment. The authors represent different areas of expertise related to these disciplines as they are applied to leisure. All these foundations together highlight how leisure can be viewed from multidisciplinary and interdisciplinary perspectives.

Many books about leisure were written in the 20th century, with most focusing on the past 40 years when predictions of a leisure society (which, by the way, has never come to fruition) emerged. Some of these books have focused on how recreation and leisure can improve the health and education of different populations. According to a noted leisure sociologist, Geoffrey Godbey, the focus early on was not necessarily on the intellectual aspects of leisure but rather on its moral importance. Another approach to leisure has focused on the social problem of dealing with free time in an industrializing world. This view largely examines leisure as juxtaposed to work as a social phenomenon. Leisure today cuts across both perspectives. Few other books have attempted to examine directly both the personal and social aspects of leisure.

This book is designed to lead you through the meanings of leisure, the vastness of the ideas, and the benefits as well as the negative implications of leisure. Not all leisure activities are good, and we hope this book will highlight the value of leisure as well as some of the concerns that leisure raises. For example, leisure that occurs in the outdoors can have negative environmental impacts. In addition to presenting academic content, the book includes a number of activities designed by the authors to help you experience leisure in different ways. Learning can be a leisure activity, although it is not always perceived in that way. We have tried to show the potential fun of learning experientially through and about leisure.

Part I examines the broad dimensions of leisure. Chapter 1 provides an overview of how leisure has been described as well as the benefits associated with it and an explanation of the broad field called "leisure industries." Chapter 2 illustrates how leisure can be studied as a social science.

Part II focuses on individuals and their lifestyles related to leisure. Chapter 3 explores how the individual dimensions of leisure affect the quality of people's lives. Chapter 4 examines how leisure is connected directly to individuals' health as well as to the health of the public. Chapter 5 looks at leisure's impact on well-being and how it contributes to many other facets of their lives.

Part III moves beyond an individual perspective to the implications of leisure for society. Chapter 6 explores the history of leisure over the centuries, providing a foundational context for understanding leisure today. Chapter 7 overviews the way leisure fits into contemporary society. Chapter 8 details specific ways that leisure and technology interface. Chapter 9 argues that leisure cannot be sustained if the environment is not considered. Because leisure is big business, the economics of leisure is addressed in chapter 10. Finally, leisure does not just naturally occur nor is it inherently good. Therefore, the interface between politics and public policy is presented in chapter 11.

Part IV focuses specifically on you as a consumer of leisure in all its dimensions. Campus and community leisure resources are described in chapter 12. Chapter 13 discusses the importance of leisure for all regardless of gender, race, socioeconomic status, or disability status. Chapter 14 examines the way that the geography of leisure plays into the experience of recreation spaces and places. Chapter 15 relates to life stages and leisure across the life span. The book concludes with chapter 16, which provides specific suggestions about how you can incorporate leisure into your life both today and into the future.

An online student resource (OSR) is also included with this book. Go to **www. HumanKinetics.com/DimensionsOfLeisureForLife** and click on View Student Resources to see supplemental materials for each chapter, such as the glossary list with and without definitions, chapter overviews, Web links, and research and response assignments.

For instructors, we have provided additional online resources, such as an instructor guide, test package, and presentation package. The instructor guide includes chapter overviews, extended learning activities, mini-case studies, and movie recommendations. The test package contains more than 290 questions, including multiple choice, true–false, and short answer. The Microsoft® PowerPoint® presentation package includes slides for each chapter, featuring some of the photos, illustrations, and tables that appear in the book.

We hope that after you read this book you will recognize that leisure is not a trivial matter. It can be examined from numerous perspectives. Making leisure scholarly does not take the enjoyment from it. The ideas of scholarship and enjoyment are not mutually exclusive. We hope that you will have some fun with this book, especially related to some of the activities that are suggested. We also hope that you recognize that leisure may be just as important to study as any other topic that prepares students for a career. One's well-being and quality of life are not trivial issues. Ironically, students spend years preparing for a career that may change a number of times during their lives. Yet, leisure education and quality of life issues are possibilities that last a lifetime. At the least, we hope some of the ideas in this book will help you understand further your own behavior and why leisure should be given its due in our society.

—Karla Henderson

Textbook Advisory Board

PART

I

Dimensions of Leisure

Importance of Leisure to Individuals and Society

Karla Henderson
North Carolina State University

Learning Outcomes

After reading this chapter, you will be able to

▶ identify the definition of leisure that is most meaningful for you,

▶ list at least five benefits of recreation and leisure,

▶ explain the relationship between quality of life and leisure,

▶ describe the differences among the three major sectors of the leisure industry, and

▶ discuss the constraints to leisure.

Vocabulary Terms

benefits	not-for-profit organizations	sports
commercial recreation	park	sport tourism
cyclical time	parks and natural resources	state of being or state of mind
enjoyment	place	
leisure	play	tourists
leisure education	quality of life	work
leisure industry	recreation	work ethic
linear time	space	

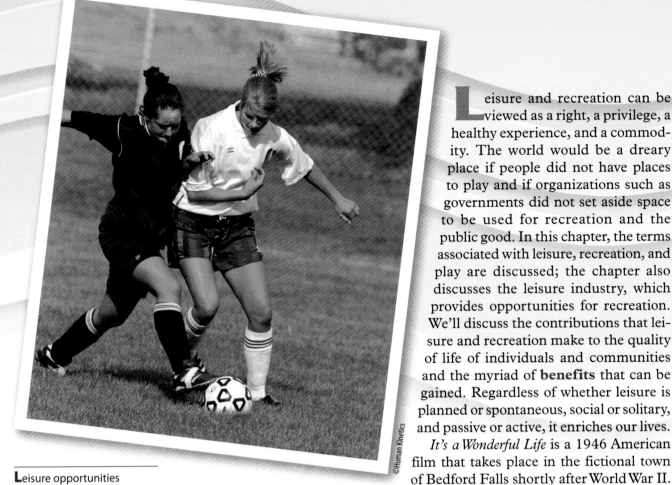
©Human Kinetics

Leisure opportunities abound throughout the world. Pick something you enjoy or have always wanted to try, and jump in!

Leisure and recreation can be viewed as a right, a privilege, a healthy experience, and a commodity. The world would be a dreary place if people did not have places to play and if organizations such as governments did not set aside space to be used for recreation and the public good. In this chapter, the terms associated with leisure, recreation, and play are discussed; the chapter also discusses the leisure industry, which provides opportunities for recreation. We'll discuss the contributions that leisure and recreation make to the quality of life of individuals and communities and the myriad of **benefits** that can be gained. Regardless of whether leisure is planned or spontaneous, social or solitary, and passive or active, it enriches our lives.

It's a Wonderful Life is a 1946 American film that takes place in the fictional town of Bedford Falls shortly after World War II. George Bailey is a businessman who has financial difficulties and considers suicide on Christmas Eve. A guardian angel is sent to help him and through a series of flashbacks shows George how many lives he has touched. By seeing what people's lives in his community would have been like without him, George realizes what a difference he has made. This story provides a way of thinking about what the world would be like without recreation and leisure. If opportunities for recreation and leisure did not exist, the world would be quite different, just as it would have been if George Bailey had never existed.

What would life be like if no one had leisure or free time? People would labor all day in the paid workforce. Stay-at-home moms would devote every waking second of their lives to house cleaning and taking care of children. Children would study and do chores at home, with no time to play. People would never retire from their jobs. College students would not be able to watch their favorite athletic events or attend concerts. Technology would be used strictly for work and not for social networking. Fitness equipment manufacturers would not exist, nor would movie theaters and sports complexes.

If people had free time but no recreation places or opportunities, their lives would be diminished. If no park, recreation, sport, arts, or outdoor opportunities existed in the United States, people would have no places to relax outside their homes. Children would have no playgrounds. Picnic areas would not be available. We would have no intramurals, no youth sports, and no baseball, softball, and other team leagues. Where would children learn to swim? Older adults would have no senior centers in which to congregate. Where would families go on vacation when they wanted an opportunity to see the natural wonders of the country? Private individuals with wealth would own the land and keep the general public out.

Musicians would have no place to play. Art would not be available to the public. People would become fatter and lazier because of fewer places to be active. Without recreation and leisure, our world would be a radically different place.

Fortunately, most people value their leisure and have access to a variety of recreation opportunities in their communities and throughout the United States. Many people take these opportunities for granted, but without them adults' and children's quality of life would be greatly diminished. The **leisure industry** is huge not only in the United States but throughout the world. Recreation, parks, tourism, sports, and other leisure opportunities are ubiquitous. However, the meanings of these opportunities and the values they provide require further exploration.

PERSONAL LEISURE

Think about what leisure opportunities you have had during the past month. Would you say you had too little, too much, or just the right amount of leisure time? What would you do if you had more time for leisure? Is having leisure a priority in your life? What are the priorities in your life?

What are your favorite things to do during your leisure? What are the primary leisure activities of your parents or grandparents? Are your preferred leisure activities like or unlike theirs? What would you say were the primary leisure activities of other students at your university during the past month? Are your leisure preferences like or unlike theirs?

DESCRIPTIONS AND DEFINITIONS

In a research study I once undertook, one of my interviewees announced that "finding leisure is much more important than defining leisure." That statement rings true. However, to understand leisure and its components, common understandings are needed through definitions. Note that *understandings* is plural because there is no single meaning of the terms associated with leisure and recreation. Recognizing the ways that scholars have used the words in research as well how these words have been described in daily lives may be useful. Such understandings allow researchers to measure phenomena such as the amount of free time people have or the economic value of an activity such as sport tourism and help us determine whether opportunities meet the expectations of participants. The following terms are discussed next to establish some common understandings: *leisure, recreation, parks and natural resources, tourism, commercial recreation, sports, play, work, space,* and *place.*

> To be able to fill leisure intelligently is the last product of civilization.
>
> *Arnold Toynbee (British economic historian and social reformer)*

Leisure

Leisure is probably the most nebulous of these ideas and has been subject to many interpretations related primarily to use of free time, participation in recreational activities, and state of mind. Leisure is often associated with social and cultural contexts of life as well. When some people think of leisure they think of "doing nothing," which in a work-oriented society

For many people, leisure activities double as a social experience.

puts leisure in a negative light. In my research, I ask women to tell me about their leisure. Often they reply that they have none, and yet they go on to describe the enjoyable times they have with friends or the super family vacation they had the previous summer. Leisure obviously is not understood in the same way by everyone nor can the concept be limited to a single definition.

As an experience interpreted by individuals within varied contexts, leisure during the 20th century has typically been discussed from three approaches: time, activity, and state of mind. In the postmodern 21st century, the approaches to and applications of leisure are expanding, as you will read about in all the chapters of this book.

Some individuals view leisure as a period of time they call free or unobligated time. Time exists as cyclical and linear. In **cyclical time**, people organize themselves around cycles or recurring events from the natural world, such as the year's seasons. **Linear time**, on the other hand, is ordered around specific beginning and ending points and is how time has been structured in the industrial and technological world. Linear time is given meaning by its applications, and thus people use calendars or PDAs to keep track of classes, tasks, and appointments. Leisure as free time emphasizes how time is used. Furthermore, defining leisure as free time defines leisure in terms of what it is not (i.e., leisure is not work) rather than what it is (i.e., an opportunity for something).

Some people see leisure as earned activities that generally occur outside paid or unpaid work activities. It's the idea that you probably heard as a child: "You can go out and play once your homework is done." The activities undertaken in leisure are generally associated with recreation and are pursued mainly for **enjoyment** or fun. **Recreation** activities can be categorized into groups that share important characteristics, such as competitive sports, cooperative games, outdoor endeavors, cultural pursuits, and socializing (Goodale & Godbey, 1988). Leisure described as recreational activity is usually measured by the distribution and frequency of participation in specific activities.

Other people conceive of leisure as an attitude, a psychological construction, or a state of being related to personal experiences. The amount of free time can be counted quantitatively as can the number of activities a person pursues. Psychological experiences or state of mind, however, have distinct qualitative connotations. For example, leisure as a state of mind connotes that it is freely chosen, not compulsory, and is done for its own sake (i.e., intrinsic motivation) and not as a means to another goal (i.e., extrinsic motivation). The concept of perceived freedom is among the best-known psychological conceptualizations of leisure. In this concept, leisure exists when people perceive themselves as freely choosing an activity that is simultaneously enjoyable and intrinsically motivated (Neulinger, 1981). Another psychological concept of leisure is optimal arousal (Ellis, 1973). In leisure, most people attempt to achieve balance and pleasant psychological states like the simple notion of enjoyment or having fun (Mannell & Kleiber, 1997). Leisure can also be characterized as a state of mind related to spiritual and psychological understandings. For example leisure has been described as "a mental and spiritual attitude" independent of time or work (Pieper, 1963, p. 40). Leisure might also elicit a sense of calm or silence, which many people find in wilderness experiences. Regardless, all definitions of leisure as a state of mind refer to relative freedom and enjoyment on some level.

Each of these three main definitions, however, raises issues. For example, free or unobligated time can be measured, but determining when you are at leisure is difficult. If you are on spring break but have nowhere to travel like your friends do, is that free time really leisure for you? You may have unobligated time between classes. Do you perceive that time as leisure? Defining leisure as certain types of activity also has problems. For example, I love to run and define jogging as a leisure activity. However, many people hate to run if it is just for exercise, so it is not a leisure activity for them. The definition of leisure as a psychological construct, a **state of being or state of mind**, is perhaps the most favored, but it has its drawbacks. Even when you're engaged in a recreation activity, you may feel guilty (e.g., because a huge project assignment is due and you are not working on it) or anxious about the future (e.g., worrying about that same assignment) and may never really experience leisure as a state of mind.

Although a slippery idea, leisure can come from any experience in which motives are more important than the activity itself or the time spent pursuing an activity. Thus, the experience of leisure generally includes relative freedom to choose what you want to do (e.g., running, reading a book, watching TV, taking a walk, updating your Facebook page). The idea of relative freedom is carefully used because any activity cannot be completely free—we all have obligations to our own well-being as well as the well-being of others. Nevertheless, leisure is undertaken because it is enjoyable and makes a person feel good physically and mentally. In other words, leisure experiences generally offer some element of satisfaction. Leisure experience may be more likely to occur during free time, but as a state of mind, leisure is not limited to a specific time or activity.

Recreation

The terms *leisure* and *recreation* are frequently used interchangeably, especially when leisure is defined as activity done for fun. Sometimes what people say they do for leisure is the same as they do for recreation. However, others do not view the words as synonymous. Recreation is undertaken because of conscious or unconscious end results. These ends might include benefits such as relaxation, stress relief, or creative expression. Recreation can also be viewed as a means to an end. For example, a person might take a walk to see the beauty of wildflowers. Generally, recreation is associated with activities that are voluntary, organized, socially redeeming, and fun and that occur during free time. Recreation generally involves participation in an activity, whether a physical activity such as basketball or hiking or a passive

©Wayne Bronson/fotolia

Recreation refers to the enjoyable activities that people do during their free time. Make the most of your free time by getting out there and doing something you love!

activity such as picnicking or seeing a movie. Recreation typically is considered beneficial to society as a whole and thus the U.S. government as well as state and local governments fund recreation opportunities in communities and in nature.

Recreation experiences usually include more than just one isolated activity. Researchers have called this notion a multiphasic experience (Stewart, 1998). On the simplest level you might anticipate or plan a recreation activity like going to the beach or attending a concert, participate in the actual activity, and then remember and reflect on some aspect of the experience, such as someone you met or a beautiful sunset.

Recreation activities are available to people in a variety of ways. Recreation is most often associated with parks and natural resources, tourism and commercial recreation, and sports. Recreation also occurs through cultural activities and performing arts, volunteer opportunities and community service, and numerous unstructured activities such as family gatherings, special interest clubs, and social networking.

Parks and natural resources refer to outdoor, nature-based opportunities for recreation activity. A **park** is typically defined as a natural or near-natural green or open space that is bounded in some way and has the purpose of natural resource conservation and preservation, human use, or both. Outdoor spaces for recreation include urban parks and greenways, state parks, and national areas such as national parks, national forests, Bureau of Land Management lands, and Army Corps of Engineers recreation areas.

Tourism is travel for mainly recreational or leisure purposes. **Tourists** are generally defined as people who travel to and stay in places outside their usual environment for the purpose of leisure rather than permanent residence or remuneration. **Commercial recreation** refers to market-driven, private-sector recreation activities for which a fee is charged by a profit-oriented enterprise. Many recreation opportunities fall into this category, such as country clubs, ski operations, restaurants, movie theaters, and health clubs.

Sports include a range of recreational and entertainment activities that involve rules, physical prowess, and contests between individuals or teams—generally with an uncertain outcome. However, the word *sport* is sometimes used to describe any type of competition regardless of physical prerequisites. Examples of these types of competition are NASCAR, poker, chess, or video games. Most people "play" sports, but sports can be work performed by professional athletes to entertain spectators during their leisure.

Play

Some people use the term **play** interchangeably with *recreation* or *leisure*. Play is usually associated more with children than with adults, although play is commonly used in a variety of contexts. Characteristics of play include spontaneity, purposelessness, and the creation of an imaginary world. Play is almost always pleasurable and self-expressive and can range from disorganized activity to structured involvement. Although play is usually associated with children, many adults like to be spontaneous and find a sense of play a refreshing break from structure of everyday living. Regardless, play refers to spontaneous and expressive activity done for its own sake with little obvious, direct extrinsic value. When play serves as a means to socialize children or to relieve stress, it certainly has instrumental value as well.

Theories of play have been proposed during the past 100 years. Before scientific research was conducted concerning play, people were assumed to play when the "spirit" moved them. However, play has been examined from several dimensions. A biological theory suggested that play was an innate need that must be met and was genetically required for survival. A Freudian analysis of play suggested that society legitimizes certain play behaviors as a way to deal with internal conflicts. For example, instead of attacking someone out of frustration, a person might kick or hit a ball. Developmental psychologists theorized that play was essential to defining the self and that a child, for example, might be socialized into society through play. Sociologists examined play as a way to maintain the values of society. Most discussions of play today blend these ideas and suggest that we need to play in order to function well and interact with our environment at an optimal level (Ellis, 1973). People express who they are and interact socially through play.

All sentient beings, including animals, children, and adults, have the propensity to play. Play is also a great mood lifter and stress reliever.

Work

For most people, the distinction between leisure, recreation, and play is seldom an issue. The greatest juxtaposition to these notions of free time and enjoyment is **work**. In contemporary Western society, people learn that work and leisure form distinct spheres in their lives, although not everyone works in traditional, economically productive ways. For example, volunteering in the community is usually called *volunteer work*, and raising children is typically seen as another form of unpaid work. Therefore, work should be defined as activity undertaken for economic gain or socially redeeming vitality.

Work can be classified as task oriented or time disciplined (Henderson et al., 2001). Task-oriented work is organized around features needed to perform particular tasks. Some tasks such as cleaning a room can be done either today or tomorrow. Although some consequences could occur in not doing the cleaning today, the task will still be there tomorrow. However, some tasks like completing an assignment for a class need to be completed or repercussions will occur. Task-oriented work can infringe upon one's time for leisure when tasks must be completed by a certain time. On the other hand, working hard and completing a task also mean that time is now available for leisure.

Time-disciplined work requires synchronizing the work of people who are performing different tasks. This work is usually scheduled and controlled. Workers must arrive at work at a certain time, work a set number of hours, take organized breaks, and leave work at a specific time. Work is not meant to occur outside those times.

For many people, work has greater meaning than just putting in one's time for a monetary reward. In other words, work can be more than a means to an end. Many people build their identities around work (e.g., being a nurse, a pilot, a social worker, a professor). Others have a great deal of social interaction during their work. Perhaps individuals could find the same meanings outside work, but work is a central aspect of what society believes people should do to be productive citizens. However, if the meaningfulness of work is uncertain and people only work because of the income and benefits (e.g., health insurance, retirement contributions), leisure may be a more important aspect of their lives.

For most people, the transition from childhood through adolescence to adulthood consists of increasingly structured preparation for an adult life of productive work, interrupted by intervals of leisure, and then a transition to a retirement ideally devoted to the cultivation of leisure. However, this pattern has numerous variations based on social and cultural patterns that are broadening our understanding of what leisure means.

Emerging Notions About Leisure

The three typical perspectives of leisure—time, activity, state of mind—focus primarily on individuals and how they experience leisure. Leisure, however, is greatly influenced by circumstances outside individuals. Our social situation and demographic characteristics, our community and natural environment, and the regulations and policies of our government affect how we encounter and make meaning in leisure. One area that has received increased attention is the physical environment—the places and spaces that define leisure opportunities.

Space and **place** have been defined many ways. One theory is that space has absolute and relative dimensions with concrete boundaries (Tuan, 1977). Thus, a recreation center or a public park is a space. Place, however, is perceptually and socially produced by individuals. Therefore, spaces become places when they mean something significant. As a space, your university is a piece of land with buildings. As a place, your university is filled with many associations and memories. A sense of place is associated with an emotional and affective bond between a person and a particular space and may vary in intensity from immediate sensory awareness to long-lasting, deeply rooted attachment (Williams et al., 1992). The physical amenity may be less important, however, than the meanings that people attach to places where they experience leisure. For example, places can promote leisure whether referring to a neighborhood coffee shop or a mountain campground. Frequently, these leisure places are also associated with other people.

Leisure is part of society and encompasses a major social cultural context in addition to individualized descriptions. Individual preferences are not independent of social and cultural influences (Henderson et al., 2001). A cultural context includes an integrated view of leisure that occurs in time and space with social connotations. People often choose activities based on their previous social experiences, such as socialization from family, as well as what others around them are doing. For example, if everyone in your college fraternity is going to Cancun for spring break, you might be more likely to go. If you live in a small town where everyone goes to the high school football game on Friday night, you might go as well. Leisure is never free from social norms. Leisure time and space are continually made and remade by the actions of people in their social worlds (Rojek, 1989).

Several leisure researchers have examined the cultural issues that surround typical Western concepts of leisure. Some believe that leisure is problematic from a global, and particularly linguistic, perspective (Iwasaki et al., 2007) and recommend that the term *leisure* not be used in research, particularly that involving people from non-Western cultures. Leisure is differently defined by various cultures and is an ethnocentric term used mostly in North American and European linear thinking. Some researchers believe that the term *leisure* has been thrust on non-Western cultures such as Asian, Latino, and aboriginal people. Perhaps a life story or folk knowledge approach should be used to understand the meanings of leisure in all cultures. For example, stories about one's life may elucidate more about what leisure means than asking people to categorize their activities as leisure or not. For people from some cultures, telling stories illustrates the value of their experiences better than talking about the amount of free time or recreation activities they have. Not using the term *leisure* may be one way to resolve some misunderstandings. However, not having a term may also make discourse and other interpretations of what leisure means difficult. The points mentioned here highlight that leisure should be considered within a cultural context. For many people, the essence of leisure

PERSONAL LEISURE

Given what you've read so far in this chapter, think further about what leisure means to you. Which definition of leisure makes the most sense to you? If you had to choose between having more leisure time or more money, which would you choose? Do you have more or less leisure than adults you know, such as your parents? Do you have more or less leisure than your classmates and friends? What type of career do you hope to have? How will it allow, or not allow, opportunities for leisure? If your friends were to describe your leisure life, what would they say about you?

lies in the relationships and identities that surround any meaningful undertaking, aside from paid work, in their lives. The relative freedom that people expect in their leisure and the potential for enjoyment exist in all cultural contexts.

WHY ARE LEISURE AND RECREATION IMPORTANT?

Several years ago the National Recreation and Park Association, which is the largest citizen and professional organization in the United States that advocates for the value of recreation, launched a campaign called "Recreation, The Benefits Are Endless." This campaign aimed to show the importance of recreation by describing benefits associated with individuals, communities and their sociocultural context, the environment, and the economy. One of the buzz words to describe the value of leisure is *quality of life*.

Quality of life can be defined as the degree to which a person enjoys the important possibilities of life (Global Development Research Center, n.d.). These possibilities reflect the interaction of personal and environmental factors. Enjoyment includes feeling satisfied and achieving something important. The three major life domains associated with quality of life are being, belonging, and becoming. *Being* addresses "who you are" and includes physical aspects such as health, nutrition, exercise, and appearance; psychological aspects related to adjustment and cognition; and spiritual aspects including standards of conduct and personal values. *Belonging* addresses a person's fit or physical belonging in an environment, such as at home, in the workplace, or at school. Social belonging includes acceptance by intimate others, work colleagues, fellow students, friends, and neighbors. Community belonging connotes access to resources such as adequate income, health services, employment, education and recreation services, and community activities. *Becoming* refers to purposeful activities concerning practical day-to-day actions such as paid work or volunteer activities; leisure, including activities for relaxation and stress reduction; and growth opportunities that improve or maintain knowledge and skills. As evident from these examples, recreation and leisure opportunities are central components of quality of life. They are certainly not the only components, but they are integral to creating quality of life. The ways that leisure and recreation contribute to this quality of life, however, are not always evident to people until they stop to consider the benefits that leisure and recreation offer. Or, as in the case of George Bailey in the movie described at the beginning of this chapter, the benefits are missed if opportunities are no longer available.

Individual Perspectives

Imagine that you have just finished a leisure activity, such as walking on a trail, making a gift for a family member, or attending a concert. The satisfaction and exhilaration that result are part of the leisure experience. The value of a leisure or recreation experience is connected to its meanings and motives. Recreation and leisure experiences can be planned or spontaneous, social or solitary, and passive or active. These multiple opportunities within the recreation experience mean that the benefits of the experience are endless.

Some of the common benefits of leisure are physiological (physical) health, psychological (mental) health, and a combination of these (referred to as psychophysiological health) (Driver et al., 1991). The physiological benefits of recreation

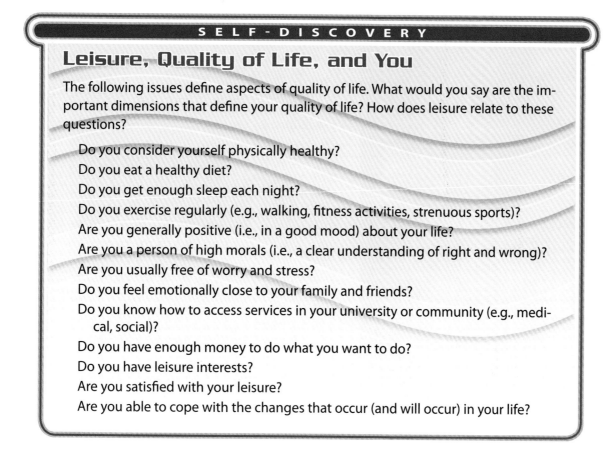

Leisure, Quality of Life, and You

The following issues define aspects of quality of life. What would you say are the important dimensions that define your quality of life? How does leisure relate to these questions?

Do you consider yourself physically healthy?

Do you eat a healthy diet?

Do you get enough sleep each night?

Do you exercise regularly (e.g., walking, fitness activities, strenuous sports)?

Are you generally positive (i.e., in a good mood) about your life?

Are you a person of high morals (i.e., a clear understanding of right and wrong)?

Are you usually free of worry and stress?

Do you feel emotionally close to your family and friends?

Do you know how to access services in your university or community (e.g., medical, social)?

Do you have enough money to do what you want to do?

Do you have leisure interests?

Are you satisfied with your leisure?

Are you able to cope with the changes that occur (and will occur) in your life?

are usually embodied in regular exercise and physical activity that often occur in free time. This idea has been referred to as "physical activity by choice" (Henderson & Bialeschki, 2005). Many of the benefits of physical activity have been documented scientifically. For example, regular physical activity reduces our risk for heart attack, colon cancer, diabetes, and high blood pressure and may reduce the risk for stroke. Regular physical activity helps us control our weight; contributes to healthy bones, muscles, and joints; reduces falls among older adults; helps to relieve the pain of arthritis; and is associated with fewer hospitalizations, physician visits, and medications. Moreover, physical activity need not be strenuous to be beneficial. For example, new guidelines from the U.S. government suggest that adults of all ages need to do two types of physical activity each week to improve health: 2 hours and 30 minutes (150 minutes) of (a) moderate-intensity aerobic activity such as brisk walking every week and (b) muscle-strengthening activities on 2 or more days a week that work all major muscle groups including legs, hips, back, abdomen, chest, shoulders, and arms (Centers for Disease Control and Prevention, 2008). Given the amount of scientific evidence about how leisure-time physical activity contributes to health, many leisure activities have great potential to contribute to our quality of life.

Many of the physiological benefits of leisure activities reduce our feelings of stress. Leisure can result in mental and physical relaxation and improve mood. Researchers have found that adolescents who participate in a broad range of physical activities are less likely to engage in risky behaviors and more likely to have positive health outcomes, like higher self-esteem (Nelson & Gordon-Larsen, 2006). In addition, the more time children spend outdoors, the more likely they

A recreation experience includes anticipating the activity, doing the activity, and recalling the memories. Scrapbooking and journaling are popular ways to preserve those good times.

©Andreas Rodriquez/fotolia

are to be active (Baranowksi & Puhl, 1993). The presence of trees and grass is related to greater use of outdoor spaces and the amount of social activity in those areas (Sullivan et al., 2004). Research on recreational activities shows that savanna-like settings are associated with self-reported feelings of peacefulness, tranquility, or relaxation (Frumkin, 2001). Other psychological benefits of leisure are enhanced self-competence, improved sense of self-worth, enhanced self-identity, and a better ability to relate to others.

Broader Social Benefits

Recreation provides benefits beyond those focused on individuals. For example, communities that provide activities and accommodations for tourists receive an economic benefit as a result of recreation. The economic impact of travel, particularly emerging activities like sport tourism, can be huge. Leisure and recreation may make us healthier and less likely to miss work because of illness, which benefits the economy.

Recreation and leisure can benefit the environment and our communities. Environmental protection has been an outgrowth of a commitment to saving outdoor recreation resources. Parks and recreation play a role in preserving green space and the biological diversity of areas. Communities benefit from recreation or leisure when people develop pride in their community—for example, when we celebrate an ethnic heritage through a recreation opportunity such as an ethnic festival.

The benefits we have discussed are sometimes difficult to measure. The value of recreation and leisure often lies in how they *prevent* problems like obesity, community decay, and environmental destruction. Prevention, however, is not easily measured. For example, it would be unethical to teach half the children in a community to swim and not the other half and then count over the years how many people drown and compare who had lessons and who did not. This case is extreme, but the point is that calculating the direct value of leisure in terms of statistics takes a long time and is not easy. Nevertheless, many agencies, organizations, and businesses promote and facilitate leisure experiences on the theory that they provide benefits.

THE UBIQUITOUS LEISURE INDUSTRY

Although leisure and recreation can occur without any equipment, programs, services, facilities, or spaces, most people at leisure use these elements, which comprise the leisure industry. The idea of an industry that includes many activity providers has its roots at the beginning of the 20th century. At that time, leisure was becoming a commodity that people wanted, and entrepreneurs recognized that they could make money by providing leisure activities. Concerns also were voiced that leisure time could become a problem if people did not use it wisely (Brightbill, 1960). Thus the leisure industry emerged, consisting of public and private enterprises that sought to provide positive structured and planned leisure opportunities to ensure that people used their leisure time appropriately and to create a positive economic impact. Citizens began to recognize that the positive outcomes of leisure could best be achieved by providing structured leisure opportunities for individuals, families, and communities. The most obvious way to promote positive use of leisure time was to provide and promote activities that could be experienced, bought, and consumed. Leisure came to be seen as a right, a privilege, a healthy experience, and a commodity.

The leisure industries that evolved in industrialized countries in the 20th century were based on the idea that people's demand for leisure creates a supply of opportunities. Similarly, a supply of activities requires that demand be created. Thus, many private, public, sports-oriented, and tourism-based opportunities, referred to as leisure industries or sectors, were initiated for people seeking ways to consume, experience, and enjoy leisure.

The leisure industry consists of three primary sectors: public or governmental agencies; not-for-profit private or nongovernmental organizations; and commercial, private, for-profit sectors. Each has a somewhat unique mission but all provide leisure experiences through sports, recreation, arts, the outdoors, and tourism opportunities. These sectors generally differ in their philosophies, objectives, facilities, financing, and membership.

Public Recreation

Public leisure agencies are governmentally supported and theoretically are available to all citizens of a community, state, region, or nation. Public recreation and the involvement of governments in leisure services stem from a concern for citizens'

Photo courtesy of Lollapalooza/Dave Mead

Festivals and concerts are a growing part of the leisure industry. Cheering for your favorite band with a huge crowd is a great way to blow off steam for a few hours . . . or days.

health and welfare and the wise use of natural resources. Democratic governments generally assume some responsibility for providing a quality of life for all citizens, and public spaces and recreation opportunities are part of that obligation.

Two primary functions are evident in the provision of leisure opportunities from a public governmental perspective (Henderson et al., 2001). The first is management of land and natural resources typically by providing opportunities for outdoor recreation while at the same time ensuring that the resources are not exploited. National and state governments have focused primarily on resource-oriented outdoor recreation, whereas local governments have provided both resources and opportunities for leisure activity.

The second function of public leisure providers is to deliver services in the form of activity instruction, competition, special events, and performances for community residents. This role is changing to brokering or facilitating recreation opportunities rather than directly providing services because so many more opportunities in the not-for-profit and private sectors now exist in many areas.

©Human Kinetics

Volunteering is an aspect of leisure that benefits not only the volunteers but also the organizations that receive the volunteer efforts. The local YMCA is a great place to volunteer.

Not-for-Profit Organizations

Not-for-profit organizations are sometimes called nonprofit, voluntary, third sector, independent sector, or nongovernmental organizations and are voluntary associations that usually focus on a particular issue, activity, or population. Not-for-profit organizations are limited in their scope based on the mission of the particular organization. The YMCA is one such example; its motto is "We build strong kids, strong families, strong communities." The YMCA mission is accomplished by a variety of recreation activities such as fitness instruction and facilities, outdoor education and camping opportunities, social clubs, child care, family nights, support groups, and volunteering. Most local YMCA organizations receive support in a number of ways including membership fees, donations, grants, fund-raising endeavors, and sometimes limited governmental backing.

The not-for-profit sector is important for many reasons (Salamon, 1999). Local groups often identify needs within their communities before governments can react. These organizations address community needs by offering membership (e.g., YMCA, Girl Scouts/Girl Guides, sports leagues) or by providing service or advocacy (e.g., environmental groups such as the Sierra Club, health-related organizations such as the Muscular Dystrophy Association, or religious groups). Some nongovernmental organizations operate solely to provide recreation, sport, and leisure opportunities. Other not-for-profit groups exist for many reasons, among which are providing leisure and recreation as a means to address other goals.

Although religious organizations are not necessarily associated with nongovernmental organizations, they are more like this sector than the other sectors. I would be remiss not to acknowledge the contributions that religious organizations such as churches, synagogues, mosques, and temples make to leisure by offering activities such as sports leagues, youth camps, and retreat centers. Regardless of an organization's purpose, many organizations use recreation to get people involved with one another, often for a specific cause.

Private Businesses

Private commercial organizations are aimed at satisfying, and often creating, a demand for recreation services and are focused on appealing to participants (customers) who purchase a product or service. Private leisure industries may be the fastest-growing sector in the leisure industry because of the commodification of leisure and the market-driven nature of the world's economy. New markets, services, and products appear almost daily. The consumption of goods and services in the United States includes a number of private recreation opportunities.

The structures of these private commercial organizations vary from small industries such as a souvenir shop run by a single owner to multinational corporations like hotel chains or amusement parks. Five service domains within the private recreation sector have been described (Bullaro & Edginton, 1986).

- Entertainment services (e.g., bowling alleys, circuses, rodeos, water parks)
- Natural resource–based services (e.g., campgrounds, marinas, ski resorts, wildlife parks)
- Retail outlets (e.g., shopping malls, dance studios, golf courses, fitness clubs)
- Hospitality and food services (e.g., hotels, resorts, convention centers)
- Travel and tourism services (e.g., tour promoters, travel agencies)

The private sector of the leisure industry is huge. These businesses provide many opportunities for investment and profit making for entrepreneurs. Because of the competitive nature of this sector, these industries are always focused on improving their services to attract participants. Satisfied customers will return to leisure experiences they have enjoyed and will tell their friends about good leisure experiences. The more positive experiences that people have, the more they are likely to seek (i.e., buy) those experiences in the future. Tourism and sports, in particular, have gained popularity in the past 50 years.

Tourism and Sport Industries

Various opportunities for tourism as well as sports occur across all sectors. Although travel for trade and religious purposes dates to ancient times, tourism is a relatively recent idea. Tourism is an outgrowth of people's desire to relax, to have new and different experiences away from their daily routines, to visit other environments, and to learn about other cultures. Not all tourism possibilities come from the private sector, but the number of such opportunities continues to grow.

Leisure Activities in the United States in 2008

- On an average day, nearly everyone age 15 and over (96 percent) engaged in some sort of leisure activity, such as watching TV, socializing, or exercising. Of those who engaged in leisure activities, men spent more time in these activities (5.7 hours) than did women (5.1 hours).

- Watching TV was the leisure activity that occupied the most time, accounting for about half of leisure time, on average, for both men and women. Socializing, such as visiting with friends or attending or hosting social events, was the next most common leisure activity, accounting for about three quarters of an hour per day for both sexes.

- Men were more likely than women to participate in sports, exercise, or recreation on any given day, 21 versus 15 percent. On the days that they participated, men also spent more time in these activities than did women, 1.9 versus 1.3 hours.

- On an average day, adults age 75 and over spent 7.6 hours engaged in leisure activities—more than any other age group; 25- to 44-year-olds spent just over 4 hours engaged in leisure and sports activities—less than other age groups.

- Time spent reading for personal interest and playing games or using a computer for leisure varied greatly by age. Individuals age 75 and over averaged 1.2 hours of reading per weekend day and 0.3 hours (17 minutes) playing games or using a computer for leisure. Conversely, 15- to 19-year-olds read for an average of 0.2 hours (10 minutes) per weekend day while spending 1.0 hour playing games or using a computer for leisure.

- Employed adults living in households with no children under 18 engaged in leisure activities 4.5 hours per day, nearly an hour more than employed adults living with a child under age 6.

Source: www.bls.gov/news.release/atus.nr0.htm

The tourism industry faces challenges for the future. One is the influence of tourism on the destination's social system and culture. Although tourism can be a huge boost to economically depressed areas, it also carries issues related to pollution, infrastructure costs, social problems, and potential seasonal unemployment. Tourism also can have a negative impact on the environment. If the environment degrades, many forms of tourism change. Sustainable tourism is an aspect that moves from a strictly socioeconomic focus toward preserving resources for the future (Fennell, 1999). Sustainable tourism means not consuming natural resources at a higher rate than they can be replaced. Ecotourism is a related area that connects tourism to the environment. Despite the potential drawbacks, however, tourism is increasing in popularity globally. Sustainable tourism can be maximized when all leisure industries work together to provide quality recreation opportunities.

Another area that often cuts across all sectors is sports. Sports can be provided by public recreation agencies (e.g., city recreation leagues), nongovernmental organizations (e.g., soccer leagues), or for-profit companies (e.g., private sports facilities that charge admission fees to spectators). Sports can range from international sporting events such as the Olympics to local sporting events like high school football games. Sports offer a means for participation as well as a venue for spectators.

Sport tourism is a fast-growing area within the leisure industry. Many people travel to watch or participate in athletic events in nearby communities as well as around the world (e.g., Olympics). Sports are an increasingly popular tourism product that can take place in urban or nonurban settings, indoors or outdoors, in all types of climatic conditions, and in all seasons (Kurtzman & Zauhar, 2003). People have engaged in sport-related travel for centuries (Gibson, 1998) in three primary domains of sport tourism: active sport tourism, whereby people travel to participate in a sport; event sport tourism, whereby people travel to watch a sport; and nostalgic sport tourism, in which people visit sports museums and famous sports venues and take part in sports-themed cruises. In the past 20 years, sport tourism popularity has increased dramatically. Sport tourism can contribute to economic development, positive image and identity, and tourism promotion and marketing.

Sports comprise a big leisure business whether done for recreation in local communities or for spectators in college, national, or international competitions.

©AP Photo/Nam Y. Huh

VALUE OF LEISURE

With the myriad of benefits of leisure and the plethora of opportunities within the leisure industries, leisure seems like it should be a top priority for all individuals and communities. However, some people do not see the value of leisure, and many people do not believe they have enough opportunities for recreation. A number of explanations can be considered, including the domination of the work ethic and trivialization of enjoyment, perceptions of work and time, technology, and the invisibility of leisure education.

The **work ethic** is still alive and well in society. People are more likely to be valued for what they "do," which usually includes gainful employment. Some of these work ideas are shaped by lingering puritanism and the traditional way work has been valued over leisure, especially in the United States. Leisure is often not considered a legitimate topic of study at the university level, which also connotes that it is not important. Much of what students study in universities relates directly to career development and not necessarily life satisfaction. The reality is that many people define themselves not by their work but by their personal relationships, like being a spouse or friend, and by what they commit themselves to and enjoy doing outside the workplace, such as church work, sports fandom, or walking in the woods.

Related to this work ethic is the devaluing of enjoyment. Based on the definitions already discussed, leisure is signified by the relative freedom to choose what you enjoy. Few opportunities are available in life for the purpose of having fun or finding enjoyment. People need to laugh, to be creative, to be passionate about living. Leisure and recreation provide those intangible intrinsic opportunities, but they sometimes get lost in the busy task- and goal-oriented lives most people live. What greater feeling is there than to be happy because of involvement in enjoyable personal activities and social relationships?

Given perceptions of use of time and its relationship to work, many people think they have limited leisure. Time, interestingly, is the most equally distributed resource. Everyone has 24 hours a day—no more and no less. How much time people perceive they have for leisure may be where the differences lie (Robinson & Godbey, 1999). Although average paid work hours have remained fairly constant in terms of the standard 40-hour work week, many Americans have increased the number of hours they work annually (Henderson et al., 2001).

©Photodisc

A key aspect of any opportunity that might be perceived as leisure is the intrinsic aspect of enjoyment. Sometimes just hanging out with friends is the best way to spend your free time.

Work hour trends, however, are not uniform throughout society. For example, women's annual work hours have increased while men's have decreased. Many women now participate in the paid workforce, but their responsibilities for unpaid work such as housework and child care have decreased little over the years, a situation that has been called "the second shift" (Hochschild, 1989). Furthermore, people with higher levels of education work more hours on average than people with less education.

Working many hours per week is the norm in some occupations. For example, professionals and managers are usually expected to work more hours than other workers, even though working more does not necessarily mean increased earnings. In some occupations people are well rewarded for their long work hours, whereas most other workers must increase their work hours simply to hold on to their present lifestyles. As people work longer hours, whether in paid or unpaid work and whether they earn more or not, they surrender more of their time. Most people want leisure time, but often it feels like a scarce resource.

Ironically, technology compromises people's perceptions about leisure. Although various forms of technology liberate people from some of the drudgery of work, technology is often expected to save time so that more work can be done. Furthermore, various uses of technology can constitute leisure, such as electronic game playing and computer-based social networking. Using technology, however, can also mean that individuals spend less time in non-technology-related activities, such as physically active recreation. The best seller *Bowling Alone* suggested that people are becoming more socially isolated even in recreation (Putnam, 2000). For example, people continue to watch a great deal of television, but that activity is not always considered leisure. Although people freely choose to watch television, some individuals do not perceive it as leisure because they do not know of other possible choices even if they have 300 channels to select. Television can be entertaining, but for some people it may not be satisfying. Thus, they crave more in their leisure than technology can provide.

People's perceptions that they don't have enough leisure may be due to their lack of skills in using their free time. **Leisure education** has not found great enthusiasm in society. Furthermore, some people think of leisure education as an oxymoron—the two words seem contradictory. Nevertheless, leisure education could be a way to contribute to better living for all. The World Leisure Organization (2005) defined the main aim of leisure education as helping individuals, families, communities, and societies to achieve a suitable quality of life and good health by using leisure time intelligently and by developing and cultivating physical, emotional, spiritual, mental, and social aspects related to the aims of education in the country and its cultural heritage. Therefore, helping children, youth, and adults make the right choices during leisure is critical to their enjoyment as well as for maintaining social civilities. In addition, leisure education may have the potential to help mitigate social problems. Perhaps if individuals were aware of and had access to interesting leisure options, they might not smoke or drink as much, or crime levels might decrease.

Another way to think about education for leisure is contextually. Recreation and leisure are learned experiences (Godbey, 1989). Some forms of leisure involve skills whereas others do not. People generally prefer doing leisure activities in which they feel competent. Thus, learning specific skills cannot be disassociated from appreciation and enjoyment in experiences. The context of leisure education certainly has connections to "active learning" and "experiential education" that contribute to quality of life.

SUMMARY

It is a wonderful life when leisure is meaningful to individuals and available in communities. A world without leisure and recreation opportunities would be a very dreary place. Leisure is important, and this book addresses many dimensions of leisure and quality of life. Several key ideas can frame our thoughts about leisure.

First, leisure is a part of life; it extends from the play of children to activities that help us age well. The basis of support for leisure opportunities is the theory that leisure can be a creative and constructive force in the lives of individuals, social groups, communities, and the global society.

Second, leisure is culturally situated; it involves individual and collective manifestations that vary from country to country as well as within the diversity of a single country. Therefore, all understanding about leisure is evolving and contextual. An intriguing aspect of leisure is that it has various meanings that are important to all people at some level. We hope this book helps you to explore what is important and enjoyable to you.

Third, opportunities for leisure are numerous. However, action is needed by individuals as well as policy makers to communicate the personal, economic, social, and environmental potential of leisure and to ensure that people have a variety of opportunities for expression of leisure.

Learning Activities

1. **20 things I love to do:** List 20 activities you enjoy. You do not need to share the list with anyone, so be honest. Next, go through your list and mark the items as follows:

   - Social Interaction—Mark each activity as *A* (an activity done alone), *P* (an activity done with people), and *AP* (an activity that can be done alone or with people).
   - Cost—Put a dollar symbol ($) by any activity that you have to pay for every time it is done.
   - Activity Level—Write *PA* for every activity that is physically active (e.g., jogging) and *RE* for every activity that is relaxing or passive (e.g., watching television).
   - Planning Level—Place *PL* for an activity that requires some amount of planning and *SP* for an activity that is spontaneous.
   - Time Duration—Write the number of minutes that you usually spend when you do this activity. For example, walking the dog might be 20 minutes or watching TV might be 3 hours (180 minutes).
   - Time Passage—Indicate the last time you did this activity with *Y* (yesterday), *PW* (during the past week), *PM* (during the past month), *PY* (during the past year), or *MY* (many years ago).
   - Work or Leisure—Mark each item as *W* (you consider the activity work) or *L* (you consider the activity to be leisure).

   Do you see any patterns in what you do? What did you learn about yourself and your leisure?

2. **Leisure candidates:** Answer yes or no to the following questions:

   - Do you feel continually rushed and pressed for time?
   - Has it been a while since you did anything fun or had time for relaxation?
   - Has it been a while since you had time for relaxation?
   - Are you neglecting your health in any way?
   - Do you feel dissatisfied or discontent with the past semester?
   - Is there a relationship in your life that needs attention?
   - Are you studying more and enjoying it less?
   - Do you believe something is missing in your life?

If you answered yes to any of these questions, you are a candidate for more leisure and you might think about how leisure and recreation could benefit you.

3. **Living leisurely:** Some people would like to live a more leisurely life. A leisurely life is not the same as a life of leisure. The following six points describe possible components of a leisurely life. Identify which of the following, if any, you would like to make a part of your leisurely life. After you have identified something that might be important, think about one thing that you could do to achieve this goal.

- Working and living under control and not always at a frantic pace
- Working at a moderate pace by putting order and planning into your life
- Enjoying life as you go rather than waiting for something big to happen (like a new job, marriage, winning the lottery)
- Allowing balance in your life
- Taking care of yourself by eating well, exercising regularly, getting enough sleep, and avoiding stressful situations
- Seeing life as a glass half full; anticipating the future as bright while living in the present

For additional assignments, Web links, and more, visit the online student resource at www.HumanKinetics.com/DimensionsOfLeisureForLife.

Review Questions

1. How do values determine what you do with your leisure? How do societal values affect the relevance of leisure?
2. What are the primary sectors that provide leisure services? Give examples of all of the ones you have participated in.
3. Why is it important to develop definitions and descriptions of leisure, recreation, and play?
4. Which of the definitions of leisure fits most closely with your personal views?
5. How has change from cyclical to linear time affected leisure?
6. Should leisure be viewed more as a right, a privilege, a healthy experience, or a commodity?
7. What benefits do you seek most often in your leisure?
8. What might be some negative impacts of leisure?
9. What needs to happen if leisure is to have a greater value in American society?
10. If you were given a choice between having more time for leisure or more money for leisure, which would you choose? In this hypothetical question, you cannot have both!
11. Why do people need to be educated about leisure?

Leisure Reading

Barr, N. Numerous mystery books centered in different National Parks throughout the United States: for example, *Firestorm* (2008), *High country* (2005), *A superior death* (2003). New York: Putnam.

Bissinger, H.G. (2004). *Friday night lights.* Cambridge, MA: Perseus.

Brown, S., & Vaughan, C. (2009). *Play: How it shapes the brain, opens the imagination, and invigorates the soul.* New York: Penguin.

Bryson, B. (1998). *A walk in the woods: Rediscovering America on the Appalachian Trail.* New York: Doubleday.

Elkind, D. (2007). *The power of play: Learning what comes naturally.* Cambridge, MA: Perseus.

Gini, A. (2003). *The importance of being lazy: In praise of play, leisure, and vacation.* New York: Routledge.

Krakauer, J. (1999). *Into thin air.* New York: Doubleday.

Krakauer, J. (2007). *Into the wild.* New York: Doubleday.

Louv, R. (2005). *Last child in the woods.* Chapel Hill, NC: Algonquin.

Rybczyski, W. (1992). *Waiting for the weekend.* New York: Penguin.

Switzer, K. (2009). *Marathon woman: Running the race to revolutionize women's sports.* New York: Carroll & Graf.

Zadoorian, M. (2009). *The leisure seeker: A novel.* New York: Dell.

Glossary

benefits—Positive outcomes associated with something.

commercial recreation—Market-driven, private-sector recreation activities for which a profit-oriented enterprise charges participants a fee.

cyclical time—Cycles or recurring events from the natural world.

enjoyment—The experience of satisfaction and achieving something important.

leisure—Meanings that people attach to enjoyable activities undertaken during their unobligated time.

leisure education—Field of study that aims to help individuals, families, communities, and societies achieve a suitable quality of life and good health by using leisure time intelligently and by developing and cultivating physical, emotional, spiritual, mental, and social aspects related to the aims of education in the country and its cultural heritage.

leisure industry—The agencies, organizations, and businesses that provide facilities, programs, services, or areas for people to enjoy in their free time.

linear time—Time that is associated with specific beginning and ending points.

not-for-profit organizations—Voluntary associations that usually focus on a particular issue, activity, or population and are limited in their scope based on the mission of the particular organization; also called *nonprofit, voluntary, third sector, independent sector,* or *nongovernmental organizations.*

park—A natural or near-natural green or open space that is bounded in some way and has the purpose of natural resource conservation and preservation, human use, or both.

parks and natural resources—Outdoor nature-based opportunities for recreation activity.

place—A location that is perceptually and socially produced by individuals and has meaning.

play—Activity undertaken by children and adults that includes characteristics of spontaneity, purposelessness, and the creation of an imaginary world. Play is almost always pleasurable and self-expressive and can range from disorganized activity to structured involvements.

quality of life—The degree to which a person enjoys the important possibilities of life that reflect the interaction of personal and environmental factors.

recreation—Activities undertaken because of conscious or unconscious enjoyable end results.

space—A geographic location denoting absolute and relative dimensions with concrete boundaries.

sports—A range of recreational and entertainment activities that involve rules, physical prowess, and contests between individuals or teams, generally with an uncertain outcome.

sport tourism—Traveling for the purpose of participating in or watching sport activities or visiting places of sports nostalgia.

state of being or state of mind—A psychological experience whereby leisure is perceived as being freely chosen, not compulsory, and done for its own sake.

tourists—People who travel to and stay in places for leisure outside their usual environment with the travel not associated with permanent residence or remuneration.

work—Activity undertaken for economic gain or social redeeming vitality.

work ethic—The valuing of activities that result in economic gain.

References

Baranowksi, J., & Puhl, J. (1993). Observations on physical activity in physical locations: Age, gender, and month effects. *Research Quarterly for Exercise and Sport, 64,* 127-133.

Brightbill, C. (1960). *The challenge of leisure.* Englewood Cliffs, NJ: Prentice Hall.

Bullaro, J., & Edginton, C. (1986). *Commercial leisure services: Managing for profit.* New York: Macmillan.

Centers for Disease Control and Prevention. (2008). *How much physical activity do adults need?* www.cdc.gov/physicalactivity/everyone/guidelines/adults.html.

Driver, B.L., Brown, P.J., & Peterson, G.L. (Eds.). (1991). *Benefits of leisure.* State College, PA: Venture.

Ellis, J.J. (1973). *Why people play.* Englewood Cliffs, NJ: Prentice Hall.

Fennell, D.A. (1999). *Ecotourism.* London: Routledge.

Frumkin, H. (2001). Beyond toxicity: Human health and the natural environment. *American Journal of Preventive Medicine, 20*(3), 237.

Gibson, H.J. (1998). Sport tourism: A critical analysis of research. *Sport Management Review, 1,* 45-76.

Global Development Research Center. (n.d.). *Notes on "quality of life."* www.gdrc.org/uem/qol-define.html.

Godbey, G. (1989). Implications of recreation and leisure research for professionals. In E.L. Jackson & T.L. Burton (Eds.), *Understanding leisure and recreation: Mapping the past, charting the future* (pp. 613-628). State College, PA: Venture.

Goodale, T.L., & Godbey, G.C. (1988). *The evolution of leisure.* State College, PA: Venture.

Henderson, K.A., & Bialeschki, M.D. (2005). Leisure and active lifestyles. *Leisure Sciences, 27,* 355-366.

Henderson, K.A., Bialeschki, M.D., Hemingway, J.L., Hodges, J.S., Kivel, B.D., & Sessoms, H.D. (2001). *Introduction to recreation and leisure services* (8th ed.). State College, PA: Venture.

Hochschild, A., with Machung, A. (1989). *The second shift.* New York: Viking.

Iwasaki, Y., Nishino, H., Onda, T., & Bowling, C. (2007). Leisure research in a global world: Time to reverse the western domination of leisure research? *Leisure Sciences, 29,* 113-117.

Kurtzman, J., & Zauhar, J. (2003). A wave in time—The sports tourism phenomena. *Journal of Sport Tourism, 8,* 35-47.

Mannell, R., & Kleiber, D.A. (1997). *A social psychology of leisure.* State College, PA: Venture.

Nelson, M.C., & Gordon-Larsen, P. (2006). Physical activity and sedentary behavior patterns are associated with selected adolescent health risk behaviors. *Pediatrics, 117*(4), 1281-1290.

Neulinger, J. (1981). *The psychology of leisure* (2nd ed.). Springfield, IL: Charles C. Thomas.

Pieper, J. (1963). *Leisure: The basis of culture* (A. Dru, Trans.). New York: New American Library.

Putnam, R. (2000). *Bowling alone: The collapse and revival of American community.* New York: Simon & Schuster.

Robinson, J.P., & Godbey, G. (1999). *Time for life: The surprising ways Americans use their time* (2nd ed.). University Park: Pennsylvania State University Press.

Rojek, C. (1989). Leisure time and leisure space. In C. Rojek (Ed.), *Leisure for leisure: Critical essays* (pp. 191-204). London: Macmillan.

Salamon, L.M. (1999). *America's nonprofit sector: A primer.* New York: Foundation Center.

Stewart, W.P. (1998). Leisure as multiphase experiences: Challenging traditions. *Journal of Leisure Research, 30*(4), 391-400.

Sullivan, W.C., Kuo, F.E., & DePooter, S.F. (2004). The fruit of urban nature. Vital neighborhood spaces. *Environment and Behavior, 36*(5), 678-700.

Tuan, Y. (1977). *Space and place: The perspective of experience.* Minneapolis: University of Minnesota Press.

Williams, D.R., Patterson, M.E., & Roggenbuck, J.W. (1992). Beyond the commodity metaphor: Examining emotional and symbolic attachment to place. *Leisure Sciences, 14,* 29-46.

World Leisure Organization. (2005). www.worldleisure.org.

Leisure Through a Social Science Lens

Erik Rabinowitz • J. Joy James
Appalachian State University

Learning Outcomes

After reading this chapter, you will be able to

▶ define social science;

▶ define how social science helps us understand leisure and leisure behaviors; and

▶ discuss leisure from a psychological, sociological, anthropological, and geographical perspective and give examples of how each helps us better understand human leisure behaviors.

Vocabulary Terms

anthropology	interpretivism	postmodernism
cross-cultural	macroeconomics	postpositivism
deviance	methodology	psychology
economics	microeconomics	sensation seeking
epistemology	ontology	social sciences
ethnography	positivism	sociology
flow		

Have you ever watched a hamster running in its wheel endlessly day in and day out or the sloth that has all the time in the world to move about? Imagine you are like this hamster, everyday rushing to each location, and your life is all work and no play. In American society, some people work all possible hours in a week, not unlike that hamster in the wheel. Other people are like the sloth, with more free time than they know how to use. Retirees, children, and underemployed or unemployed people may have around two thirds of their time available for leisure (Reid, 1995). The average time spent in leisure activities for those who are unemployed or over the age of 64 is approximately 7 hours (Bureau of Labor Statistics, 2009). How do the hamster and sloth metaphor relate to leisure and social science? The disparity in time is what makes studying the social sciences and leisure fascinating.

The **social sciences** are about people, how they act individually and in a group. This chapter discusses areas of study at both levels. Individually, people's lives—their food, employment opportunities, health, and leisure activities—are shaped by environmental, social, psychological, and biological factors. Examination of these areas will help us understand the impact leisure has on our lives individually and as a society. For example, the psychological basis for why we chose certain leisure activities over others will be explored. We use psychological theories every day without even being aware; for example, we drive past the doughnut shop and like Homer Simpson may have a biological response of our mouths drooling. This is very similar to the famous psychological study by Pavlov. For most of us, this response, which we may not notice, happens when we see pictures of our favorite recreation and leisure activity, such as a whitewater kayaker may have as she passes a roaring river. This response may be amplified if the kayaker passes the river and notices four of her good friends out kayaking; this is a sociological behavior elaborated on later in the chapter. Our biological systems and the role of our genetic makeup versus the role of nature, or the product of our environment, also may play a significant role in our leisure choices. Imagine if no leisure activities existed: The impact on our society could be detrimental from an individual, a social, and even an economic perspective. Some countries are completely dependent on leisure for their economic survival. As a group, we are living through a major transformation in society, and the traditions that hold it together often revolve around leisure participation. Four centuries BC, Aristotle wrote, "Just as we make war in order to have peace, the reason we labor is to have leisure." Certainly you have heard the phrase "money makes the world go round," but maybe the quote should be "leisure makes the world go round"; without leisure, people probably would be very disinterested in making money.

In this chapter, we examine what it means to be a social scientist and how social science helps us in our daily lives. Social science draws from numerous disciplines of study: This chapter examines some of the major fields of social science as well as the application of major theories from these fields, specifically in relationship to leisure behavior. The final sections discuss the benefit social science has on leisure and society as a whole.

WE ARE ALL SOCIAL SCIENTISTS

Every day you draw from sociology, political science, economics, anthropology, geography, history, psychology, and other related disciplines that provide an integrated view of your world. This interdisciplinary understanding helps you to make connections between, and to think critically about, issues both past and present. The social sciences differ from the so-called hard sciences by focusing on human behavior. For example, in daily conversation have you heard of or used the expression "it's not rocket science" to indicate that a concept is easily understood? Although this cliche makes its point, rocket technology is actually thousands of years old: Put some sulfur, saltpeter, and charcoal powder in a tube; light; and run for cover. A little trigonometry will tell you precisely where the rocket will land. Although this is basic Newtonian physics and math, the most difficult work scientists have attempted is to understand humans and human behaviors, which is social science (i.e., social scientists are interested in the cliche rather than the physics and math).

To understand social science, we must first understand how we come to truth or our "assumptions about knowledge and how it is attained" (Samdahl, 1999, p. 119). The story of the blind men and the elephant illustrates this point well (and points out the fallacy of learning by experience only). In this story, the blind men surround the elephant at different points. Each firmly believes in the truth of what he can touch and perceive. The man at the trunk believes the elephant is elongated and quite flexible like a snake. The man at the tail perceives the elephant as a string and possibly as quite smelly. The man touching the tusk believes the elephant is smooth and pointy, maybe a spear. The man touching the elephant's ears and feeling air move thinks the elephant is a fan. Each draws on previous experiences and values to frame his sensory experience and then puts it forward as truth. Each has his own idea of what the elephant is and believes he has the truth. None of the men are wrong nor are they completely right. What is the truth or reality of the elephant?

Social science provides us a way to learn about things. Growing out of skepticism and created to test speculations, social science offers a systematic way to discover truth. "The goal of social research is to discover, understand, and communicate truth about people in society" (Henderson, 1991, p. 9). The goal of social scientific theory is in discovering patterns in social life (Babbie, 2002).

> What one theory conceals, another illuminates.
>
> *M.P. Driscoll*

One could think of social science research as a puzzle. The researcher is akin to a puzzle solver (Henderson, 1991). By piecing together the social puzzle, the researcher attempts to discover, explain, and predict social patterns. Unfortunately, the researcher is working without a specific picture to determine how the puzzle pieces fit together. The picture that the researcher does have is based on observations, experience, paradigm, and previous research.

SOCIAL SCIENCE PERSPECTIVES

The paradigm or worldview that a researcher has determines how he will put together the puzzle. In the story about the six blind men, each illustrates a different paradigm. To understand how each blind man approaches the truth, one must investigate their paradigms from three perspectives. The first perspective is **ontology**: What is the blind man's belief of reality? Is truth universal or are there multiple realities? The second perspective is **epistemology**, the blind man's beliefs about how to get information or how the blind man believes the puzzle should be put together. The third perspective used to investigate the blind man's paradigm (worldview) is **methodology**. This consists of the procedures and techniques that are used to collect information to help put the puzzle together. These three perspectives determine the blind man's paradigm.

Paradigm is at the heart of how the social scientist strategizes putting the puzzle pieces together. In social science there are many paradigms, such as positivism, postpositivism, interpretivism, and postmodernism. Let's continue with the story of the blind men trying to put the pieces of the puzzle together to determine what is an elephant.

The paradigm of **positivism** offers that there is one elephant (or truth). When one is attempting to solve a puzzle, objectivity is of utmost importance. The scientific method involves inquiry by gathering evidence through observation, measurement, or empirical data to discover the "truth." We are all familiar with this paradigm at an early age—think back to your elementary school science fair. You determined a topic to investigate and then came up with a research question. You conducted a review or literature search for what was known about the phenomenon. Then you picked a methodology to conduct your experiment. The results were gathered and an analysis was conducted. Then you were the expert on this research and presented it at the school science fair!

A person using **postpositivism** when viewing the elephant would suggest that although there is one truth we cannot prove it but can show it is false. This paradigm recognizes that you cannot separate the knower and the known; in other words, the knowledge that the blind man had of a snake informed his interpretation of the elephant's trunk. This realization of our own bias opens the doors for other research methods. A postpositivistic researcher would continue to use the scientific method but has less faith in the method than the positivists. So the postpositivist might use some or all of the blind men to confirm the reality of the elephant. In this paradigm, the researcher is still the expert but also recognizes her own shortcomings.

Using the paradigm of **interpretivism**, the social scientist would agree that all the blind men are viewing their own reality or truth of what is an elephant. There are many realities, which implies that objectivity of positivism is not practical. "The researcher should try to understand the contextual realities and subjective meanings that shape people's interactions with their world" (Samdahl, 1999). In the interpretivist paradigm, the participant, rather than the researcher, is viewed as the expert on the phenomenon that is being researched (Henderson, 1991; Samdahl, 1999). This view allows the researcher to put the puzzle together by considering how people define their experience. The interpretivist researcher is trained to conduct research whereby an understanding of the phenomenon emerges from the people being studied.

The scientist using the **postmodernism** paradigm would question the reality of the elephant. This point of view illustrates there is really no answer to the question, only various points of view (as in the case of the blind men and the elephant). Therefore, all the images of the elephant are equally true (Babbie, 2002). This paradigm is skeptical of grand theories that try to explain everything.

There are other paradigms of social science (e.g., constructivist, critical theory, participatory), more than we can discuss in this chapter. What is important is that each paradigm has its own assumptions, values, methods, and criticisms. Each of the social science disciplines (e.g., psychology, sociology, economics, anthropology, geography) can encompass all the paradigms discussed. Thus, there are many perspectives with which to view the elephant, and one must understand the assumptions that the individual makes when conducting investigations.

THEORIES TO PRACTICE

In this section we examine the fields of psychology, sociology, economics, anthropology, and geography and how they apply to leisure and leisure behaviors. Examining these theories will help us understand how leisure enriches our lives and how it is essential to human existence.

Psychological Theories and Leisure Application

One of the major fields of study that influence social science is psychology. **Psychology** is the study of the way the human mind works and how it influences behavior. We all use the principles of psychology daily without realizing it. When we reward ourselves with a night at the movies for doing something good, we are using psychology's learning principle of positive reinforcement. When we get nervous right before we drop in from the top of a skateboard ramp, we are activating our autonomic nervous system. When we talk to ourselves in our heads, telling ourselves to calm down, work harder, or give up, we are using psychological cognitive approaches. These examples illustrate psychology as the study of humans' thoughts, emotions, and behavior.

If you examine the definition of psychology closely, you can see that it is heavily entrenched in leisure and leisure behaviors. For example, why does one person choose to jump out of a plane whereas another person says, "Look at that idiot jumping out of a perfectly good plane." One of the psychological theories at play in these scenarios is the theory of sensation seeking. **Sensation seeking** is "the need for varied, novel and complex sensations and the willingness to take physical and social risks for the sake of such experiences" (Zuckerman, 1983, p. 10). According to the theory of sensation seeking, four subcomponents make up how much a person desires sensation-seeking attributes and opportunities:

- Thrill and adventure seeking, which relate to the willingness to take physical risks and participate in high-risk sports

©Valeriy Pistryy

That nervous feeling you get right before participating in a challenging activity is a sign that your body's autonomic nervous system is gearing up. This is an example of a psychological principle you unconsciously use on yourself.

- Experience seeking, which relates to the need for new and exciting experiences
- Disinhibition, which relates to a willingness to take social risks and engage in health risk behaviors (e.g., binge drinking or having unprotected sex)
- Boredom susceptibility, which relates to intolerance for monotony and repetitive activities

PERSONAL LEISURE

Are you a sensation seeker? How would you rate yourself? Go online and take a quick questionnaire to see how you score on the Sensation Seeking Scale: www.bbc.co.uk/science/humanbody/mind/surveys/sensation/

Have you ever participated in a leisure activity such as snowboarding, playing the guitar, or meditating, where you lost all sense of time; your ability and the challenge were perfectly matched; you became totally unaware of your surroundings; or you just seemed to get into the rhythm of things, on the ball, in the zone, or in the groove? This is called the flow theory. The nine factors of **flow** are these:

1. The challenge level and skill level are matched.
2. A high degree of concentration is present.
3. Self-consciousness is lost.
4. Sense of time is distorted.

5. Successes and failures are apparent.

6. Clear and obtainable goals are present.

7. The person has a sense of personal control.

8. The experience is intrinsically rewarding.

9. The person becomes absorbed in the activity.

Not all of these factors are needed for flow to be experienced. When an expert skier skis on a bunny hill she is likely to be bored; when a beginner is on a black diamond hill, she is likely to feel anxiety. The optimal situation for flow is when the person is in the middle, matching her skill level with the challenge. The borrowing and merging of psychological theories and leisure are too expansive to discuss in this text; however, you can almost take any major theory of psychology and use the theory to better understand leisure behaviors.

SELF-DISCOVERY

Can you remember a time you were in flow? What made that situation ideal for flow, and could you replicate those conditions to put yourself in flow? How does the person next to you answer these questions?

The psychological perspective of leisure shows us that leisure is a time for building purpose in our lives, is individually determined, and should have beneficial results. Some of the psychological benefits of leisure might include, but are not limited to, increases in self-actualization, self-identity, self-esteem, or self-concept; personal enjoyment and growth; reduction of anxiety and depression; enhanced feelings of spirituality; and improvements in overall psychological well-being. Additionally, it is well documented that as a result of leisure engagement, people make significant gains in informational knowledge, visual learning, problem solving, creativity, and recognition memory. Interestingly, much of the research to support these statements comes not only from human trials but also from psychological studies on animals.

Sociological Theories and Leisure Application

Cliques, team sports, social clubs, parties, social networking sites, and religious holidays are all components of **sociology**, which is the systematic study of social behavior and human groups. For example, sociologists study things such as race or ethnicity, social class, gender roles, family, deviance, and crime. **Deviance** consists of actions or behaviors that differ from cultural norms. Many people participate in leisure pursuits that society may deem socially inappropriate or deviant. Bondage, graffiti, and entering in the Cannabis Cup (a festival held in the Netherlands focused on marijuana) are just a few of these types of leisure pursuits that may be deemed deviant. The specific culture matters in whether a leisure activity is considered deviant. For instance, in Amsterdam the Cannabis Cup is not considered socially deviant because it is part of the social norms; this is an example of what social scientists call **cross-cultural** differences. Another instance is whistling loudly during a music concert in the United States to show your appreciation; in Europe,

©AP Photo/Carolyn Kaster

Could this be a possible future MVP of the World Series?

whistling shows disapproval, like booing. A sociologist looking at leisure from a gender perspective may find that many women today are not allowed to participate in many leisure and recreation pursuits, like some Islamic women who are limited by the prevailing culture in which they live. Or sometimes women are just treated differently: Appalachian State University has a "girl rule" in coed intramurals, where a woman receives 3 points per basket whereas a man receives the traditional 2 points. Not until 1974 were girls even allowed to play in Little League baseball (Little League of America, 2003). American society has gained speed in the push for equal treatment for women. This sociological trend is an example of how society can flourish and nurture leisure opportunities; for example, girls can now play in Little League. One of the most important examples of a law affecting society in regard to equal treatment for men and women is Title IX of the Education Amendments of 1972 (sometimes called the Equal Opportunity in Education Act), which protects against discrimination on the basis of sex. Again, there are too many components of sociology and leisure to discuss in this chapter.

For leisure to flourish, society must encourage and support it. This is where sociology becomes a significant player in our understanding of the benefits of leisure to our society. Some of the sociological benefits that result when a family has common or shared leisure activities are improved family bonding, increases in marital and family satisfaction, and stability. People who work for companies that offer leisure opportunities for their employees (e.g., Google and Texas Instruments) are more likely to have high job satisfaction and to enjoy their work; the companies benefit through reduced health care costs, fewer on-the-job accidents, and a lower rate of employee turnover. Communities that provide citizens with many leisure opportunities, such as Seattle, Washington, show increases in quality-of-life assessments, higher community involvement and satisfaction, and lower crime rates than communities that offer fewer such opportunities.

RESEARCH TO REALITY

Make a list of socially appropriate and questionable leisure pursuits and discuss why U.S. norms consider these activities deviant or not. Would other cultures view these practices differently than Americans do? Does society perceive these practices differently according to gender? How might this view of social deviance change over time?

Economics Theories and Leisure Application

Economics examines the production, distribution, and consumption of goods and services. How many of us work all week so we can play on the weekend? Imagine if you added up all the money you spent in the last year on leisure activities. The economic impact of leisure can be substantial; in some areas the economy is partially or even completely dependent on tourism and the offering of leisure escapes. North Dakota, which has a little over 600,000 residents, lists tourism as its third largest industry (North Dakota Department of Commerce Tourism Division, 2009)!

P E R S O N A L   L E I S U R E

List all your expenses from the past week (e.g., food, rent, recreation, utilities, savings). What portions of your expenses went to recreational activities like drinking, renting movies, playing pool, and going out? How does this amount compare with the rest of your expenditures? Are you spending too much or not enough on leisure activities? Does this make you rethink any of your spending habits?

Most economists examine economics through two major theories: microeconomics and macroeconomics. **Microeconomics** looks at how individuals, families, organizations, and some states make decisions to spend their money, whereas **macroeconomics** looks at the total of economic activity (growth, inflation, and unemployment) of a national or regional economy as a whole. From a leisure perspective, microeconomics looks at the relationship between a person's economic state of affairs and her leisure choices. If an unemployed worker has $100 left after paying all his monthly bills and chooses to take the kids putt-putt golfing, this is a microeconomic issue. Leisure and macroeconomics examine the growth of leisure needs and demands on the economic system. For example, if unemployment is high then available time for leisure activities may also be high, but money for expenditures on leisure is low; this is a macroeconomic scenario. The economy of some countries is dependent on tourism, and leisure is directly connected to this; in Jamaica, for example, 23.7 percent of total employment or 1 in every 4.2 jobs is related to the tourism industry (World Travel and Tourism Council, 2009). In the United States, expenditures on recreation goods and services account for more than 14 percent of personal consumption expenditures and nearly 8 percent of the total gross domestic product. Additionally, most states rank tourism as one of their top 10 major industries (e.g., Colorado, Florida, and Hawaii) (U.S. Forest Service, 2005). People do not think about the economic impact leisure has on our society, but could you imagine if all the leisure opportunities in a country like Jamaica were nonexistent? Although poverty exists in this country now, what would it be without tourism?

Imagine how economics plays a role from the perspective of recreation and leisure providers. Every day they are presented an economics-based question. For example, if an amusement park has long lines, the managers are forced to reflect on numerous questions. Should they raise the price of admittance? Should they expand the park? Even if they decide to do nothing, what impact will that decision have? Although economic considerations should not be the only criteria used to answer these questions, economics has a significant influence on the decisions.

Anthropology Theories and Leisure Application

Are you curious about why sports fans paint their faces, why people follow bands around the country, or why people play at all? This is the type of curiosity that would inspire an anthropologist to investigate. The field of **anthropology** is the study of humankind. Everything in culture and society—traditions, values, leisure, language, beliefs, economics, and more—can be investigated. Anthropologists want to understand humans' impact on society and on other humans. The fanatical sports devotee and the band groupie are of interest to anthropologists, as is the way humans play. The anthropologist's paradigm is to study and learn directly from people through ethnographic methods. Anthropology prioritizes understanding people from their unique perspective, which is quite a different perspective from other social sciences.

In studying and describing all aspects of people, anthropologists use the method of **ethnography**. "Rather than *studying people*, ethnography means *learning from people*" (Spradley, 1980, p. 3). Although leisure studies have benefited from many social science fields (e.g., psychology, social psychology, economics), the contribution of anthropology to the field has been small (Chick, 1998). What has been studied in the leisure field has come from ethnographies describing cultures' games, sports, and recreation. It has been suggested that leisure ethnography will help us to understand the nature and distribution of leisure as well as its validity as a concept in other cultures (Chick, 1998). Using ethnographic methods and cultural theory, one researcher studied how regular participation in pickup basketball develops values and community (McLaughlin, 2008). This study helps us understand informal recreation activity participation and the nuances that are involved within the community of participants. Cross-cultural understanding of leisure can be found through ethnography of anthropology. Why is this important? From a social science perspective, anthropology offers descriptions of society and culture that can provide insight into benefits and challenges of leisure for a pluralistic society.

©Human Kinetics

Anthropologists would want to learn from these sports fans to understand why they paint their bodies.

Geography and Leisure Application

Have you ever visited a national, state, or local park and thought about how important it is to set aside lands for this experience?

In using these lands, we must balance our desire for positive leisure experiences and our need to protect the lands for future generations. Geography is the study of the earth and its features and of the distribution of life on the earth, including human life and the effects of human activity. Geography has not always been considered a social science, and many geographers do not consider themselves social scientists. But with the improvements and accessibility of geographic information system (GIS) technology, interesting social science issues are being examined. For example, figure 2.1 is a map of the population within 350 miles of Adirondack Park. Access to this map allows the park managers to watch for changes in population

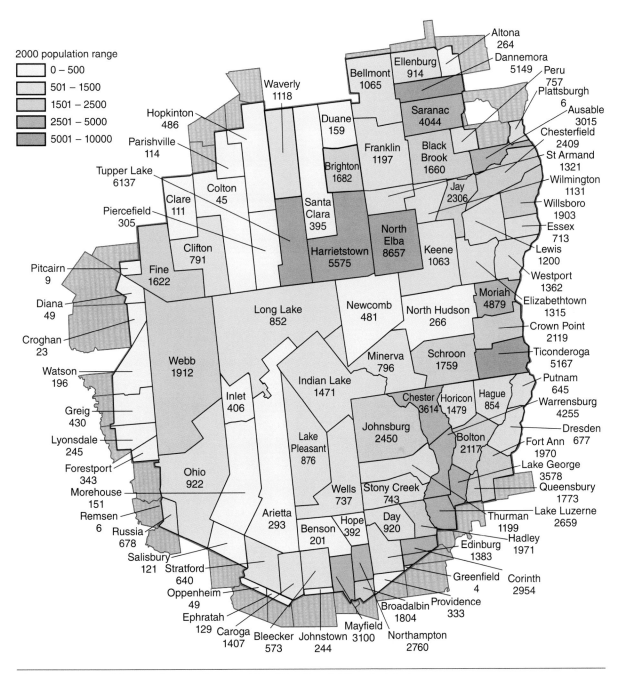

Figure 2.1 Map of the populations of towns within 350 miles of Adirondack Park.
Reprinted from http://www.apa.state. ny.us/gis/index.html.

growth and urban sprawl and make informed decisions on all sorts of things, like resource management, accessibility, and staffing needs.

BENEFITS OF SOCIAL SCIENCE

Knowledge is a social product. Social science is also a social product, and its intent is to discover patterns of social life. The presumption that there is one way of knowing is a bit arrogant. Each of the social science disciplines offers explanations, descriptions, or theories related to the human condition. Through understanding these disciplines and their research, practitioners can work on solutions to the challenges and issues facing their constituency.

Social science provides information to inform policy making and management decisions on the personal, community, national, and global levels. Communities benefit from social science through initiatives that improve management information (through technological advances), allocation or budgetary efficiency, and institutional change. For example, information on products and quality of sports equipment can improve consumer choices as well as policy for implementing youth sport programs (Smith, 1998). Social science, whether prompted by curiosity of the researcher or by public need, can reveal patterns of behavior and provide potential solutions. For example, when studying human relations, researchers changed lighting and ventilation of work areas to see whether worker performance would improve. To the researchers' astonishment, performance improved in both the experimental group and the control group (where no changes were made). This was the discovery of the Hawthorne effect, which "refers to an increase in performance caused by

©Human Kinetics

Researchers have determined that outdoor adventure programs help improve participants' self-confidence.

the special attention given to employees, rather than tangible changes in the work" (Lussier, 2005, p. 13). This discovery changed how managers view motivation in their employees. Think about the top 10 companies to work for—what do they offer to help motivate their employees? The Hawthorne effect was the beginning in changing management's view on how to work with and motivate employees!

For many years it was thought that recreation was good for you or would enhance human development, but this was anecdotal evidence. To garner resources (e.g., money, facilities, or employees) for an organization or agency, benefits of recreation needed to be determined empirically (i.e., determined through research methods of observation and experimentation). The recreation field turned to social science (e.g., psychology, sociology, economics) to help generate evidence of both economic and noneconomic benefits of leisure. For example, researchers investigating benefits of participation in outdoor adventure programs suggested that participants improve their self-concept (Burton, 1981; Ewert, 1982), whereas other researchers indicated that self-confidence was an outcome (Kaplan, 1984; Nye, 1976). These findings can be used to demonstrate benefits of programs such as Outward Bound or National Outdoor Leadership School.

Social science research has been used to determine pricing for programs, crowding capacity in natural areas or parks, and ways to garner financial resources for youth-at-risk programs. Beyond our field, social science offers insight into potential partnerships and collaborations. For instance, education research demonstrates that playing chess can improve academic performance of students by increasing concentration and raising test scores (Root, 2008). An urban recreation center that works with at-risk youth can use this information to create a chess club, partner with schools, and ultimately affect students' academic performance. The ability to demonstrate leisure's benefits beyond casual observations requires good methodology from social science. Although most of us know from personal experience that leisure is beneficial to our quality of life, social science will help us know empirically where, how, when, and for whom this is true.

Think about the person on the hamster wheel. There are only 108 waking hours in a week: If a person spends 60 hours working, she also spends 48 hours doing something else (besides sleeping). This leaves roughly 30 hours for leisure time, assuming the person spends 18 hours on personal care and daily chores. According to social scientists, without those 30 hours of leisure the person will most likely be unhappy (psychology), alone (sociology), and a workaholic (anthropology) but financially okay (economics); however, what is the point of having money if you do not have time to spend it? U.S. trends over the last 80 years have shown that generally we are *not* more likely to get on the hamster wheel; our work hours have decreased and conversely leisure time has increased. At the beginning of the 20th century a workweek averaged 50 to 60 hours, and since that time the standard workweek has declined to 35 to 40 hours, thereby increasing other time, including leisure time, from 53 hours in the past to 70 hours today. With this knowledge from social science, recreation practitioners can provide programs and help people understand their choices in both work and leisure.

The human condition is like a puzzle with some missing pieces. We can see the picture as a whole but not always the nuances that provide information. By investigating the missing pieces of the social puzzle, the researcher attempts to discover, explain, and predict social patterns. Let's think of the puzzle as the elephant and the blind men as social scientists. The men can feel the shape of the elephant and some of the body, but each "sees" the elephant from a different perspective (i.e., psychology, economically, sociologically, or anthropologically) and offers explanations that are accurate. If the blind men share their knowledge they all can better understand the phenomenon of the elephant. Like the elephant in the puzzle, the human subject is neither quantifiable nor qualifiable. Social sciences offer the ability to move beyond our blindness and use knowledge from a systematic approach to better understand the human condition.

SUMMARY

The value of studying people is paramount to recreation professionals. Through social science we can begin to understand how employment opportunities, culture, health, and leisure choices are shaped by environmental, social, psychological, and biological factors. That is, social science helps us understand the human equation. This chapter provides context on social science and its impact on leisure behaviors.

The social sciences are about people: how they act individually and in a group. Social science encompasses disciplines such as psychology, sociology, economics, anthropology, and geography. All of these disciplines can provide insight into leisure behaviors. Also important to social science is the understanding of the paradigm or worldview of the researcher. The major paradigms discussed are positivism, postpositivism, interpretivism, and postmodernism. Ontology, epistemology, and methodology are the determinants of a social scientist's paradigm (or worldview). These perspectives determine how research is conducted within the paradigm.

Social science draws from numerous disciplines of study. Psychology, the study of individual human behavior, can offer insight into why a person participates in a recreational activity. Sociology, the study of two or more human behaviors, can provide insight into group behavior, such as at a baseball game (e.g., when fans do the wave). Economics, which examines the production, distribution, and consumption of goods and services, is at the heart of pricing recreational activities, the basis of the tourism industry for some countries. Anthropology, the study of humankind and cultures, can best inform a national park or heritage site of the culture being preserved. Geography, the study of earth's lands, inhabitants, and features, provides data for natural resource and land management decisions.

Social science provides tangible benefits for leisure and society. Social science research informs policy making and management decisions. Communities benefit from social science through initiatives that improve quality of life through technological advances, allocation or budgetary efficiency, and institutional change. Social science provides empirical evidence to substantiate the provision of fiscal resources, staffing, and facilities for recreation.

Learning Activities

1. Choose any recreation or leisure activity and find literature on how the activity is being examined through a social science lens. Look for the psychological, social, economic, anthropological, and geographical issues, benefits, and constraints.

2. Put on your imaginary lab coats and be a social scientist. With the advent of social networking Web sites (like Facebook, Twitter, and MySpace), leisure interactions have changed. Using one of the major areas of social science, examine the benefits, constraints, and negative aspects of leisure

participation. Write a two-page report and be ready to discuss your findings and thoughts. Here are some questions to think about before beginning this assignment: How would scientists in your chosen area of social science approach this problem? How might they examine this issue? What do you suspect the results of their study might be? How has leisure changed as a result of these social networking sites? What are some examples from the area of social science you have chosen?

3. Attend a social event. Examine how each field of the social sciences interacts, explains, or plays a role in the success and failure of the event. Write a one-page paper, providing examples of how each of the following fields was important: psychology, sociology, economics, anthropology, and geography.

4. Form a group with four fellow students. Each student picks an article that addresses the benefits of leisure through each field of social science: psychology, sociology, economics, anthropology, and geography. After each student writes a one-page summary of the benefits, hold a roundtable discussion of all members' findings. Find common themes in everyone's findings and note how these themes were examined in their field. *Benefits of Leisure* (Driver et al., 1991) is a good starting place for finding literature to review, but the student article must be dated post 1991.

For additional assignments, Web links, and more, visit the online student resource at www.HumanKinetics.com/DimensionsOfLeisureForLife.

Review Questions

1. In social science, there are many paradigms such as positivism, postpositivism, interpretivism, and postmodernism. Explain each.

2. One of the major fields of study that influences social science is psychology. Explain this influence through a leisure example.

3. What may a sociologist who looks at leisure from a gender perspective find with regard to women and recreation pursuits? Explain and support your answer.

4. Explain micro- and macroeconomics as they apply to leisure.

5. How do ethnographies help social science?

6. Discuss the benefits of leisure from a psychological, social, economics, anthropology, and geography lens.

Leisure Reading

Dyson, M.E. (1997). *Race rules: Navigating the color line.* New York: First Vintage Books.

Dyson, M.E. (2003). *Open mike: Reflections on philosophy, race, sex, culture and religion.* New York: Basic Civitas Books.

Howell, J.T. (1973). *Hard living on Clay Street: Portraits of blue collar families.* Chapel Hill, NC: Bantom Doubleday Dell.

Liebow, E. (2003). *Tally's corner.* Lanham, MD: Rowman and Littlefield.

Mills, C.W. (2000). *The power elite.* New York: Oxford Press.

Putman, R. (2000). *Bowling alone.* New York: Simon and Schuster.

Schor, J.B. (1992). *Overworked American: The unexpected decline of leisure.* New York: HarperCollins.

Stack, C.B. (1974). *All our kin: Strategies for survival in a black community.* New York: Perseus Books.

Terkel, S. (1997). *The good war: An oral history of World War II.* New York: The New Press.

West, C. (2001). *Race matters.* Boston: Beacon Press.

Glossary

anthropology—Study of humankind including everything in culture and society: traditions, values, leisure, language, beliefs, and economics.

cross-cultural—Referring to any idea, tradition, or social norm that spans more than one culture.

deviance—Actions or behaviors that differ from cultural or social norms.

economics—Study of the production, distribution, and consumption of goods and services.

epistemology—A person's belief about how to get information or how things should be put together.

ethnography—Field of study that relies on learning from people rather than studying people.

flow—State when a person's skill level and challenge are exactly matched and the person loses a sense of time and is "in the zone."

interpretivism—Paradigm that all knowledge is a matter of interpretation and in social science the participant rather than the researcher is viewed as the expert.

macroeconomics—Study of the total of economic activity (growth, inflation, and unemployment) of a national or regional economy as a whole.

methodology—Procedures and techniques that are used to collect information.

microeconomics—Study of how individuals, families, organizations, and some states make decisions to spend their money.

ontology—What is known about reality and existence; the study of being and existence.

positivism—Paradigm that posits that knowledge is based on natural phenomena and their properties and relations as verified by the empirical sciences.

postmodernism—Paradigm that is skeptical of explanations that claim to be valid for all groups; postmodernists focus instead on the relative truths of each group.

postpositivism—Paradigm in which the knower (researcher) and known cannot be separated, emphasizing the importance of multiple measures and observations in social science.

psychology—Study of the way the human mind works and how it influences behavior.

sensation seeking—Need for varied, novel, and complex experiences; willingness to take physical and social risks for the sake of such experiences.

social sciences—Sciences that focus on people and how they act individually and in a group.

sociology—Systematic study of social behavior and human groups.

References

Babbie, E. (2002). *The basics of social research*. Belmont, CA: Wadsworth Thompson Learning.

Bureau of Labor Statistics. (2009). *American time use survey—2008 results*. Washington, DC: Bureau of Labor Statistics. www.bls.gov/news.release/atus.nr0.htm

Burton, L.M. (1981). A critical analysis and review of the research on Outward Bound and related programs. *Dissertation Abstracts International, 42,* 158-B.

Chick, G. (1998). Leisure and culture: Issues for an anthropology of leisure. *Leisure Sciences, 20,* 111-133.

Driver, B.L., Brown, P.J., & Peterson, G.L. (Eds.). (1991) *Benefits of leisure*. State College, PA: Venture.

Ewert, A. (1982). *Outdoor adventure and self-concept: A research analysis*. Eugene: University of Oregon, Department of Recreation and Park Management.

Henderson, K.A. (1991). *Dimensions of choice: A qualitative approach to recreation, parks and leisure research*. State College, PA: Venture.

Kaplan, R. (1984). Wilderness perception and psychological benefits: An analysis of a continuing program. *Leisure Sciences, 6*(3), 271-290.

Little League of America. (2003). *Little League to mark 30th anniversary of decision allowing girls to play*. www.littleleague.org/media/newsarchive/06_2003/03_30thgirls.htm

Lussier, R.N. (2005). *Human relations in organizations: Applications and skill building*. Boston: McGraw-Hill Irwin.

McLaughlin, T. (2008). *Give and go: Basketball as a cultural practice*. New York: State University of New York Press.

North Dakota Department of Commerce Tourism Division. (2009). *2009 N.D. tourism annual report*. www.ndtourism.com/uploads/resources/793/2009-annual-report-for-web.pdf

Nye, R. Jr. (1976). *The influence of an Outward Bound program on the self-concept of the participants*. Unpublished doctoral dissertation, Temple University.

Reid, D.G. (1995). *Work and leisure in the 21st century: From production to citizenship*. Toronto, ON: Wall and Emerson.

Root, A. (2008). *Science, math, checkmate: 32 chess activities for inquiry and problem solving*. Westport, CT: Libraries Unlimited/Teacher Ideas Press.

Samdahl, D.M. (1999). Epistemological and methodological issues in leisure research. In E.L. Jackson & T.L. Burton (Eds.), *Leisure studies: Prospects for the twenty-first century* (pp. 119-134). State College, PA: Venture.

Smith, V.H. (1998, July). *Impact assessment discussion paper no. 2: Measuring the benefits of social science research*. Washington, DC: Director General's Office International Food Policy Research Institute. www.ifpri.org/publication/measuring-benefits-social-science-research

Spradley, J.P. (1980). *Participant observation*. Fort Worth, TX: Harcourt.

U.S. Forest Service. (2005). *The forest service program forest and rangeland resources: A long-term strategic plan*. Washington, DC: U.S. Department of Agriculture.

World Travel and Tourism Council. (2009). *Tourism impact data and forecasts*. www.wttc.org/eng/Tourism_Research/Economic_Research/index.php

Zuckerman, M. (Ed.). (1983). *Biological bases of sensation-seeking, impulsivity, and anxiety*. Hillsdale, NJ: Lawrence Erlbaum.

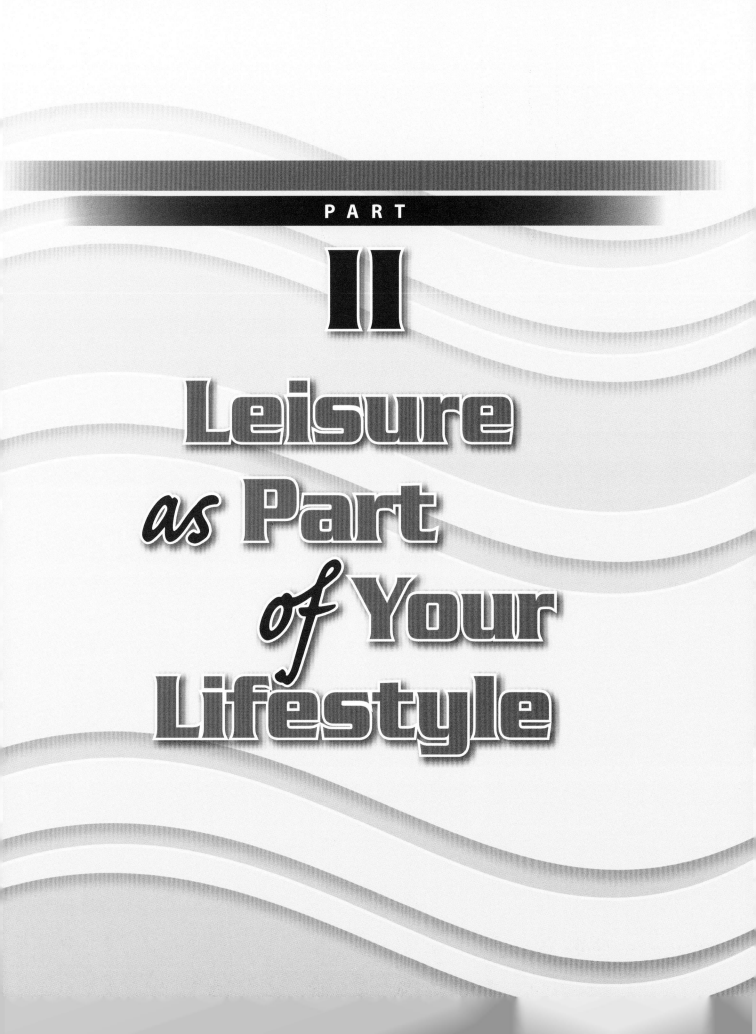

PART

II

Leisure *as* Part *of* Your Lifestyle

Leisure and Quality of Life

Ariel Rodríguez • Dovie Gamble
Arizona State University • University of Florida

Learning Outcomes

After reading this chapter, you will be able to

▶ understand how leisure affects your quality of life,

▶ explain the relationship between leisure and other domains of life, and

▶ locate leisure resources that may improve your quality of life.

Vocabulary Terms

autonomy	physical health	social embeddedness
community	prevention	social network
competence	relatedness	social support
coping	sacrilization	spiritual health
mental health	serious leisure	transcendence
neighborhood	social climate	

©Photodisc

Throughout the day we may find our minds wandering to those favorite leisure pastimes that help us to deal with stress, get physically healthier, or simply enjoy life. Despite school demands, we can't help but think about what leisure activities we would like to do after we have finished our required tasks.

You have been studying for your exam for what feels like a lifetime. You know that your exam will be in less than an hour, but you cannot help but think about what you will do afterward. You think about texting your friends to see whether you can get a group to grab some food at the union. Perhaps you are in the mood to go to the student recreation center and get in a cardio workout. You quickly text your best friend and ask her to meet you at the gym after your exam. Within a few seconds, she texts, "c u there." Although you are tired from studying and stressed about the exam, you cannot help but smile as you look forward to relaxing and meeting up with your friends after the exam.

Throughout this chapter, we introduce a number of conceptual and theoretical frameworks to help explain how leisure affects your quality of life. Because leisure is intertwined with many aspects of life, the discussion focuses on those parts of your life that may be most important to your quality of life. These include a person's health, spiritual well-being, employment, social support, and community and neighborhood.

The pursuit of happiness is the right of all citizens of the United States of America according to the Declaration of Independence. Yet, many things in our life may hinder this pursuit. For instance, your life today may be filled with daily stressors such as the demands of studying, participation in clubs and organizations, volunteering, and part-time or full-time jobs. Leisure may provide you with a variety of ways to cope with daily stressors, prevent illnesses (maintain good health), and even overcome difficulties associated with challenging life experiences. Leisure brings about these benefits in many different ways, including buffering the effects of stress; providing an avenue to develop stronger relationships with family, friends, and loved ones; providing an outlet for needs not satisfied during employment; providing opportunities to be active in an array of different recreation facilities; and providing an opportunity to become more spiritually healthy. These are a few ways in which leisure contributes to your happiness and quality of life.

DEFINING QUALITY OF LIFE

To understand how leisure influences quality of life, it is important to first understand what quality of life is and what influences it. When people use the term *quality of life*, they are often determining the worth or value of some aspect of a person's life. The aspects of life often focus on what have been termed "important domains of life." Many aspects of a person's life are important, and seven key or salient domains have been identified (Cummins, 1996):

1. Health: physical and mental

2. Material well-being: items such as a house, clothes, a car, income, and savings

3. Productivity: employment and other paid work, school, vocations, and housework

4. Intimacy: social support, such as friends, partner, children, and family

5. Safety: the amount of privacy, degree of control over your life (including financial and legal), and level of physical safety you have

6. Community: the place where you live (i.e., neighborhood) or where you predominantly interact with others

7. Emotional well-being: leisure or recreation activities including those done as hobbies, for spiritual or religious reasons, or simply for fun

Engaging in meaningful activities with people who provide strong social support is an important contributor to the quality of a person's life.

This chapter focuses on describing the relationships between leisure and various important life domains.

INDIVIDUAL HEALTH AND PREVENTION OF ILLNESS

Your health is a critical component of your overall quality of life. As such, it is important to incorporate measures that help prevent illnesses and keep you in good health. Although this may seem like common knowledge, often people are not aware of how leisure may help prevent and even treat illnesses. To understand how leisure affects your health, it is important to understand what health is. For instance, from a holistic model, health refers to physical, mental, and social well-being (i.e., the health of the whole person), as opposed to simply the absence of disease, illness, and disability (Larson, 1991).

> Regarding the question if I'm happy . . . the answer is yes . . . and not because I've reached happiness, but because I now realize that it's not like a place, but more like a path.
>
> *Carlos in the movie 7 Mujeres, 1 Homosexual, y Carlos, 2004; translated by Dr. Ariel Rodríguez*

Consistent with the holistic model's perspective of health, at least three ways have been identified in which leisure influences health and well-being: prevention, coping, and transcendence. Each of the concepts has unique implications (Caldwell, 2005). For instance, **prevention**

©Photodisc

Getting back to normal is a difficult thing to do after experiencing a traumatic event. Becoming grounded through your leisure activities can help you to enjoy life once again.

refers to the ability of leisure to prevent illnesses. **Coping** refers to the ability of leisure to help people cope with negative daily stresses, whereas **transcendence** refers to the ability of leisure to help a person overcome a traumatic life event.

Physical Well-Being

Being physically healthy means having a healthy body, which helps prevent numerous illnesses. Many things contribute to a healthy body, including what you eat and drink, the amount of regular physical activity you integrate into your daily life, and the amount of rest you take. Participation in an activity that is physically demanding, such as jogging or swimming, positively affects your physical well-being as long as you do not overdo it. Muscle fatigue and injury along with joint injuries can set your physical activity participation back. The scientific evidence is strong that regular participation in physical activities can help to promote joint functioning, muscle strength, and appropriate body weight (Kahn et al., 2002; Miilunpalo, 2001; Wankel & Berger, 1991). There is also evidence that being physically active can reduce your number of illnesses and even expand your life span (Pedersen & Clemmensen, 1997; Schnohr et al., 2003). Being physically healthy is a very strong indicator of your quality of life. Think back on the last time you went to the gym and pushed yourself a little too far. Perhaps you had not worked out in some time and decided to work out like you never had before. What happened the next day? Perhaps you were in such pain that every step was extremely demanding. Maybe even lifting a pencil was difficult. On that day were you able to do all the things that you normally do? How did you perform even mundane tasks, such as brushing your teeth or using the restroom? When your body is in pain or you are so physically weak that you cannot do even mundane tasks, your quality of life suffers. You may not want to go out with friends; you might limit all of your interactions to online interactions; you may not be able to go to work or school; and you definitely would have difficulty doing any physical activity outside the house. In other words, when you are not physically healthy, every other aspect of your life is at risk. If you are physically ill, your work might be at risk; your friendships might be at risk, because you will not be able to spend quality time with friends; and you may not even be able to do your personal hobbies or may have to change them. This list goes on and on.

We are in the midst of an epidemic that has the potential of influencing our **physical health,** the obesity epidemic. The U.S. population has demonstrated a steady increase in obesity over the past 50 years (U.S. Department of Health and Human Services, 1996, 2000). Being obese increases your odds of developing a

©AP Photo/Michael Sohn

With each stroke, the swimmer feels her body gliding through the water. Many recreation activities can help us maintain or enhance our physical health. In this case, the swimmer is becoming more physically healthy one stroke at a time.

disease that may reduce your physical health. These diseases include, but are not limited to, high blood pressure, stroke, heart attack, cancer, and type 2 diabetes.

Mental Well-Being

Being mentally healthy is being emotionally and cognitively healthy. Leisure activities and their settings can help you maintain emotional stability and cognitive well-being. It has already been established that physical activities done for leisure can improve physical health. The same kinds of activities have been associated with reducing anxiety and tensions as well as depression (Biddle et al., 2000; Mutrie, 2000). Physical activity as an adjunct therapy has been effective in the treatment of disorders like schizophrenia, developmental disorders, somatoform disorders, substance abuse disorders (e.g., alcohol and drug addiction), smoking cessation, and sleep apnea (Fox et al., 2000). Despite the various positive outcomes of leisure experiences, there are times in which a person may not enjoy these experiences. For example, high performance expectations without the appropriate skills can cause a person anxiety instead of pleasure. Likewise, a person who has played and beaten a specific video game so many times may become bored because the challenge is not there anymore. In leisure studies, flow theory has been used to help explain optimal experience levels (Csikszentmihalyi, 1990).

SELF-DISCOVERY

Think about what activities or hobbies have helped you to relax and relieve stress throughout your life. Are they still a part of your life? Through life transitions and life challenges we can often look to these activities to help bring a sense of balance to our lives. What are you doing today to maintain these activities in your life?

Coping

The stresses of everyday life, such as those experienced from work or school, may be emotionally and psychologically taxing. These stresses may make you irritable, decrease your ability to concentrate, increase the frequency of headaches, and increase your muscular tension. Prolonged exposure to stress may cause depression, ulcers, digestive issues, and cardiovascular illnesses. Therefore, the management of stress is critical for a healthy life.

As a form of coping, leisure can be an important buffer against stress from daily life (Coleman & Iso-Ahola, 1993; Iso-Ahola & Park, 1996; Iwasaki, 2001). "As stress levels increase, leisure coping strategies appear to act as a buffer against the negative impact of stress to help people maintain good physical health" (Iwasaki, 2003, p. 106). Two coping strategies that may buffer the negative effects of stress on your health are participating in leisure activities that provide you with social support and facilitating participation in activities that you determine and have self-control over (Coleman & Iso-Ahola, 1993).

A task is self-determined when it fulfills your needs for autonomy, competence, and relatedness. **Autonomy** refers to choice, such as when you want to participate in an activity or have a specific experience. **Competence** generally refers to whether you are knowledgeable enough to get what you want from an activity or experience. **Relatedness** refers to the desire to feel connected to others, such as loving or caring for others along with being loved and cared for (Deci & Ryan, 2000; Ryan & Deci, 2000).

©Human Kinetics

Have you ever needed someone's help? When we are in these situations and we get the help we need, it can improve our quality of life in many different ways. The opposite also tends to be true: When we reach out but no one is there to grab our hand, this can decrease our quality of life.

Transcendence

Some events can cause a severe amount of stress. These traumatic events may involve life-threatening situations, such as being assaulted or losing a loved one. These events are often so horrifying to the person that memories of the event make a person feel he is reliving the event. Such flashbacks may bring back the same feelings of helplessness and fear once experienced during the event. Life episodes such as the terrorist acts of September 11, 2001, can be traumatic. After September 11, it seemed as though our lives had changed and would never be the same again.

As a form of transcendence, "someone uses leisure to find new meaning to life and becomes reborn in a way that allows for a fuller realization of one's potential" (Caldwell, 2005, p. 15). In other words, leisure is a way to deal with negative life events (e.g., natural disaster or loss of a loved one). More specifically, "leisure is a resource for the self-protective effects of emotion-focused and problem-focused coping, and that such experience may be the foundation for adjustment and personal growth following a negative life event" (Kleiber et al., 2002, p. 225). Leisure activities buffer the impact of negative life events by distracting us from our problems, generating optimism about the future, and aiding in the reconstruction of a life story that is continuous with the past (Kleiber et al., 2002).

Grief Gone Wild is an example of a leisure program aimed at helping youth transcend difficult life experiences. Specifically, it helps teens deal with grief in their lives. The program is an outdoor recreation experience, or better described as a wilderness adventure experience, which takes teens on a 5-day river rafting expedition through the San Juan River in Utah. The program is offered by the City of Phoenix Parks and Recreation Department and is designed to help grieving teens accept and eventually learn to live with their loss (Tousley, 2006).

Spiritual

Spiritual health and well-being have been found to contribute to people's quality of life. People who are spiritually healthy have a sense of purpose in their life and feel connected to other people and nature. They are committed to something greater than themselves, have strong spiritual beliefs and values, and are filled with love, happiness, and peace (Hawks, 1994). **Spiritual health** is marked by "a high level of faith, hope, and commitment in relation to a well defined worldview or belief system that provides a sense of meaning and purpose to existence" (Hawks, 1994, p. 6). At least three factors contribute to spiritual health: having a worldview that provides

We can connect with nature in many ways, such as camping, hiking, fishing, and hunting. Many people who have hectic lives use their time in nature to simply relax and get in touch with their true selves.

©RÉmy MASSEGLIA

meaning and purpose to life, feeling connected to others, and maintaining a strong commitment to and personal faith in one's worldview (Hawks, 1994).

Spiritual health and well-being are possible outcomes of leisure experiences. For example, camping and other outdoor activities in nature and in the wilderness are often associated with spiritual values. Many organizations that provide leisure services, such as the YMCA, have spiritual components. Additionally, many people participate in spiritual activities, such as going to a spiritual or religious facility, during their leisure time. Researchers have provided a model showing the theorized relationship between leisure and spiritual health, such as the model of leisure and spiritual well-being (Heintzman, 2002).

SELF-DISCOVERY

Think about your spiritual health. What activities help you get in tune with your spirituality? Do you consider yourself spiritual? What presence does spirituality have in your life?

The model of leisure and spiritual well-being theorizes that there is a somewhat homeostatic level of spiritual well-being that is unique to each person. There are times when people feel alienated from their spiritual energy and consciously or unconsciously suppress their spiritual self. During these times, a person may need assistance to get her spiritual level back to normal. Two techniques identified in the model are sacrilization and resacrilization. **Sacrilization** is the process of sensitizing a person to her spiritual self; resacrilization involves sensitizing a person who was sensitized previously but has consciously or unconsciously moved from her spiritual self. Many leisure activities can provide assistance with sacrilization and resacrilization, such as meditation, rhythmic breathing techniques, creative visualization, and relaxation exercises. Conversely, there are times when people get spiritual energy boosts, moments in their life when their spiritual energy is higher than normal and they become off-centered. Having elevated levels of spiritual energy may occur because of a spiritual emergency or a time in your life when your personal growth at a spiritual level becomes overwhelming or even chaotic. The model recommends using grounding techniques to get spiritual levels back to normal. Some leisure activities that help ground people include gardening, tai chi, and walking (Heintzman, 2002).

Work is often associated with the disruption of spiritual energy. If you have had a job, you have inevitably felt the pressures involved in working, such as pressure from dealing with a demanding customer or boss. Work also limits the amount of time that you have for leisure. If you are trying to get through school while working a part-time or full-time job, then you are probably very familiar with how much strain work may put on your life, including your leisure life. The next section discusses the relationship between leisure and work.

LEISURE AND WORK

Many students find it more difficult to pay for their education than was true in the past. With budget cuts at the federal level affecting all aspects of government, including student loans, more students are turning to part-time jobs (and some even full-time jobs) to help pay for their education. With their dual roles as students and employees, students have a dwindling amount of time for leisure activities. The relationship between work and leisure is often similar to a one-sided relationship where one person gets his way and the other person is put to the side. This conflict between leisure and work is part of the foundation of the United States. To understand this conflict, one need go no further than the historic inauguration speech by President Barack Obama. While discussing historical elements of the United States, he stated: "Our journey has never been one of shortcuts or settling for less. It has not been the path for the faint-hearted—for those who prefer leisure over work" (CNN, 2009). There is a strong belief in the United States that work signifies achievement whereas leisure signifies laziness or nonproductivity, but there is also a body of literature that contradicts this belief.

Spillover Theory and Compensation Theory

Your job provides you with income, a network of colleagues, and friends to socialize with. But how does your work influence your leisure? Researchers have analyzed two primary theories predicting the relationship between work and leisure: spillover theory and compensation theory. Spillover theory states that people participate in leisure activities similar to their work, and thus work activities spill over into leisure activities. For instance, people who are computer savvy, such as computer programmers, may have a higher likelihood of playing computer games during their free time than playing basketball or volleyball.

LEISURE AWARENESS

Think about your typical week. How much time do you spend at work, and how much time do you spend doing the leisure activities you love? Does work influence the amount of time you participate in leisure activities? Does it affect the types of leisure activities you select?

Compensation theory purports that people participate in leisure activities that are dissimilar from their work, activities that help people meet the needs that are not met at work. For example, a person who has a high-risk job, such as racecar driving, would probably have leisure activities that are not as risky, such as fishing. Of the two theoretical frameworks, spillover tends to have more support than compensation theory in predicting the relationship between work and leisure (Mannell & Reid, 1999).

Serious Leisure

Sometimes a leisure activity is more than something to just pass the time; it is something that resembles work. Leisure researchers refer to this phenomenon as **serious leisure** and define it as "the systematic pursuit of an amateur, hobbyist, or volunteer activity that participants find so substantial and interesting that, in the typical case, they launch themselves on a career centered on acquiring and expressing its special skills, knowledge, and experience" (Stebbins, 1999, p. 69).

©Ric Tapia/Icon SMI

There are many instances in which people transform leisure activities into careers, like Ryan Sheckler did with skateboarding. The key is that when you started this activity, you did it for leisure purposes.

There are six distinctive qualities of serious leisure: perseverance, career-related results, generation of knowledge, achievement of intrinsic rewards, identification, and unique ethos. People who engage in serious leisure pursuits have had to persevere. There may have been difficult times when they even contemplated giving up their pursuit but instead continued. These people wish to find a career in their leisure pursuit, and for many people, this is a turning point at which their level of involvement increases. For example, many high school athletes must make a conscious decision to pursue their sport as a possible career. Many students decide to not pursue their sport careers and instead focus on another profession. People who have serious leisure pursuits make genuine efforts to obtain more knowledge and skills concerning their leisure pursuit. This may come in many forms. For example, an amateur woodworker may begin to buy magazines focused on furniture building, or a gardener might take classes about different plants.

For these people, the leisure pursuit is self-gratifying; they engage in it because they love it. Moreover, these people identify strongly with their leisure pursuit. Finally, these people engage in what is termed a *unique ethos,* a special culture that is based around the leisure pursuit. An example of this is the culture that revolves around online games, such as World of Warcraft. In the game, a unique language has developed that is consistent with online gaming but unique to the game. If an outsider were to read an online conversation between players, she would have major difficulties understanding the language.

Three types of people engage in serious leisure (Stebbins, 1999): amateurs, hobbyists, and volunteers. Amateurs often are referred to as people who pursue a pastime, such as a sport, art, science, or entertainment, without pay. Some leisure researchers believe that it is very difficult to differentiate between amateurs and professionals because their passions and fields of interest are so closely linked. Hobbyists tend to differ from amateurs in that they do not wish to be professionals. There are at least five distinct categories of hobbyists: collectors; makers and tinkerers; participants, such as birdwatchers, who engage in a rule-based but noncompetitive activity; players, people who play sports and games that have no professional counterpart, such as field hockey; and enthusiasts, who are interested in the liberal arts. Finally, a volunteer is a person who performs voluntary or service-oriented work (Stebbins, 1999).

Unemployment

According to the U.S. Department of Labor, Bureau of Labor Statistics (2009), "From April to July 2009, the number of employed youth 16 to 24 years old increased by 1.6 million to 19.3 million." On the other hand, "the proportion of young people who were employed in July was 51.4 percent, the lowest July rate on record for the series, which began in 1948" (U.S. Department of Labor, 2009). It is clear that although youth want to work, the current economic situation is making it difficult for young people to find employment. For instance, "In July 2009, 4.4 million youth were unemployed, up by nearly 1.0 million from July 2008. The youth unemployment rate was 18.5 percent in July 2009" (U.S. Department of Labor, 2009). Although youth in general are being affected by the weak job market, not all youth are being affected equally. "The July 2009 unemployment rates for young men (19.7 percent), women (17.3 percent), whites (16.4 percent), blacks (31.2 percent), Asians (16.3 percent), and Hispanics (21.7 percent) increased from a year earlier" (U.S. Department of Labor, 2009). It is clear from the data that blacks and Hispanics are disproportionately affected by the poor job market.

Although many in the United States believe that leisure does not serve an important purpose, others believe it serves numerous important purposes. As mentioned in this chapter, leisure has the ability to help prevent numerous illnesses, buffer the stresses of everyday life, and even help people overcome traumatic events. When a person loses her job and is left unemployed, this may cause severe stress and even trauma. During these critical times, leisure plays an important role.

Researchers have found that leisure provides a source of well-being for unemployed young adults, including those in minority ethnic and racial groups (Melamed et al., 1995). For instance, it has been found that unemployed young adults who participated in leisure activities that were more challenging and active had higher levels of psychological well-being than those who did not (Haworth & Ducker, 1991). As noted, how people use their leisure influences the wellness outcomes people derive from leisure. Another example comes from a study of the mental health of unemployed men (Kilpatrick & Trew, 1985). Unemployed men who spent their leisure time doing passive activities, such as watching television, had the poorest psychological well-being. Unemployed men who were active, such as through volunteering and actively pursuing leisure interests outside the home, had higher levels of psychological well-being.

Material Well-Being

The money that we make while employed helps us sustain our current lifestyles and move into new lifestyles. The relationship that we have with money is interesting. Money is necessary to purchase food and clothes, keep a roof over our head, have access to transportation, or simply enjoy leisure activities. Being a student without money is difficult because you are living month to month trying to figure out how to pay the next bill. This stress may take its toll on you, and your quality of life may suffer because of it. There are many examples showing how money plays an important role in your life, but the relationship is not simple. For instance, although money increases the quality of your life, once you have enough money to meet daily necessities, making more money does not affect your quality of life as much. Findings such as these have stimulated thought about other indicators of quality of life.

At least nine factors affect our quality of life: cost of living, leisure and culture, economy, environment, freedom, health, infrastructure, risk and safety, and climate (InternationalLiving.com, 2009). According to these indicators, in 2009 France was identified as the country with the highest level of quality of life followed by Switzerland, the United States, Luxembourg, and Australia. Interestingly, Italy had the highest score on leisure and culture, followed by France, Japan, and the United States.

SOCIAL SUPPORT

Going to college is often a major transition for many students. Many students leave their homes and relocate to their university. As part of the relocation, students often leave behind the social support that they have had throughout their lives. For instance, although some friends from your high school may attend your new university, many other friends simply move on. Although your family might still be there for you, they may be miles away. The wonderful dinners you grew accustomed to at home may now be replaced with microwave noodles or cheap pizza to save some money. You are on your own to do your laundry, pay bills, clean your apartment, and do all the other chores that we often take for granted when we live at home. Moreover, all those places you used to visit when you were younger that

©Stockdisc Royalty Free Photos

Few groups provide us with as much social support as our family. During your college years, you may notice many students building stronger bonds with their families. As we mature, we tend to realize just how important our family is, in particular through the more difficult times in our lives.

brought you peace and happiness, especially when you were feeling down, may be too far for you to visit with any consistency. In other words, your social support has changed. This stripping of a person's social support often makes the first year of college quite difficult. Yet, all is not gloom; in your first year at a university, you also meet new friends, perhaps visit your family a few times, and even begin to make deep connections with the leisure places you experience.

Spending time with people, in particular those who care about you, such as your family, friends, and significant others, has consistently been associated with better physical health, **mental health**, and quality of life throughout the life span (Bovier et al., 2004; Cummins, 1996; Langford et al., 1997). For instance, social support helps decrease depression, increase personal competence during stressful life events, and influence positive affect, sense of stability, recognition of self-worth, and life satisfaction (Langford et al., 1997). Think about your friends in college. How often have they stepped up to the plate when you needed someone to hang out with, grab a quick bite with, or simply talk to? If you answered "very often," this is a good indicator that you have strong social support. A study of undergraduate students found that the very happiest students were highly social and had stronger romantic and other social relationships more often than did less happy students (Diener & Seligman, 2002).

Social support has been defined as "the assistance and protection given to others, especially to individuals" (Langford et al., 1997, p. 95). Assistance can come in many forms, such as lending money or providing a person with a place to call home. Social support may include providing someone with emotional support after a breakup, following a bad exam, or when he just needs some encouragement. Protection refers to what one may envision a shield doing for a knight; a person may protect another by shielding her from threats, such as life stresses.

Necessary Components for Social Support

At least three components are necessary to foster social support: social networks, social embeddedness, and social climate (Langford et al., 1997). To understand a **social network**, envision a car traveling along a road. The road represents the social network: It provides a path for social support to function. Having large social networks, such as having an interstate highway system, to continue the analogy, does not necessarily mean that you have a greater amount of social support, but smaller social networks would limit your social support; only so many cars can fit on a small strip of road.

Social embeddedness refers to the connectedness people have to others within their social network, the depth and strength of relational ties between people in a social network (Langford et al., 1997). Imagine two separate roads, one with a sheet of ice over it and the other without. Lower levels of social embeddedness are more like a road with ice, where cars or people slip in and out of the road or network with little keeping them together. Social embeddedness is necessary for strong social support to develop.

Social climate refers to the personality of people in a social network (Langford et al., 1997). In keeping with the driving analogy, it is the difference between driving on a road with courteous drivers or drivers who conduct themselves in dangerous and inappropriate ways on the road. Social networks with more "courteous drivers" tend to foster more positive social support.

WHAT DO YOU THINK?

Think about your first year of college. Did you feel alienated and out of place at first? Did it take long to form a social support network away from your family and home-town friends?

Leisure and Social Support

It has been well documented that leisure participation often is social and is organized around groups of family members or friends (Coleman, 1993; Coleman & Iso-Ahola, 1993; Godbey et al., 2005). As such, an important role of leisure activities and programs is to provide people an opportunity to develop companionship and friendships (Coleman & Iso-Ahola, 1993). These opportunities can promote social support because they increase people's social networks in a safe and fun environment. For example, researchers have found that people who are more involved in sport and recreation activities develop larger networks of friends, receive more social support, and are more likely to socialize with other people (Coleman & Iso-Ahola, 1993). Given that leisure participation involves some form of active involvement by participants, people have the opportunity to interact with each other, which may promote social embeddedness. Leisure programmers often strategically integrate icebreakers to overcome any initial social awkwardness that may be present when groups of people meet for the first time. Many leisure activities naturally provide a social climate that promotes an exchange of assistance or helpfulness and protection, as are integral to social support. For instance, sport-based activities such as team basketball, baseball, softball, soccer, football, and volleyball have rules and regulations that encourage group and team unity. It is by playing together that teams have advantages. As the saying goes, "There is no *I* in *team*."

COMMUNITIES AND NEIGHBORHOODS

The communities and neighborhoods in which we regularly interact influence our quality of life (Allen, 1990; Baker & Palmer, 2006; Sirgy & Cornwell, 2002). For instance, if you are not satisfied with where you live or where you spend most of your day, this may have a negative effect on your quality of life. This lack of satisfaction may come in many different forms. You may simply not feel safe in your community, or you may not like that the closest gym is more than 5 miles away. Perhaps you live too far away from your friends. There are many reasons for not being satisfied with your community. **Community** has been defined as "an area in which individuals and groups regularly interact to integrate various attributes, opportunities and services for the fulfillment of subsistence needs and the establishment of a sense of community" (Allen, 1990, p. 184) and **neighborhood** as "the area immediately adjacent to a resident dwelling" (Allen, 1990, p. 186). In other words, our neighborhood is where we live, whereas our community is where we primarily interact with other people.

Key Community Elements

Researchers have identified at least five key components of a community that significantly predict increases in quality of life: recreation participation, community involvement, residency, community pride, and community elements. Recreation participation includes participation in activities for educational or self-improvement purposes, outdoor activities, artistic activities, and active recreation activities. Participation in these recreation pursuits is directly linked to increases in community pride and quality of life. Community involvement includes items such as being involved in making community decisions and working together with other community members to get things done. Residency includes the number of years a person lives in both her community and her neighborhood. Community pride is composed of two main items: how attached residents are to their community and how satisfied they are with their community. Finally, community elements focus on social and physical leisure opportunities within a community, such as special events and festivals, parks and open spaces, clubs and organizations, and general entertainment and recreation opportunities. Both community pride and community elements are directly linked to quality of life (Baker & Palmer, 2006).

Key Neighborhood Elements

Researchers have identified the elements of a neighborhood that promote higher levels of quality of life among their residents. These have been broken down into three categories: physical, social, and economic. Physical elements include satisfaction with the upkeep of homes and yards, landscapes in the neighborhood, street lighting, crowding and noise level, nearness to needed facilities, and the overall quality of the environment. Social elements include satisfaction with social interactions with neighbors, outdoor play spaces, people living in the neighborhood, ties with people, crime, race relations, and a sense of privacy at home. Finally, economic elements include satisfaction with a home's value in the neighborhood,

©Human Kinetics

Serving the community is one way in which we build a stronger relationship with those in the community. This may come in many ways but involves reaching beyond ourselves to help someone else.

WHAT DO YOU THINK?

Think about where you live now. Is it similar to or different from where you would like to live in the future? What features in your neighborhood are must-haves in your future residence? How would it affect your quality of life in the future if your neighborhood did not have these features?

cost of living, socioeconomic status of neighborhood, and neighborhood improvements (Sirgy & Cornwell, 2002).

Recreation Facilities and Programs

As part of both key community and neighborhood elements, the recreation facilities near a person's home or within the community are important contributors to that person's quality of life. Three sectors provide recreation facilities and programs: public, nonprofit, and private. Public recreation facilities span most leisure activities imaginable. At the local level, such as cities, townships, counties, and special districts, this may include traditional parks, skate parks, dog parks, playgrounds, museums, fitness centers, convention centers, aquatic facilities, or hiking trails. For instance, in Phoenix, Arizona, South Mountain Park/Preserve provides more than 51 miles of primary trails for horseback riding, hiking, and mountain biking on more than 16,000 acres of land (City of Phoenix Parks and Recreation Department, 2009). At the state and federal levels, facilities primarily focus on outdoor recreation and tourism-oriented activities. For instance, within the U.S. Department of the Interior, the National Park Service manages numerous national parks, such as Yellowstone and the Grand Canyon, which attract more than 200 million visitors each year (National Park Service, 2009). The Bureau of Land Management manages more than 250 million acres of public lands for recreation purposes where people can do just about any outdoor recreation activity imaginable, including birding, boating, camping, climbing, fishing, hang gliding, hiking, horseback riding, hunting, mountain biking, off-road driving, photography, and whitewater rafting (Bureau of Land Management, 2009).

The nonprofit and private sectors provide a number of programs and facilities for recreation. We can join the YMCA and work out in the gym or volunteer in the local 4-H to increase our participation in and pride in our community. We can attend a private concert with a loved one, go to a health spa to relax, or take a trip to Disney World with our family.

SUMMARY

Happiness is not so much a destination as a journey. Leisure influences your life journey in a number of ways and, ultimately, your quality of life. Leisure affects health in three ways: prevention, coping, and transcendence. For instance, being physically active in many leisure pursuits, such as biking or playing tennis, increases muscle strength, improves joint functioning, and helps us manage our body weight. As a form of coping, leisure helps to buffer the negative stress that people often encounter. Moreover, leisure helps people to transcend very negative life events by providing distraction, generating optimism about the future, and aiding the reconstruction of people's life stories. Leisure can promote spiritual well-being as well. Leisure activities such as meditation and relaxation exercises increase our spiritual levels, whereas activities such as gardening, tai chi, and walking help to ground us when spiritual levels are too high. People are likely to have leisure pursuits consistent with skills obtained during their work. Unemployment may influence our quality of life if our basic needs are not met. By providing us opportunities to find social support, leisure may alleviate some of the negative effects of unemployment. Leisure increases the size of social networks and encourages social embeddedness within positive social climates. Within communities and neighborhoods, leisure is important in promoting positive quality of life. Participation in recreation and leisure pursuits helps to promote community pride, which is directly linked to increases in quality of life.

Learning Activities

1. **Online activity:** Participate in a social or chat room of common recreation or leisure activities (e.g., reading club, cycling club, or an official club either on campus or out of campus) with other classmates. Post discussions at least once a week pertaining to club activities and experiences.

2. **Application activity:** Discuss with at least 3 other people in your class the changes they are making in their lives based on what they have learned from the chapter. The intent is to apply the new understanding you have about leisure and its role and function in your life and lifestyle.

3. **Dealing with stress:** Describe a period in your life when you felt a high level of stress. How did you reduce your stress? Did leisure play a role in this stress reduction? If yes, how? If not, how might it have helped reduce your level of stress?

4. **Social networking:** Describe the last time you volunteered (if you have not volunteered, find someone close to you who has and ask him or her the following questions). Describe the volunteering experience: Where did it take place? What was the cause? With whom did you volunteer? Describe how this volunteering experience made you feel. Was it a meaningful experience? What would have made this experience more meaningful to you? How might a volunteering experience such as the one you had positively influence the physical, mental, and spiritual health of a person who is unemployed?

5. **Journal or diary activity:** Complete an activity journal or diary that contains work, leisure, school, and social activities and involvements for 7 days. Each day, document how the activities in each category contribute to your quality of life, including your physical, mental, and spiritual health. After 7 days, decide whether there are any activities that you would like to discontinue, activities that you would like to do more of, and activities that you would like to include in your daily life and why.

For additional assignments, Web links, and more, visit the online student resource at www.HumanKinetics.com/DimensionsOfLeisureForLife.

Review Questions

1. Describe the three ways in which leisure influences health and well-being.

2. Describe the competing relationships between leisure and work.

3. Will making a great deal of money automatically lead to a higher level of quality of life? Explain.

4. What leisure activities should you do if your spiritual energy is too high? Too low?

5. How do your neighborhood and community influence your quality of life?

Leisure Reading

Honore, C. (2005). *In praise of slowness: Challenging the cult of speed.* New York: HarperOne.

Layard, R. (2005). *Happiness: Lessons from a new science.* New York: Penguin Books.

Glossary

autonomy—An inner endorsement of one's action; personal choice.

community—An area in which individuals and groups regularly interact to integrate various attributes, opportunities, and services to fulfill subsistence needs and establish a sense of community.

competence—Feeling of capability.

coping—Process of managing difficult circumstances.

mental health—Emotional and cognitive health.

neighborhood—The area immediately adjacent to a resident dwelling.

physical health—State of a person's body, including presence or absence of disease.

prevention—Any activity that reduces the chances of poor health or other risk factors.

relatedness—The desire to feel connected to others; to feel a sense of belonging.

sacrilization—State of being sensitized to one's spiritual self.

serious leisure—The systematic pursuit of an amateur, hobbyist, or volunteer activity that participants find so substantial and interesting that, in the typical case, they launch themselves on a career centered on acquiring and expressing its special skills, knowledge, and experience.

social climate—Atmosphere resulting from the personalities of people in a social network.

social embeddedness—The connectedness people have to others within their social network.

social network—The set of relationships between people.

social support—The assistance and protection given to others, especially to individual people.

spiritual health—State of a person's faith, hope, and commitment in relation to a well-defined worldview or belief system that provides a sense of meaning and purpose to existence.

transcendence—The ability of leisure to help a person overcome a traumatic life event.

References

Allen, L.R. (1990). Benefits of leisure attributes to community satisfaction. *Journal of Leisure Research, 22*(2), 183-196.

Baker, D.A., & Palmer, R.J. (2006). Examining the effects of perceptions of community and recreation participation on quality of life. *Social Indicators Research, 75,* 395-418.

Biddle, S.J.H., Fox, K.R., Boutcher, S.H., & Faulkner, G.E. (2000). The way forward for physical activity and the promotion of psychological well-being. In S.J.H. Biddle, K.R. Fox, & S.H. Boutcher (Eds.), *Physical activity and psychological well-being* (pp. 154-168). New York: Routledge.

Bovier, P.A., Chamot, E., & Perneger, T.V. (2004). Perceived stress, internal resources, and social support as determinants of mental health among young adults. *Quality of Life Research, 13,* 161-170.

Bureau of Land Management. (2009). *Recreation and visitor services.* www.blm.gov/wo/st/en/prog/ Recreation.html

Caldwell, L.L. (2005). Leisure and health: Why is leisure therapeutic? *British Journal of Guidance & Counseling, 33*(1), 7-26.

City of Phoenix Parks and Recreation Department. (2009). *Hiking trails: South Mountain Park/ Preserve.* http://phoenix.gov/parks/hikesoth.html

CNN. (2009). *Obama's inaugural speech.* www.cnn.com/2009/POLITICS/01/20/obama.politics/ index.html

Coleman, D. (1993). Leisure based social support, leisure dispositions, and health. *Journal of Leisure Research, 25*(4), 350-361.

Coleman, D., & Iso-Ahola, S.E. (1993). Leisure and health: The role of social support and self-determination. *Journal of Leisure Research, 25*(2), 111-128.

Csikszentmihalyi, M. (1990). *Flow: The psychology of optimal experience.* New York: Harper & Row.

Cummins, R.A. (1996). The domains of life satisfaction: An attempt to order chaos. *Social Indicators Research, 38,* 303-328.

Deci, E.L., & Ryan, R.M. (2000). The "what" and "why" of goal pursuits: Human needs and the self-determination of behavior. *Psychological Inquiry, 11*(4), 227-268.

Diener, E., & Seligman, M.E.P. (2002). Very happy people. *Psychological Science, 13*(1), 81-84.

Fox, K.R., Boutcher, S.H., Faulkner, G.E., & Biddle, S.J.H. (2000). The case for exercise in the promotion of mental health and psychological well-being. In S.J.H. Biddle, K.R. Fox, & S.H. Boutcher (Eds.), *Physical activity and psychological well-being* (pp. 1-9). New York: Routledge.

Godbey, G., Caldwell, L.L., Floyd, M., & Payne, L. (2005). Contributions of leisure studies and recreation and park management research to the active living agenda. *American Journal of Preventive Medicine, 28,* 150-158.

Hawks, S. (1994). Spiritual health: Definition and theory. *Wellness Perspectives, 10,* 3-13.

Haworth, J.T., & Ducker, J. (1991). Psychological well-being and access to categories of experience in unemployed young adults. *Leisure Sciences, 10,* 265-274.

Heintzman, P. (2002). A conceptual model of leisure and spiritual well-being. *Journal of Park and Recreation Administration, 20*(4), 147-169.

InternationalLiving.com. (2009). *2009 quality of life index.* www.il-ireland.com/il/qofl2009/

Iso-Ahola, S.E., & Park, C.J. (1996). Leisure-related social support and self-determination as buffers of stress-illness relationship. *Journal of Leisure Research, 28*(3), 169-187.

Iwasaki, Y. (2001). Contributions of leisure to coping with daily hassles in university students' lives. *Canadian Journal of Behavioral Science, 33*(2), 128-141.

Iwasaki, Y. (2003). The impact of leisure coping beliefs and strategies on adaptive outcomes. *Leisure Studies, 22,* 93-108.

Kahn, E.B., Ramsey, L.T., Brownson, R.C., Heath, G.W., Howze, E.H., Powell, K.E., et al. (2002). The effectiveness of interventions to increase physical activity: A systematic review. *American Journal of Preventive Medicine, 22*(4 Suppl. 1), 73-107.

Kilpatrick, R., & Trew, K. (1985). Lifestyles and psychological well-being among unemployed men in Northern Ireland. *Journal of Occupational Psychology, 58,* 207-216.

Kleiber, D.A., Hutchinson, S.L., & Williams, R. (2002). Leisure as a resource in transcending negative life events: Self-protection, self-restoration, and personal transformation. *Leisure Sciences, 24*(2), 219-235.

Langford, C.P.H., Bowsher, J., Maloney, J.P., & Lillis, P.P. (1997). Social support: A conceptual analysis. *Journal of Advanced Nursing, 25,* 95-100.

Larson, J.S. (1991). *The measurement of health: Concepts and indicators.* New York: Greenwood Press.

Mannell, R.C., & Reid, D.G. (1999). Work and leisure. In E.L. Jackson & T.L. Burton (Eds.), *Leisure studies: Prospects for the twenty-first century* (pp. 151-165). State College, PA: Venture.

Melamed, S., Meir, E.I., & Samson, A. (1995). The benefits of personality-leisure congruence: Evidence and implications. *Journal of Leisure Research, 27*, 25-40.

Miilunpalo, S. (2001). Evidence and theory based promotion of health-enhancing physical activity. *Public Health Nutrition, 4*(2B), 725-728.

Mutrie, N. (2000). The relationship between physical activity and clinically defined depression. In S.J.H. Biddle, K.R. Fox, & S.H. Boutcher (Eds.), *Physical activity and psychological well-being* (pp. 46-62). New York: Routledge.

National Park Service. (2009). *Frequently asked questions.* www.nps.gov/faqs.htm

Pedersen, B.K., & Clemmensen, I.H. (1997). Exercise and cancer. In B.K. Pedersen (Ed.), *Exercise immunology* (pp. 171-201). Austin, TX: Landes.

Ryan, R.M., & Deci, E.L. (2000). Self-determination theory and the facilitation of intrinsic motivation, social development, and well-being. *American Psychologist, 55*(1), 68-78.

Schnohr, P., Scharling, H., & Jensen, J.S. (2003). Changes in leisure-time physical activity and risk of death: An observational study of 7,000 men and women. *American Journal of Epidemiology, 158*(7), 639-644.

Sirgy, J.M., & Cornwell, T. (2002). How neighborhood features affect quality of life. *Social Indicators Research, 59*, 79-114.

Stebbins, R.A. (1999). Serious leisure. In E.L. Jackson & T.L. Burton (Eds.), *Leisure studies: Prospects for the twenty-first century* (pp. 69-79). State College, PA: Venture.

Tousley, M. (2006). *Grief Gone Wild—Grief healing discussion groups.* http://hovforum.ipbhost.com/index.php?showtopic=1591&pid=8910&st=0&#entry8910

U.S. Department of Health and Human Services. (1996). *Physical activity and health: A report of the Surgeon General.* Atlanta, GA: U.S. Department of Health and Human Services, Centers for Disease Control and Prevention.

U.S. Department of Health and Human Services. (2000). *Healthy People 2010* (2nd ed.). Washington, DC: U.S. Government Printing Office.

U.S. Department of Labor, Bureau of Labor Statistics. (2009). *Employment and unemployed among youth—summer 2009.* www.bls.gov/news.release/pdf/youth.pdf

Wankel, L.M., & Berger, B.G. (1991). The personal and social benefits of sport and physical activity. In B.L. Driver, P.J. Brown, & G.L. Peterson (Eds.), *Benefits of leisure* (pp. 121-144). State College, PA: Venture.

4

Leisure, Health, and Physical Activity

Jason N. Bocarro • Michael A. Kanters
North Carolina State University

Learning Outcomes

After reading this chapter, you will be able to

▶ identify some of the major trends and statistics relating to physical inactivity as well as the consequences of these trends,

▶ understand how the leisure services field can facilitate active living and positively contribute to addressing this public health issue, and

▶ understand how leisure behavior can contribute to personal health and wellness.

Vocabulary Terms

health
leisure-time physical activity

Photo courtesy of Brad Allen

Leisure time physical activity can take many forms, and it benefits all ages.

©Human Kinetics

Have you ever wondered why most exercise DVDs and videos remain in their packages and are never used? Why do so many people sign up for gym memberships and never go to the gym? Why do the people who do go to the gym watch TV and listen to iPods when they work out? Although most people in Western society believe that physical activity has health benefits, many do not find exercise to be fun and either look for distractions to make it more palatable or simply never get around to it. There is a disconnect between knowledge and action.

Looking to a purely medical solution to this problem discounts the potential contribution of the parks and recreation profession. We are trained to understand what motivates people to engage in leisure experiences. We are the so-called experts in creating leisure experiences that are both enjoyable and meaningful for participants. By acting as integral partners in solving the crisis of physical inactivity, obesity, and health in our society, parks and recreation professionals are more likely to find solutions that people will accept.

Parks and recreation services have the potential to improve everyone's health and physical activity levels. Furthermore, as the two photographs shown here illustrate, services and programs offered by the parks and recreation profession attract a wide segment of the population. This is why many public health professionals and policy makers interested in increasing the physical activity level of Americans look to the parks and recreation profession.

The potential for leisure amenities and programs to help people become physically active (i.e., to engage in active recreation), and thus healthier, is great. Sports programs, parks, trails and greenways, and outdoor adventure activities are just some examples of how the leisure services industry enhances all people's personal health and wellness.

This chapter begins by outlining recent physical activity trends and some of the health and economic ramifications that have occurred as a result of inactivity. The chapter describes how leisure activities, leisure services, and leisure professionals can play an integral role in addressing this public health crisis. We end by sharing some real-life examples of how recreation and leisure professionals are implementing health strategies and making a difference in their communities.

PHYSICAL ACTIVITY TRENDS

Obesity and the associated health costs have become a major worldwide concern. According to the World Health Organization (WHO, 2005), rates of obesity for both children and adults have reached pandemic levels. According to projections by WHO, there are 1.6 billion overweight and 400 million obese adults worldwide, and this organization predicts that by 2015 these numbers will increase to 2.3 billion overweight and 700 million obese adults. In the United States, the Centers for Disease Control and Prevention (CDC) reports that 65 percent of adults and 16 percent of children and adolescents are overweight or obese. Obesity prevalence is also rising in countries throughout the world, reaching 20 to 30 percent in some European countries and 70 percent in Polynesia (Kumanyika et al., 2008). One of the primary reasons for these higher rates of obesity is increasingly sedentary lifestyles. For an interesting slideshow documenting these trends, see www.cdc.gov/obesity/data/trends.html.

> Many of us think of health as only the absence of illness. It is much more than that. It is a state of being, which extends beyond just "feeling good" and enters the "plus" margin of physical, mental, and social well-being.
>
> *Charles Brightbill*

As figure 4.1 shows, sedentary living and obesity across all age, social, ethnic, and economic categories have reached epidemic proportions in the United States. The CDC reports that 65 percent of adults and 16 percent of children and adolescents are overweight or obese (Hedley et al., 2004). Recent data from the CDC (2004) show that from 1980 to 2002, the rate of obesity among children aged 6 to 11 climbed from 7 to 16 percent, and among adolescents aged 12 to 19 obesity tripled from 5 to 16 percent.

Trends regarding sedentary living and obesity have attracted much media and political attention because sedentary living substantially increases the risk of significant diseases including heart attacks, breast and colon cancer, osteoporosis, stroke, and numerous other life-threatening illnesses (see Calle & Kaaks, 2004; CDC, 1997; Must et al., 1999; Visscher & Seidell, 2001). As figure 4.2 shows, this can have a profound economic cost.

The percentage of overweight adults, adolescents, and children has increased so significantly that the CDC and numerous other U.S. federal, state, and local agencies have identified the reduction of obesity as one of the nation's top health priorities. The field of parks and recreation can make a major, positive contribution in addressing this public health challenge.

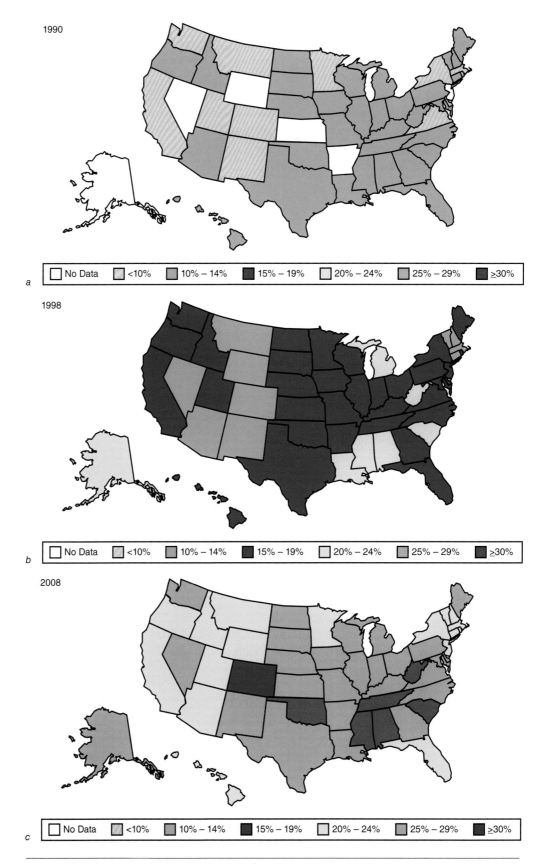

Figure 4.1 Obesity trends among U.S. adults, from Behavioral Risk Factor Surveillance System (BRFSS): *(a)* 1990, *(b)* 1998, and *(c)* 2008.

From CDC.

FIGURE 4.2

Economic Consequences of Obesity

As obesity increases, so does the use of health care services (36 percent increase in annual costs to the individual).

Estimates of cost to the nation range from $69 to $117 billion per year:

- $61 billion in direct costs
- $56 billion in indirect costs

Cost to employers is approximately $13 billion annually:

- $8 billion in health insurance expenditures
- $2.4 billion in sick leave
- $1.8 billion for life insurance
- $1 billion for disability
- Indirect quality of life costs, lost human potential, premature loss of life, and other nonmeasurable, noneconomic consequences

WHAT IS HEALTH?

The World Health Organization defines **health** as "a complete state of physical, mental and social well being, and not merely the absence of disease or infirmity." Thus, it is important to recognize that the dimensions of health include physical, social, emotional, and psychological aspects. WHO recognizes that governments have a responsibility for the health of their people that can be fulfilled by the provision of adequate health and social measures. Increasing physical activity is a key component of improving people's health.

Benefits of Regular Physical Activity

- Reduce the risk of premature death
- Improve aerobic endurance and muscular strength
- Favorably affect risk factors for cardiovascular disease
- Decrease blood pressure in adolescents with borderline hypertension
- Increase physical fitness in obese children

SELF-DISCOVERY

Think about what you did last week. How much physical activity did you engage in? How would you categorize your physical activity (e.g., moderate, vigorous)? Review the CDC guidelines for physical activity online (www.cdc.gov/physicalactivity/everyone/guidelines/index.html) and then evaluate whether your physical activity in the past week met these guidelines. Then determine whether you need more physical activity in your life. What specific changes could you make to satisfy these guidelines?

©Photodisc/Getty Images

Opportunities for physical activity are often prevalent on college campuses, but are they being used?

- Decrease degree of overweight in obese children
- Increase of self-esteem and self-concept
- Reduce anxiety and stress

As the list indicates, physical activity carries numerous benefits. Most people are at least aware of some of these benefits. However, as was the case with previous public health challenges (like smoking and AIDS), translating knowledge into action requires a coordinated effort by a variety of agencies and policy initiatives. Parks and recreation is considered a profession that can play a pivotal role.

PARKS AND RECREATION: MAKING A DIFFERENCE

The role of parks and recreation in helping people to become physically active has seemed obvious since the recreation movement began well over a century ago (Bocarro et al., 2009). However, that role has become more pronounced since the emergence of some key political reports and research. For example, every 10 years, the U.S. Department of Health and Human Services initiates a health promotion and disease prevention plan for the country called *Healthy People*. The most recent plan, *Healthy People 2010* (U.S. Department of Health and Human Services, 2000), challenges individuals, communities, and professionals to take specific steps to ensure that good health and a long life are enjoyed by all. It has two overarching goals:

Goal 1: To help people of all ages increase life expectancy and improve their quality of life

Goal 2: To eliminate health disparities among different segments of the population

Healthy People 2010 emphasizes that the design of communities and the presence of parks, trails, and other public recreational facilities affect people's abilities to reach the recommended 30 minutes of moderate-intensity physical activity or 20 minutes of vigorous activity each day. The document specifically mentions two objectives that affect sedentary leisure behavior:

- Reduce the proportion of adults who engage in no leisure-time physical activity
- Reduce the proportion of adolescents who view television two or more hours on a school day

Other landmark reports have pointed to the importance of parks and recreation in increasing physical activity. A review of environmental and policy approaches for increasing physical activity found that creating and enhancing access to places for physical activity and providing informational outreach can increase by 25 percent the number of people who exercise three times or more per week (Task Force on Community Preventive Services, 2002). In a national survey of city managers in the United States, 89 percent indicated that the primary governmental agency responsible for helping to address the obesity problem is parks and recreation (International City/County Management Association, 2005).

As park and recreation professionals design programs and interventions to address levels of physical inactivity within their communities, it is important to be aware of some of the following trends.

People 12 to 21 Years Old

- Fifty percent do not engage in regular, vigorous physical activity.
- Fourteen percent report no recent physical activity.
- Inactivity is more prevalent among females (14 percent) than males (7 percent).
- Inactivity is more prevalent among black females (21 percent) than white females (12 percent).
- People in urban areas tend to be less overweight or obese than those in rural areas, putting them less at risk for the health risks associated with overweight or obesity (e.g., stroke, high blood pressure, diabetes, and so on).
- Physical activity declines with age.
- Enrollment in physical education classes is declining.
- Funding for after-school and community-based programs continues to be a challenge.
- Approximately 80 percent of physical activity occurs outside of school (in community-based programs).

Adults (22 and Older)

- Six of 10 adults do not engage in the recommended amount of activity.
- One of four adults reports no physical activity at all.
- Physical inactivity is more prevalent among women than men.
- Physical inactivity is more prevalent among African American and Hispanic adults than whites.
- Physical inactivity is more prevalent among older adults than younger adults.
- Physical inactivity is related to affluence (less affluent people are less active, more affluent people are more active).

Parks and recreation professionals must consider statistics such as these. For example, understanding why certain segments of the population (e.g., people from rural communities, African Americans and Hispanics) are less physically active is an important determinant to consider before programmatic, environmental, or policy changes are enacted or resource allocations are made.

> ### WHAT DO YOU THINK?
>
> Look at the Self-Discovery sidebar on page 71 and consider your current levels of physical activity. Now think back to your childhood and the community in which you lived. Describe your patterns of **leisure-time physical activity** and the community resources that facilitated your activity levels. How much did your leisure-time physical activity depend on the resources provided by your community's parks and recreation services (i.e., parks and open spaces, swimming pools, community centers, sport facilities, walking trails)? What improvements would you recommend for your childhood community to better facilitate an active leisure lifestyle for its residents?

LEISURE AND LIFE STRESS

For more than two decades stress has been identified as a significant health issue. In 1983, *Time* magazine declared that stress was "the epidemic of the 80s" (Wallis et al., 1983). Since then our lives have been further influenced by the Internet, cell phones, text messaging, 24-hour news from around the world, a global economy, self-managed retirement plans, changing expectations in the home and at work, and a growing list of things we can't control, like global warming, terrorism, and the ever-changing causes of cancer. Ask any adults between the ages of 20 and 60 to use one word to describe their lives and themselves, and odds are it wouldn't be *calm, serene,* or *content.* According to a recent survey by the American Psychological Association (APA), nearly half of all Americans report that stress has a negative impact on both their personal and professional lives. Results of their survey also indicated that many Americans had experienced physical symptoms (77 percent) and psychological symptoms (73 percent) related to stress in the previous month (APA, 2007). The question before us then is not whether we will experience stress in our lives but rather how we will cope with stress when it arrives. (See chapter 5 for more in-depth discussion of coping with stressors.)

Most leisure researchers acknowledge that leisure activities can have both positive and detrimental effects, but there is a growing consensus that leisure can act as a protective factor against negative events that occur and can contribute to a person's general state of resiliency (Caldwell, 2005). Efforts to understand why some people stay healthy and others become ill when negative life events occur indicate that people with a higher degree of resiliency or balance between risk and protective factors tend to be healthier. It also seems evident that leisure is a general protective factor and the specific outcomes of leisure participation can also be protective. Common leisure-related protective factors include these (Caldwell, 2005):

- Benefits of personally meaningful or intrinsically interesting activity
- Social support, friendships, and social acceptance
- Competence and self-efficacy
- Experiences of challenge and being totally absorbed in an activity
- Feelings of self-determination and control over one's life

- Feeling relaxed, disengaging from stress, and being distracted from negative life events through leisure
- Continuity in life after experiencing disability

It seems clear that leisure activities can be therapeutic and can decrease the negative health effects of stressful life events. How leisure contributes to stress-related coping responses at different ages and across various ethnic and socioeconomic groups is unclear; however, it does seem evident that leisure in and of itself does not yield the desired outcomes. The environment in which leisure occurs and the leisure choices people make can either maximize or minimize the protective nature of leisure. It also seems clear that people need help to maximize the benefits of leisure activities (Caldwell, 2005). Leisure education at an early age can help children develop a repertoire of healthy leisure activities and avoid the many potential negative outcomes of physical inactivity.

Therefore, a community's resources for leisure-time physical activity affect people's amount of activity. Well-designed parks and recreation facilities and programs can help shape behavior patterns in the following ways, which provide greater stress-buffering properties:

- Activities can foster social interaction and friendships.
- Developmental sport and leisure activity programs that incorporate well-designed skill acquisition properties can help people develop a repertoire of leisure skills, fostering feelings of competency and self-efficacy.
- Aesthetically pleasing and nature-based outdoor spaces can provide opportunities for relaxing, which fosters disengagement from stressful environments or negative life events.

Community parks and recreation facilities and services provide an endless array of benefits. Not only do they help make our communities better places to live, but if designed well, these facilities and services can also provide protective factors against life's many negative and stressful events.

PROMOTING LIFELONG RECREATION AND ACTIVE LIVING

The importance of theories as well as the notion of theory guiding practice has long been debated. A simple explanation of the importance of theories is that they have been empirically tested and provide some understanding of outcomes given specific circumstances. These theories can then help us use available resources to effect specific outcomes. In the case of physical activity promotion, the leisure repertoire theory is useful in understanding why people do or don't engage in certain leisure activities.

Leisure researchers highlight the importance of involving people in a variety of leisure activities at a young age (see figure 4.3). The leisure repertoire theory suggests that people who develop a wide spectrum of activities during childhood are more likely to continue to participate in activities as they get older because of their broader leisure repertoire (and more activities to draw from). Thus, a person's leisure repertoire usually consists of activities in which they participate on a regular basis and do well.

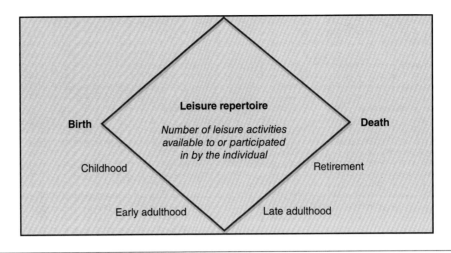

Figure 4.3   Leisure repertoire model.
Adapted from Iso-Ahola, Jackson, Dunn 1994.

Applying this theory one can see that an important predictor of lifelong participation in leisure activities does not appear to be the volume of leisure involvement as a child but rather the number of different leisure activities that young people are taught (Roberts & Brodie, 1992). As adults we become more conservative about our leisure lifestyle and tend to make leisure choices from our own repertoire of skilled activities (Iso-Ahola et al., 1994; Roberts, 1999). For example, adults in their 30s and 40s tend to have more family and work commitments and therefore less leisure time. Thus, they are more likely to engage in leisure activities that are accessible and that they have enjoyed previously in their lives. Consequently, the greater the repertoire of choices, the more likely people will remain committed leisure participants when moving from adolescence to adulthood.

Some studies have found a positive association between participation in youth sports and increased physical activity in later life (e.g., Green et al., 2005; Taylor et al., 1999; van Mechelen et al., 2000). However, children who had negative experiences in youth sports and were forced (by their parents) to exercise were less likely to be physically active as adults. Thus, although participation in youth sports helps prevent both youth and adult obesity, it may also be a detriment depending on a child's experience (see figure 4.4). Sport participation itself may yield immediate benefits in the form of increased physical activity, yet long-term benefits such as positive attitudes toward sport participation and physical activity may be more dependent on the environment in which sport participation occurs.

The ultimate purpose of physically active leisure programs is to promote active lifestyles and lifelong participation in physical activity (Fairclough et al., 2002). By age 16 most adolescents have adopted a pattern of leisure activities that will form the foundation of their adult leisure lifestyle (Roberts, 1999). For example, in a study of men and women, the main characteristic of adults who had become committed to sport was that they had participated in several (usually three or more) games or activities during their lives (Roberts & Brodie, 1992).

Therefore, researchers and policy makers have begun to examine the long-term ramifications of youth involvement. These results have suggested that enjoyable participation in activities during childhood and adolescence can result in a "leisure for life" philosophy. Young adults are not likely to participate in sport if they have

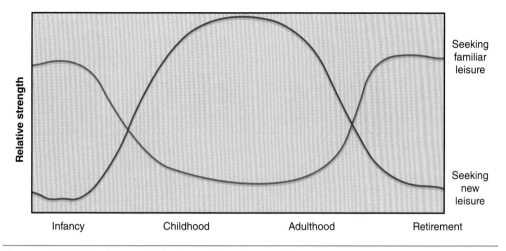

Figure 4.4 Tendencies to seek familiar and new forms of leisure.
Adapted from Iso-Ahola, Jackson, Dunn 1994.

not participated in the past (Perkins et al., 2004). Thus, youth are more likely to continue participation in an activity if they begin participating at a young age.

EXAMINING FACTORS THAT INFLUENCE BEHAVIOR

Many policy makers and practitioners have struggled with how to create interventions that make people healthier. In the past, strategies have focused on trying to make individual people healthier or more physically active and have not accounted for other important factors that may reinforce both healthy and unhealthy behaviors. For example, a parks and recreation department may successfully educate a teenager about the benefits of engaging in physically active leisure programs. However, if that teenager's peer group or family thinks that these programs are a waste of time or if the programs are situated in an area that is perceived as unsafe, the department's efforts will have limited success.

One model that has guided the design of interventions is the social ecological model (McLeroy et al., 1988). The social ecological model recognizes that multiple levels influence people's health and well-being. The model has five levels:

1. Interpersonal and individual factors
2. Interpersonal processes
3. Institutional (organizational) factors
4. Community factors
5. Public policy

The following sections discuss each of these in more detail.

Intrapersonal and Individual Factors

Interpersonal and individual factors primarily focus on individual characteristics such as psychological, developmental, and biological variables. Intervention strategies at this level tend to focus on educating people in order to change individual

Courtesy of the NHL

The Hockey Is for Everyone program combines hockey skills instruction with life skills instruction and is rooted in positive youth development practices. The program targets underserved youth, introducing them to a sport that they may not have been exposed to before.

behavior, influencing their attitudes, and challenging their beliefs. There are numerous examples of park and recreation programs attempting to persuade an individual to change his behavior. On college campuses, campus recreation programs try to convince faculty and students to change their behavior and become more physically active by using their facilities. In 2009, the National Hockey League established the Hockey Is for Everyone program, which focused part of its efforts on persuading people from less affluent communities that hockey could be a viable, healthy, and enjoyable leisure activity.

Interpersonal Processes

Interpersonal processes relate to primary social groups such as a person's family, friends, and peers. Intervention strategies focus on educating family members and peers and involving them in helping people change their behaviors. Examples are providing parents with information about recreation programs to encourage the parents to support their children's physical activity.

Institutional (Organizational) Factors

Institutional factors examine the policies, practices, and physical environment of an organization (typically the workplace or school) and how the organization supports healthy behavior change. For example, Moore Square Middle School in Wake County, North Carolina, decided that the interscholastic, highly competitive sport model was excluding many children from participating in sport. Furthermore, they felt that the interscholastic sport model often limited children to traditional sports such as basketball, football, and cheerleading. The school decided to implement an intramural sport program, giving every child at the school the opportunity to participate in a wide assortment of sports. Other examples of institutional factors include company incentives for employees to work out, time devoted to recess and physical education, and facilities provided within an organization to encourage physical activity.

Community Factors

Community factors involve the relationships among different organizations and social networks within a defined area. This may involve coordination of efforts among members of a community (schools, citizen groups, and community leaders). For example, the CDC recommends that schools and communities form partnerships so that school facilities can be used for recreation programs and physical activity opportunities after school hours, thereby increasing daily physical activity opportunities among adolescents. Schools have been recommended as a safe and accessible place for physical activity to occur within the community (American Academy of Pediatrics, 2006), and numerous communities across the country have established partnerships for the construction and joint use of school facilities. For example, all school grounds in Berkeley, California, are open to the public, and in Pitt County, North Carolina, local public school facilities are kept open to allow community use of school facilities through their schools and recreation program (Spengler et al., 2007). Other examples are coalitions and community groups formed to create green spaces, safe recreation areas, and parks within communities.

©Bananastock

Campus recreation facilities often provide easy access for college students to experience new or familiar leisure activities.

Public Policy

Public policy focuses on laws and policies at local, state, and national levels that promote physical activity. This includes physical education curricular legislation and government funding of facilities to promote physical activity patterns. For example, many local and state governments have the power to make communities healthier by implementing laws and policies that support more walking- and biking-friendly streets. When communities adopt this type of policy, they change how streets are designed and built so that residents of all ages and abilities can travel easily and safely along community streets, whether they are walking, biking, or riding the bus. The National Policy & Legal Analysis Network to Prevent Childhood Obesity (http://nplanonline.org) is an organization that has been established to help communities, advocates, and leaders navigate the complex world of policy as well as provide fact sheets, toolkits, training, and technical assistance to explain legal issues related to childhood obesity.

Previously, many strategies focused primarily on intrapersonal and interpersonal factors. However, focusing physical activity intervention strategies on intrapersonal factors and interpersonal processes can have limited or even no impact. For example, data may show that a particular strategy increases the population's knowledge about the benefits of physical activity, increases people's willingness to engage in physical activity (intrapersonal factors), and increases the level of support a person receives from his social support system (interpersonal processes), but that will have limited impact if a person's economic situation prohibits him from being physically active or his community has no safe environments in which citizens can be physically active. Research has shown that interventions designed to affect multiple levels of the social ecological model are much more effective at bringing about behavioral change within a community. Although it is rare for any one intervention to put into practice every level of the social ecological model, the more levels that a program or initiative contains the more effective the change will be.

The social ecological approach may be particularly prevalent when we work with underserved or specific populations with unique issues (e.g., poor people in rural areas, certain minority populations, elderly people, people with disabilities). Thus, the social ecological framework recognizes that different factors influence a person's ability to change her physical activity behavior. The model strongly supports the notion that everyone lives within an environment influenced by social systems that influence healthy behavior patterns.

EXAMPLES OF PHYSICAL ACTIVITY INITIATIVES

In the last few years, the National Recreation and Park Association has engaged in a number of physical activity initiatives. The number of studies examining the impact of parks and recreation facilities on people's physical activity levels has also increased. The following section shows three examples of research being put into action. The initiatives discussed here are strongly guided and influenced by the social ecological model.

North Carolina Senior Games

Engaging seniors and elderly adults in regular physical activity can have a number of benefits (Payne et al., 1999). However, the CDC has shown that only a third of persons aged 65 years and older participate in regular, sustained physical activity. The North Carolina Senior Games (NCSG) was designed to encourage year-round participation in local communities for people aged 55 years and older. It consists of local games run by local organizations, all under the NCSG umbrella. In 2006, more than 60,000 participants in 52 local games programs were served in all 100 counties of North Carolina. Most of the programs were delivered through a local parks and recreation department.

The NCSG program emphasizes educating people about the benefits of senior games (intrapersonal level) and often works through local resources like senior centers to engage senior peer groups (interpersonal level). This is important, because research has shown that many older adults participate in physical activity programs that are available through local community organizations (Orsega-Smith et al., 2003). Furthermore, many older adults like to participate in group-based physical activity programs (King, 2001). NCSG is successful in highlighting a third dimension of the social ecological model—the community (having a local infrastructure to support this change). Physical activity for these older participants is encouraged and maintained through NCSG, which is a locally based community organization. Research has shown the importance of providing supportive environments in which people can be physically active, such as community settings, facilities, and programs (Sallis et al., 1998). The results of research focused on NCSG have been encouraging. Researchers who compared the attitudes of NCSG participants with the CDC's measures found that NCSG participants reported feeling more healthy and engaged in more daily physical activity (Cardenas et al., 2009).

LEISURE HEALTH

How would you use the knowledge given here to advise your grandparents to become more physically active? What would you say to them? If you were charged with getting older citizens in your community involved in physical activity, how would you use some of the information provided here to create programs for these older adults?

Youth Sport Programs That Encourage Physical Activity

Youth sport has the potential to increase physical activity among children and play a major role in improving their health. Although it seems obvious that participation in youth sport would enhance children's health, the outcomes associated with youth sport participation are often contradictory. The book *The Last Child in the Woods* indicates that the increase in child obesity has "coincided with the greatest increase in organized sports for children in history" (Louv, 2005, p. 47).

Critics of sport question whether sport is addressing the public health challenge posed by obesity. There may be several reasons for the apparent positive association between child obesity and organized youth sport opportunities. One is that fewer options are available for students who are not advanced athletes (Koplan et al., 2005). Another reason is that some children find sports no longer fun, given the competitiveness of organized sports (Seefeldt et al., 1992). For whatever reason, participation in youth sport has declined significantly among both boys and girls during middle school years (see Hedstrom & Gould, 2004; President's Council on Physical Fitness and Sport, 1997). Following are other reasons for declining participation in youth sport:

- Students want to participate in other activities (Seefeldt et al., 1992).
- The distance from children's homes to their schools has increased. Because local school systems are building bigger schools on the outskirts of communities, where land is cheaper, students are faced with longer commuting times. For example, students who lived more than 5 miles from their school

had significantly lower levels of activity than children who lived within that radius (Cohen et al., 2006).

- Student have less free time given increasing commuting times, bus schedules, and excessive quantities of homework; environmental barriers exist as well (e.g., bad weather, no equipment) (Allison et al., 1999).
- Children have an increasingly negative attitude toward physical activity as they get older (Trudeau & Shepherd, 2005).
- Teenagers' preoccupation with technology has increased; recent statistics show that 71 percent of teenagers (ages 12-17) own cell phones, 77 percent own a game console (e.g., an Xbox or PlayStation), 74 percent own an iPod or MP3 player, 60 percent own or have access to a desktop or laptop computer, and 55 percent own a portable gaming device (Lenhart, 2009).

A growing body of research that has examined declining physical activity patterns in youth has led to calls for schools to introduce (or reintroduce) intramural programs (see Bocarro et al., 2008; Koplan et al., 2005). The primary motivation for implementing intramural programs is to reengineer sporting opportunities around children's motives for participating in sport. For example, when asked why they participate in sport, children rate "wanting to win" as eighth, behind factors such as "to have fun," "to stay in shape," "to learn and improve skills," and "to play as part of a team" (Seefeldt et al., 1992).

Although interscholastic competitive sport programs have strong roots within North American culture, they often serve only the most elite youth athletes—kids who make the school team. These programs also require participants to give up a significant portion of their free time to practice, travel, and participate in games, and in some cases the programs preclude participation in other sports. In other cases, students in certain grades are excluded from participation altogether (e.g., sixth-grade students in North Carolina are not allowed to try out for school teams). Remember previously in this chapter when we talked about the leisure repertoire theory. Think about the ramifications of excluding children from sport and leisure opportunities at a time when they are open to engaging in new activities that may provide a platform for lifetime involvement.

The intramural school sport philosophy incorporates the social ecological model in a number of ways. First, it provides more children with a diverse array of activities, taking into account some of the factors identified previously (intrapersonal level). Intramurals are often socially oriented, and mixed-gender participation is allowed (interpersonal level). This is important, given that a school social climate that supports girls' sports has been seen as a critical variable in influencing girls' levels of physical activity (Barr-Anderson et al., 2007; Birnbaum et al., 2005). Finally, intramural school sport programs provide an ecological context for shaping physical activity participation at the organizational or institutional level.

PERSONAL LEISURE

How many of you have given up participating in a sport because of some of the reasons described here? What could have been done to keep you engaged in these sports? On the other side, how many of you love participating in a sport and still do? Why?

Parks, Greenways, and Trails

Parks, trails, and greenways are community resources that have tremendous potential to contribute to people's overall health. Research shows that having access to these resources increases a person's physical activity levels (regardless of a person's income, age, race, or gender). That is because parks, greenways, and trails are typically free and accessible to all residents. Furthermore, these outdoor environments often make unique contributions that cannot be achieved in indoor settings such as gyms or at home (Shores & West, 2008). At the interpersonal level, research has shown that youth living in communities with parks and playgrounds tend to be more physically active than those living in communities with fewer parks (Davidson & Lawson, 2006). At the intrapersonal level, low-income youth who had access to supervised parks were found to be significantly more active than those without such access (Farley et al., 2007).

However, it is important to consider other factors within the social ecological model. For example, at the community level, proximity to parks, greenways, and trails as well as perceived neighborhood walkability is associated with higher use and rates of physical activity. Conversely, parks that have low ratings of maintenance, have high rates of physical incivilities (e.g., empty beer bottles, evidence of drug use), and are located near industrial sites are linked to lower use and lower levels of physical activity.

The NCSG; youth sport programs; and parks, trails, and greenways are just three examples. However, the number of physical activity initiatives continues to increase as community leaders begin to see the role and value of parks and recreation in addressing the public health challenge posed by obesity.

Physical activity initiatives have other tangential benefits. As we have seen, having access to parks, trails, greenways, and other recreation programs can help people maintain higher levels of physical activity, which decreases both individual and societal health costs. Think about where you would like to live when you graduate from college. Many community leaders have started to ask themselves what makes their community attractive, knowing that some of the most educated people want access to physical activity opportunities for their families because of the health benefits described here.

©Stephen Coburn/fotolia

Having access to greenways and trails has been shown to encourage more physical activity and is a desirable amenity for most people.

SUMMARY

Over the past decade, obesity in children and adults across all sectors of our population has become one of the top health priorities in the United States. Parks and recreation programs and leisure services have great potential to affect the health of the population. The dimensions of health extend beyond physical characteristics and include social, emotional, and psychological aspects. Although numerous factors affect individual responses to stress, leisure activities can both directly and indirectly moderate negative stress responses. Indeed, the engagement, challenging, or relaxing characteristics of leisure activities can directly minimize stress responses. It is important to engage people as early as possible in leisure activities—research shows that children who develop a wide spectrum of activities are more likely to continue to participate in activities as they get older relative to more inactive children. The social ecological model has helped policy makers, researchers, and practitioners develop strategies to improve individual health behaviors through parks and recreation programs and leisure services.

Learning Activities

1. **Community analysis of leisure facilities and recommendations for improvement:** Select a community that you are familiar with and have access to (avoid large cities). Summarize that community's parks and recreation resources from the perspective of facilitating physical activity. What recommendations would you make for improvements? Submit a PowerPoint presentation with recorded audio and a brief (two-page) summary report.

2. **Personal opinions:** Interview some people from different backgrounds, races, ethnicities, and cultures. How would you describe the leisure-time physical activity patterns of your subjects? Do cultural differences affect variations in leisure-time physical activity patterns? (two-page maximum)

For additional assignments, Web links, and more, visit the online student resource at www.HumanKinetics.com/DimensionsOfLeisureForLife.

Review Questions

1. What are the current trends in physical activity and obesity across the United States? Is there cause for concern?

2. How do leisure services facilitate active living and make a major contribution in addressing this public health issue?

3. How do leisure and community leisure services moderate the negative relationship between stress and health?

4. How can leisure behavior contribute to personal health and wellness?

Leisure Reading

Cloud, J. (2009, August 17). The myth about exercise. *Time*, pp. 42-47.

Critser, G. (2003). *Fat land: How Americans became the fattest people in the world.* London, England: Penguin.

Finkelstein, E., & Zuckerman, L. (2008). *The fattening of America: How the economy makes us fat, if it matters, and what to do about it.* Hoboken, NJ: Wiley.

Kluger, J. (2008, June 12). How America's children packed on the pounds. *Time*. Available at: www.time.com/time/health/article/0,8599,1813700,00.html

Oliver, J.E. (2006). *Fat politics: The real story behind America's obesity epidemic*. New York: Oxford University Press.

Glossary

health—The state of complete physical, mental, and social well-being and not merely the absence of disease.

leisure-time physical activity—Exercise, sports, recreation, or hobbies that are not associated with activities as part of one's regular job duties, household, or transportation.

References

Allison, K.R., Dwyer, J.J.M., & Makin, S. (1999). Perceived barriers to physical activity among high school students. *Preventive Medicine, 28,* 608-614.

American Academy of Pediatrics. (2006, January). *Promoting physical activity: Basic recommendations for promoting activity.* www.aap.org/family/physicalactivity/physicalactivity.htm

American Psychological Association (APA). (2007). *Stress in America.* Washington, DC: American Psychological Association.

Barr-Anderson, D.J., Young, D.R., Sallis, J.F., Neumark-Sztainer, D., Gittelsohn, J., Webber, L., et al. (2007). Structured physical activity and psychosocial correlates in middle school girls. *Preventive Medicine, 44*(5), 404-409.

Birnbaum, A.S., Evenson, K.R., Motl, R.W., Dishman, R.K., Voorhees, C.C., Sallis, J.F., et al. (2005). Scale development for perceived school climate for girls' physical activity. *American Journal of Health Behavior, 29*(3), 250-257.

Bocarro, J.N., Casper, J., Henderson, K., Floyd, M.F., Moore, R., Kanters, M.A., et al. (2009). Physical activity promotion in North Carolina: Perceptions of public park and recreation directors. *Journal of Park and Recreation Administration, 27*(1), 1-16.

Bocarro, J.N., Kanters, M., Casper, J., & Forrester, S. (2008). School physical education, extracurricular sports, and lifelong active living. *Journal of Teaching in Physical Education, 27*(2), 155-166.

Caldwell, L.L. (2005). Leisure and health: Why is leisure therapeutic? *British Journal of Guidance & Counseling, 33*(1), 7-26.

Calle, E.E., & Kaaks, R. (2004). Overweight, obesity and cancer: Epidemiological evidence and proposed mechanisms. *Cancer, 4,* 579-590.

Cardenas, D., Henderson, K.A., & Wilson, B.E. (2009). Experiences of participation in senior games among older adults. *Journal of Leisure Research, 41*(1), 41-56.

Centers for Disease Control and Prevention (CDC). (1997). Guidelines for school and community programs to promote lifelong physical activity among young people. *Morbidity and Mortality Weekly Report, 46,* 1-36. Available at: www.cdc.gov/mmwr/preview/mmwrhtml/00046823.htm

Centers for Disease Control and Prevention (CDC). (2004). *Behavioral Risk Factor Surveillance System.* www.cdc.gov/brfss/

Cohen, D.A., Ashwood, S., Scott, M., Overton, A., Evenson, K.R., Voorhees, C.C., et al. (2006). Proximity to school and physical activity among middle school girls: The trial of activity for adolescent girls study. *Journal of Physical Activity & Health, 3*(1), S129-S138.

Davidson, K.K., & Lawson, C. (2006). Do attributes of the physical environment influence children's level of physical activity? *International Journal of Behavioral Nutrition and Physical Activity, 3*(19), 1-17.

Fairclough, S., Stratton, G., & Baldwin, G. (2002). The contribution of secondary school PE to lifetime physical activity. *European Physical Education Review, 8*(1), 69-86.

Farley, T.A., Meriwether, R.A., Baker, E.T., Watkins, L.T., Johnson, C.C., & Webber, L.S. (2007). Safe play spaces to promote physical activity in inner-city children: Results from a pilot study of an environmental intervention. *American Journal of Public Health, 97*(9), 1625-1631.

Green, K., Smith, A., & Roberts, K. (2005). Young people and lifelong participation in sport and physical activity: A sociological perspective on contemporary physical education programs in England and Wales. *Leisure Studies, 24*(1), 27-43.

Hedley, A.A., Ogden, C.L., Johnson, C.L., Carroll, M.D., Curtin, L.R., & Flegal, K.M. (2004). Overweight and obesity among US children, adolescents, and adults, 1999-2002. *Journal of the American Medical Association, 291,* 2847-2850.

Hedstrom, R., & Gould, D. (2004). *Research in youth sports: Critical issues status.* East Lansing, MI: Institute for the Study of Youth Sports.

International City/County Management Association. (2005). *Active living approaches by local governments, 2004.* www.icma.org/upload/library/2004-07/%7B05AB7A74-29FB-47E6-AA2B-B5497BE4E0A6%7D.pdf

Iso-Ahola, S.E., Jackson, E., & Dunn, E. (1994). Starting, ceasing, and replacing leisure activities over the life-span. *Journal of Leisure Research, 26*(3), 227-249.

King, A.C. (2001). Interventions to promote physical activity by older adults. *Journals of Gerontology Series a-Biological Sciences and Medical Sciences, 56,* 36-46.

Koplan, J.P., Liverman, C.T., & Kraak, V.I. (2005). *Preventing childhood obesity: Health in the balance.* Washington, DC: National Academies Press.

Kumanyika, S.K., Obarzanek, E., Stettler, N., Bell, R., Field, A.E., Fortmann, S.P., et al. (2008). Population-based prevention of obesity—The need for comprehensive promotion of healthful eating, physical activity, and energy balance: A scientific statement from American Heart Association Council on Epidemiology and Prevention, Interdisciplinary Committee for Prevention (formerly the Expert Panel on Population and Prevention Science). *Circulation, 118*(4), 428-464.

Lenhart, A. (2009). *Teens and mobile phones over the past five years: Pew Internet looks back.* www.pewinternet.org/Reports/2009/14--Teens-and-Mobile-Phones-Data-Memo.aspx

Louv, R. (2005). *The last child in the woods.* Chapel Hill, NC: Algonquin.

McLeroy, K.R., Bibeau, D., Steckler, A., & Glanz, K. (1988). An ecological perspective on health promotion programs. *Heath Education Quarterly, 15,* 351-377.

Must, A., Spadano, J., Coakley, E.H., Field, A.E., Colditz, G., & Dietz, W.H. (1999). The disease burden associated with overweight and obesity. *Journal of the American Medical Association, 282*(16), 1523-1529.

Orsega-Smith, E., Payne, L.L., & Godbey, G. (2003). Physical and psychosocial characteristics of older adults who participate in a community-based exercise program. *Journal of Aging and Physical Activity, 11*(4), 516-531.

Payne, L.L., Orsega-Smith, E., Spangler, K., & Godbey, G. (1999, October). For the health of it. *Parks and Recreation,* pp. 72-77.

Perkins, D.F., Jacobs, J.E., Barber, B.L., & Eccles, J.S. (2004). Childhood and adolescent sports participation as predictors of participation in sports and physical fitness activities during young adulthood. *Youth & Society, 35*(4), 495-520.

President's Council on Physical Fitness and Sport. (1997). *Physical activity and sport in the lives of girls: Physical and mental health dimensions from an interdisciplinary approach.* University of Minnesota: Center for Research on Girls & Women in Sport.

Roberts, K. (1999). *Leisure in contemporary society.* Wallingford, United Kingdom: CABI.

Roberts, K., & Brodie, D. (1992). *Inner-city sport: Who plays and what are the benefits?* Culemborg, The Netherlands: Giordano Bruno.

Sallis, J.F., Bauman, A., & Pratt, M. (1998). Environmental and policy interventions to promote physical activity. *American Journal of Preventive Medicine, 15*(4), 379-397.

Seefeldt, V., Ewing, M., & Walk, S. (1992). *Overview of youth sports programs in the United States.* Washington, DC: Carnegie Council on Adolescent Development.

Shores, K.A., & West, S.T. (2008). The relationship between built park environments and physical activity in four park locations. *Journal of Public Health Management and Practice, 14*(3), e9-e16.

Spengler, J.O., Young, S.J., & Linton, L.S. (2007). Schools as a community resource for physical activity: Legal considerations for decision makers. *American Journal of Health Promotion, 21*(4), 390-396.

Task Force on Community Preventive Services. (2002). Recommendations to increase physical activity in communities. *American Journal of Preventive Medicine, 22*(4S), 67-72.

Taylor, W.C., Blair, S.N., Cummings, S.S., Wun, C.C., & Malina, R.M. (1999). Childhood and adolescent physical activity patterns and adult physical activity. *Medicine and Science in Sports and Exercise, 31*(1), 118-123.

Trudeau, F., & Shepherd, R.J. (2005). Contribution of school programs to physical activity levels and attitudes in children and adults. *Sports Medicine, 25*(2), 89-105.

U.S. Department of Health and Human Services. (2000). *Healthy People 2010: Understanding and improving health.* Washington, DC: U.S. Government Printing Office.

van Mechelen, W., Twisk, J.W.R., Post, G.B., Snel, J., & Kemper, H.C.G. (2000). Physical activity of young people: The Amsterdam longitudinal growth and health study. *Medicine and Science in Sports and Exercise, 32*(9), 1610-1616.

Visscher, T., & Seidell, J. (2001). The public health impact of obesity. *Annual Review of Public Health, 22*, 355-375.

Wallis, C., Mehrtens, R., & Thompson, D. (1983, June 6). Stress: Can we cope? *Time,* pp. 48-54.

World Health Organization. (2005). *Risk factor projects. Overweight and obesity.* www.who.int/chp/chronic_disease_report/part2_ch1/en/index16.html.

CHAPTER

Leisure and Well-Being

Colleen Hood • Cynthia Carruthers
Brock University • University of Nevada at Las Vegas

Learning Outcomes

After reading this chapter, you will be able to

▶ describe the essential dimensions of well-being,

▶ identify and discuss three strategies for managing distress,

▶ describe the three principal determinants of happiness,

▶ compare and contrast the contributions of pleasurable experiences and the gratifications to well-being,

▶ identify the critical qualities of leisure that link the leisure experience to well-being, and

▶ describe the five strategies for enhancing the value of leisure in supporting well-being.

Vocabulary Terms

distress

emotion-focused coping

gratifications

habituation

hedonists

intentional activity

intrinsic motivation

person–activity fit

pleasures

problem-focused coping

savoring

virtues

well-being

©Brand X Pictures

Filling your life with joy is an important step in creating a good life.

Imagine that you have a day off from your studies. It is spring and the sun is shining and warm. You and a friend decide to hike out to the cliffs by the ocean. You start off with high expectations; you are excited about getting outside, about being physically active, and about doing something fun with your friend. As you reach the trail head, you decide to leave your worries behind. You step out of the car onto the trail with an open and clear mind and become very aware of the sounds of the birds, insects, and rustling branches—and the quiet of being away from the city. In the distance you can hear the rumbling of the ocean. As you begin to walk, you are aware of warming up and you can feel your blood pumping through your body. It reminds you of the many times you went hiking and camping with your family. It reminds you of how important the outdoors is to you. You notice the smells of damp earth and decay and they remind you of the renewal that comes with spring. You notice that your friend is struggling a bit with the slope and the pace. You go back to offer assistance and find a walking stick to help him manage the slippery parts of the slope. You slow down and point out the various signs of spring to him as you are working your way up the slope. As you move forward, you feel your mood improving and a smile start to spread across your face. You know the climb to the cliffs will be difficult, particularly after a long winter of studying, but you look forward to the challenge and know that you will feel great after. You feel alive and excited and can't wait to see the ocean, smell the sea air, and hear the sound of the waves crashing against the shore.

The person in the preceding story is engaged in a leisure experience that supports well-being. This chapter introduces a number of concepts that link leisure involvement to well-being and creating a good life. Leisure involvement can either be supportive of well-being or detrimental to well-being; this chapter invites you to examine your own leisure practices and to be purposeful about your leisure choices and experiences.

In the scenario described, the person hiking has made a number of choices that help the experience contribute to her well-being. She was intentional in leaving behind her worries and in being fully present in the current experience. She chose a leisure experience that has been important to her in the past and that she has enjoyed before. She chose a leisure experience that is physically demanding yet within her capabilities. She focused on the sounds, smells, and bodily sensations that accompanied her experience. She was aware of the challenge ahead but felt confident in her ability to manage those challenges. She wanted to support her friend and to help him see the **pleasures** in the experience as well. She anticipated enjoyment and happiness in both the journey and the destination.

In the last 20 to 30 years, there has been a growing interest in what is necessary to live a good life. This interest in the good life has resulted in a dramatic increase in the number of researchers who are examining what is required to create a life of happiness, meaning, and fulfillment, and this interest has spread to a number of disciplines that have traditionally focused on problem resolution (such as medicine, psychology, and other allied health professions). The positive psychology movement of the last 10 years has certainly put the issue of understanding well-being in the foreground of psychological research (Ryan & Deci, 2001; Seligman, 2002). This movement emphasizes the importance of understanding human strengths, capacities, and happiness as avenues through which to help citizens create better lives for themselves. This movement has influenced many other fields in terms of the ways they approach working with people and has made the notion of "strengths-based" practice one of interest to many professions whose practitioners work with people, including recreation and leisure studies (Carruthers & Hood, 2004, 2005, 2007; Hood & Carruthers, 2007), social work (Saleeby, 1997; Sharry, 2004), psychology and counseling (Fava & Ruini, 2003; Smith, 2006), education (Lopez & Louis, 2009), and nursing (McAllister, 2003).

> Leisure time should be an occasion for deep purpose to throb and for ideas to ferment. Where a man allows leisure to slip without some creative use, he has forfeited a bit of happiness.
>
> *C. Neil Strait*

Leisure professionals have traditionally been interested in the value of leisure for people in terms of health, social involvement, and personal and community well-being. Leisure has many benefits, but some members of the public do not recognize the value of leisure in building a life of meaning. Given that leisure is seen as a discretionary experience that occurs in "free time," people often bypass leisure in order to accomplish tasks of daily living and work. However, we must not underestimate the importance of leisure in creating a balanced, healthy life that supports overall well-being (Carruthers & Hood, 2004). This chapter explores the relationship between leisure and well-being and provides an overview of the concept of well-being; the relationships among stress, coping, and well-being; and the relationship between leisure and well-being, including leisure choices that both undermine and support well-being. The chapter ends with a discussion of strategies that can be used to increase the value of leisure in supporting well-being and building the best possible life.

UNDERSTANDING WELL-BEING

Well-being has been studied from a number of different perspectives, including philosophy, psychology, geography, sociology, and political science. As a result of the breadth of interest, the term **well-being** has many definitions, and many factors have been found to affect well-being. In a philosophical sense, well-being refers to how well a person's life is going. In a medical sense, well-being refers to the status of a person's physiological being. In an economic sense, well-being refers to how satisfied a person is in terms of income, financial stability, and material goods. In a psychological sense, well-being refers to the degree to which a person experiences positive emotion and fulfillment (Csikszentmihalyi, 1993; Keyes & Lopez, 2002; Pollard & Rosenberg, 2003). People who experience psychological well-being feel happy more often than they feel sad, develop their strengths and capacities, and use those strengths and capacities in service of something greater than themselves (Seligman, 2002).

Some of the factors that influence well-being include your cultural background and connection, physical and social environment, socioeconomic status, family status and structure, age, and gender. Interestingly, these factors often influence the experience of leisure as well (Allison & Schneider, 2000). Although these factors may have a significant effect on well-being, they are often not within our direct control. However, we may be able to control other factors. In fact, many researchers suggest that well-being is often a result of the choices we make (Nix et al., 1999; Ryan & Deci, 2001). For example, the experience of more positive emotion than negative emotion on a daily basis directly affects your sense of well-being and is influenced by several factors. The way you focus your attention on the events of daily life influences how much positive emotion you feel. This focus of attention is something that you can actively address and modify by practicing activities that highlight the positive events in life, such as gratitude exercises, and by monitoring your focus and directing your attention toward the positive. Positive emotion is often generated by participating in physical activity, so choosing physically active leisure is a way to increase the amount of positive emotion you experience. Exercising personal control and autonomy, seeking contexts in which you can feel competent, creating and sustaining a social world that is rich and fulfilling, maintaining moderate levels of physical activity, and engaging in experiences that develop and express your true self are all examples of ways to improve your well-being and are a result of personal lifestyle choices (Fava & Ruini, 2003; Foster & Lloyd, 2007; Kobasa et al., 1985; Mas-

©rgbspace/fotolia

Well-being is supported by engagement in expressive activities like music that allow you to develop yourself fully.

simini & Delle Fave, 2000; Reis et al., 2000; Ryan & Deci, 2000). These factors are also directly related to leisure involvement and can be supported and enhanced through leisure engagement (Kleiber, 1999; Kleiber et al., 2002).

Creating a life that is rich with positive emotion, fulfillment, and expression of personal capacities has many significant benefits. People who experience more positive emotion than negative tend to be more resilient to challenges in life—they bounce back more quickly in the face of adversity (Fredrickson & Joiner, 2002). They tend to be more optimistic and believe that even when they experience difficulties, perseverance and tenacity will pay off—they are much less likely to give up in the face of difficulties. These people tend to look for the good in situations and people and seek out and focus their attention on the aspects of life that support their hopeful, optimistic perspective (Carver & Scheier, 2002). People who have fulfilling lives tend to live longer and live better—they get sick less often, and when they do get sick, they recover more quickly (Charnetski & Brennan, 2001; Vaillant, 2002). Their neural complexity and adaptability are greater than those of people who do not have rich and fulfilling lives; thus, positive people are more flexible in problem solving and maintain cognitive function longer as they age (Danner et al., 2001). Positive emotion also affects social connectedness and relationship satisfaction; people who experience lives that are rich also have strong relationships with family, friends, and partners (Harker & Keltner, 2001). It seems obvious that a focus on building a life of meaning and well-being, including positive emotion and the cultivation and expression of strengths, creates a positive spiral of capacities and resources that support ongoing engagement and satisfaction with life.

STRESS AND WELL-BEING: THE IMPORTANT ROLE OF COPING

No matter how happy and fulfilled people are, it is inevitable that they will experience stress at some point. In fact, to avoid stress is to avoid life. Not all stress is negative, and, in fact, stress can support development in important ways. This form of stress, called *eustress* (Selye, 1975), arises from positive events, such as marriage, the birth of a baby, starting a new job, or going away to university for the first time. Eustress also encompasses those events that are perceived as challenging but in which the challenge is perceived as manageable. Think for a moment about studying for an exam. The anxiety associated with exam writing can result in sleeplessness, difficulty concentrating, and irritation. On the other hand, exam anxiety in a class where you perceive that you have the capacity to do well tends to enhance cognitive functioning, performance, and memory. The key factor is whether the stress is perceived as something you can manage and is somewhat short term in nature. The types of experiences that generate eustress vary by individual, but the outcomes tend to be similar—increased motivation, improved performance, and increased excitement and engagement.

Not all stress results in enhanced performance, however. When stress leads to negative outcomes, it is referred to as *distress* and is often based on how we perceive the situation. Among its many other benefits, well-being creates a greater capacity for dealing with the challenges and hardships of life (Carruthers & Hood, 2007). If people want to improve their well-being, they can do so by constructively engaging their emotions and building a life of meaning (Ben-Shahar, 2007). People who are experiencing positive emotion and developing their strengths are less likely to interpret situations as stressful, and they are more likely to believe that they have

©Getty Images/Stockbyte Platinum

A life filled with joy allows us to cope better with everyday stresses.

the resources necessary to meet life's challenges (Carruthers & Hood, 2005). They are also more likely to have a repertoire of coping skills upon which to draw, as well as the ability to know when and how to use these skills.

When people believe that they do not have the ability to deal with the challenges of their lives, the resulting negative stress, called **distress**, can have many negative physical and emotional consequences (Davis et al., 2008). Distress is created by a perception or appraisal of threat (Hood & Carruthers, 2002). That perception creates a physiological stress response that is called *flight or fight* (Frydenberg, 2002). This evolutionary response protected our ancestors from disasters and dangers by preparing them to run from or fight immediate environmental threats (Davis et al., 2008). However, in contemporary society people cannot always fight or run from the stressors, nor would running or fighting serve as an effective coping strategy. However, the physiological response to threat remains the same today. If people do not have the contemporary coping skills necessary to deal with the stressors in their lives, their bodies are stuck in the chronic stress state, which has negative consequences for physical and mental health (Davis et al., 2008). If people are able to successfully adapt or respond to a stressor so that it is no longer perceived as threatening, the flight or fight response is turned off. Their bodies return to a relaxed state, ready for the next challenge.

MANAGING STRESS TO ENHANCE WELL-BEING

The stressors in one's life can be managed in three ways (Hood & Carruthers, 2002). First, people can target the thoughts or perceptions of threat that trigger the flight or fight response and the related feelings. Second, people can take action to address directly the environmental challenges. Third, people can pursue activities that reduce the physiological stress response. People cannot be simultaneously physiologically stressed and relaxed.

Emotion-Focused Coping

One's perceptions or thoughts are the primary source of distress (Lazarus & Folkman, 1984). People who experience chronic distress may have distorted and irrational thoughts (Burns, 1999). Some people are genetically predisposed to overreact to stress (Lykken & Tellegen, 1996). **Emotion-focused coping** strategies target the thoughts and feelings associated with distress (Smith & Carlson, 1997). When people use emotion-focused coping strategies, they might examine the ways in which their irrational thoughts contribute to their negative emotions (Lazarus & Folkman, 1984). For example, a young woman who is anxious about going to college parties may be afraid that she will make a social blunder and others will judge her harshly. She can recognize and challenge that negative self-talk and replace it with rational, constructive thoughts or just realize that her distorted thoughts are not reality and let them go. She can learn to keep situations in perspective and not overreact emotionally to life events.

Another example of emotion-focused coping is distraction (Lazarus & Folkman, 1984). Distraction is the process of diverting attention away from one issue and focusing attention on another. If a person is not thinking about a potential threat, the physiological stress response will be turned off, resulting in the relaxation response. When people believe there is nothing that they can do to change the situation, it does little good to think about it. In fact, the distress created by thinking about it can result in physical and emotional harm (Davis et al., 2008). Under these circumstances, it may be helpful to turn one's mind to an enjoyable, engaging leisure activity (Kleiber et al., 2002; Lyubomirsky, 2008). Leisure experiences that are personally meaningful, challenging, and enjoyable are optimal experiences for disengaging from everyday routines and worries (Hood & Carruthers, 2002). To reap the reward of this coping response and turn off the physiological stress response, it is important to immerse oneself in the leisure experience as completely as possible.

A final example of emotion-focused coping is acceptance (Lazarus & Folkman, 1984). Like distraction, this coping strategy is used when people believe that there is little that they can do or should do to change a situation. Many things in life are out of our control; it is simply not within our power to change them. Worrying and fretting about them will just create chronic stress and undermine our physical and mental health. Acceptance of a situation is experiencing it for what it really is, without defense or distortion, and letting it be (Kabat-Zinn, 1990). Mindfulness meditation is a leisure activity through which acceptance can be cultivated. The focus of mindfulness meditation is to see and accept things as they are, moment by moment.

LEISURE HEALTH

Think for a moment about a situation in your life that is likely to create high levels of stress—for example, writing a final exam in a class at school. What were the signals from your body that indicated you were experiencing stress (did you have trouble sleeping, increases in heart rate, muscle tension)? What, if any, emotion-focused coping strategies did you use? Did you try to change your thinking about the exam (e.g., did you tell yourself that you are a good student and that you can be successful on the exam)? If so, how effective was this strategy? Did you try to distract yourself from the stressful situation (e.g., go out with friends to take a break from studying)? How effective was this strategy? Finally, did you try to accept the situation (e.g., tell yourself that exam time is just stressful and that this too shall pass)? How effective was this approach?

Problem-Focused Coping

A second strategy for coping is problem-focused coping. **Problem-focused coping** involves taking action to directly address the challenges of life. For example, problem-focused coping strategies for the stress associated with writing a final exam might include joining a study group, setting aside 2 hours a day to study, and getting a good night's sleep before the exam. Problem-based coping requires a realistic assessment of actions that can be taken to improve a situation and the willingness to act. The development of one's personal strengths and resources contributes to one's ability to cope with life's demands (Carruthers & Hood, 2002; Hood & Carruthers, 2002). Enhancing or developing resources can be seen as a proactive approach to coping. The cultivation of physical resources, such as health, fitness, and energy, can contribute to one's coping capacity. The development of emotional resources, such as a belief in one's own competence, worth, and purpose, can contribute to one's coping capacity: Engagement in optimally challenging, meaningful leisure can enhance these emotional resources (Iwasaki, 2008). The creation and maintenance of social resources, such as social connections and support, can also contribute to one's coping repertoire. Leisure is an important area for the cultivation of these social networks (Iwasaki, 2008).

LEISURE HEALTH

Think for a moment about a situation that creates stress for you—for example, having a fight with your girlfriend, boyfriend, or best friend. What if any problem-focused strategies did you use? How effective were the strategies you used in helping you to get the stress under control?

Relaxation

A third strategy for coping is to pursue activities that facilitate the relaxation response. Relaxation allows for physiological and emotional recuperation from stress (Fredrickson, 2000), and leisure is an important path to attaining a relaxed state. Leisure can serve as a context for engaging in personal reflection, gaining a sense of perspective and appreciation, and living in the moment (Kleiber, 1999). Engaging in physical leisure activities decreases anxiety and depression (Lyubomirsky, 2008). Experiencing nature through activities such as walking in nature preserves and hiking in the wilderness has a restorative effect (Hartig et al., 2003). Involvement in leisure activities that are nontaxing and enjoyable, such as watching television or listening to music, also induces the relaxation response. After immersing ourselves in optimally challenging activities that require our full concentration, we often feel refreshed. The full attention required to engage in the activity helps us disengage from our ruminations and distress (Lyubomirsky, 2008). Finally, activities such as meditation, yoga, and tai chi can directly reduce the physiological stress response (Olson, 2006).

Leisure-Based Coping

A fourth strategy for coping includes three specific forms of coping that are leisure based: leisure palliative coping, leisure mood enhancement, and leisure companion-

©pixhunter.com/fotolia

An important way of getting the most out of life is taking time now and then to appreciate the good things in life.

ship (Iwasaki & Mannell, 2000). Leisure palliative coping might include activities like running, cycling, or hiking that give us temporary relief from stress and an opportunity to regroup and gain perspective. Leisure mood enhancement activities might include watching a funny movie or playing a game with friends. Leisure companionship would include any activities that involve social interaction that facilitates a supportive social network of friends. With each of these leisure coping strategies, the activities we select to cope with stress will likely reduce stress but may not necessarily improve our health and well-being. Leisure mood enhancement activities could include excessive alcohol consumption or drug use. Leisure companionship might include promiscuous sexual activity, and leisure palliative coping might include engaging in reckless or dangerous activities.

Leisure involvement clearly can support a person's ability to cope with stress (Hutchinson et al., 2008). Certain qualities of the leisure experience are particularly important for supporting well-being and building a life of meaning and purpose. These qualities support both the experience of happiness and positive emotion and the development and expression of one's full potential (Carruthers & Hood, 2007).

PARTICIPATING IN MEANINGFUL LEISURE TO ENHANCE WELL-BEING

In examining the connection between leisure experience, coping, and well-being, we must consider some of the essential defining qualities of the experience. When most people think of leisure, they think of experiences like relaxing at the beach, talking on the phone, or watching TV. Recreation activities are viewed by most people as those activities that "look" like recreation, such as sports, crafts, hobbies, and games. These activities are a form of leisure but do not represent the full range of leisure experiences. Many leisure researchers have suggested that the quality of the experience and the perception of the participant determine whether the experience is leisure and whether it has value and benefit to the participant. Thus, it is not the activity that is most important in defining an experience as leisure or recreation but rather the participant's subjective assessment of the activity (Kleiber, 1999).

The defining qualities of leisure that are most closely related to well-being are positive emotion or pleasure, perception of freedom and control, intrinsic motivation, and change in level of engagement from the activities and experiences that surround leisure. The positive emotion associated with leisure, either in anticipation, experience, or recollection, creates a direct link to well-being. The freedom inherent in leisure allows the participant to choose and modify the situation to create the most rewarding and meaningful experiences possible. This sense of freedom and control over your own experience often allows you to appreciate those experiences and craft the experiences in such a way as to bring about the greatest pleasure and benefit. **Intrinsic motivation,** or the desire to participate in an activity for the rewards inherent in that experience, supports well-being and reinforces the importance of the **person–activity fit**. Activities that "feel right" are those that have the greatest value and tend to occur frequently in leisure experiences.

Leisure involvement is often experienced in contrast to other daily experiences. This contrast may occur in terms of level of engagement, such as shifting from studying to going for a run. The contrast may involve a shift from an individual experience to a social experience, or it may involve a shift in sense of obligation, such as taking a break from studying to call a friend or family member. Regardless of the nature of the shift, leisure is often experienced in contrast to what was going on before and what will happen after the "leisure interlude" (Kleiber, 1999). Interestingly, engaging leisure experience can lead to a disengagement from daily life concerns while simultaneously fostering a full immersion in the present moment. The capacity for leisure to support disengagement from daily life concerns and engagement in personally meaningful, pleasurable activities is an important way that leisure supports well-being (Hutchinson & Kleiber, 2005; Kleiber, 1999; Stebbins, 2006).

DETERMINANTS OF HAPPINESS

Many scholars have worked to understand what determines happiness and well-being. They have found that there are three principal determinants of happiness: genetics, circumstantial factors, and intentional activities (Sheldon & Lyubomirsky, 2004). The significant role of leisure in the construction of enduring happiness is discussed within this framework.

Genetics

The first principal determinant of happiness is genetics and inherited tendencies. There is much evidence that people differ in their genetically determined ranges of happiness. A landmark study of identical twins showed that about 50% of the happiness that a person experiences every day is genetically determined (Lykken & Tellegen, 1996). Most of us know people who are perpetually happy, with little change from day to day. Although these people experience the same challenges and disappointments as everyone else, they return relatively quickly to a state of happiness. We also know people who are unhappy, with little change from day to day. Their perpetual unhappiness often exists despite apparent good fortune.

Although they may experience brief increases in happiness as a result of positive life events, they will most likely return to their usual state—in a low range of happiness. The genetic set point, by its very nature, is resistant to change. However, recent research suggests that one's genetic predispositions and environment interact (Klein, 2006). For example, a stressful family home may trigger depression in a child with a genetic predisposition for depression, whereas the depression gene may not be expressed if the child is in a loving, stress-free home. The key to well-being is to operate at the most optimal levels of one's own genetic range (Lykken & Tellegen, 1996; Lyubomirsky, 2008).

S E L F - D I S C O V E R Y

Think about the people you know. Do you think you are happier or unhappier than most of your friends? In daily life, are you quick to smile and laugh; do you often see the bright side of things? Or are you more likely to be disappointed with the little things, tending to feel a little blue? Each of us comes with a genetically "set" range of happiness—some people are just born happier than others! Do you want to know how happy you are compared with others? Go to www.authentichappiness.org and create an account (it is free). Complete the Fordyce Emotions Questionnaire to determine how your level of happiness compares with that of others.

Circumstantial Factors

The second principal determinant of happiness involves circumstantial factors, such as health, marriage, socioeconomic status, or geographic location. One's life circumstances account for approximately 10% of a person's happiness level. Why do the circumstances of a person's life contribute so little to the happiness equation? Although changes in life circumstances can temporarily boost happiness levels, the impact of these factors typically fades over time (Sheldon & Lyubormirsky, 2004, 2006). For example, getting an A on an exam, buying a new cell phone, or getting a new roommate may give you an immediate boost in happiness, but it tends to be relatively short lived. You will soon drift back to your set point of happiness. If your set point of happiness is low, you will forget the A as you turn your attention to the next test; the features of the new phone become mundane; the flaws of the new roommate begin to surface.

This lessening of effects seems to be due to the fact that people quickly grow habituated to or dissatisfied with their new circumstances (Sheldon & Lyubomirsky, 2004). **Habituation** occurs when we become accustomed to the new circumstances and our nervous systems no longer register the experience as novel or worthy of notice (Seligman, 2002). New circumstances might affect happiness levels immediately and dramatically, but due to habituation, they have few long-term effects. A good example of the impact of circumstantial factors on happiness is the research on lottery winners (Brickman et al., 1978). This study found that lottery winners were no happier 1 year later than they had been before winning. This relationship is also demonstrated in the face of negative life events; people who acquired a spinal cord injury that required the use of a wheelchair were also found to return to their preinjury levels of happiness over time (Allman, 1990).

Ironically, people often live their lives believing that external circumstances will bring happiness (Seligman, 2002). They pursue money, large homes, fancy cars, prestigious jobs, and beauty with the belief that once they obtain these things, they will be happy. Yet there is much evidence that this road is a dead end. In fact, the pursuit of money and material possessions often contributes to unhappiness (Lyubomirsky, 2008).

Intentional Activities

Although changing our genetic makeup is impossible and changing our external circumstances tends to have little effect on long-term happiness, we still have the power to change our happiness levels (Lykken, 1999). The third principal element that determines well-being or happiness is **intentional activity** (Lyubomirsky, 2008). Intentional activities, defined as effortful, goal-oriented endeavors, account for approximately 40% of a person's happiness level (Lyubomirsky, 2008). Interestingly, the effects of these intentional activities are much less likely to fade over time and thus result in lasting changes to happiness. People can incorporate many types of activities into their lives to increase their happiness level; however, the activities that increase one person's happiness may have little impact on the happiness of another. The selection of intentional activities is very individualized. Leisure provides a rich source of activities through which people can intentionally cultivate well-being (Carruthers & Hood, 2004).

There are two general types of intentional activities that can increase one's level of happiness or well-being (Ben-Shahar, 2007). The first is engagement in activities that bring positive emotion, such as joy, excitement, humor, pleasure, contentment, satisfaction, and relaxation, into one's day-to-day life. People who are experiencing well-being feel happy more often than they feel sad (Carruthers & Hood, 2004). Oftentimes people in our society get so caught up in creating a positive future for themselves that they do not enjoy the process or journey (Ben-Shahar, 2007). Enjoying the present moments of one's life is an essential component of happiness (Csikszentmihalyi, 1990).

Happiness in the present can be created through involvement in pleasurable activities (Seligman, 2002). These activities often have a strong sensory component to them. For example, pleasure may be obtained by eating a piece of decadent chocolate cake, taking a warm bubble bath, or cuddling with your partner in front of a fireplace. Pleasurable activities may be sought because they are arousing, such as riding a roller coaster or bungee jumping, or soothing, such as sitting on a beach or listening to music. These types of activities are important to well-being. However, many people do not intentionally build such activities into their lives. To get the full happiness boost from pleasurable activities, people must be fully present for those moments. People also should have a variety of "happy habits" (Lykken, 1999). Doing the same pleasurable activity repeatedly leads to habituation; an activity that is done too often loses its pleasurable impact. Eating three pieces of decadent chocolate cake in one day is no longer the same treat.

The second general type of intentional activity that can increase one's level of happiness or well-being is engagement in meaningful experiences that result in the cultivation of one's full potential (Ben-Shahar, 2007; Keyes, 2003). Clear distinctions have been made among leading a pleasant life, a good life, and a meaningful life (Seligman, 2002). A pleasant life is one in which people experience pleasure regularly in their day-to-day lives. They savor and live mindfully those "momentary delights." However, these pleasurable experiences do not alone constitute a good

W H A T   D O   Y O U   T H I N K ?

What kinds of things do you do each day to make your life happier and more fulfilling? What practices add the most happiness to your day? What do you do to bring more pleasure into your life? What leisure activities, if any, do you engage in that help you grow as a person and develop skills and capacities? In what ways do you see yourself making a contribution to the world through your leisure, if any? When you think about your life, what kinds of choices do you consciously make that support your happiness and fulfillment?

life. A good life is one in which people cultivate and invest their signature strengths and virtues in their relationships, leisure, and work. This investment of the best of self in challenging, meaningful activity or **gratifications** increases a person's capacity for growth and feelings of competence, satisfaction, and well-being. Last, a meaningful life is one in which people use their "signature strengths in the service of something larger" than themselves (Seligman, 2002, p. 249). Authentic happiness is ultimately constructed by investment in meaningful activity through which people can realize their full potential as human beings. Although experiencing positive emotion is important, most of us want more from life than just to feel good (Ben-Shahar, 2007; Seligman, 2002). The evolution of self occurs through engaging in ongoing self-discovery, creating contexts and opportunities for self-development, and making meaning in our lives (Fava & Ruini, 2003).

Although leisure is not the only life domain in which people can cultivate their signature strengths and create a meaningful life, it is an important one (Carruthers & Hood, 2007). Leisure offers many opportunities to seek out optimal challenges and realize one's full physical, emotional, social, intellectual, and spiritual potential. When people engage in activities that are totally engrossing and stretch their capabilities, they often experience an enjoyment that draws them back to the activity over and over again. The challenges inherent in the activity demand the participant's full attention to be successful; she becomes immersed in the activity and experiences a feeling of flow (Csikszentmihalyi, 1990). People experiencing flow activities are unlikely to habituate. To continue to be optimally challenged, they must seek out increasingly complex or engaging opportunities. Rock climbers traverse a higher mountain. Artists investigate other media or subjects. Travelers explore new landscapes.

Finding activities that allow you to express important aspects of yourself is central to building a life of meaning.

LEISURE CHOICES THAT UNDERMINE WELL-BEING

Just as fire can warm a home or burn it down, leisure can enhance well-being or undermine it. By definition, leisure is behavior that is chosen because it will result in pleasure, enjoyment, or satisfaction (Neulinger, 1981). However, people who pursue pleasure at the expense of challenging and meaningful activity, take leisure behaviors to an extreme, or regularly disengage from their lives through leisure may be undermining their well-being (Csikszentmihalyi, 1990; Seligman, 2002). The term "purple recreation" refers to a type of leisure that challenges societal norms and is detrimental to the participant, to others, or to the community (Curtis, 1988).

Humans are genetically programmed to seek positive emotion and to avoid negative emotion (Klein, 2006). When we desire something, neurotransmitters are released that energize and drive us (Nettle, 2005). When we satisfy our desires, neurotransmitters are released that cause the sensation of pleasure, spurring us to future pursuit of the next best experience (Klein, 2006). This genetic programming causes us to pursue sensory pleasure and strive for excellence (Nettle, 2005).

People have a finite amount of time and energy. Pleasurable activities can contribute to well-being but if overdone can undermine engagement in the meaningful experiences that result in the cultivation of one's full potential. Watching television, for example, can reduce physiological stress. However, Americans spend the majority of their leisure time watching television (Russell, 2005). Television viewing is associated with less involvement in physical and social activities, both of which contribute to long term well-being (Layard, 2005). America's common culture is based on entertaining or amusing ourselves (Russell, 2005).

Hedonists take the pursuit of pleasure and the avoidance of pain to an extreme. They believe that happiness "is reducible to a succession of pleasurable experiences" (Ben-Shahar, 2007, p. 20). They seek immediate gratification with little concern for future well-being or sometimes find pleasure in doing nothing rather than in engaging in positive experiences (Ben-Shahar, 2007). If something that these people desire requires hard work, effort, sacrifice, or overcoming difficulties, they will avoid it (Seligman, 2002). Unfortunately, the happiness that results from the pursuit of challenging and meaningful goals escapes the hedonist. After all, the best moments in life "usually occur when a person's body or mind is stretched to its limits in a voluntary effort to accomplish something difficult and worthwhile" (Csikszentmihalyi, 1990, p. 3).

PERSONAL LEISURE

Most people at some time or another overindulge in pleasurable activities. Sometimes, we drink too much, sometimes we eat too much, sometimes we exercise too much, sometimes we shop too much, sometimes we watch too much TV. Thinking about the past few months: Have you overindulged in a leisure activity that you usually enjoy? How did you feel after you overindulged? How was your enjoyment of the experience affected by overdoing it? Did your overindulgence in one activity take time away from an activity that might have been more meaningful?

Overindulgence in pleasurable leisure experiences poses other threats to well-being. Ideally, people are able to balance the desire for happiness in the present with a commitment to the cultivation of a meaningful, satisfying life (Ben-Shahar, 2007). However, some people lose the ability to maintain the balance. They begin to compulsively pursue experiences such as drinking alcohol, gambling, shopping, playing video games, or having indiscriminant sex with little regard for the long-term consequences (Goldstein, 2005; Klein, 2006). They lose their ability to control their behaviors, regardless of the negative consequences. The same neurotransmitter systems that cause humans to seek pleasure and avoid pain are engaged. These compulsive experiences, many of which could be considered purple recreation, can significantly harm a person's physical, emotional, social, intellectual, and spiritual well-being as well as the well-being of his community.

APPROACHES AND STRATEGIES TO ENHANCE THE VALUE OF LEISURE FOR WELL-BEING

The defining qualities of leisure make it an ideal context and experience through which to enhance well-being and to develop capacities associated with living a life of meaning. Given that leisure is freely chosen, supports a sense of autonomy and competence, generates pleasure and positive emotion, and is motivated by a desire for the experience alone, leisure is an essential domain for engagement in intentional activities that support well-being (Carruthers & Hood, 2004, 2007; Hood & Carruthers, 2007).

However, not all leisure experiences are equal in their capacity to support well-being nor do all people possess the ability to gain the greatest benefit of leisure. What approaches can we use to enhance the quality of the leisure experience in supporting well-being? Five broad approaches to gaining the greatest benefit from leisure experiences have been identified: savoring leisure, authentic leisure, leisure gratifications, mindful leisure, and virtuous leisure (Hood & Carruthers, 2007).

Savoring Leisure

One critical approach for enhancing the value of leisure in creating a life of well-being is savoring leisure. **Savoring** leisure is defined as "paying attention to the positive aspects of, and emotions associated with, leisure involvement and purposefully seeking leisure experiences that give rise to positive emotions" (Hood & Carruthers, 2007, pp. 310-311). The premise of savoring leisure is that we often participate in activities without paying much attention to the actual participation. We may be thinking about other things, we may be so accustomed to the activity that we don't have to pay attention to it, or we could be experiencing negative emotions such as stress or anger that overwhelm the positive aspects of the experience (Bryant & Veroff, 2007). Savoring leisure can help us become more aware of the positive aspects of leisure experience.

Savoring leisure is linked directly to well-being through the experience of positive emotion. Strategies or practices associated with savoring leisure include these: (1) purposefully selecting experiences that will generate positive emotion (such as nature, music, art, good conversation); (2) purposefully discovering a set of experiences that generate positive emotion and building them into daily life in novel

Don't forget to slow down and smell the flowers in life! When you're feeling stressed, a simple change in scenery can help you refocus and feel more calm.

and interesting ways to avoid habituation; (3) paying conscious attention to the positive aspects and outcomes associated with an experience; (4) recreating those positive emotions and experiences through reminiscing and storytelling; and (5) selecting experiences that require active engagement (mind, body, or emotion) (Ben-Shahar, 2007; Fredrickson, 2000; Lykken, 1999; Lyubomirsky, 2008; Seligman, 2002; Sheldon & Lyubomirsky, 2004). Passive activities or casual leisure experiences can be powerful in generating positive emotions, but a balance of active and passive leisure is needed to create a life of well-being (Hutchinson & Kleiber, 2005). Regardless of the nature of involvement, the positive emotions associated with leisure involvement are central and necessary for our well-being.

Authentic Leisure

A second important approach for enhancing the value of leisure in supporting a life of well-being is consciously and purposefully selecting leisure experiences that "feel right." Researchers have identified the importance of person–activity fit in their discussion of the role of intentional activities in enhancing happiness (Sheldon & Lyubomirsky, 2004). They stated that "not all activities will help a particular person become happier. People have enduring strengths, interests, values, and inclinations, which predispose them to benefit more from some activities than others" (p. 138). In fact, one researcher stated that "if there's any 'secret' to becoming happier, the secret is in establishing which happiness strategies suit you best" (Lyubomirsky, 2008, p. 70). She suggested that as we attempt to determine which activities suit us best, we can evaluate them in terms of the degree to which the activity feels natural, is enjoyable, has inherent value for us, does not involve guilt or obligation, and is not done because of the requirements and expectations of the situation.

The notion of person–activity fit is woven into the conception of authentic leisure (Hood & Carruthers, 2007). Authenticity has been described as experiencing and expressing oneself in ways that are consistent and true to the inner experience (Harter, 2002). Authentic leisure is a blend of person–activity fit and authenticity, and it is proposed that leisure is an ideal context in which to construct and engage in authentic experience. Leisure is a potent context in which to both come to know your preferences, capacities, and interests as well as to express those essential aspects of the self in meaningful engagements. The relative freedom inherent in leisure choices allows people to experiment with experience to learn about themselves (Kleiber, 1999) and then to purposefully select and engage in experiences that allow them to express important aspects of the self (Carruthers & Hood, 2007).

©iStockPhoto/Krzysztof Kwiatkowski

Participating in leisure experiences that involve a social world is very important for well-being.

An additional strategy for engaging in authentic leisure that builds more happiness into life is finding or creating a social world around authentic leisure experiences (Carruthers & Hood, 2007). Leisure has an important role in identity development and expression (Kleiber, 1999), and it has been suggested that engagement in social worlds that are created around leisure experiences is central to human development and well-being. For example, if a person becomes interested in taekwondo and finds that this leisure activity "fits" with her needs, interests, and capacities, then participation in taekwondo can support her happiness and well-being. As she becomes more experienced and involved in the activity, she will learn the language, etiquette, and culture of taekwondo enthusiasts and will soon begin to identify herself through this involvement. The sense of attachment to and engagement in a social world related to a preferred, meaningful activity creates a set of reciprocal relationships, a sense of belonging, and a unique identity associated with the social world surrounding the activity (Stebbins, 2006). All of these qualities are associated with greater well-being.

Leisure Gratifications

Participation in leisure experiences that give rise to positive emotion and that "feel right" set the stage for engagement in activities that require investment of attention and result in an ongoing upward spiral of skill and capacity development. These types of activities are referred to as leisure gratifications by Hood and Carruthers (2007) and are very similar in nature to the concept of flow developed by Csikszentmihalyi (1990). Leisure gratifications are defined as "leisure experiences that are optimally challenging and engaging, and that lead to sustained personal effort and commitment to the experience" (Hood & Carruthers, 2007, p. 314). This conception of leisure is based on the premise that people want to be happy

Push your limits; never stop challenging yourself.

and they want to develop themselves in meaningful ways (Seligman, 2002).

People can engage in a set of strategies designed to enhance the possibility of experiencing leisure gratifications. Probably one of the most important decisions about activity engagement is to select activities that are a good fit with interests and capacities and that afford degrees of skilled performance; thus, as skills increase, greater challenge can be undertaken to avoid boredom. These types of skill-based activities also allow for early skill development without experiencing anxiety and frustration. Take, for example, the popular video game Guitar Hero. The beginning levels of Guitar Hero are designed to help new players become competent with the techniques necessary to play various songs. The finger movement is simplified in the beginner level, and a slower pace of player response is needed. As skills increase, players can move up levels that increase in complexity, speed, and challenge. These types of experiences are designed to engage players and to keep them coming back even as their skills increase. This balance of challenge and skills sets the stage for an upward spiral of development of skills related to the specific activity as well as more general skills related to tenacity, problem solving, and perseverance. As skills increase, greater and greater challenge is undertaken to achieve the sense of flow and full engagement that is so rewarding for most people (Csikszentmihalyi, 1990).

Matching one's goals for engagement with the possibilities presented by the activity is an important way to manage the level of engagement. For example, if you are participating in an activity where your skills exceed the demands of the activity, boredom is likely. As a result, you can either modify the way you engage in the activity, to increase the challenge, or you can modify your reasons for engagement (e.g., social connection rather than competition). If the demands of your chosen activity exceed your skills, then anxiety may result. In this situation, you can either modify the activity so the demands are not so great or change your goals for involvement (e.g., enjoyment and laughter rather than demonstration of skills).

Leisure gratifications fulfill an important role in supporting personal development and capacity development. Engagement in these kinds of experiences also produces significant feelings of satisfaction, pleasure, and fulfillment. These two dimensions of experience, positive emotion and self-development, are the cornerstones of well-being.

Mindful Leisure

A conscious and direct focus on the positive aspects of an experience reflects the approach called savoring leisure. Mindful leisure takes this conscious engagement in an experience and broadens it to include attention to the entirety of the current experience coupled with a simultaneous disengagement from daily life concerns (Brown & Ryan, 2003). Thus, although savoring leisure involves narrowing attention to the positive aspects of the experience, mindful leisure involves focusing one's full attention on the current experience and not attending to worries about the future or other issues of concern. "It is difficult to attend to the pleasurable aspects of any experience if one is focused on the future and/or functioning automatically, 'without much thinking.' Shifting attention back to the experience at hand significantly impacts the degree to which the person truly experiences the fullness of one's own life, including positive emotions" (Seligman, quoted by Hood & Carruthers, 2007, p. 315).

Becoming more mindful in leisure requires us to increase our capacity to attend to the present moment. We can learn to pay attention to the present moment by slowing our thought processes through such activities as breathing exercises, mental imagery, yoga, and relaxation techniques (Fredrickson, 2000). These allow us to quiet our minds and physiological responses so we can be fully present in the current experience. In addition, full engagement can be supported by examining the habits of thought that interfere with being fully present in the moment. Examining negative self-talk habits, ruminations and worry, and other habits of thought can be extremely helpful in disengaging from those thoughts and engaging fully in the current experience. Finally, full engagement can be supported by selecting leisure activities that are personally meaningful and optimally challenging (Sheldon & Lyubomirsky, 2004). These types of activities are often so engaging that they result in a momentary disengagement from the concerns of daily life. Thus, mindful leisure can be experienced through purposeful engagement in experiences that build capacity for mindful involvement in the present (controlling anxiety and enhancing relaxation) as well as through purposeful engagement in leisure experiences that are so fully absorbing that they don't allow daily concerns and anxieties to affect the experience.

Virtuous Leisure

The term *virtuous* comes from the work of Seligman (2002), who discussed the importance of "using one's strengths and virtues in the service of something much larger than you are" (p. 263). **Virtues** are characteristics that are viewed as universally "good" and that support individual and collective well-being. It has been suggested that life has the greatest meaning when a person has many opportunities to use her personal strengths and virtues in the service of something greater than herself. Thus, virtuous leisure was defined as "the capacity to engage in leisure experiences that develop and/or mobilize personal strengths, capacities, interests, and abilities in the service of something larger than oneself" (Hood & Carruthers, 2007, p. 316).

Experiences that would be considered virtuous leisure include obvious leisure engagements such as volunteering. They may also include less obvious forms of engagement such as helping a neighbor, participating in an environmental cleanup, teaching others a skill that you possess, or planting a beautiful garden that brings others pleasure. Finding contexts in which a person can use his or her strengths in service is central to engaging in virtuous leisure. Experiencing these acts of service and reflecting on the positive outcomes is also necessary. Interestingly, the research associated with volunteering clearly demonstrates that the greatest benefit occurs for the person providing the service rather than the person receiving the assistance

©Ints Vikmanis/fotolia

The greatest gift you can give yourself is to give to others.

(Pillavin, 2003). Finally, finding opportunities to be of service in the community can help us develop reciprocal interdependent relationships with other community members and allow us to feel connected to and needed by our community.

SUMMARY

Leisure has some direct and powerful connections to building a life of meaning and well-being. However, not all leisure has the same benefit, and some leisure experiences may be detrimental to well-being. The freedom of the leisure context and experience sets the stage for the possibility of engaging in leisure in such a way as to maximize its benefits. However, for many people, this type of leisure engagement requires effort and knowledge and must be purposeful—that is, people need to engage in leisure with conscious attention to the nature of their engagement and the resultant benefits. Leisure services professionals can help citizens engage in leisure that is personally meaningful, that allows for engagement and disengagement, that is pleasurable, and that allows participants to develop and express their best selves while feeling connected and important to their communities, families, and friends. These supports may include educational opportunities to learn about the potent connection between leisure engagement and well-being; they may include providing opportunities to experience various types of leisure and the resultant effects on feelings of well-being; or they may involve the creation of communities and places where enriched opportunities for leisure experiences are part of the daily fabric of life.

Learning Activities

1. Play the Tim McGraw song "Live Like You Were Dying." Discuss the message of the song as it relates to leisure, relationships, and well-being (e.g., positive emotion, personal growth, and meaning).

2. Locate a volunteer opportunity in your community in which you are interested (e.g., community cleanup, political rally, charity event, marathon support, soup kitchen). Volunteer at the event and really pitch in. Write a brief paper reflecting on your reactions to the virtuous leisure experience. Share your reactions with your classmates.

For additional assignments, Web links, and more, visit the online student resource at www.HumanKinetics.com/DimensionsOfLeisureForLife.

Review Questions

1. Provide an example of a stressful situation from your own life and explain how you drew from more than one type of strategy to manage the stressor. How successful were you in managing the stress?

2. How does each of the two types of intentional activities contribute to overall well-being?

3. Describe a personally meaningful leisure experience in which you have recently engaged. Thinking about the five broad strategies identified to increase the value of leisure for well-being (savoring leisure, authentic leisure, leisure gratifications, mindful leisure, and virtuous leisure), identify strategies that you could use to increase the value of that experience for you.

Leisure Reading

Fitzgerald, F.S. (1996). *The great Gatsby.* Cambridge, UK: University of Cambridge.

Fox, M.J. (2009). *Always looking up: The adventures of an incurable optimist.* New York: Hyperion.

Frankl, V.E. (1959). *Man's search for meaning.* New York: Washington Square Press.

Gilbert, E. (2007). *Eat, pray, love.* New York: Penguin.

Glossary

distress—Physiological response resulting from perception or appraisal of threat.

emotion-focused coping—Strategies that target the thoughts and feelings associated with distress.

gratifications—Immersive experiences that result in personal growth.

habituation—Becoming accustomed to or adapting to experiences.

hedonists—People who pursue pleasure as life's primary goal.

intentional activity—Effortful, goal-directed endeavors.

intrinsic motivation—Participation in an activity based on anticipation of rewards that come from within the person.

person–activity fit—Finding the activities that are congruent with the person's interests, capabilities, and needs.

pleasures—Emotionally positive, momentary, often sensory experiences.

problem-focused coping—Active strategies to address directly the problems that create a given distress.

savoring—Paying attention to the positive aspects of, and emotions associated with, an experience.

virtues—Characteristics that are viewed as universally good and that support individual and collective well-being.

well-being—The degree to which a person experiences positive emotion and fulfillment.

References

Allison, M.T., & Schneider, I.E. (Eds.). (2000). *Diversity and the recreation profession: Organizational perspectives.* State College, PA: Venture.

Allman, A. (1990). *Subjective well-being of people with disabilities: Measurement issues.* Unpublished master's thesis, University of Illinois.

Ben-Shahar, T. (2007). *Happier.* New York: McGraw-Hill.

Brickman, P., Coates, D., & Janoff-Bulman, R. (1978). Lottery winners and accident victims: Is happiness relative? *Journal of Personality and Social Psychology, 36,* 917-927.

Brown, K.W., & Ryan, R. (2003). The benefits of being present: Mindfulness and its role in psychological well-being. *Journal of Personality and Social Psychology, 84,* 822-848.

Bryant, F., & Veroff, J. (2007). *Savouring: A new model of positive experience.* Mahwah, NJ: Erlbaum.

Burns, D. (1999). *The feeling good handbook.* New York: Penguin.

Carruthers, C., & Hood, C. (2002). Coping skills for individuals with alcoholism. *Therapeutic Recreation Journal, 36,* 154-171.

Carruthers, C., & Hood, C. (2004). The power of the positive: Leisure and well-being. *Therapeutic Recreation Journal, 38,* 225-245.

Carruthers, C., & Hood, C. (2005). Research update: The power of positive psychology. *Parks and Recreation, 40,* 30-38.

Carruthers, C., & Hood, C. (2007). Building a life of meaning through therapeutic recreation: The leisure and well-being model, part I. *Therapeutic Recreation Journal, 41,* 276-297.

Carver, C., & Scheier, M. (2002). Optimism. In C. Snyder & S. Lopez (Eds.), *Handbook of positive psychology* (pp. 231-256). New York: Oxford University Press.

Charnetski, C., & Brennan, F. (2001). *Feeling good is good for you.* New York: Rodale.

Csikszentmihalyi, M. (1990). *Flow: The psychology of optimal experience.* New York: Harper & Row.

Csikszentmihalyi, M. (1993). Contexts of optimal growth in childhood. *Daedalus, 122,* 31-56.

Curtis, J.E. (1988). Purple recreation. *Society of Park and Recreation Educators Annual on Education, 3,* 73-77.

Danner, D., Snowden, D., & Friesen, W. (2001). Positive emotions in early life and longevity: Findings from the nun study. *Journal of Personality and Social Psychology, 80,* 804-813.

Davis, M., Eshelman, E., McKay, M., & Fanning, P. (2008). *The relaxation and stress reduction workbook.* Oakland, CA: New Harbinger.

Fava, G., & Ruini, C. (2003). Development and characteristics of a well-being enhancing psychotherapeutic strategy: Well-being therapy. *Journal of Behavioral Therapy and Experimental Psychology, 34,* 45-63.

Foster, S., & Lloyd, P. (2007). Positive psychology principles applied to counseling psychology at the individual and group level. *Consulting Psychology Journal: Practice and Research, 59,* 30-40.

Fredrickson, B. (2000). Cultivating positive emotions to optimize health and well-being. *Prevention and Treatment, 3,* Article 0001a. http://journals.apa.org/prevention/volume3/pre0030001a.html

Fredrickson, B., & Joiner, T. (2002). Positive emotions trigger upward spiral toward emotional well-being. *Psychological Science, 13,* 172-175.

Frydenberg, E. (2002). Beyond coping: Some paradigms to consider. In E. Frydenberg (Ed.), *Beyond coping: Meeting goals, visions, and challenges* (pp. 1-18). New York: Oxford University Press.

Goldstein, J. (2005). Desire, delusion, and DVD's. In S. Kaza (Ed.), *Hooked: Buddhist writings on greed, desire, and the urge to consume* (pp. 17-26). Boston: Shambhala.

Harker, L., & Keltner, D. (2001). Expressions of positive emotion in women's college yearbook pictures and their relationship to personality and life outcomes across adulthood. *Journal of Personality and Social Psychology, 80,* 112-124.

Harter, S. (2002). Authenticity. In C.R. Snyder & S.J. Lopez (Eds.), *Handbook of positive psychology* (pp. 382-394). New York: Oxford University Press.

Hartig, T., Evans, G., Jamner, L., Davis, D., & Garling, T. (2003). Tracing restoration in natural and urban field settings. *Journal of Environmental Psychology, 23,* 109-123.

Hood, C., & Carruthers, C. (2002). Coping skills theory as an underlying framework for therapeutic recreation services. *Therapeutic Recreation Journal, 36,* 154-161.

Hood, C., & Carruthers, C. (2007). Enhancing leisure experience and developing resources: The leisure and well-being model, part II. *Therapeutic Recreation Journal, 41,* 298-325.

Hutchinson, S., Bland, A., & Kleiber, D. (2008). Leisure and stress-coping: Implications for therapeutic recreation practice. *Therapeutic Recreation Journal, 42,* 9-23.

Hutchinson, S., & Kleiber, D. (2005). Gifts of the ordinary: Casual leisure's contributions to health and well-being. *World Leisure Journal, 47,* 2-16.

Iwasaki, Y. (2008). Pathways to meaning-making through leisure-like pursuits in global contexts. *Journal of Leisure Research, 40,* 231-249.

Iwasaki, Y., & Mannell, R. (2000). Hierarchical dimensions of leisure stress coping. *Leisure Sciences, 22,* 163-181.

Kabat-Zinn, J. (1990). *Full catastrophe living: Using the wisdom of your body and mind to face stress, pain, and illness.* New York: Bantam Doubleday.

Keyes, C. (2003). Complete mental health: An agenda for the 21st century. In C. Keyes & J. Haidt (Eds.), *Flourishing: Positive psychology and the life well-lived* (pp. 185-204). Washington, DC: American Psychological Association.

Keyes, C., & Lopez, S. (2002). Toward a science of mental health: Positive directions in diagnosis and interventions. In C.R. Snyder & S. Lopez (Eds.), *Handbook of positive psychology* (pp. 45-59). New York: Oxford University Press.

Kleiber, D. (1999). *Leisure experience and human development: A dialectical interpretation.* New York: Basic Books.

Kleiber, D., Hutchinson, S., & Williams, R. (2002). Leisure as a resource in transcending negative life events: Self-protection, self-restoration, and personal transformation. *Leisure Sciences, 24,* 219-235.

Klein, S. (2006). *The science of happiness: How our brains make us happy—and what we can do to get happier.* New York: Avalon.

Kobasa, S., Maddi, S., Puccetti, M., & Zola, M. (1985). Effectiveness of hardiness, exercise and social support as resources against illness. *Journal of Psychosomatic Research, 29,* 525-533.

Layard, R. (2005). *Happiness: Lessons from a new science.* New York: Penguin Press.

Lazarus, R., & Folkman, S. (1984). *Stress, appraisal, and coping.* New York: McGraw-Hill.

Lopez, S.J., & Louis, M.C. (2009). The principles of strengths-based education. *Journal of College and Character, 10,* 1-8.

Lykken, D. (1999). *Happiness: The nature and nurture of joy and contentment.* New York: St. Martin's Griffin.

Lykken, D., & Tellegen, A. (1996). Happiness is a stochastic phenomenon. *Psychological Science, 7,* 186-189.

Lyubomirsky, S. (2008). *The how of happiness: A scientific approach to getting the life you want.* New York: Penguin Press.

Massimini, F., & Delle Fave, A. (2000). Individual development in a bio-cultural perspective. *American Psychologist, 55,* 24-33.

McAllister, M. (2003). Doing practice differently: Solution-focused nursing. *Journal of Advanced Nursing, 41,* 528-535.

Nettle, D. (2005). *Happiness.* New York: Oxford University Press.

Neulinger, J. (1981). *The psychology of leisure.* Springfield, IL: Charles C Thomas.

Nix, G., Ryan, R., Manly, J., & Deci, E. (1999). Revitalization through self-regulation: The effects of autonomous and controlled motivation on happiness and vitality. *Journal of Experimental Social Psychology, 35,* 266-284.

Olson, E. (2006). *Personal development and discovery through leisure.* Dubuque, IA: Kendall/Hunt.

Pillavin, J. (2003). Doing well by doing good: Benefits for the benefactor. In C. Keyes & J. Haidt (Eds.), *Flourishing: Positive psychology and the life well-lived* (pp. 227-248). Washington, DC: American Psychological Association.

Pollard, E., & Rosenberg, M. (2003). The strength-based approach to child well-being: Let's begin with the end in mind. In M. Bornstein & L. Davidson (Eds.), *Well-being: Positive development across the life course* (pp. 13-32). Mahwah, NJ: Erlbaum.

Reis, H., Sheldon, K., Gable, S., Roscoe, J., & Ryan, R. (2000). Daily well-being: The role of autonomy, competence, and relatedness. *Personality and Social Psychology Bulletin, 26,* 419-435.

Russell, R. (2005). *Pastimes: The context of contemporary leisure* (3rd ed.). Champaign, IL: Sagamore.

Ryan, R., & Deci, E. (2000). Self-determination theory and the facilitation of intrinsic motivation, social development, and well-being. *American Psychologist, 55,* 68-78.

Ryan, R., & Deci, E. (2001). On happiness and human potentials: A review of research on hedonic and eudaimonic well-being. *Annual Review of Psychology, 52,* 141-166.

Saleeby, D. (1997). *The strengths perspective in social work practice.* New York: Longman.

Seligman, M. (2002). *Authentic happiness.* New York: Free Press.

Selye, H. (1975). Confusion and controversy in the stress field. *Journal of Human Stress, 1,* 37-44.

Sharry, J. (2004). *Counseling children, adolescents, and families: A strengths-based approach.* Thousand Oaks, CA: Sage.

Sheldon, K., & Lyubomirsky, S. (2004). Achieving sustainable new happiness: Prospects, practices, and prescriptions. In P. Linley & S. Joseph (Eds.), *Positive psychology in practice* (pp. 127-145). Hoboken, NJ: Wiley.

Sheldon, K.M., & Lyubomirsky, S. (2006). Achieving sustainable gains in happiness: Change your actions, not your circumstances. *Journal of Happiness Studies, 7,* 55-86.

Smith, C., & Carlson, B. (1997). Stress, coping, and resilience in children and youth. *Social Science Review, 71,* 231-256.

Smith, E. (2006). The strength-based counseling model. *Counseling Psychologist, 34,* 13-79.

Stebbins, R.A. (2006). *Serious leisure: A perspective for our time.* New Brunswick, NJ: Transaction.

Vaillant, G. (2002). *Aging well.* Boston: Little Brown.

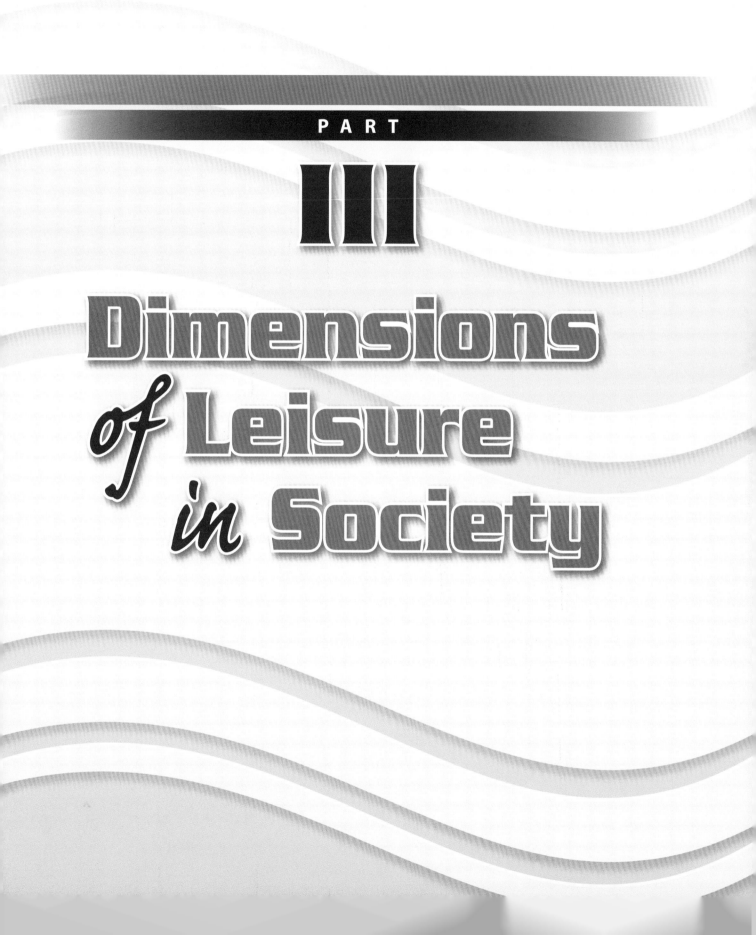

PART

III

Dimensions of Leisure in Society

6

Leisure History and Heritage

Lee J. deLisle
Western Michigan University

Learning Outcomes

After reading this chapter, you will be able to

▶ understand the role of leisure in human evolutionary development;

▶ describe and give examples of the relationship between leisure and threats to survival;

▶ identify sociological and technological practices that expand leisure opportunities;

▶ describe the relationship between leisure and work;

▶ discuss the similarities and differences in leisure behavior in ancient cultures;

▶ discuss the influence of ancient cultures on our contemporary understanding and use of leisure;

▶ describe political, religious, and economic influences on leisure behaviors;

▶ describe the cultural and economic conditions that led to the Playground Movement; and

▶ identify the stages of development in the formation of recreational services in the United States.

Vocabulary Terms

arête	Dark Ages	Pax Romana
blood sports	Enlightenment	Playground Movement
bread and circuses	evolution	Renaissance
civilization	festivals	*schole*
creation	Industrial Revolution	threats to survival

The control of fire provided heat, light, protection, and cooked food, which greatly enhanced the quality of life of early hominids.

Almost one million years ago a group of hominids sat around a fire in a cave in what is now Iraq. Their home had light and heat, there were animal skins spread on the floor for comfort, and the group lived together peacefully while struggling against the forces of nature that challenged their very existence. After finishing their meal they split the long bones of the animal they had hunted that day and enjoyed the sweet marrow within each bone. This simple pleasure, dessert, is an indication that they had some time to enjoy this leisure activity. As each subsequent generation of humans evolved, additional leisure activities, such as art, storytelling, dance, religion, and sport, contributed to their group culture and the development of the human race.

Social realities such as ritual and religion, slavery, technology, economic development, and the enhancement of the human intellect through play and formal education all contributed in positive ways to our present understanding of what it means to be human. Equally important in human development are the negative influences of war, greed, corruption, superstition, and social and physical disease on the quality of life experienced in past epochs and the subsequent rate of human development. In this chapter we examine the emergence of Western civilization through an understanding of the role of leisure in this unending human drama.

UNDERSTANDING LEISURE FROM A HISTORICAL PERSPECTIVE

Leisure can be described in many ways, both objectively and subjectively, depending on context and intent. To study leisure from a historical perspective we need a common point of reference. For the purpose of this chapter *leisure* is best defined as "free or unobligated time." This value-neutral concept can be understood across temporal and cultural boundaries.

The influential book *Leisure: The Basis of Culture* positions leisure as the most critical element in the formation and continuation of personal and communal culture (Pieper, 1963). Contemplation, celebration, and community, according to this book, are based in our use of leisure. How we experience leisure defines who we are as individuals and as a society. What we do with our leisure says something about our interests, our character, and our understanding of what it means to be fully human. Free time constructively used advances societies, enhances individual lives, and produces cultural development over time.

The relationship of leisure to personal and communal cultural development in past epochs can be seen as the interplay between activities needed for survival and time free from threat. This relationship between leisure and **threats to survival** is germane to our understanding of history but is also observable in contemporary societies. Despite all the technological advances in our modern world, we still face threats to survival. The most obvious examples are floods, hurricanes, and other natural forces that are beyond our control. Unfortunately, human activity such as war, military occupation, terrorism, and other threats continue to constrain individual and communal leisure.

The amount and quality of leisure are inversely related to the level of threat to survival that is experienced by an individual or community. As threats increase, leisure tends to decrease. As we individually and communally master or overcome these threats, we have more free time at our disposal, allowing for creative and cooperative behaviors that enhance our quality of life and deepen the cultural foundations of society.

This chapter takes us on a journey from prehistoric times to our modern understanding of leisure and recreational services. We will begin in your own backyard.

Imagine that in the course of digging a garden in your backyard you unearth what turns out to be a human settlement that is determined to be more than 10,000 years old. As you sift through the remnants of this prehistoric site you may discover artifacts that, with a little bit of insight and creative thinking, could help you understand the amount of leisure that this group might have enjoyed. We know that leisure is needed for creative activity.

> There can be no high civilization where there is not ample leisure.
>
> *Henry Ward Beecher*

LEISURE AWARENESS

Ancient Signs of Leisure

See how many items you can identify in the box below that may be an indication of leisure, including the following words: *tools, fire pit, cloth, jewelry, pottery, weapons, flute, drum, artwork, animal bone.*

```
Y R L E W E J P D Q
A C L O T H P O R K
T O O L S U I T U R
W E A P O N S T M O
F I R E P I T E W W
E T U L F R E R G T
D V H O R L M Y K R
E N O B L A M I N A
```

EVOLUTION OR CREATION?

Although we cannot scientifically describe the very origin of the human species, there is sufficient evidence to suggest that humans evolved over hundreds of thousands of years through both physical and cultural change. **Evolution** is a process of successful existence through natural selection, environmental adaptation, mutation, and survival. The debate continues between those who attribute human development to a natural process of adaptation and survival and those who ascribe the process of human history as being based in **creation** (created and controlled by an intelligent and, some would say, benevolent supreme being). You are encouraged to identify your own feelings about issues like creationism, intelligent design, and evolution and attempt to arrive at a place of informed knowledge. Others have managed to find humor in the controversy.

SELF-DISCOVERY

Is it possible to accept both the theory of evolution and the faith-based assertions of creation? Explain how this might work for you.

A number of creation stories have been preserved from ancient civilizations. Creation myths attempt to explain the origins of the world in ways that are relevant and understandable to a certain group of people. Many stories also emphasize the role of rest in relationship to work. Consider the creation story of the book of Genesis in the Judeo-Christian tradition.

> And on the seventh day God finished his work which he had done, and he rested on the seventh day from all his work which he had done. So God blessed the seventh day and hallowed it, because on it God rested from all his work which he had done in creation. (Book of Genesis 2:1-3 RSV)

According to this story, God worked to create all the elements of the cosmos in six days and on the seventh day rested. It should be noted that humans (man) arrived on the scene on the sixth day. If we subscribe to the existence of "days" as presented in the story, then the first day on earth for man was the Sabbath, a day of rest, a day of leisure. The idea of the original condition of human existence to be one of leisure is significant in our understanding of later religious practices that attempt to address issues related to use of free time. At this point in our study of human development we understand that leisure was considered by some to be the natural and original or primal state of human existence. This is sometimes referred to as the *primacy of leisure*.

IMPORTANCE OF FIRE AND ITS EFFECT ON THE DIVISION OF LABOR

There is evidence that approximately 1.2 million years ago pre-humans learned to control fire. Controlling fire allowed humans to master their environment to a much greater degree by using fire as protection against attacks from wild animals, as a means to cook and preserve food, and to provide heat and light to extend the day. These extra hours provided time for tool making and for basic communication between group members. It was a time to reflect on the events of the day and plan the next's day's hunt or a move to a new camp. This leisure brought greater organization and stability to the group, contributing to communal well-being, reducing threats to survival, and allowing for the creation of forms of self-expression such as language, art, music, and dance.

PERSONAL LEISURE

Technology continues to affect leisure in our lives. Make a list of 10 or more items around your home or apartment that create opportunities for more free time in your life.

Along with the development of tools and language and the controlled use of fire was the emerging ability of humans to plan and organize tasks. The fastest, strongest men became warriors and hunters, finding food for cooking and storage and protecting the settlement. Others, including women and theatre majors, stayed closer to the camp and foraged for edible plants and roots and maintained the communal living amenities. Job responsibilities became more specialized. This division of labor allowed for periods of work and periods of rest—leisure was on the increase. One result of this increase in free time was the celebration of festivals. **Festivals** marked special times in the ancient lunar calendar, times that were sacred, *sacro* (set apart), from the rest of the year (deLisle, 2009). Festivals also commemorated past events, oftentimes spiritual or religious, providing a cyclical understanding of time, an enormous advance in ancient culture. One insightful book on human festivity tells us that what makes a festival time special is the cessation of normal daily activities to allow for access to something extraordinary, even otherworldly (Pieper, 1999).

LEISURE AWARENESS

Identify festivals that take place in your hometown. What is the purpose of each event? How do these events add to the quality of your life and that of your community?

MEANWHILE, BACK AT THE CAVE . . . AGRICULTURAL ALTERNATIVES

As humans sought to infuse their existence with meaning through creation stories, the development of taboos and requisite punishments, and the nascent emergence of creative activities, there remained some very basic concerns about survival. Hunter-gatherers were required to follow their source of food, animal herds, as they migrated according to the seasonal food supply. For the humans, there were certainly times of starvation and death due to a lack of food provided by animals. Other natural factors, including competition from other human groups, forced these clans to defend themselves or die.

Early humans gradually found that certain plants and fruits were edible. As this process developed over the centuries there was a shift from hunter-gatherer strategies to a dependency on agriculture. This was not a universal and complete change, because we still today find hunter-gatherer societies in remote places in the world. Life for these early farmers revolved around the activities needed for effective farming, with work becoming cyclical, based on the planting, growing, and harvesting seasons. This shift represents a major milestone in human development because it affected both the work and leisure patterns of society. There was a time for each needed activity and time for rest, recuperation, and celebration.

The formation of communities led to the growth of technology, more sophisticated means of communication, an increase in creative and artistic endeavors, and a sense of prosperity for those communities that were well managed and benefitted from their efforts to progress. With the relative stability of community living, many threats to survival were reduced or altered, creating more leisure. However, other threats arose, including barbaric behaviors.

The greatest threat to survival came from the actions of neighboring communities that used force to attack and conquer others. It is a cycle that continues into the 21st century. In ancient times war often resulted in the taking of property and the bondage of slavery for the defeated group. This was not a slavery based on race or ethnicity but one based on the rules of war in ancient civilizations. Slave labor, regardless of our modern feelings about it, supported civilizations that have produced some of the most valued contributions to Western **civilization**. Democratic governance, architecture, science, the arts, philosophy, and religion all benefitted from the additional leisure realized by free men as a result of the enforced labor of conquered civilizations.

RISE OF CIVILIZATION

By 4000 BCE, farming, building, and trading communities were spread across the Middle East. There remained some groups who wandered as hunters and herders but the majority had settled into the stability of agricultural and commercial life. The Fertile Crescent, or Fertile Triangle, situated between the Tigris and Euphrates rivers (a region called Mesopotamia, "the land between the rivers") was a focal point of civilization for 3,500 years. This area, which is today the country of Iraq, was the most sophisticated and powerful nation in the ancient world. Mesopotamia is remembered for many positive contributions to the advancement of civilization, including the first written code of laws, the Code of Hammurabi, and the first public park, the Hanging Gardens of Babylon. As is the case in all settled areas, Mesopotamia was the site of repetitive warfare; the region was invaded and ruled by the Sumerians, Akkadians, Babylonians, Assyrians, and Chaldeans during those 3,500 years. Each group assimilated the cultural practices of their subjects and introduced new elements to the advancement of civilization.

Advancements during this time included the development of a numbering system, calendars, techniques for measurement, irrigation, currency, and written contracts for business transactions. Aesthetic advancements included arts and crafts, reading and writing, sculpture, and ornate architectural features such as columns, arches, and domes. Governmental structures became more sophisticated, and commercial organizations were formed to share their expertise. Efforts were made to make life more enjoyable for free men including the staging of festivals and celebrations that satisfied the religious needs of the community and brought a welcome break from the ordinary demands of daily life. Hunting was pursued as a leisure activity, as were competitive sport activities that prepared men for war and provided amusement for participants and spectators. The first truly organized state or kingdom familiar to us is that of Egypt.

LEISURE IN THE LAND OF THE PHARAOHS

Egypt, a confederacy of cities along the Nile River, is a great example of how civilization and culture are closely related to leisure. Egypt benefitted from a strategic location both militarily and economically, the existence of a religious system that helped to control behaviors through a belief in the rewards of an afterlife, personal and communal wealth, and slave labor that freed citizens from much of the hard work of the kingdom. All of these positive factors reduced threats to survival, thereby increasing leisure.

The amount of leisure available to the population was inversely proportional to one's place in society (figure 6.1). The leisure class had great land holdings and grew wealthy from agricultural enterprises. Peasants labored daily for the benefit of the upper classes. When the Nile flooded, however, it was festival time, a religious occasion when all work paused long enough for everyone to celebrate with feasts, games, and rituals. The dynasties of Egypt are critical to our understanding of Western civilization because we see the positive effect of stability and order on the advancement of culture.

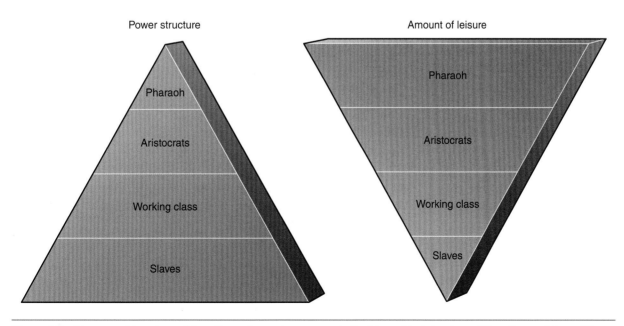

Figure 6.1   The pyramid, an icon of Egyptian culture, also represents the hierarchical structure of Egyptian society and the amount of leisure available to each group.

EMERGENCE OF GREECE

By 1000 BCE the Greeks were developing an alphabet, were sailing to foreign shores for trade and colonization, and had a class system in society that provided much leisure for the wealthy citizens. Women were not a part of society in terms of rights and privileges but ranked a little higher than the working class or slaves. Slavery was important in the development of the leisure class of ancient Greece. The practice was highly accepted, and no guilt was associated with the keeping of slaves.

The Greeks are best identified through the cultural developments brought by their position in the ancient world. Philosophy, mathematics, logic, government, the arts, music, theater, literature, sport, and so many other aspects of a thriving society were developed to work toward the ideal of perfection. Deeply embedded in the ideals of heroism, satire, education, political awareness, and aesthetics was the need for and use of leisure. Most Greek men spent time in the *gymnasia,* a community building that allowed for physical activity, sports, and education. For adult males it was the right use of leisure—to improve the mind, keep fit, and engage in social dialogue. It is interesting to note that the Greek word for leisure, **schole**, is the root for our word *school.* This reminds us that the Greeks dedicated their leisure to self-improvement rather than merely amusement. Leisure was used to better the human condition, to contribute to one's community, to bring about intellectual and physical stimulation and learning, and to improve on the art of living.

The Greek ideal of **arête** suggested that all pursuits, including recreational activities, be performed excellently, with complete mastery. *Arête* was the pursuit of perfection; it combined noble actions with noble thoughts. This concept of unity of mind and action to achieve perfection found its way into the very foundation of the Greek code of living. There is no real English translation of *arête* except for "proud and valorous behavior"—our classical sense of sportsmanship would illustrate a portion of this concept. The Olympic ideals were founded on the sense of *arête*—human perfection and nobility (Shivers & deLisle, 1997).

RESEARCH TO REALITY

The Greeks developed many schools of philosophy as guides to living. Research the following schools of philosophy and define their approach to leisure: Stoicism, Hedonism, Epicureanism, Eudaimonism.

CAPUT MUNDI: THE GLORY OF ROME

The Roman era begins with the arrival of the Etruscans to central Italy. The citizens of Rome, who numbered close to one million during the pre-Christian era, established their city and its surrounding environs as the capital of the entire known Western world. Rome was truly the leader of the world: *caput mundi.* Rome became the strongest military power in the Western world. These conquests led to an increase in wealth for some and a greater gap between rich and poor. A new leisure class arose. The wealthy and the urban middle class enjoyed a good lifestyle whereas the peasants and slaves suffered. So many slaves were available that the wages of citizen workers declined. The well-to-do no longer performed manual labor or lived the simple life of their ancestors. Although there was decadence and a distinct level of brutality, there was also great development of the arts and sciences.

Leisure Activities in Imperial Rome

Romans set aside time for games, races, gladiatorial contests, and other amusements. Public festivals and entertainment were numerous and varied for both rich and poor. Gladiatorial combats, theatrical performances, horse racing, and acrobatics were some of the events held to entertain the people. History, poetry, oratory, and the didactic essay were integral parts of Roman literature. Architecture, sculpture, and painting flourished. Roman architecture formed a style of its own.

Romans enjoyed feasts, public entertainment, and the public baths. The Roman baths were recreational centers built on a grand scale. Often covering hundreds of acres, these facilities offered bathing pools of varying temperatures, saunas, restaurants, rooms for massage, and sexual partners of all ages and persuasions. These pleasure palaces were a sign of the sophistication of Roman culture as well as a contributing factor to Rome's eventual downfall. Several theories about the fall of Rome

Photo courtesy of Lee deLisle

The Coliseum or Amphitheater of Flavius in Rome was the site of gladiatorial battles and other blood sports, holding more than 55,000 spectators and offering free entertainment for all.

attribute its decline to the misuse of leisure. The early Christians would not attend the blood sports or the baths and were thereby viewed as a threat to the order of the empire, resulting in their execution by the Romans.

Leisure and the Politics of Social Control

Throngs of foreigners came to Rome. The rulers, politicians, and policy makers saw the inherent danger of a large population of underpaid, overworked nonresidents in their midst. To maintain the **Pax Romana**, the relative peace experienced in Rome, the leaders controlled the citizens' behavior through planned special events intended to entertain, educate, inspire, and distract the masses. **Bread and circuses** is the term used to describe the strategy of the ruling class to control the lower classes by offering them a ration of food each week and the spectacles of the amphitheaters like the Coliseum, the circuses, and racetracks of Rome. The **blood sports** of ancient Rome provide us with some understanding of the lack of respect for human life that characterized Roman culture.

Rome was in decline for several hundred years, effectively losing its influence by the 4th century CE. The reasons for this decline have been the subject of hundreds of books and research articles. What can be said with some confidence is that the use of leisure by the ruling class and the masses certainly contributed to the moral and cultural devolution of this great society.

MEDIEVAL PERIOD: CASTLES, CHURCHES, AND THE PEASANT CULTURE

The thousand years between the fall of the Roman Empire (455) and the Renaissance (1455) are referred to as the medieval period or the Middle Ages. The downfall of the Roman Empire in the West brought the scourge of barbarism to Europe. This time is also referred to as the **Dark Ages**, because the European continent was subject to endless war, constant migration, food shortages, poor living conditions, and diseases such as the bubonic plague of 1347 to 1350, which produced more death and destruction than any preceding war or natural disaster. Twenty-five percent of the population of Europe was destroyed in this 3-year period, a rate of 1,000 deaths per day (Deaux, 1969). The disease, commonly seen as a punishment from God, was spread through fleas that transmitted the disease from the burgeoning rat population in urban areas to unsuspecting residents. The disease caused red, swollen circles called *buboes* and damaged the respiratory systems of the victims. If untreated, people died within 4 to 7 days of contracting the disease. Children attempted to reconcile this horror through games and songs. The game "Ring Around the Rosie" was based on their experience of the plague. The original song was this:

> *Ring around of roses*
>
> . . . describing the red swollen circles on the skin;
>
> *A pocket full of posies*
>
> . . . many people carried flowers in their pockets and would then press them to their nose to mask the smell of dead bodies;
>
> *Achoo, Achoo, (or ashes, ashes) we all fall down*
>
> . . . because the disease compromised the respiratory system, the momentary cessation of the heart during a sneeze could cause an afflicted person to die on the spot. The ashes referred to the burning of bodies, because there were too many for traditional burials.

The Dark Ages, filled with fear, disease, warfare, and very difficult living conditions, challenged the human spirit and threatened the continued cultural development of the human race. Considering the relationship between threats to survival and the amount and quality of free time available, it is no wonder that cultural advancements all but ceased during this difficult period.

One saving grace during these difficult times was the rise of institutional Christianity and the birth of Islam on the Arabian Peninsula and subsequent formation of an Islamic empire. Organized religion supported literacy and, in the case of Islam, retained and disseminated the scientific knowledge of the previous 2,000 years. Islamic scholars collected and protected the classical works of knowledge and became a ready source for translation when reason replaced superstition. The monastic system of early Christianity led to the development of the great universities of Western Europe, fostering the reengagement of the populace with learning and scientific advancement.

The plague was a catalyst for change in Europe. Economic, social, governmental, and ecclesial practices, accepted and endured for centuries, were no longer held to be valid or effective means of making sense of life's experiences. The plague set the stage for economic and social change that would be realized during the following two centuries.

Feudalism, the prevalent economic system of the time, and town autonomy permitted the emergence of the European fledgling nation-states. Banking, accounting, and public finance were invented. Trade, travel, and industry augmented economic development.

Leisure in the Middle Ages

Leisure, as in past times, was determined by wealth and class and was controlled to some degree by the Christian Church. Peasants' work was relieved by the Sabbath, church festivals, holidays, and aristocratic largess. At one point the Roman Church provided over 185 holy days or saint's days, creating leisure opportunities for the overworked peasantry. Sports, gambling, music, dance, and drinking were favorite pastimes for men. Women socialized in groups in the home. Children, when not working for their families, enjoyed simple games, rhymes, and stories. Protestant sects also had an impact on leisure, usually by restricting the types of activities that were allowed during free time.

Aristocrats benefitted from the peasant labor and enjoyed riding, hunting, reading, and great feasts. On feast days the aristocrats invested in parades and heraldry, providing entertainment for the peasants while reinforcing aristocratic control over the social structure of the community.

Fairs and Trading

Another respite from the hard labor of peasant life was fairs and markets that visited locales to sell or barter crafts and goods. Fairs were held on a regular basis near urban areas, allowing the citizens a break from their business and exposure to new ideas and products that were brought to town by the traveling merchants. Fairs were a time for lavish display booths. Dancing bears, wrestling contests, stage shows, mountebanks selling the latest snake oil, and an occasional hanging or other form of public punishment contributed to the leisure amusement of travelers.

RENAISSANCE: A RESURGENCE OF CLASSICAL VALUES

The **Renaissance** marked the rebirth of the classical values of ancient Greece and Rome. People were conscious of a changing world around them and reveled in the idea that they were part of this evolution. The old anchors of feudalism and

Photo courtesy of Lee deLisle

This mural on the wall of a palazzo in Tivoli, Italy, extols the virtues of reading, education, and fine arts for men and women of social means.

dedication to religion were slowly giving way to the emerging nation-states and the revival of interest in ancient Roman legal and literary studies. The center of this intellectual movement on the Italian peninsula between 1350 and 1525 was the city of Florence.

The Renaissance was an age of spectacles, filled with the mock combat of festival sports, the pomp and circumstance of processions, and the uproar of great citywide celebrations. Almost any occasion—a saint's day, the arrival of visiting nobility, the anniversary of a great battle, even the political reverses of some feared or hated prince—was reason enough for crowds to fill the streets with revelry.

When there were no opportunities to celebrate, the people found outlet in hunts, ball games, horse races, boxing matches, snowball fights, racket games, gambling, dancing, musical entertainments, and banquets. The energy and enthusiasm of the Renaissance found expression in a wide variety of sports and games. Schoolmasters considered physical activity an essential part of the curriculum. Exercise was deemed a necessity for both young and old. The forerunners to tennis, baseball, and bowling were very popular. Physical activity was both utilitarian and enjoyable. It provided for the sound body in which a sound mind could exist, and it was fun.

The mature Renaissance gave way to an even more rationally oriented philosophy. Scientific evidence and the Enlightenment were the underlying bases for the emergence of a humanist, romantic, secular philosophy that counteracted stoicism, asceticism, and religiosity. The **Enlightenment** was an 18th-century philosophical movement that freed people's minds from dependence on the supernatural and otherworldly rewards. Religious rule was replaced by an insistence on human reason rather than divine law, natural rights instead of supernaturalism, the scientific method rather than faith-based truths, social contracts and personal liberty rather than authoritarian mandate, and a humanitarian and democratic belief rather than aristocratic rule.

This was a time for learning based on scientific inquiry. The humanist-oriented concept that the human, not God, is the measure of all things played a great part in the recovery of leisure as an important aspect of human life.

INDUSTRIAL REVOLUTION

The **Industrial Revolution** was the movement toward centralized workplaces—factories that brought together large number of skilled and unskilled workers and great technological innovations in the production of goods. Factory work caused a previously unimagined segmentation of leisure. A farmer or craftsman working at home could take a break when needed, stop for lunch, and enjoy the company of family while completing his work tasks. Factory work settings broke the basic fabric of life, because free time was controlled by the employer in terms of both the amount of time available daily or weekly and the physical location of the worker. Leisure became segmented by gender, age, time of day, and day of the week. Leisure was further segmented by economic status, because the factory worker's life was similar to a form of economic slavery. Workers' rights were not considered, and eventually women and children (as young as 9 years of age) entered the factory setting to contribute to the economic well-being of the family. Education for the young was an afterthought, and many social problems arose from the lack of supervision of children during the long work day of the parents. This problem led to the intervention of churches and philanthropic organizations and governmental agencies that addressed social issues by providing recreational services in urban settings.

The effects of the Enlightenment and the Industrial Revolution, a heightened awareness and reliance on science and reason, and the emergence of a large middle class produced inventions and discoveries and new cultural paradigms at an unprecedented pace. Distant unknown lands beckoned, and those with the financial ability sought to explore new worlds. The settling of North America by the Spanish, Dutch, English, and French created new opportunities for religious and economic advancement. With this new adventure came many of the problems of the Old World. Social problems arising from the difficulties of living and working in newly found cities were addressed in some respects by the development of private and public philanthropic services, including the provision of spaces and programs to meet the leisure needs of a new world.

The course of human history has seen several notable, major shifts in the basic character of social and communal living. Early humans, hunter-gathers, slowly embraced an agrarian lifestyle that allowed for the formation of societies and nation states. Peasants and their rulers embraced the system of feudalism until the lower classes sought more autonomy from aristocratic controls. From the guilds and cottage industries of Europe and the growth of the new colonies in America came a technological and industrial revolution that continues to affect our lives today.

ORIGINS AND DEVELOPMENT OF RECREATIONAL SERVICES IN THE UNITED STATES

With parents working up to 18 hours a day in factories, children were often left to fend for themselves in new cities along the east coast of America. Churches and social leaders sought to remedy this situation initially by providing safe places for children to play, to literally get them off the streets. A philanthropic church-based effort to provide safe places for urban children to recreate, called the **Playground Movement**, began in the late 1800s. In 1868, the first outdoor playground was established in Boston under the guidance of the First Church of Boston. It was situated next to a public school and was associated with a vacation program. Nearby Brookline, Massachusetts, purchased land for the expressed desire of creating playgrounds in 1871. This was followed by the designation of meadows in Chicago as a play area in 1876. Tennis courts, baseball diamonds, and other facilities

©Library of Congress

Factory work greatly enhanced economic growth in the United States but did so at great cost to individuals and families.

were added in later years. In 1898, New York City opened 31 playgrounds under the supervision of the Board of Education.

By 1900, only a few U.S. cities provided public playgrounds. Today nearly all cities have recreational areas available, some with highly organized programs supervised by professional practitioners.

Along with the growth of social service–based recreational programming there was, despite the efforts of the churches, an enormous increase in commercial amusements and recreation in early America. Drinking, theater performances, professional and amateur sports, and travel all captivated the imagination of the urban populations. Leisure activity, as was the case in so many other previous cultures, was delineated by class and wealth. Spectator sports ranged from loosely organized professional sports to the emergence of college sports and amateur events. Betting was common, and drinking was a part of the experience. Participative activities included athletic clubs, lawn sports such as tennis or croquet, bicycling, skating, and outdoor pursuits like hiking, fishing, camping, and visiting parks and natural sites. The health movement of the 19th century emphasized the value of outdoor experiences, particularly the seashore and natural spas, as restorative experiences for stressed-out city dwellers. Examples such as the Muscular Christianity movement of the 19th century emphasized the importance of active physical activity over passive entertainment. This focus on exercise and sport influenced other organizations, such as the YMCA, to include recreational sports as a part of their program. Early support of recreational sports eventually led to the development of new sports such as basketball and volleyball.

By the early 20th century, a thriving leisure-based economy had emerged, fueled by government-sponsored recreation sites, commercial amusements, and travel experiences. Labor unions fought to reduce the workweek to 5 days per week and 8 hours per day, providing workers with increasing opportunities to participate in leisure activity. In the past 100 years, the hours of factory labor have been reduced in some industries from 60 per week to 40. State and federal legislation has imposed restrictions upon the number of hours children can work. White-collar and professional workers have enjoyed similar reductions in hours.

Labor-saving devices, competitive decreases in the cost of entertainment, better and faster transportation, improved communication—all served to expand leisure and its opportunities. Much of this wealth has been reinvested and consumed in the processes of further production; much has been wasted in wars and other enterprises that produced few social values; and much has been expended on social betterment, education, and recreational experience.

A recognition of the importance of leisure and recreational activities in terms of human and social value gained general acceptance. As work receded from its preeminent place in Western culture, religious leaders reconsidered the place of leisure in human life. The churches incorporated leisure into their philosophy and theology. The Puritan tradition, which viewed work as the antithesis of leisure, had been largely dispelled. Churches often support leisure and recreational activities, adopting techniques developed by practitioners in the field of recreational service. Methodists encouraged the camp meeting movement, which became permanent settlements in places like Oak Bluff on Martha's Vineyard and Ocean Grove, New Jersey. Chautauqua, originally a place to train Sunday school teachers in upstate New York, became the site for educational summer experiences that were the model of wholesome recreation for individuals and families. Catholic youth centers and Jewish community centers grew from the identified need to provide wholesome recreational opportunities for their respective communities.

Eight transitions of play and recreation help explain early developments in the provision of recreational services (Rainwater, 1922):

1. From the provision of recreational services for little children to provision for people of all ages

2. From facilities operated during the summer only to those maintained throughout the year

3. From outdoor equipment and activities only to both outdoor and indoor facilities and events

4. From congested urban districts to both urban and rural communities

5. From philanthropic to community support and control

6. From "free" play and miscellaneous events to "directed" play with organized activities and correlated activities including manual, physical, aesthetic, social, and civic projects

7. From the provision of facilities to the definition of standards for the use of leisure

8. From individual interests to group and community activities

The social service foundation of recreational services intended to address urban issues in the immigrant neighborhoods of large East Coast cities has been linked to the greater appreciation of the value of leisure services for all citizens in an environment of increased professional standards and practices (Rainwater, 1922). Almost 20 years later, five more transitions were identified (Hjelte, 1940):

1. From a "play" movement to a "recreational" movement

2. From a local municipal movement only to a state and national movement

3. From programs detached from public education to programs integrated with the educational curriculum and system

4. From organizations limited to urban communities to organizations that included suburban and rural areas as well

5. From an organization largely under quasi-public control with subsidies from public funds to full acceptance of recreational service as a public function

To these observations we can now add the following transitions (Shivers & deLisle, 1997):

1. From programs operated by laypeople to those operated by professionally prepared and, in most instances, highly qualified practitioners

2. From an amenity service to one considered essential to the health, welfare, and cultural development of all

3. From a voluntary service to a professionalized occupational field of applied social science

4. From a relatively universal dependence on the merit system of civil service classification for the employment of personnel in the field to a mistrust of such procedures, at least in many urban centers

5. From a reliance on a career ladder process to the use of seasonal, contractual, and specialist personnel

6. From a nonpolitical position to a highly sophisticated use of political procedures to gain departmental advantages

7. From an effort to serve most of the constituency to the initiation of a few well-publicized projects designed to satisfy high-profile, special interest groups

8. From a position of serving only those who have the physical and mental capacity to seek service to an attempt to identify and serve all populations with nontraditional needs, either through mainstreaming or through specialized grouping and programming

RESEARCH TO REALITY

Research the history of recreational services in your town or city. When were programs first offered? What has been the focus of community efforts to provide recreational services?

During the 20th century, diverse entities began to address the need for professional preparation of recreational service providers, which led to the joining of these diverse groups of park and nature enthusiasts, sports leaders, youth social service providers, and recreation business leaders to eventually form the leading association for recreation professionals in the United States, the National Recreation and Park Association.

HERITAGE OF THE NATIONAL RECREATION AND PARK ASSOCIATION

A natural outcome of the development of parks and play spaces was the formation of an organization of individuals whose profession was supervising and maintaining public parklands. The first such meeting took place in Boston in 1898, marking the beginning of the New England Association of Park Superintendents. In 1904, the group was expanded and was referred to as the American Association of Park Superintendents. In 1921, the group promoted itself to the

©Library of Congress

Playgrounds provided children the freedom to explore their personal and communal potential in a safe environment.

lofty title of the American Institute of Park Executives. Sounds like they must have all received a raise!

In a parallel development, the Playground Association of America was founded in Washington, DC, in 1906. This group was based on a social service model focusing on the provision of recreational services and programs. By 1911, the group saw the need to change its name to the Playground and Recreation Association of America. In 1926, a training school for recreational leadership was established to train executives in the profession of recreational management. In 1930, the name was again changed to the National Recreation Association. These newly trained professionals formed their own group, the Society of Recreation Workers of America, in 1938 and experienced growth in specific areas of recreational services including state, industrial, armed forces, rural, and hospital settings as well as a branch dedicated to professional education.

A merger of interests and organizations took place in 1965 with the formation of the National Recreation and Park Association. The NRPA is the leading advocate for the promotion of recreational services and park related activities in the United States. Annual conferences held in major cities throughout the United States provide more than 8,000 professionals with the opportunity for continuing education, professional development, and access to new equipment, programming ideas, and technologies. For a more extensive review of the development of the recreation and parks movement in the United States, visit the Joseph Lee Memorial Library and archives online at www.NRPA.org.

Recreational activity is now universally recognized as one of the basic needs of human life. When a need is deemed significant to society, then government, as well as private and philanthropic enterprise, takes responsibility to meet that need for the mutual benefit and welfare of all concerned. Recreational activity is such an important aspect of life that modern society would suffer an inestimable loss without it.

LEISURE, RECREATION, AND QUALITY OF LIFE

From the social service foundations of recreational services in the late 19th century, we now recognize parks and recreation as an integral part of many communities providing year-round activities and special events that contribute to our quality of life. Since the 1950s, recreational services have grown in importance. Several trends since World War II have shaped the recreational services profession, including a growing concern for the protection of the natural environment; a stronger emphasis on the role of recreational activities in combating poverty and racial tension; additional recreational programming for girls and women; specialized disciplines within the profession to address the needs of military groups (morale, welfare, and recreation); programs for individuals with differing abilities; dedicated facilities and programs for the elderly; and the constant adjustment of the profession to the economic realities of the time (McClean et al., 2005). Although all admit that recreational services are not the answer to the world's problems, recreational professionals continue to improve the quality of life of individuals and communities.

Increased expectations for quality leisure experiences and well-planned services create the need for professionally prepared individuals to address the social, physical, environmental, and economic requirements of the recreational industry. These services can be loosely grouped into three categories:

1. Governmentally based services, such as national and state parks, municipal parks and recreation departments, and other taxed-based entities
2. Nonprofit organizations such as the Boys and Girls Clubs, Scouting, and faith-based organizations with a social imperative to improve the quality of life for citizens
3. Commercial enterprises that seek to provide recreational experiences combined with a private profit motive

During the past 25 years, recreational service provision in the public and nonprofit sectors has adopted many practices of the commercial approach to recreation. Community recreation departments have accepted the importance of marketing both the message of the benefits of recreation and the specific programs offered in their communities. Self-sufficiency typified by an entrepreneurial approach to service provision has allowed programs to grow despite governmental budget reductions. A majority of recreational programs now include a fee to cover some or all of the costs of operating a program or facility. There has been much debate over this, because public-based recreation must continue to provide services to all citizens while operating in a financially responsible manner. Private commercial enterprises have become more involved in providing recreational programs and services to local communities. The growth of the consumer mentality has coincided with the commodification or commercialization of recreational experiences for many families.

Recreational activity involves one third of our time, one third of our money, and one third of our land. It has been become a major force in contemporary society. Recreational service providers in the 21st century are confronted by the same social and economic challenges that are present in the larger society. The statement that the future is not what it used to be illustrates the challenges ahead. Geopolitical upheavals such as war, occupation, and terrorism have made the future seem not quite as secure as it seemed several decades ago. The economic system based on the free market economy has faltered to the point of creating a lack of confidence in the current practices of large financial institutions. Although these challenges may be perceived as threats to survival, the average person continues to seek out meaningful expression through leisure activities. Variables including the environment, technology, demography, changing value systems, economics, health, and work versus free time have been identified as important factors in determining the future path of leisure services (Godbey, 1997). Leisure service providers in the current environment must become more agile and innovative: They must seek out cooperative relationships with competitors, make greater use of outsourced or contractual collaborators, analyze the product of their efforts in terms of benefits provided to the individual and the community, and become both entrepreneurial and "interpreneurial" by identifying and sharing common goals (Godbey, 1997). Service providers will need to provide customized services that meet the ever-changing needs of an increasingly diverse customer base. All of this will need to be accomplished while adapting to and incorporating new technologies that shape both the interests of the public and the means of delivering leisure services. Recreational professionals must shape the future of this long-standing relationship between leisure and human development.

SUMMARY

Leisure and recreational activities both define and contribute to the advancement of human culture. Leisure and its use have added great value to life. The roots of education, the arts, and commercial entertainment are found in the perceived value of leisure and the activities associated with its use. Political and religious ideologies were formed and supported through the control of leisure.

Ancient tribes and civilizations were confronted with threats to their survival that limited the amount and quality of leisure made available to them. History tells us that when people had the luxury of leisure, they often made great strides in cultural and technological advancement.

Leisure resulted in the establishment of the greatest civilizations on earth. The Egyptians, Greeks, and Romans, through their use of leisure, created the foundations of Western civilization. Theater, the arts, philosophy, politics and government, sports, and amusements all emanated from the use or misuse of leisure.

When the machinations of war and internecine strife were in the forefront, leisure was reduced and civilization's advancement came to a halt. Peace and security are critical to human advancement and the realization of the benefits of leisure opportunities. As rationalism replaced superstition and humans created stable systems of government and land distribution, leisure reemerged, bringing an enlightened populace to new heights of discovery. At that time the threats to quality living became economic rather than natural phenomena, yet war continues to limit our potential as individuals and communities.

The last quarter of the 20th century in America was an age of massive human leisure. In no epoch of the past has there ever been such a distribution of free time. The development of civilization, with organization, division of labor, mechanization, mass production, and automation, brought leisure within the grasp of all.

Recreational service, mirroring the evolution of human culture, has evolved from a private and personally directed leisure experience to a highly complex, governmentally administered organization. Public, commercial, and voluntary institutions work side by side to provide essential opportunities for all members of a community.

But like the societies of the ancient world, there are obvious differences in the interests and activities of the various groups within any community. Western societies are constantly challenged by the possibilities that leisure presents. Are we to embrace the *schole* of ancient Greece and use our free time for contemplation of all that is good, to better ourselves and our communities through education and community service? Or are we to embrace only the *bread and circuses* of ancient Rome, with an emphasis on passive entertainment, conformity, and the devolution of social and moral standards?

We each must confront the challenge of leisure as we seek to define ourselves and our relationship to our communities. For those entering the recreational services profession, the challenge is to lead, to serve, and to inspire.

Learning Activities

1. **Focus on leisure:** Building relationships is an important element in the success of a leisure service organization. This project presents several opportunities to experience this with classmates, social agencies, and the subjects of your study. You will be identifying and increasing your understanding of the diversity of leisure behavior in the community by synthesizing personal observations and experiences with photos in order to effectively present your findings. Working in pairs, plan your approach to recording community involvement in leisure activities. Your project should include photos of youth, young adult, family, and older adult activities. (If photos are taken on private property, permission must be obtained prior to the photo shoot. Individual release forms must be made available if participants are identifiable in the photos.) The study must also include both indoor and outdoor, group and individual, and special population activities. If you speak to your subjects try to learn more about them: why they are participating in a particular activity and what they perceive to be the benefits of their participation. A written analysis of your findings (two pages) should accompany your results.

2. **Leisure in the community:** Develop a theory or hypothesis about the understanding of leisure by various age groups. This will be based on information presented in class and your own insight into the topic. Create a 10-question survey that will aid you in understanding the level of awareness that various age groups have regarding leisure and recreation. Conduct interviews with at least two individuals in each age category:

   - Under 10 years old
   - 11 to 14 years old
   - 15 to 18 years old
   - 19 to 23 years old
   - 24 to 35 years old
   - 36 to 55 years old
   - 55 to 75 years old

   All subjects should be asked the same questions. All answers should be recorded on a survey sheet. Identify the person by age, gender, and primary use of time (i.e., school, work, retired), not by name. Record your findings in a report that will be presented to the class in a 5-minute presentation, and turn in your results (a two-page written analysis of your findings).

3. **Your leisure history:** If leisure is the basis of culture, you can analyze your personal culture by recording and analyzing your leisure use. Construct a spreadsheet to record all your daily activities for a 7-day period. The chart will include a cell for each of the 24 hours for all 7 days. Indicate what you did for each hour (e.g., sleep, classes, shopping, computer time, homework, various social or recreational activities). Classify activities as obligatory or discretionary. Summarize your findings, identifying quantitative (numerical descriptions) and qualitative observations about your activities. Identify what you have learned about your behaviors through this exercise.

For additional assignments, Web links, and more, visit the online student resource at www.HumanKinetics.com/DimensionsOfLeisureForLife.

Review Questions

1. Explain why leisure is considered the basis of culture. Give three examples of how leisure shapes personal and communal culture.

2. Why do we consider leisure to be free time?

3. How do threats to survival affect leisure? Compare one ancient threat to survival to a contemporary threat from your own life experiences.

4. Identify some prehistoric activities that may have enhanced leisure for early humans.

5. What was *schole* and how does it help us to understand ancient Greek leisure activity?

6. Give two examples of the Greek idea of *arête* in modern society.

7. What role did slaves play in the accumulation of leisure in ancient societies?

8. Describe a positive and a negative effect that religion had on leisure use.

9. How did the Pax Romana contribute to leisure in ancient Rome?

10. How was leisure used by the Roman rulers as a form of social control?

11. What were blood sports all about? Provide a 21st-century example of our continued fascination with this type of entertainment.

12. When it comes to leisure and recreation, would you rather have been a Greek or Roman?

13. What was so dark about the Dark Ages? How did this period affect leisure?

14. *Renaissance* means "rebirth"; what was reborn during this era? How did this affect leisure?

15. How did the Enlightenment improve people's ways of thinking?

16. How did the Industrial Revolution permanently alter our way of life relative to leisure?

17. Identify the major transitional points in the development of the recreational movement in the United States.

18. What are the three categories of organizations that typically provide recreational services? Provide one example of each.

19. Why is it important for students of the 21st century to understand the leisure attitudes and practices of past civilizations?

20. How can this knowledge help you to maximize your own leisure?

Leisure Readings

Alboher, M. (2008, May 5). Why leisure matters. *New York Times*. http://shiftingcareers.blogs. nytimes.com/2008/05/05/why-leisure-matters/

Bronson, P. (2006, June 18). Just sit back and relax! *Time*. www.time.com/time/magazine/ article/0,9171,1205369,00.html

Bureau of Labor Statistics. (2009). Recreation workers. *Occupational outlook handbook, 2010-11 edition*. http://stats.bls.gov/oco/ocos058.htm

Lee, Y. (1999). Research update: How do individuals experience leisure? *Parks and Recreation, 34*(2), 40-46.

Parsons, Y. (2001, September). Whatever happened to leisure? *Southwest Airlines Spirit*, pp. 108-115.

Glossary

arête—Greek ideal suggesting that all pursuits, including recreational activities, be performed excellently, with complete mastery; the pursuit of perfection. *Arête* combined noble actions with noble thoughts.

blood sports—Roman competitions that resulted in injury and often death that were enjoyed by most Romans until the introduction of Christianity.

bread and circuses—Weekly distribution of bread to the citizens of Rome, which combined with the free access to Roman games and competition was used to placate the population of Rome. In this manner, leisure was manipulated for political purposes.

civilization—State brought about by invention and sustained by the need for organization, cooperation, and communication. All civilizations have institutional forms of government, economics, religion, and symbolic devices for language.

creation—Process of human history based in life created and controlled by an intelligent and, some would say, benevolent supreme being.

Dark Ages—Period of approximately 1,000 years during which life was influenced by war, disease, migration, and a decided lack of cultural development due to the threats to survival that arose during this time.

Enlightenment—An 18th-century philosophical movement that freed people's minds from dependence on the supernatural and otherworldly rewards.

evolution—A process of successful existence through natural selection, environmental adaptation, mutation, and survival.

festivals—Events that mark the cessation of normal daily activities to allow access to something extraordinary, even other worldly.

Industrial Revolution—The movement toward centralized workplaces—factories that brought together large numbers of skilled and unskilled workers and great technological innovations in the production of goods.

Pax Romana—The approximately 200 years of peace begun by Caesar Augustus.

Playground Movement—A philanthropic church-based effort, began in the late 1800s, to provide safe places for urban children to recreate.

Renaissance—An intellectual and artistic period that sought to resurrect the values and styles of ancient Greece and Rome.

schole—The Greek word for *leisure,* meaning "free time."

threats to survival—Natural and human events that increase risk to human existence, including natural disasters, climatic conditions, war, terrorism, and military occupation.

References

Deaux, G. (1969). *The Black Death 1347.* New York: Weybright and Talley.

deLisle, L. (2009). *Creating special events.* Champaign, IL: Sagamore Press.

Godbey, G. (1997). *Leisure and leisure services in the 21st century.* State College, PA: Venture.

Hjelte, G. (1940). *The administration of public recreation.* New York: Macmillan.

McClean, D., Hurd, A., & Rogers, N. (2005). *Kraus' recreation and leisure in modern society.* Sudbury, MA: Jones & Bartlett.

Pieper, J. (1963). *Leisure: The basis of culture.* New York: Random House.

Pieper, J. (1999). *In tune with the world: A theory of festivity.* South Bend, IN: St. Augustine Press.

Rainwater, C. (1922). *The play movement in the United States.* Chicago: University of Chicago Press.

Shivers, J., & deLisle, L. (1997). *The story of leisure.* Champaign, IL: Human Kinetics.

Contemporary Leisure

Virginia Dilworth
Utah State University

Learning Outcomes

At the end of this chapter, you will

▶ understand the impact of constraints on your leisure,

▶ realize the impact of technology on your life,

▶ understand the importance of active leisure,

▶ know the benefits of volunteering, and

▶ understand today's popular culture.

Vocabulary Terms

constraints	interpersonal constraints	leisure
extrinsic rewards	intrapersonal constraints	popular culture
Generation Y	intrinsic rewards	structural constraints

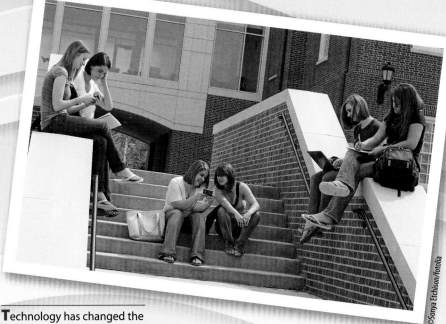

©Sonya Etchison/fotolia

Technology has changed the way we communicate at work and at leisure.

Walk around your campus or a shopping mall and observe how people spend their time there. People are talking on cell phones, listening to their iPods, or text messaging their friends, including those who are also in the mall. Fast forward to a college campus, where students call or text message their friends and family regularly throughout the day. Want to meet a friend for lunch after class? Send a text or place a call. Off campus is no different. Going for a walk? Bring your phone and stay in touch. We participate in many of the same activities as previous generations, such as socializing, shopping, and playing in the outdoors; however, how we use this discretionary time has changed.

What does **leisure** mean to you? Is it what you do, when you do it, or your psychological state? In examining the challenges of the 21st century, this chapter approaches leisure from two perspectives: our free time and what we do with that time. The increasing demands on our time make the pursuit of leisure an ever-increasing challenge. How we manage this time has a significant impact on the quality of our lives. Examining these perspectives is in line with the definition of leisure as "the combination of free time and the expectation of preferred experience" (Kleiber, 1999, p. 3).

The concept of free time can be elusive. It has become somewhat of a source of pride in America to be busy, and this is reflected in many aspects of our economy: doctors who offer early-morning and evening appointments, coffee cups that are designed to fit the cup holders in our cars, home exercise equipment, and, of course, fast food (Nazareth, 2007). All of these modern tools are designed to facilitate multitasking and allow us more time to work. The challenge in today's world is

---

PERSONAL LEISURE

How much free time do you have? How do you spend this time? What does this say about your life? For one full week (7-day period), keep a record of your time use in 1-hour intervals. Tally the amount of time spent in various life activities (e.g., work, maintenance, leisure). Write an analysis about your time use and the implications this has for your leisure lifestyle and quality of life.

Some of the questions you should ask yourself are these: How much time do I spend playing video games? Watching television? Texting my friends? Do I exercise regularly? These are some of the issues that lead to the infamous "freshman 15" (gaining 15 pounds during one's freshman year).

to recognize the constraints on your time and to learn to navigate these challenges to maximize your quality of life.

As displayed in the opening scenario, technology has had a significant impact on the way we use our leisure time. Children obtain technological tools and toys at an increasingly younger age; thus, by the time students arrive at college technology is a completely accepted aspect of their lives. The challenge, as indicated here, is to use these tools to maximize the quality of life when not at work. This line is blurred somewhat for college students, but both class attendance and the accompanying study hours, and any job a student has, account for his hours of work. It is the rest of your time on which we focus here.

> It is in his pleasure that a man really lives; it is from his leisure that he constructs the true fabric of self.
>
> *Agnes Repplier*

DO YOU FIT THE DESCRIPTION OF GENERATION Y?

People referred to as **Generation Y** include those currently in college; they have also been called Gen Y, Millennials, Generation Next, the Echo Boom, and the Digital Generation (American Sports Data, 2006). The dates of birth that are used to identify Gen Y tend to range from 1977 to 2000, although the beginning and ending dates are under some dispute (Nazareth, 2007). Your parents are the baby boomers (born 1946-1964), and they are viewed as one of the most powerful generations in terms of spending that the United States has ever seen (Krotz, 2003).

Although the involvement of parents in the lives of Gen Yers has led to an examination of helicopter parents, Gen Yers are also one of the most educated generations, because attending college has become the accepted norm (U.S. Department of Education, 2009). Some of the differences between Gen Y and previous generations follow.

SELF-DISCOVERY

The defining characteristics of Gen Y include being technologically savvy and racially and ethnically diverse; members of Gen Y tend to have been raised in a family-centered culture. A family-centered culture is one in which the most important focus of one's life is the family, which takes precedence over other social groups (e.g., friends, colleagues) to which one belongs. For example, if a conflict arises between social obligations to one's family and work, such as having to choose between an important outing with your family (e.g., birthday) or an obligation at work, family comes first. Furthermore, Gen Yers expect that their bosses will work with them on this and understand the importance of their family obligations. The importance of family also plays a part in the so-called helicopter parent phenomenon; these are the parents who "hover" over their children and are involved in every aspect of their lives. Although parents' involvement in their child's life is looked upon favorably by society, the extreme actions of a helicopter parent, such as a parent who calls her college-aged child's school to complain about a grade, is a different story. Does this describe you? How many characteristics of this cohort describe you?

The oldest of the baby boomers are reaching retirement age. According to the New Retirement Survey, baby boomers' view of retirement differs from earlier generations in that many boomers intend to mix work and play in their retirement years; the primary reasons for this are a need for continued earnings and a desire to remain cognitively active (O'Brien, n.d.). This generation is aware of the importance of maintaining an active lifestyle; however, although boomers seek a more active lifestyle than did their parents, they are more inclined to participate in low-impact activities such as walking (Johnson & Bungum, 2008).

Generation X (the generation preceding yours; born between 1965 and 1977) is most often labeled the *slacker generation*, but these people are in fact defined by a much more intriguing social construct. They grew up in a world of expanding choices, during the breakdown of gender and racial stereotypes (Holtz, 1995). They also started their careers in a world where job security was a thing of the past, as fewer in the workforce were staying with the same company throughout their careers. Moreover, Generation Xers were more inclined than their predecessors to demand time off from work for leisure (Nazareth, 2007), a trait that may enable them to appreciate that demand from Gen Y.

"Such shared experiences during one's youth unite and shape a generation" (McCrindle, 2007, p. 2). How does this affect leisure? The dominant changes seem to be the advances in technology and its integration into our everyday lives, which have had a profound impact on leisure time. Tools such as cell phones and handheld devices (e.g., PDAs) have made multitasking part of Gen Yers' lives. Take a picture, talk to a friend, surf the Internet—all of these activities can be performed with a phone; when the parents of Gen Yers were growing up, they used a telephone only to make phone calls, and only from a land line.

RESEARCH TO REALITY

Research these experiences that the following generations shared. How did these experiences shape each generation's view of leisure and recreation?

Baby Boomers (1946-1964)
- Increasing popularity of television
- Introduction of rock and roll
- The Cold War and the Vietnam War
- Introduction of the threat of nuclear war

Generation X (1965-1977)
- Growth of the personal computer
- AIDS
- Increase of single-parent families
- Increase of multiculturalism
- Corporate downsizing

Generation Y (1977-2000)
- The age of the Internet
- Cable television
- The age of globalization
- Terrorism attacks of September 11, 2001
- Environmentalism an accepted practice

THREE TYPES OF CONSTRAINTS TO LEISURE

Time is not the only obstacle to enjoying leisure for students today. Three types of **constraints** can explain a lack of leisure, or at least less fulfilling leisure than desired. The three types of constraints are intrapersonal, interpersonal, and structural (Crawford & Godbey, 1987).

Intrapersonal Constraints: The Challenge of Your Inner Self

Intrapersonal constraints are internal perceptions or beliefs that affect one's intentions. For example, many children are taught to believe that boys play with toy soldiers and girls play with dolls. Ironically, boys tend to believe that it is perfectly acceptable to play with action figures, which are a type of doll, regardless of how they are marketed by the toy companies.

Interpersonal Constraints: The Challenge of Others

Interpersonal constraints are the result of interactions between people. Using the same example as we used previously, let's assume that a young boy played with dolls at home before he was school aged. He was not taught that this was inappropriate; therefore, he did not have a preconceived notion that dolls were meant for girls. Once he entered school, however, he was ridiculed by other children for playing with dolls and so he stopped playing with them. His constraint is interpersonal, because the interaction with the other children halted his participation in this activity.

Intrapersonal constraints continue to impede leisure choices as children grow to adulthood.

Effective time management is necessary to navigate the demands of a hectic life.

WHAT DO YOU THINK?

College students in the United States come from all over the country as well as the rest of the world. Do you have different beliefs than your roommate? Did your friends come to school with a different view of certain activities? Two examples are male cheerleaders and female football players.

Some people believe they are too uncoordinated to participate in sports or dancing. If a person believes that he cannot be good at something, then he may never attempt to participate. However, intrapersonal constraints can be overcome: A person can overcome a fear of heights and take up rock climbing or overcome a fear of water and learn to swim.

Interpersonal constraints evolve as children grow through the teenage years and into adulthood. If you and your friends go to a movie, who decides what you should see? Do you vote? If it is not unanimous, do the minority go anyway, because this is an outing with their friends? We often make the decision that time spent with friends is worthwhile, regardless of the activity chosen.

Structural Constraints: General Challenges

The third type of constraint is structural. These are constraints that interfere with participation in an activity rather than in one's attitude toward the activity. Examples

©Royalty-Free/Corbis

It can be very rewarding to face your fears, such as stage fright, and overcome intrapersonal constraints.

of **structural constraints** include lack of time, money, equipment, or access. As discussed earlier in the chapter, the time crunch forces us to make decisions. A student who works and goes to school may not have time to participate in every desired activity. There is, after all, only so much time in the day. If you only have a few free hours in a given day, what do you do with that time? Watch a movie? Read a book? Participate in intramural sports?

Lack of money can also be a problem for students. Can you afford to go to every concert that interests you? What will you do on spring break? Trips to southern beaches and ski resorts are popular choices, but many students can't afford such trips. Access to certain activities may also affect participation. If you go to school or live in a warm climate, going to the beach may be within your reach. Going skiing, however, may not. The reverse is true for those who reside in winter sport areas. However, finances may dictate your choice as well, given that not all people who live near a ski resort can enjoy this activity as often as they like; it tends to be an expensive leisure choice.

Not all constraints have the same impact for all people in all situations. Some constraints may be relatively permanent, such as geographic location. Other constraints may be temporary; a broken leg could impede participation, but this is a condition from which a person will recover. Constraints in terms of free time tend to evolve as you move through the life cycle. Preschool children will have more free time than high school or college students, who in turn may have more free time than a working person or a parent. Once children leave home, their parents may rediscover additional free time. Research in this area has revealed several patterns (Jackson, 2000), including the following:

- People experience constraints at different levels of intensity. Although a deficiency of time and money tends to rank highest in terms of impact, the impact on people is relative to each situation.

- Constraints vary among groups as well; no subgroup of the population is completely free from constraints, and patterns tend to reveal themselves over time. For example, young people may have more free time, but they tend to face greater financial constraints. Although older adults may also have free time, they tend to have more financial resources. However, older adults face a decline in skills as well as lack of companionship.

- Age is not the only factor that reveals differences; income, race, and ethnicity provide different challenges.

Why does it matter if your participation or desire to participate is constrained? Meaningful participation in leisure has proven to enhance quality of life and produce healthier and happier people. Thus, it is important to both recognize constraints that affect your leisure and learn to negotiate these constraints. Learning to negotiate constraints will maximize your leisure experiences. Constraints do not

PERSONAL LEISURE

Take a few minutes to think about your personal leisure constraints. Do you run into excuses or obstacles that prevent you from engaging in meaningful leisure activities? What can you do to overcome these challenges or limitations?

always lead to lack of participation (Shaw et al., 1991), and awareness of these constraints can help you plan around them (Kay & Jackson, 1991). The challenge in today's hectic world is to determine what benefits you most desire, what leisure activities will help you achieve those benefits, and how to negotiate any constraints to participation in your chosen activities.

TRENDS IN CONTEMPORARY LEISURE

As discussed earlier in this chapter, different generations have various shared experiences. Gen Y has technology, environmentalism, and terrorism. It is important to understand the evolving trends and how they may affect your leisure. For example, checking in at an airport is much more time consuming than it was before September 11, 2001; going through security checks, producing the required documentation, and dealing with restrictions on carry-on items have increased the time necessary to check in for a flight. Technology is ever evolving, and this plays a significant role in emerging leisure activities, such as social networking and virtual reality games. Environmentalism and sustainable practices have also affected how students use their leisure time. In addition to these three defining characteristics, an increasing awareness of health and wellness marks the emergence of several leisure trends.

Gen Y and the Shrinking World

Gen Y inhabits a world that has become much smaller in terms of identities and access. News about world events quickly spreads via the Internet, creating a culture of citizens of the world and promoting a sense of obligation and awareness beyond one's own borders. Furthermore, the Millennials, as Gen Y is sometimes called, are wired to a greater extent than previous generations. A 2008 study found that more than 80 percent of undergraduates own laptops, more than 50 percent own desktops, and approximately one third own both (Caruso & Salaway, 2008). Laptop ownership, in particular, has increased recently; "only" 65.9 percent of undergraduates in the 2006 study reported ownership of a laptop. Recreation-related activities

©Monkey Business/fotolia

Technology has changed the way we work and play.

that use technology such as social networking sites (e.g., MySpace, Facebook) were reported by more than 85 percent of undergraduates in the 2008 study, more than 46 percent contributed content to Web sites such as YouTube, and more than 30 percent accessed the Internet from their cell phone or PDA. More than 90 percent of students aged 18 to 24 use social networking sites. Students belonging to the Net Generation rely on multiple forms of technology to communicate and socialize with their peers (Caruso & Salaway, 2008). Thus, it may not be surprising to hear that they are deemed "smart, but impatient" (Carlson, 2005, p. A54).

Certainly one of the greatest impacts on contemporary leisure is the constantly evolving technologies that we embrace. Gaming devices (e.g., Xbox), GPS units in cars and boats, and PDAs, for example, have created a subculture unto themselves. For example, geocaching, an electronic treasure hunt, has been used by teachers as a learning tool and by leisure service providers as a form of recreation. What does this mean in terms of leisure? Although technology and leisure are discussed in depth in chapter 8, we mention technology here because its importance cannot be overemphasized; technology has become embedded in our culture and plays an integral role in how members of Gen Y manage their lives. It can be found in popular culture such as on-line voting for reality shows, increasing use of video games and gaming toys, and the related impact on the health of young people in the United States.

SELF-DISCOVERY

Make a list of the leisure activities you most enjoy. What is it about these activities that makes them valuable to you? What benefits do you derive from them?

Health and Wellness

One of the repercussions of the technology available today is that more and more leisure time is spent playing video and virtual reality games instead of engaging in physical activity. These high-tech games may challenge the mind, but most do not challenge the body. Thus, it has become increasingly important to make time for active leisure. A 2007 study revealed that more than 38 percent of college seniors engaged in less than 2 hours of exercise per week (Spinosa et al., 2008). According to the Office of the Surgeon General, this is not a healthy level of physical activity

LEISURE AWARENESS

Keep a daily diary of your physical activity for 2 weeks. Assess the amount of time and the level of effort you exerted during this period. Do you meet the Surgeon General's recommendations for active adults? Are you consistent with your workouts? Do you have a set schedule? If you fall short of the guidelines, what might you do to increase your level of activity? For the following 2 weeks, increase your activity level to meet (or exceed if you already met) the standards. Keep a diary of your experiences and reflect on your health and wellness. Do you think that increasing your physical activity improved your physical and mental health and well-being?

(U.S. Department of Health and Human Services, n.d.). For adults ages 18 to 65, the keys to good fitness include avoiding inactivity; engaging in a minimum of 75 to 150 minutes of physical activity per week, depending on the intensity level; and undertaking muscle-strengthening exercises at least twice a week.

Environment and Health

An aspect of health concern for young people is the lack of outdoor experiences. Given that the benefits of leisure include the prevention and reduction of stress, it is important to note that nature offers restorative opportunities. Nature provides these opportunities in terms of the reduction of mental fatigue (Kaplan et al., 1998) and recovery from stress (Ulrich et al., 1991). One author examined this in depth in terms of saving the younger generations from "nature-deficit disorder," which he described as "the human costs of alienation from nature, among them: diminished use of the senses, attention difficulties, and higher rates of physical and emotional illnesses" (Louv, 2006, p. 34). Several studies have shown that access to green space and participation in outdoor activities benefit one's health and well-being (Kaplan, 1995; Tennessen & Cimprich, 1995). This applies in particular to children with attention deficits; one study found that a simple walk in the park can improve concentration (Faber Taylor & Kuo, 2008).

The concern about our lack of exposure to nature is shared by federal land managers. As noted by the U.S. Forest Service, "Our most important resource in this country is not forests, vital as they are. It is not water, although life itself would cease to exist without it. It is people" (U.S. Forest Service, 2008, para. 1). The concern in the apparent disconnect from the land that is evident among young people today does not end at the border of federally managed lands. Although environmental issues are discussed more completely in chapter 9, we note here some of the programs geared toward our nation's youth.

The U.S. Forest Service has a long tradition of programs that target children, dating back to Smokey the Bear. Its programs today include NatureWatch, the purpose of which "is to provide children and adults the opportunity to safely view, and participate in, activities and programs that raise their level of awareness and understanding of wildlife, fish, and plants, and their connection to ecosystems, landscapes and people" (U.S. Forest Service, 2008, para. 7). The concern is for the future of these resources, in terms of both young people who might seek a career in this area and young people who might gain an appreciation for these resources as recreational visitors to the forests.

RESEARCH TO REALITY

National Tree Day promotes planting trees to improve your community. As a class project do one or both of the following:

- Identify places in town that lack trees. Map out these locations and present a proposal to the town or city council.
- Organize a National Tree Day event. Select a site with a tree deficit, raise the funds to support your efforts, and plant a tree for your community.

For more ideas, see http://treeday.planetark.org/documents/doc-47-ntd08-benefits-of-trees.pdf.

The U.S. National Park Service has also recognized this challenge. Many national parks offer a Junior Ranger program, and the National Park Service now offers a WebRanger program for kids, as well as Park Fun, another on-line program for kids. As of early 2009, more than 66,000 children were registered WebRangers; more than 2,500 of these had completed all the activities, thus earning WebRangers patches (National Park Service, n.d.). Activities such as these allow the Net Generation to learn about and become interested in these resources and, it is hoped, become enticed to go outdoors. A recent initiative, H.R. 1612, The Public Lands Service Corps Act, has been proposed to develop a volunteer corps that will focus on the improvement of public lands (Farnor, 2009). If passed, this will provide excellent opportunities for college students to gain valuable experience while helping to protect their public lands. The Student Conservation Association provides internship opportunities for college students who want "to learn from resource management professionals, gain tangible skills and experience, and make a contribution to our natural and cultural treasures" (Student Conservation Association, 2009, para. 1).

Sustainable practices are increasingly evident in many aspects of our society. Wind farms are just one example.

©Art Explosion

Sustainable practices are receiving increasing attention from today's students. Sustainable practices are those that ensure that today's resources will be available for future generations. Students can become involved with numerous organizations, such as the Student Sustainability Committee at the University of Illinois. Its focus is on funding energy-efficient projects such as solar panels and green roofs (Bollinger, 2009).

Popular Culture

Popular culture covers a variety of aspects of a culture that are prevalent and predominant among members, and the exact definition appears to be elusive. One definition of popular culture is that which is "widely favored or well-liked by many people" (Storey, 2006, p. 4). Another way of viewing popular culture is as "mass produced commercial culture" (p. 5). We use these definitions in the following discussion and examine those artifacts that represent dominant features of the current popular culture including video games, entertainment, and sports.

It is simplistic to assert that all sedentary activities (e.g., watching television, playing video games) are related to childhood obesity. In fact, one study found that although a child's weight was related to the amount of time spent playing video games, it was not related to the amount of time spent watching television (Vande-water et al., 2004). Video games have also been linked to aggressive behavior in adolescents (Anderson, 2004; Anderson & Bushman, 2001), as has television in adolescents and young adults (Johnson et al., 2002). Of course, this depends on the types of programs and games being viewed or played.

As noted earlier in this chapter, Gen Y is an established tech generation; a 2003 study of college students found that 65 percent were regular game players and 20 percent of these reported that they made or sustained friendships via gaming activities (Jones, 2003). However, in the 2007 studies of college freshmen and seniors, approximately 48 percent of freshmen and 60 percent of seniors reported that they did not play video games during a typical week (Liu et al., 2008; Spinosa et al., 2008). There are distinct differences between male and female participation in computer games. Male college students tend to spend more time on computer games than do female students (Lucas & Sherry, 2004; Ogletree & Drake, 2007), as do younger males in general (Wright et al., 2001). Males also play more sports games than do females (Wright et al., 2001), and females are less likely to prefer violent games (Hartmann & Klimmt, 2006). What is certain is that college students depend more and more on the Internet for access to information and for socializing, via Web pages, e-mail, social networking sites, and blogs. Regardless of how, and how often, Gen Yers use the Internet to access information or each other, they are wired and will remain so. What does this mean for other aspects of popular culture?

The number of reality shows is ever increasing, and audience participation via electronic sources has become an established part of the game. Shows such as *American Idol* and *Dancing With the Stars* use audience feedback via texting or on-line voting to help determine the winner. This generation has come to expect to be part of the action. Each show has its own Web site, blogs and fan sites arise, and the days of merely watching a game show on television appear to be gone. Everyone, it seems, wants their 20 seconds of fame. This is substantiated by the popularity of YouTube. What has the impact of this type of media been on the population at large? Some television shows take the viewer into a family's life. Many reality shows take you into the inner workings of the family; in most cases you can even submit questions for them on the show's Web page. What drives viewers to follow the lives of others? Do people watch because they identify with these families, because they want to learn something, or because they want to feel better about themselves? It has been found that reality television viewers watch these shows in order to experience a sense of superiority; these are people who place a high importance on status, and the experiences of ordinary people such as themselves starring in these shows may indicate that they, too, are important (Reiss & Wiltz, 2004).

Sports

Another aspect of popular culture is the dominance of sports in America today. This is not a new phenomenon, but as with reality shows, sports have become multimedia events. Fans do not simply follow their home team: Cable television, sports packages, and the Internet have made it possible to follow as many teams as one might desire, and channels are dedicated to a specific sport, such as NFL Network, MLB Network, the Tennis Channel, and the Golf Channel. Because of expansion the cellular network, we can access Web sites, podcasts, and aspects of sports-related channels through a cell phone or PDA. Fantasy leagues and mock drafts reach across a broad spectrum of sports, including the National Football League, Major League Baseball, the Professional Golf Association, and NASCAR. NFL-based fantasy football, for example, merges reality and fantasy; participants act as general managers and coaches, selecting their players from actual NFL rosters to create their teams and then running the games by selecting plays. By 2007 approximately 27 million American adults were participating in fantasy sports leagues (Fantasy Sports Trade Association, 2009).

Action Sports

A dominant part of this type of popular culture is the X Games activity, also known as extreme sports. Traditional X Games sports such as snowboarding, bicycle motocross, and mountain biking have become mainstream in part because of their inclusion in the Olympics. These sports have been allotted their own page on ESPN, which also televises the games along with their affiliates and reported record viewership in 2009 across their multimedia platform (e.g., Internet, television, video on demand, mobile access); ESPN reported that the 2009 Winter X Games 13 was the most viewed since the inception of the X Games, averaging 900,000 homes across the eight telecasts. Two of the competitions (Ski Big Air and Snowboard Big Air) involve viewer voting; more than 100,000 text-messaged votes were received during each of these competitions in the 2009 Winter X Games (Gorman, 2009).

©Human Kinetics

Extreme sports are an integral part of leisure in popular culture.

In sports today, whether traditional, fantasy, or extreme, the consumer must have an opportunity to participate at some level—not just in terms of playing but in terms of interacting with athletes as well. Although fantasy leagues allow participants to run their own game, viewers of traditional sports can participate in the outcome via podcasts, blogs, and voting opportunities. In that sense, sports events can be viewed as another form of reality television. This is becoming a prevalent aspect of popular culture in America.

As we have discussed, popular culture, much of which involves electronic media of one form or another, has changed the face of how we spend our leisure time. Virtual participation has allowed people to broaden their exposure to others around the world and has made the world a smaller place in this sense. Perhaps that is why another international endeavor, volunteering, is also increasing in popularity.

SERVICE LEARNING AND VOLUNTEERISM

Volunteer activities, particularly in terms of spring break trips around the world to help others, have become a way for college students to learn more about the world and themselves. These experiences provide Gen Yers with valuable social and practical skills and enable them to share their talents during their leisure time.

PERSONAL LEISURE

Many of you may have first volunteered in high school, when volunteering can be a required activity. These projects may have ranged from helping elderly members of the community to tutoring other students. What types of volunteer service did you perform? Was it truly voluntary, or was it required by a class? Did this entice you to continue to volunteer? What benefits did you obtain from these experiences? Would you call such an experience a leisure activity?

Becoming involved in volunteer service is a good way to become invested in your community, but many students would not consider it to be leisure. Thus, is participation truly a leisure activity, or it is something one engages in for extrinsic rewards? There are indications that some young people do engage in volunteer service without the promise of extrinsic rewards. Participation in volunteer work by 15- to 25-year-olds dropped from 44 percent in 2002 to 36 percent in 2006, whereas participation by the over-25-year-old group increased from 32 percent to 34 percent during the same time period (Lopez et al., 2006). As discussed next, this may be related to life stage more than desired benefits.

Extrinsic Rewards

Extrinsic rewards are tangible outcomes such as grades or, in the case of high school seniors, stocking one's resume with community service to increase one's chances of getting into college. Data from the 2005 College Student Survey (Saenz & Barrera, 2007) and 2007 College Senior Survey (Spinosa et al., 2008) show that 67 percent and 61.4 percent, respectively, of seniors participated in volunteer work. However, 49.3 percent of seniors in 2005 and 50.3 percent of seniors in 2007 reported that participation in community service was a class activity, and only 15.9 percent and 14.1 percent, respectively, projected that they would participate in volunteer work 6 months after graduating (Saenz & Barrera, 2007; Spinosa et al., 2008). After college, participation decreases further in terms of the proportion of the age group (over 25), but this older group tends to participate more regularly (Lopez et al., 2006). For example, a high school student may participate once a year for a community project or a college student once per semester for a class project, whereas an over-25-year-old may volunteer weekly for a community group. Perhaps one's life stage affects the types of benefits sought.

Intrinsic Rewards

Intrinsic rewards benefit you internally. No one pays you or gives you a grade for participating—your reward is the experience itself. Those over-25-year-olds who continue to volunteer are no longer fulfilling a course requirement. They have found something that they are passionate about and are using their discretionary time to act on that passion.

Our discussion raises the question of whether intrinsic and extrinsic rewards can be combined in one activity. It is possible to find internal satisfaction in an activity that also helps someone else. Just because a college student receives course credit or a resume builder from participating in a service project does not mean

©AP Photo/Coeur d'Alene Press, Jerome A. Pollos

Volunteering can provide extrinsic benefits (such as experience) as well as intrinsic benefits (such as self-satisfaction).

PERSONAL LEISURE

Ask yourself the following questions:

- How often did I volunteer in high school? Where? What types of service? How did I benefit?
- How often do I volunteer now that I am in college? Where? What type of service? How did I benefit?
- Has my volunteer service increased? Decreased?
- Has the type of service I engage in changed?
- Did my benefits change? How?
- What do the changes say about myself and the way I use my leisure time?

that she cannot enjoy and appreciate the experience. For example, of increasing popularity among college students is the volunteer vacation or alternative spring break. These long-distance volunteers tend to be especially dedicated volunteer participants and usually are without ties (e.g., unmarried volunteers are more likely to participate in long-distance activities than are those who are married or have children). Furthermore, younger volunteers make up a larger percentage of long-distance volunteers than they do overall volunteers (Corporation for National and Community Service, 2008). The students get to visit a new place, meet new people, and feel good about what they have done. They help another community by building a home or school, teaching English, or teaching life skills to children.

Numerous opportunities are available on college campuses to lend a helping hand, most of which take place outside of course requirements. These opportunities arise through formal organizations such as fraternities, sororities, and other clubs as well as general campus-wide events such as a food drive.

LEISURE AWARENESS

Thousands of volunteer organizations can use your services at any time of the year. Following are several that offer spring break opportunities.

Break Away: The Alternative Break Connection (www.alternativebreaks.org)

Campus Compact (www.compact.org)

i-to-i Life Changing Travel (www.i-to-i.com/volunteer/)

United Way Alternative Spring Break (www.liveunited.org/asb/)

WHAT HAVE YOU LEARNED ABOUT YOUR LEISURE AND YOURSELF?

The most important knowledge you can gain in college is an understanding of who you are and what you want to do, both at work and at leisure. Gen Y is tied together by positive and negative events including exposure to technological tools and toys, terrorism as part of daily life, and environmentalism. Your sense of self, along with how you negotiate the constraints that confront you, plays a significant role in the way you address these challenges and augment your quality of life.

Your choices also play an enormous role in the way you interact with the world around you. Do you spend all your time in front of the television or playing computer games, or do you use your technological skills to improve your community, for example, by offering to design a Web page for a local nonprofit organization? Do you spend all your time indoors, or do you take advantage of the great outdoors? Do you live a healthy life in terms of exercise and sustenance? Many habits that you accrue or refine while in college will remain your tendencies throughout your adult life. Have you started on the right path?

SUMMARY

Leisure in the 21st century is a complicated endeavor. Although the modern time crunch has affected our lives, technology has enabled us to complete tasks more quickly. It has also opened up a world of new opportunities, providing us with even more options for spending our time. The key to a healthy and satisfying lifestyle seems to be moderation; entertainment has become highly interactive because of an explosion of technology, but spending all of one's time glued to a computer may not produce the most satisfying lifestyle. Technology has also enabled us to stay in touch with one another while away from the computer and to access our choice of leisure activities, yet a failure to maintain more traditional forms of leisure, beginning with basic physical exercise, may result in a less healthy self. Gen Y's task is to negotiate the constraint of diminished time and find a way to healthy and happy lives.

Learning Activities

1. **Benefits of leisure:** For one week, keep a list of leisure activities in which you participate (you may use the first activity of the chapter: *How much free time do you have?*). For each activity that you list, ask yourself why you participated in that activity. What benefits did you derive from it? Do you receive a variety of benefits across your leisure choices? Can you identify a possible benefit of leisure that you are not obtaining? What activities might you engage in to address this need?

2. **Constraints to leisure:** Make a list of the leisure activities you typically engage in during the school year. Next, list the activities you engage in while not in school. How do these differ? What types of constraints are impeding participation? For example, do you play racquetball at school but not at home because there are no available courts? Does your family go on vacation during the summer? Do you go with them, or do you have to work? Does your family go on vacations when you are in school, and if so, are you able to negotiate the constraints of your schedule to join them?

   Discuss your constraints in small groups with your classmates. How many of you face the same constraints? How do different people within your group negotiate similar constraints?

3. **Sustainability:** Utah State University's Sustainability Pledge asks students, faculty, and staff to take the challenge of becoming more sustainable by doing one or more of the following:

   Walk, bike, carpool, or take transit.

   Drive a fuel-efficient vehicle.

   Shrink the travel distances in your daily life—live near work or school.

   Teleconference instead of driving (or flying) to your meetings and conferences.

   Keep your tires inflated to save gas.

   Plant native trees and perennials.

   Recycle and use recycled products.

   Eat meat-free meals 1 day a week.

   Drink local water. It is fresh, pure, and delicious!

   Eat locally produced foods whenever possible.

   Replace chemical pesticides on your lawn, garden, and houseplants with nontoxic alternatives.

   Use environmentally friendly products or make your own cleaning products.

Buy less stuff!

Purchase clothes and household items at secondhand stores.

Reduce home heating and electricity use by 10 percent, by committing to any of the following:

- Check walls, doors, and windows for drafts and seal them up—up to 40 percent of heat loss is from these areas.
- Turn down the thermostat.
- Buy renewable energy.
- Insulate everywhere—the roof, floors, walls, basements. This will keep you cooler in the summer and toastier in the winter.
- Any electronic gizmo that has a clock, digital timer, remote control, or standby mode is sucking energy when it's not being used (it's called "phantom electricity," and it's scary how much of it there is!). If you're not using them, yank them!
- Use sleep mode on your computer, or turn it off if you are not using it.
- Set up a "charging station" for equipment that needs charging—plug everything into a power bar and turn that off until you actually need to charge something.
- Switch to compact fluorescent light bulbs (CFLs). They're 75 percent more efficient than conventional bulbs.
- If you're buying a home, be sure it meets R-2000 standards (which means it will use two thirds of the energy of a conventional home). R-2000 costs a little more up front, but in the long run, the design saves money on utility bills and boosts resale value (that's a lot of energy saved and a wad of money for your wallet).
- Choose Energy Star appliances—they're way more efficient than their ancestors. A new refrigerator, for example, uses 40 percent less energy than a model produced before 1993 (and saves you cash on utilities).
- When you shop for electronics of any kind, tell sales staff you are looking for energy efficiency. The more people demand this feature, the more pressure there is for companies to supply.
- Think twice before you buy any electronic toys and gadgets. Even though lots of us choose more efficient models, home energy use is actually increasing just because we keep loading up on more electrical devices!
- Go for a walk instead of watching TV or booting up your computer. It'll do you and the whole planet a lot of good.

How many of these actions do you already do? How many could you begin to do? Try to add at least one of these actions to your life and examine the impact it has on you.

For additional assignments, Web links, and more, visit the online student resource at www.HumanKinetics.com/DimensionsOfLeisureForLife.

Review Questions

1. Explain the three types of constraints and provide an example of each using your own experiences.

2. Examine how you use technology in your everyday life. Does this enhance or inhibit your leisure experience?

3. What is the importance of active leisure? Examine your weekly practices and assess whether you need to alter your physical activity.

4. What are the benefits of volunteering? What types of constraints might you face when pursuing these benefits? Do you achieve extrinsic benefits, intrinsic benefits, or both when you volunteer?

5. What aspects of popular culture have emerged for Gen Y? What impact does participation in these activities have on your life?

Leisure Reading

Johnson, S. (2005). *Everything bad is good for you: How today's popular culture is actually making us smarter.* New York: Penguin.

Louv, R. (2006). *The last child in the woods.* Chapel Hill, NC: Algonquin Books.

McMillon, B. (2009). *Volunteer vacations: Short-term adventures that will benefit you and others* (10th ed.). Chicago: Chicago Review Press.

Nazareth, L. (2007). *The leisure economy.* Mississauga, ON: Wiley.

Glossary

constraints—Barriers to leisure participation.

extrinsic rewards—Tangible outcomes; outcomes that are measurable.

Generation Y—People born between approximately 1977 and 2000; defining characteristics include being technologically savvy and racially and ethnically diverse; these people tend to have been raised in a family-centered culture. Also called *Millennials, Generation Next,* the *Echo Boom,* and the *Digital Generation.*

interpersonal constraints—Constraints that are the result of interactions between people.

intrapersonal constraints—Constraints that are the result of internal perceptions or beliefs that affect one's intentions.

intrinsic rewards—Benefits that are internal to the individual and are not measurable.

leisure—Time free from obligation.

popular culture—Cultural elements that are widely favored or well liked by many people; mass-produced commercial culture.

structural constraints—Constraints that interfere with participation in an activity rather than in one's attitude toward the activity.

References

American Sports Data. (2006). *A stereotype of Generation Y.* www.americansportsdata.com/dev/pr-generation-y.asp

Anderson, C.A. (2004). An update on the effects of playing violent video games. *Journal of Adolescence, 27*(1), 113-122.

Anderson, C.A., & Bushman, B.J. (2001). Effects of violent video games on aggressive behavior, aggressive cognition, aggressive affect, physiological arousal, and prosocial behavior: A meta-analytic review of the scientific literature. *Psychological Science, 12*(5), 353-359.

Bollinger, L. (2009, April 20). ECE graduate student leads student sustainability committee. *ECE Headline News.* www.ece.illinois.edu/mediacenter/article.asp?id=148

Carlson, S. (2005). The Net Generation goes to college. *Chronicle of Higher Education, 52*(7), A54.

Caruso, J., & Salaway, G. (2008, October). *The ECAR study of undergraduate students and information technology, 2008.* www.educause.edu/ers0808

Corporation for National and Community Service. (2008). *Long distance volunteering in the United States, 2007.* Research brief, July 2008. Washington, DC: Author. www.volunteeringinamerica. gov/assets/resources/Long-Distance_Volunteering.pdf

Crawford, D.W., & Godbey, G. (1987). Reconceptualizing barriers to family leisure. *Leisure Sciences, 9,* 119-127.

Faber Taylor, A., & Kuo, F.E. (2008, August 25). Children with attention deficits concentrate better after walk in the park. *Journal of Attention Disorders.* http://jad.sagepub.com/cgi/ rapidpdf/1087054708323000v1.pdf

Fantasy Sports Trade Association. (2009). *Welcome to the official site of the FSTA.* www.fsta.org

Farnor, S. (2009, April 21). *NRPA: We need a service corps for the parks.* Message posted to NRPA mailing list. http://act.npca.org/npca/notice-description.tcl?newsletter_id=17190892

Gorman, B. (2009, February 2). ESPN winter X-Games 13 sets records across platforms. Released via *ESPN Press Release.* http://tvbythenumbers.com/2009/02/02/espn-winter-x-games-13-sets-records-across-platforms/12008

Hartmann, T., & Klimmt, C. (2006). Gender and computer games: Exploring females' dislikes. *Journal of Computer-Mediated Communication, 11*(4), article 2. http://jcmc.indiana.edu/vol11/ issue4/hartmann.html

Holtz, G.T. (1995). *Welcome to the jungle.* New York: St. Martin's Press.

Jackson, E.F. (2000). Will research on leisure constraints still be relevant in the twenty-first century? *Journal of Leisure Research, 32*(1), 62-68.

Johnson, J.G., Cohen, P., Smailes, E.M., Kasen, S., & Brook, J.S. (2002). Television viewing and aggressive behavior during adolescence and adulthood. *Science, 295*(5564), 2468-2471.

Johnson, M.L., & Bungum, T. (2008). Aging adults learning new avocations: Potential increases in activity among educated Baby-Boomers. *Educational Gerontology, 34,* 970-996.

Jones, S. (2003). *Let the games begin: Gaming technology and college students.* Pew Internet & American Life Project. www.pewinternet.org/Reports/2003/Let-the-games-begin-Gaming-technology-and-college-students.aspx

Kaplan, R., Kaplan, S., & Ryan, R.L. (1998). *With people in mind: Design and management of everyday nature.* Washington, DC: Island Press.

Kaplan, S. (1995). The restorative benefits of nature: Toward an integrative framework. *Journal of Environmental Psychology, 15*(3), 169-182.

Kay, T., & Jackson, G.A.M. (1991). Leisure despite constraint: The impact of leisure constraints on leisure participation. *Journal of Leisure Research, 23,* 301-313.

Kleiber, D. (1999). *Leisure experience and human development.* New York: Basic Books.

Krotz, J.L. (2003, January). *Touch customers: How to reach Gen Y.* www.microsoft.com/smallbusiness/ resources/marketing/market_research/tough_customers_how_to_reach_gen_y.mspx?id=c0008

Liu, A., Sharkness, J., & Pryor, J.H. (2008). *Findings from the 2007 Administration of Your First College Year (YFCY): National aggregates.* Report from the UCLA Higher Education Research Institute, May 2008. www.gseis.ucla.edu/heri/PDFS/YFCY_2007_Report05-07-08.pdf

Lopez, M.H., Levine, P., Both, D., Kiesa, A., Kirby, E., & Marcelo, K. (2006). *The 2006 civic and political health of the nation.* Tufts University's Center for Information and Research on Civic Learning and Engagement. Report issued October 2006. College Park, MD: Center for Information and Research on Civic Learning and Engagement.

Louv, R. (2006). *The last child in the woods.* Chapel Hill, NC: Algonquin Books.

Lucas, K., & Sherry, J.L. (2004). Sex differences in video game play: A communication based explanation. *Communication Research, 31*(5), 499-523.

McCrindle, M. (2007). *Understanding Generation Y.* The Australian Leadership Foundation. http://innovationfeeder.files.wordpress.com/2007/08/understandinggeny.pdf

National Park Service. (n.d.). *WebRangers.* www.nps.gov/webrangers/

Nazareth, L. (2007). *The leisure economy.* Mississauga, ON: Wiley.

O'Brien, S. (n.d.). *How baby boomers will change retirement.* http://seniorliving.about.com/od/retirement/a/newboomerretire.htm

Ogletree, S.M., & Drake, R. (2007). College students' video game participation and perceptions: Gender differences and implications. *Sex Roles, 56*(7-8), 537-542.

Reiss, S., & Wiltz, J. (2004). Why people watch reality TV. *Media Psychology, 6,* 363-378.

Saenz, V.B., & Barrera, B.S. (2007). *Findings from the 2005 college student survey (CSS): National aggregates.* Report from the UCLA Graduate School of Education and Information Studies, February 2007. www.gseis.ucla.edu/heri/PDFs/2005_CSS_REPORT_FINAL.pdf

Shaw, S.M., Bonen, A., & McCabe, J.F. (1991). Do more constraints mean less leisure? Examining the relationship between constraints and participation. *Journal of Leisure Research, 23,* 286-300.

Spinosa, H., Sharkness, J., Pryor, J.H., & Liu, A. (2008). *Findings from the 2007 Administration of the College Senior Survey (CSS): National aggregates.* Report from the UCLA Higher Education Research Institute, May 2008. www.gseis.ucla.edu/heri/PDFs/CSS_2007%20Report.pdf

Storey, J. (2006). *Cultural theory and popular culture: An introduction* (4th ed.). Athens: University of Georgia Press.

Student Conservation Association. (2009). *Internships.* www.thesca.org/serve

Tennessen, C.M., & Cimprich, B. (1995). Views to nature: Effects on attention. *Journal of Environmental Psychology, 15,* 77-85.

Ulrich, R., Simons, R.F., Losito, B.D., Fiorito, E., Miles, M.A., & Zelson, M. (1991). Stress recovery during exposure to natural and urban environments. *Journal of Environmental Psychology, 11,* 201-230.

U.S. Department of Education. (2009). *Digest of education statistics, 2008.* National Center for Education Statistics. http://nces.ed.gov/programs/digest/d08/

U.S. Department of Health and Human Services. (n.d.). *Childhood overweight and obesity prevention initiative.* www.health.gov/paguidelines/guidelines/chapter1.aspx

U.S. Forest Service. (2008). *Kids in the woods. United States Forest Service emphasis areas.* www.fs.fed.us/emphasis/kids.shtml

Vandewater, E.A., Shim, M., & Caplovitz, A.G. (2004). Linking obesity and activity level with children's television and video game use. *Journal of Adolescence, 27*(1), 71-85.

Wright, J.C., Huston, A.C., Vandewater, E.A., Bickham, D.S., Scantlin, R.M., Kotler, J.A., et al. (2001). American children's use of electronic media in 1997: A national survey. *Journal of Applied Developmental Psychology, 22*(1), 31-47.

Leisure and Technology

Paul A. Schlag
Western Illinois University

Learning Outcomes

After reading this chapter, you will

- ▶ understand historical and contemporary perspectives of technology and leisure,
- ▶ understand technology's impact on leisure,
- ▶ consider how technology affects your leisure,
- ▶ learn how technology can add to or detract from wellness, and
- ▶ consider how you can improve your life through appropriate use of technology during leisure.

Vocabulary Terms

communication technologies
deviant leisure
digital technologies
discretionary time
domestic technologies
idea technologies

Internet addictions
leisure spaces
Moore's law
motion-sensing technologies
narcissism
obesity

product technologies
social networking
technology
transport technologies
virtual communities
virtual reality

The bottle in *The Gods Must Be Crazy* was a new technology that greatly changed the tribe's way of life.

Imagine your life without modern technologies. How would it be different if there were no airplanes, cars, televisions, microwaves, cell phones, iPods, video games, computers, or the Internet? Obviously your life would be drastically affected if you did not have access to these modern technologies. The leisure pursuits in your life would be different as well.

In the 1980 movie *The Gods Must Be Crazy,* a tribesman in the Kalahari Desert encounters modern technology for the first time when a pilot drops a glass bottle from his airplane. The tribesman takes the bottle back to his people, and they use this new technology in a variety of ways such as curing snake skins, making music, preparing food, and playing games. However, the members of the tribe quickly begin to fight over the bottle, so the tribesman decides to get rid of the object by throwing it off the end of the earth. Before this new technology dropped from the sky, the tribe experienced no crime, no punishment, and no violence. They did not have laws, police, judges, rulers, or bosses. They shared everything because the tools and materials that they used came from their natural surroundings. However, the bottle could not be shared because there was only one of it, and this disrupted the tribe. One of the underlying themes of this movie is that the introduction of new technology into a society has profound effects on that society and its members.

In this chapter we learn about past technologies that have affected leisure, society, and individual lives. Next, we consider contemporary technologies with the aim of understanding how they affect leisure and individual lives as well. We then critically examine technology's impact on leisure and wellness. Pay special attention to how technology can affect social, physical, spiritual, and intellectual development, or lack thereof. We also consider **deviant leisure** with regard to technology. Finally, ideas are presented for using technology during leisure to enhance your quality of life.

The Gods Must Be Crazy aims to help you think critically about how technology affects your life. This chapter's examination of how technology affects you begins by defining technology and then turns to how historical and contemporary technologies affected and still affect leisure.

HISTORICAL AND CONTEMPORARY TECHNOLOGIES

Before delving into past and contemporary technologies, you need to understand what technology means. **Technology**, in its most basic sense, involves applying current knowledge for some useful purpose. We most often think of technology as the tools developed to be used in a practical manner. However, there are two different types of technology—**product technologies** and **idea technologies** (Hooper & Rieber, 1995). Henry Ford's assembly line is one example that will help you to distinguish a product technology from an idea technology. The concept of an assembly line is an idea technology, but the conveyor belts and workstations that make the assembly line work are product technologies. **Virtual reality** is another example of an idea technology, but virtual reality headsets and motion-sensing gloves are examples of product technologies. Although this chapter does not explicitly distinguish between the two types of technologies, it may be useful for you to think about which technologies mentioned in the chapter are idea technologies and which are product technologies. Understanding technology in these terms will broaden your perception of what constitutes technology and sensitize you to concepts that greatly affect your life and have influenced humankind in the past.

> The real problem is not whether machines think but whether men do.
>
> *B.F. Skinner, American psychologist (1904-1940)*

Past Technologies

Think of past technologies that have greatly affected leisure. Throughout the ages technological advances have often been aimed at making life easier for humankind. If one considers Maslow's hierarchy, many technological advances have to do with the basic, underlying needs shown in the triangle (see figure 8.1). However, those same advances affect the more complex needs of love, self-esteem, and self-actualization. More is discussed later in the chapter about using technology for these complex needs. For now, focus on historical technological advances related to the primitive needs and how they affected leisure.

Past technological advances have greatly affected individual lives and society in many ways (see table 8.1). These advances often led to an increase in **discretionary time**. Innovations related to food production, such as irrigation, tilling equipment, and hunting tools, freed up time for primitive peoples to explore other pursuits. Advances in producing pottery, textiles, and glass (**domestic technologies**) lessened time spent on domestic production and also freed up time for other pursuits. As construction became more advanced and sophisticated, community spaces for religious and civic purposes began to appear. Such public spaces provided forums for sharing of knowledge and resources and for social contact. Advancements

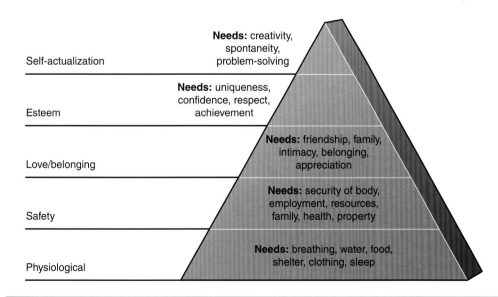

Figure 8.1 Maslow's hierarchy of needs.

TABLE 8.1   Historical Areas of Technological Advancement

Areas	Advances	
Food	• Irrigation • Tillage • Hunting and weapons	• Fishing • Domesticating animals
Domestic needs	• Pottery • Textiles • Woodworking • Leatherworking	• Glass • Weaving • Clothing
Tools	• Woodworking • Leatherworking • Metalworking • Agricultural	• Hunting • Protection and weapons • Hydraulics
Buildings	• Shelter • Religious buildings	• Community buildings
Power	• Wind • Waterwheels • Use of animals	• Steam • Chemistry • Electricity
Transport	• Wheel • Use of animals • Steam engine • Combustion engine	• Trains • Boats • Cars • Airplanes
Communication, sound, and optics	• Musical instruments • Writing instruments • Printing • Phonograph	• Record player • Optics • Photography • Cinema

in power allowed for more efficient transport and increased labor-saving devices. **Transport technologies** increased the efficiency of movement, which encouraged specialization of production and gave people access to more goods and services. This freed people from having to rely solely on agriculture or hunting for sustenance. **Communication technologies** have also increased for millennia, allowing people to share knowledge, ideas, and concepts more efficiently.

Each successive advancement enabled humans to more efficiently meet physiological and safety needs. Thus, people were able to either focus on or ignore Maslow's more advanced needs related to relationship development, esteem, and self-actualization. This is important because many of the needs in these three areas are closely tied to leisure. For instance, relationships can be strengthened through wholesome recreational activities, esteem can be enhanced through mastery of and involvement in leisure pursuits, and self-actualization can be reached through creative uses of leisure.

Technological advances not only affected how humans organized time with regard to leisure but also influenced access to leisure activities and influenced the leisure experience. Technological enhancements in transport have been important in providing access to **leisure spaces** such as beaches, mountains, resorts, and getaways.

Travel and communication technologies have increased cultural awareness and global cooperation (Bryce, 2001). Obviously, the ability to be transported great distances influences our ability to visit leisure spaces.

Tools and technologies available and accessible in the past, such as film and television, also influence the leisure experience. The phonograph, film, and television have also made it possible "to revise ordinary orientations of leisure by dramatically increasing our sense of interdependence and our access to information and entertainment" (Rojek, 2000, p. 24). Films further highlight how technologies can be used for passive leisure or for participative leisure. A person could use technology to develop a family film as part of her creative leisure or could merely be entertained by watching a film. This is the crux of how past technologies have affected the leisure experience: Some have been used for passive leisure pursuits and others have been used for creative leisure pursuits.

Sales Equipment Co., Detroit/Library of Congress

The invention of the automobile affected leisure in many ways.

To summarize, past technological advances have influenced leisure in three main ways: They increased the amount of discretionary time, affected access to leisure spaces, and influenced the leisure experience. Having considered past technological advances, we now consider the next phase of technological development, or the next technological revolution (Wojick, 1979)—digital and contemporary technologies.

Contemporary Technologies

Moore's law states that the number of transistors that can be placed on an integrated circuit has doubled every 2 years (Moore, 1965). Many have taken this to mean that computing capacity doubles every 2 years. Thus, there has been an incredible explosion in new computing technologies, a trend that appears to be continuing. *National Geographic* (2003) reported that researchers at the California Institute of Technology developed a new data transfer method that is 153,000 times faster than a modem. This means that you could download a full-length DVD in less than 5 seconds! This illustrates the speed at which digital technologies are increasing. As a result, it seems that the speed of living is also increasing.

In *The Gods Must Be Crazy,* the movie mentioned earlier, the narrator describes how civilized humans refuse to adapt to the environment but rather change the environment to suit them. In contrast, in the past many humans adapted their way of life to suit the environment. Therefore, civilized humans build cities, roads, machines, and vehicles to make life easier. Power lines and power sources were developed to run these devices. The narrator describes how the more humans tried to improve their environment, the more complicated their lives became. This complication leads to children being "sentenced" to 10 to 15 years of school to learn how to make it in the hazardous and complicated world to which they were born. The narrator concludes his monologue by asserting that humans who refused to adapt to their natural environment instead created a complete environment to which they are forced to readapt every hour of every day.

Obviously, this is indicative of many people's lives in the context of the digital revolution. Information from trillions of sources is literally available at one's fingertips, and people are bombarded with information in quantities unimaginable a few decades ago. Consider CNN's news format, which sports a scrolling news bar at the bottom of the screen, a commentator pontificating in the middle of the screen, the stock market ticker in one corner, the date and time in another corner, and moving graphics everywhere. At one point in time this format might have been overwhelming to viewers, who would have had a hard time ignoring what was not relevant. Now, people are often comfortable watching Fox News, with the same schizophrenic format as CNN, while browsing the news or checking e-mail on their smart phone. In only a few years, many people adapted to the hectic digital environment that currently envelops us.

LEISURE AWARENESS

Similar to past advances, contemporary technologies influence discretionary time, access to leisure, and the leisure experience. As you read about some of these technologies, think about how they affect these three areas.

1. Do technologies free up or take away time for your leisure pursuits?
2. Do they increase or decrease your access to your leisure pursuits?
3. How do they affect your leisure experiences?

Answering these critical questions will help you determine whether contemporary technology is influencing your life and leisure for better or worse.

Contemporary Technologies That Influence Leisure

What are some of the contemporary technologies that influence leisure in your life? Obviously, **digital technologies** have vastly influenced communication. Digital technologies now allow information to be shared in a variety of formats (printed, audio, video) in an efficient and relatively inexpensive manner. Many people now have almost instant access to any information they seek. Similarly, communication media have changed the way people interact socially (e.g., text messaging, video chatting). Communication technologies further influence leisure by helping people to be more productive at work, sometimes increasing and sometimes decreasing discretionary time. Furthermore, communication technologies affect the leisure experience. Communication media operate at speeds that overcome the obstacles of time and space. It is now possible to video chat with a friend in Africa instantaneously. However, this constant connection with others might limit the availability of deeper connections with people that go beyond a superficial relationship based on texting.

Contemporary Technologies and Where Leisure Occurs

Current digital technologies and transportation technologies have greatly affected where leisure occurs. In the past, travel was limited and costly. Now, convenient transportation is available to many Americans, enabling them to visit distant leisure spaces such as theme parks or foreign countries. Digital technologies have also affected leisure spaces. Not long ago people went to a movie theater to enjoy a cinematic experience. Now, that same type of experience is available from home in high definition with digital surround sound. In fact, it isn't even necessary to go out to rent a movie anymore. You can simply download it from the Internet. Another example of how digital technologies have affected leisure is through gaming. People interested in video games used to have to visit the arcade. Now, video games are readily accessible in the home and allow gamers with similar interest to play and connect over the Internet.

The Internet, video games, and cable television have also affected where leisure occurs. Children used to play outside and use their creativity to avoid boredom. Now, digital technologies keep many children and others inside and occupied.

Labor-saving devices in the home and power tools for the yard have perhaps freed up more time for homeowners. Consider the microwave oven and microwavable meals. Whereas preparing a meal used to take entire afternoons (and sometimes still does), you can now pop lasagna into the microwave and have a meal in 15 to 20 minutes. Similarly, consider how people used to mow the lawn with a manual mower. It took a long time and was backbreaking work. Now, people are able to mow the lawn with self-propelled mowers or riding mowers. Such advances in mowing freed up a great deal of time and energy. Conceivably, all of these technologies affect leisure because less time is being spent on domestic needs.

Computers and Internet Technology

Naturally, computer technology has affected every aspect of peoples' lives in industrialized societies. Consider the percentage of computer users listed in table 8.2.

TABLE 8.2 Computer and Internet Users (in Percentages)

	2002 computer users	2005 computer users	2002 Internet users	2005 Internet users
Canada	75	79	68	71
Great Britain	59	76	47	71
United States	74	76	64	70
Germany	63	67	47	60
France	60	61	41	57
Lebanon	50	53	36	37
Poland	33	46	20	38
Turkey	23	39	18	32
Russia	19	35	7	15
Jordan	30	31	25	20
India	6	21	3	14
Indonesia	12	16	5	7
Pakistan	7	9	4	5
China	35	—	24	33

Question asked: "Do you use a computer at your workplace, at school, at home, or anywhere else at least on an occasional basis?"

Adapted, by permission, from A. Kohut, R. Wike, and N. Speulda, 2006, *Truly a World Wide Web: Globe going digital* (Washington, DC: The Pew Global Attitudes Project).

This table illustrates that computer ownership is increasing throughout the world. The number of Internet users is also increasing yearly.

The Internet is no longer only for the young, although young people are typically more active on the Internet than are older people (Kohut et al., 2006). With the proliferation of computers and Internet access, it is conceivable that people are using computers for information and leisure pursuits in greater and greater measure.

The ECAR Study of Undergraduate Students and Information Technology provides information on the technology behaviors, preferences, and attitudes of undergraduate students in the United States (Salaway et al., 2008). The study reported that more than 80 percent of students own laptops, 54 percent own desktops, and one third own both a laptop and a desktop. Furthermore, 66.1 percent of students own Internet-capable cell phones. Students reported spending an average of 19.6 hours per week online for work, school, and recreation. Startlingly, 7.4 percent of students surveyed spent more than 40 hours per week on the Internet. Table 8.3 refers to some of the activities in which undergrads are engaged while using computers.

TABLE 8.3   **Student Computer and Internet Activities**

Activities	Percentage of students engaged	Median frequency of use
Using presentation software	93.4	Weekly
Making spreadsheets	91.9	Monthly
Participating in social networking Web sites	85.2	Daily
Text messaging	83.6	Daily
Using course management systems	82.3	Several times per week
Downloading music or videos	77.3	Weekly
Using graphics software	73.9	Monthly
Instant messaging	73.8	Several times per week
Contributing content to photo or video Web sites (Flickr, YouTube)	46.6	Monthly
Contributing content to wikis	38.2	Monthly
Contributing content to blogs	34.1	Monthly
Using software to create videos	32.9	Once per quarter or semester
Using software to create audio tracks	32.5	Once per quarter or semester
Using the Internet from a cell phone or PDA	30.8	Weekly
Playing online multiuser computer games (World of Warcraft, poker)	29.4	Monthly
Watching or listening to podcasts	29.1	Monthly
Watching or listening to Webcasts	25.0	Monthly
Using social bookmark or tagging (e.g., delicious.com)	16.7	Monthly
Accessing online virtual worlds	8.8	Once per quarter or semester

Reprinted, by permission, from G. Salaway, J.B. Caruso, and M. Nelson, 2008, *The ECAR Study of Undergraduate Students and Information Technology 2008,* No. Research Study, Vol. 8 (Boulder, CO: EDUCAUSE Center for Applied Research).

These activities clearly indicate that computer technology is not being used solely for productive purposes (homework, research, work) but also is being used during leisure (accessing virtual worlds, gaming, and **social networking**).

It is possible that all of the technologies mentioned here encourage us to take on more and more responsibilities and tasks, thus reducing leisure time and making our lives more complicated. However, these technologies are also used for leisure activities and pursuits. Sufficient for the discussion here is to understand that all contemporary technologies have a dramatic effect on leisure.

The preceding are just a few modern technologies that affect time for leisure, where leisure occurs, and leisure experiences we engage in. How, how much, and how often you use these technologies are especially poignant questions in analyzing whether these technologies affect your life positively.

Does technology enhance connectedness, or is it a distraction from deeper connections?

TECHNOLOGY'S EFFECT ON LEISURE AND WELLNESS

It is difficult to understand technology's impact on your life if you fail to think critically about this topic. There is no avoiding the impact of technology on your life, and it is to your detriment to regard technology as something neutral. In the book *The Great Brain* (Fitzgerald & Mayer, 1967), the father of the Great Brain is someone who always has to have the latest and greatest technology. His is the first home in the small town to have an indoor toilet and the first to have a toaster. He is an example of someone who embraces technology for technology's sake. You should think critically about technology's role in your life, embrace the good aspects and reject the bad. One way to examine the impact of technology on your life is to consider how technology relates to wellness.

It is well known that leisure is closely tied to wellness and quality of life (Godbey, 2003; Kleiber, 1999; Russell, 1996). Well-being is often related to different aspects of your life that affect you psychologically. Technology's impact on your life may affect you socially, emotionally, physically, spiritually, and intellectually. A close study of each of these areas in your life will illuminate how you might use technology for your development or to your detriment.

Social Impacts of Technology

With the proliferation of technologies that are able to overcome the obstacles of time and space (e.g., airplanes, cars, the Internet), one would think that these tools would be used to gain an understanding of other cultures, meet people all over the world, maintain and strengthen familial relationships, communicate effectively with others, and help people to become more socially adept. However, some technological advances cause people to be distracted, overly stressed, and increasingly isolated. Many people are involved in an abundant number of relationships through technology, but sometimes the quantity of these associations leaves people feeling qualitatively empty. Obviously, technology has had a profound impact on what it means to be social.

W H A T   D O   Y O U   T H I N K ?

How have social networking sites affected your relationships? Do they enable you to get to know people on a deep level or a superficial level? Does the time you spend on a social networking site help you to develop relationships or does it distract you from existing relationships?

Courtesy of One Laptop Per Child organization

People of all ages enjoy connecting to a virtual world while the real world is all around them.

Society is likely on the cusp of a social revolution, during which it will be important to redefine socially appropriate and acceptable behaviors (with regard to digital or virtual interaction). We are at a point in history where very few people have given critical thought to new social realities created by technology and what those realities mean for the individual and society. In this section we closely examine a few social technologies that influence leisure. The section first looks at **virtual communities**, social networking sites, and today's communication tools. Then we critically reflect on gaming and television. Think about how each technology affects your social life and social skills. Keep in mind that these are only a few of the technologies that may affect you socially. A comprehensive list is not feasible here.

A study of students and information technology found that 85 percent of undergraduates surveyed used social networking sites (Salaway et al., 2008) (see figure 8.2). Many of the respondents reported using such sites daily. Figure 8.3 indicates how undergraduate students use social networking sites. This report found indications that use of these sites is increasing yearly. Let us now look critically at whether this trend is positive.

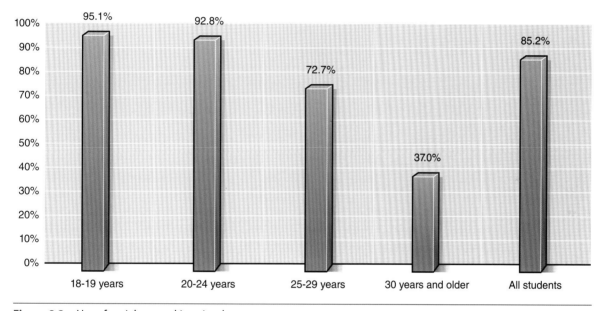

Figure 8.2 Use of social networking sites by age.
Data from Salaway, Caruso, and Nelson 2008.

The use of social networking sites has both positive and negative consequences. It is amazing how someone can find a long-lost friend through a social networking site, enabling them to reconnect. In a society where people have become quite mobile and family and friends are often geographically separated, it is convenient to keep in touch through technology.

However, one need not look far to find problems associated with social networking sites. There is a lively debate about whether **Internet addictions** are real. To me it appears to be a real problem (perception is often reality in a social context) with which people have to grapple. Some assert that these Web sites contributed to cheating on significant others, often leading to divorce. People have been fired from their jobs or put under pressure because they use these sites at work or because something is posted on a site that undermined the person's professional standing.

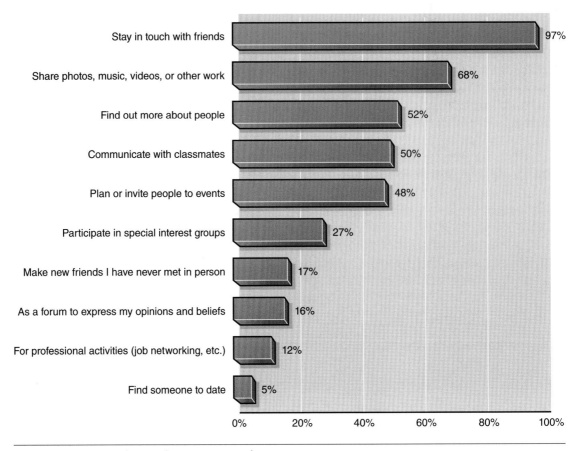

Figure 8.3 How social networking sites are used.
Data from Salaway, Caruso, and Nelson 2008.

Although divorce and loss of employment are serious issues, perhaps they are not as common as other problems that have the potential to stem from social networking sites. **Narcissism**—excessive interest in one's appearance and in oneself—is sometimes manifested on social networking sites. These Web sites have been found to be an avenue for people to display their narcissistic traits online (Buffardi & Campbell, 2008). I often wonder whether people use these sites to display their popularity to the world rather than use them as a vehicle to develop meaningful relationships.

Creating meaningful relationships is often about sharing our lives with others, and technology can allow us to do so through photos, videos, text, and music. In conducting research for my doctoral dissertation, I looked at how eight senior citizens used technology and how it affected their lives. My hope was to find that they used technology to stay in touch with friends, family, and people with similar interests. Although the participants did use e-mail to stay in touch with family and friends, almost all of the study participants talked about how vapid chat rooms and discussion boards seemed to be. Most had tried chatting a few times and then gave up because they viewed it as a waste of time (similar reasons were given by undergraduates in the ECAR study who did not use social networking sites). However, one participant was a chat room monitor for a fantasy baseball site. As he spent more time in that chat room he began to realize that it was not as shallow as he first imagined. People were in that virtual community because of a shared or common interest. Gradually he got to know people and care about their lives. He was eventually able to meet some of these new, online friends in person and said they connected as if they had known each other for years.

While working on my dissertation I visited many chat rooms and discussion boards that catered to older adults. After visiting many such sites, I began to be discouraged because of the inane nature of many of the conversations. However, I stumbled on one online discussion board in which two World War II veterans wrote about their experiences in the war. They also lamented the fact that where they lived, there were no more veterans of that war left. They felt alone and isolated, but this chat room was a forum where they fit in again. They were able to share similar interests and experiences.

Perhaps overcoming a sense of isolation is one of the greatest features of online communities and virtual worlds. Someone might feel like an outcast in her own community or family but might find someone online with similar hobbies, pursuits, and interests. Consider someone who enjoys photography as a serious leisure pursuit. This person would be able to share that passion with people all over the world by using the Internet and its powerful tools (e-mail, video chat, discussion boards, online video, family Web sites). However, simply sharing common interests and pursuits with people through technology does not necessarily have a positive impact on social skills and social development.

Gaming and Social Development

Gaming is an instance where you may encounter potentially serious social setbacks. I lead a group of Boy Scouts who share a love of a certain online virtual world game. This game seems to be all they talk about. When given other opportunities for deep, respectful, meaningful conversation, these boys are sometimes rather inept. Although linking their online gaming to poor social skills might be spurious, studies show negative social impacts of some video games. One study tested whether high exposure to video games increased aggression over time. It was found that playing violent video games is a significant risk factor for later physical aggression in both Japan and the United States—for boys and girls (Anderson et al., 2008).

However, linking video games to poor social skills and behaviors often misses the bigger picture. People might participate in other activities (take football, for example) in which the social problems that arise from the activity may be the same or even worse than those of gaming. Evidently it is not enough to simply blame the medium. In fact, in many instances, gaming may aid in relationship building. The 13th Annual MediaWise Video Game Report Card (Walsh & Gentile, 2008) indicated that 75 percent of gamers play with other people. Since my family received a Wii as a gift, we have spent countless hours of enjoyment playing together. Naturally, overindulgence in this one activity would have deleterious results, but the limited time we do spend playing together seems to strengthen our family.

Television and Social Development

Television is another technology that has mixed reviews with regard to social skills and social lives. Some researchers suggest that spending a limited amount of time watching wholesome programs can strengthen families and friendships. Others believe that television contributes to the downfall of social values in this country. It does seem that many people spend less time with others in their community than they do with the people they watch daily on television. Television tends to be a passive medium, which requires little skill and thought on our part (although some programming bucks this trend). Therefore, television provides little opportunity for meaningful interaction while watching. Watchers simply sit there and ingest what is presented to them without having to respond or react to another person. Obviously this can have serious effects on people's social skills because viewers are not practicing how to relate to and deal with other people.

Exposure to what is viewed on television can have some other serious effects on people's social lives. For example, exposure to television shows with sexual content may increase the chance of teen pregnancy (see figure 8.4) (Chandra et al., 2008). Furthermore, when some people see violence, sex, and all manner of lasciviousness on television, they may be prone to mimic the behavior and think that it is acceptable. Were everyone to copy the social behaviors portrayed on television, our society would lack morals, and many levels of individuals' lives would be destroyed.

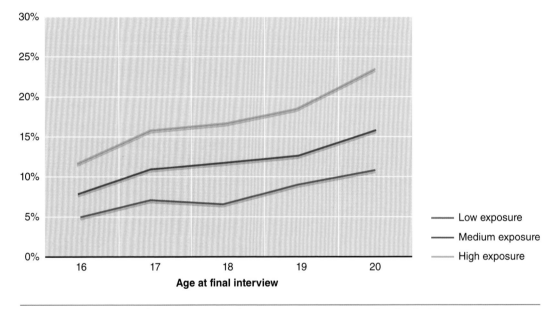

Figure 8.4   Percentage of teens expected to become pregnant compared with television sexual content exposure.
Data from Chandra et al. 2008.

It is apparent that technology has the potential to harm or enhance your social skills and social life. The key is to analyze how technology affects you socially. Do technologies help you build positive, meaningful relationships, or do technologies hinder this process? Are you better able to communicate, listen, and share because of the technologies in your life? Do you use technologies to improve your relationships and build new ones? Are you letting a few choice people know who you are and what you contribute to this world, or are you merely distracting yourself with shallow pursuits? Does technology increase or decrease your concern for others, your compassion for others, and your desire to serve them? Such are the critical questions regarding technology and social development.

Emotional Impacts of Technology

Something should be said here about emotional development. Emotional development has to do with how you feel about yourself, what your moods are, and how you feel in response to external influences. Many psychologists combine emotional and social development into a category called socioemotional development.

P E R S O N A L   L E I S U R E

Have you ever spent an entire day watching television? How did you feel afterward? Television is not necessarily bad for us emotionally, but perhaps overindulgence is. However, sometimes television can have a positive impact on how you feel.

It has been found that children laugh 400 times a day whereas adults laugh about 15 times a day (Palmer, 2007). Laughter has a variety of positive effects on people's lives; therefore, people need to do more of it. Television programming can sometimes be uplifting or funny. Many people share the favorite pastime of watching bloopers and other funny videos on YouTube. Such technology can help you laugh, help inspire you, and help you feel better emotionally. However, you need to be acutely aware of how your use of technology affects you emotionally and shape your use accordingly.

Let us now look at how technology may affect you physically.

Physical Impacts of Technology

In the 1800s and early 1900s, farming and ranching were two of the major occupations in the United States. As such, food production and domestic preparations required a great deal of physical exertion. Almost every aspect of daily living required people to move and use human energy. Plowing was not done from the climate-controlled cab of a tractor.

Preparing food meant more than simply removing the cellophane from a pre-cooked meal. Going to the store involved more than just getting in a car and pushing some pedals. Entertainment was often more than sitting on a chair and pushing a button every half hour to ward off boredom. Farmers walked behind the plow; women spent most of the day preparing food and mending and washing clothes; a trip to the store required either walking or hitching up the wagon, a physical exercise in itself; and entertainment often involved dancing, racing, or baseball.

Obviously much has changed since the 1800s. Frank Lloyd Wright, a famous American architect, educator, and author, presciently stated, "If it keeps up, man will atrophy all his limbs but the push-button finger." Technology has gotten us to the point that much of daily living requires little exertion on our part. Furthermore, many of the technologies used for entertainment keep us from moving our bodies, exercising our hearts, and using our muscles. This has serious implications for our physical health, which is often directly tied to the quality of our lives.

Chapter 4 discussed the **obesity** epidemic in the United States. Although Americans' eating habits have something to do with this trend, a lack of exercise also contributes to the problem. According to one study, 22 percent of Americans

L.W. Hine/Library of Congress

Before industrialization most occupations were labor intensive, thus providing natural physical exercise.

exercise regularly, which potentially leaves 78 percent of the population inactive (Blair, 1993). If people are not physically active at work, at home, or during leisure, they are likely to have health problems at some point in their lives. What, if any, impact does technology have on people physically?

Technology has made the tasks of daily living easier and less physically demanding. It has largely shifted work from manual labor to information management. Transportation has been made easier and more convenient through technology. Technology has made more indoor entertainment available with very little physical interaction required. Thus, technology has made people more sedentary in general, so people have to go out of their way to stimulate muscles and increase heart rate. Is technology therefore inherently bad for people physically?

Again, the answer depends on how you use technology in your life. In 2008, Wii Fit sold more than 8.7 million units (Walsh & Gentile, 2008). Wii Fit is a game console that allows players to use their body movement to improve balance, increase strength, and experience an aerobic workout through various activities. Other **motion-sensing technologies** (e.g., Nintendo Wii, iPhone) have endless possibilities for entertaining people while helping them to be active. However, instead of playing tennis on the Wii, why not go outside and play real tennis?

This all comes down to critically examining your life to determine whether the technology you use is helping or hindering your physical fitness. If passive technology is dominating your life at school, at work, at home, and in your entertainment, you will likely encounter physical problems at some point during your life that will detract from your sense of well-being. The problems and diseases related to sedentary lifestyles also increase the cost of health care for everyone. Therefore, you must be creative in changing your life to include more healthy physical exertion. Technology might even make exercise fun!

Although considering the impacts of technology on physical well-being is important, it is vital that you not forget to ponder technology and spiritual matters.

Spiritual Impacts of Technology

When was the last time you gazed at the stars and contemplated your place in the universe? Have you ever thought about where you came from, why you are here on earth, and what happens to you when you die? What are you going to accomplish on this earth and to what end? These are the weightier matters of existence, and often technology drowns out the drive to seek answers to life's great questions. Unfortunately, sometimes the answer to these questions is "I really don't think about them at all."

In our highly technical society, silence and stillness must be sought out. Think of the noise and confusion brought about by the technology around you. In your home music might constantly be playing, climate control systems purring, computers humming, appliances running, and the television blaring. Even outdoors you can almost constantly hear the din of traffic passing, the drone of airplanes overhead, and the commotion of a mobile society. How is meditation possible when it is so difficult to find a quiet spot of repose?

Technology in and of itself is not detrimental to spiritual growth. Think of how lucky you are to have the wisdom of the ages, magnificent art, and an abundance of spiritual music at your fingertips. The Internet and books are readily accessible with all of the major spiritual writings of recorded history. In fact, the Internet is full of uplifting and spiritual media that can aid you in finding and sharing meaning. Furthermore, technology has the capability of freeing up some of your time, enabling you to drive to the lake to watch the sunset and contemplate service to your fellow human beings. Again, technology can either hinder you through distraction from your

©Photodisc

When was the last time you pondered life's universal questions?

P E R S O N A L   L E I S U R E

Think of the last time you put aside technology to deeply think about the questions of life. Is your life constantly filled with texting, e-mailing, surfing the Net, watching television, gaming, or other technological pursuits? When was the last time that, rather than texting your friend about the latest movie, you went with that friend to a secluded spot to talk about life and how you fit in it? One would think that the convenience of modern technologies would make our lives less complicated because we would have more time. However, it seems that technologies have merely enabled us to live in hyperdrive. We constantly fill our time with things that are readily accessible but rather unimportant in the grand scheme.

spiritual pursuits or can increase your leisure time and help you find information for life's journey.

Intellectual Impacts of Technology

One would think that with all of the information available to us through technology, your generation would be one of the brightest, smartest, and most informed generations of all time. Whether this is the case is arguable, but it is apparent that contemporary technologies can greatly influence our intellectual development.

In the past few centuries, information was largely available through books and newspapers. To have information published in these formats required a great deal of time, thought, and editorial oversight. There were a number of gatekeepers who tried to ensure that the information being communicated was accurate. Now, anyone can publish anything on the Internet without any type of oversight. An overwhelming amount of information is available on virtually any topic. This makes it increasingly difficult to evaluate sources for validity and reliability. Therefore, people need to be skeptical of information and learn how to evaluate sources for accuracy.

A number of tools, games, and programs can help people to learn in multimedia-rich environments. In Second Life you can visit a virtual replica of the Sistine Chapel, click on the frescoes, and learn about each painting. Many interactive games are available that stimulate thinking and problem solving. Documentaries about history, countries, and any topic imaginable are available on television and DVD. Podcasts from the world's best professors are available through iTunes U and other sites.

In addition to consuming learning resources created by others, you could use technological tools to develop resources for others. The Burns Film Center (www. burnsfilmcenter.org) has a program called Unscripted where 16- to 17-year-old students produce films about senior citizens. This teaches the students about history in an interactive manner and is just one example of how technology can be used to aid intellectual development. In short, there are innumerable ways to use technology to increase one's intellectual abilities.

However, even with the multitude of intellectual resources out there, several obstacles can stand in the way of using them for your development. First, people often use technology for distraction or mere entertainment. Although disengaging from life is sometimes healthy, doing so on a frequent or continuous basis can hinder physical and intellectual development. If you pursue technologies that allow you to simply shut off your brain while programs and entertainment are force-fed to you, you will lose intellectual processing capabilities. The second aspect of technology that can stand in your way regarding intellectual development is information overload. In a frenzied intellectual environment, it often becomes difficult to filter out irrelevant or misleading information. It is a daunting task to find information that is pertinent to what one wants to learn and to evaluate its efficacy.

Again, you must seriously examine how you are using technology in your life to determine whether your pursuits are increasing your intellectual capacity. Are you using technology to increase your recall, your knowledge, and your problem-solving skills? Are your technology pursuits merely distractions that teach you something inane or teach you nothing at all? I hope you will use the technology available to you to learn how to create a better world for yourself and for others.

POTENTIALLY HARMFUL USES OF TECHNOLOGY

To this point you have learned about technology and how it can help or hinder social, emotional, physical, spiritual, and intellectual development. However, some technological pursuits seem particularly maladaptive—pursuits that keep you from appropriately adapting to the world around you. These maladaptive activities can lead to unhealthy lifestyles and greatly hamper your sense of well-being.

WHAT DO YOU THINK?

Many young people say they can't afford to attend college, travel, or move out of their parents' homes, yet they are able to purchase the latest and greatest technologies (stereos, MP3 players, smart phones). Are young people's long-term goals and well-being in danger because they want to fit in, look good, keep up, or have the latest toys? How does this desire for instant gratification affect their lives?

Watching television to excess can produce a general apathy toward life. Spending a large amount of time using the Internet can also consume people to unhealthy levels. Gambling and pornography on the Internet present real dangers to quality of life. Gaming has the potential to undercut productive lives as well. In the recent past, it was relatively difficult to gain access to deviant leisure. For instance, one would have to seek out and visit an adult store to purchase pornography. Now, deviant and unhealthy pursuits are a click away and are available for consumption in virtual anonymity. Why are these pursuits dangerous? They can destroy healthy, meaningful relationships; they can lead to physical atrophy; they are spiritually inhibiting; they destroy one's sense of right, wrong, and decency; they undercut productivity (societal and individual); and they can lead to intellectual degeneration. Fortunately, help is available from licensed professionals for those who pursue deviant leisure through technology.

SUMMARY

Contemporary technologies affect your social, emotional, physical, spiritual, and intellectual development in positive or negative ways. Thus, technology affects leisure in significant ways. It is your responsibility to scrutinize your life to determine how you use technology appropriately during leisure, how you use it detrimentally, and how you can use it better.

Too often it seems that people use technology for passive pursuits during leisure. It is conceivable that to get the optimal experience out of technological leisure pursuits, creativity must be involved. You could video chat with family members who live far away or with someone from another culture to develop socially. You could develop a personal Web site where family and friends keep up with what is happening in your life. You could use Wii Fit to become more physically active. You could even use technology productively at work and home to free up time to play a game of real tennis with a friend or significant other. You could load your iPod with spiritual music and visit a mountain stream to reflect on matters of spiritual import. You could develop a video podcast on an area of interest and post it on the Web. Or, you could use technology to research how other communities have dealt with issues that also affect your community.

There are many ways you can use technology to increase the quality of your life and the lives of those around you. It is up to you to assess your uses of technology and determine whether any of them make your life more complicated or less fulfilled. You need to find those leisure pursuits that can help you grow and develop into a happy, well-adjusted human being.

Learning Activities

1. List 15 labor-saving devices in your home. How would your life be different without them? How would your leisure time be affected?

2. Make a list of things you would like to accomplish before you die. Describe which accomplishments are related to technology. Describe ways technology could help you reach these accomplishments. Now explain how technology could hinder your quest.

3. For an entire week, write down every time you use any type of technology. Come to class prepared to discuss how prevalent technology is in your life. Be prepared to discuss whether these technologies contribute to or hinder your social, emotional, physical, spiritual, and intellectual development.

For additional assignments, Web links, and more, visit the online student resource at www.HumanKinetics.com/DimensionsOfLeisureForLife.

Review Questions

1. List six major technological advances from the past 150 years. Discuss how those new technologies have affected leisure.

2. In groups of three or four, share with each other aspects of your life that are greatly affected by technology. Discuss the following:

   - How has a certain technology affected your leisure (positively or negatively)?
   - Has that technology added to or detracted from your well-being?
   - How can you change your technology use to promote social, emotional, physical, spiritual, or intellectual development?

3. Develop a plan to use technology that would help you socially, emotionally, physically, spiritually, or intellectually. Come to class prepared to share your plan with others.

Leisure Reading

Bradbury, R. (2006). *Fahrenheit 451* (50th anniversary ed.). Pacific Palisades, CA: Vagabond Books.

Frankl, V.E. (1984). *Man's search for meaning: An introduction to logotherapy* (3rd ed.). New York: Simon & Schuster.

Huizinga, J. (1970). *Homo Ludens: A study of the play element in culture.* London: Maurice Temple Smith.

Huxley, A. (1932). *Brave new world.* Garden City, NY: Doubleday Doran.

Orwell, G. (1983). *1984.* New York: New American Library.

Talbot, S. (2007). *Devices of the soul: Battling for our selves in an age of machines*. Sebastopol, CA: O'Reilly Media.

Thoreau, H.D., Stern, P.V.D., & Thoreau, H.D. (1970). *The annotated Walden: Walden; or, life in the woods*. New York: Bramhall House.

Glossary

communication technologies—Tools that allow people to share information, knowledge, ideas, and concepts efficiently and quickly.

deviant leisure—Any pursuit that does not contribute to social, emotional, physical, spiritual, or intellectual development.

digital technologies—Tools that use numbers to share, display, represent, and communicate information.

discretionary time—Time that a person can use as she chooses.

domestic technologies—Tools that aid in tasks of daily living by making such tasks easier and faster.

idea technologies—New concepts or knowledge discoveries that have no tangible form (e.g., the concept of an assembly line).

Internet addictions—Obsession with any aspects of the Internet or features of the Internet itself (pornography, gambling).

leisure spaces—Places where leisure occurs.

Moore's law—Law whereby the number of transistors that can be placed on an integrated circuit doubles every 2 years. Some have taken this to mean that computing capacity doubles every 2 years.

motion-sensing technologies—Tools that sense a person's movements and translate that motion to a graphic representation of some kind.

narcissism—Excessive interest in one's appearance and in oneself. This is sometimes manifested on social networking sites.

obesity—Body weight that is greater than what is generally considered healthy for a given height. Research has identified ranges of weight that increase the likelihood of certain diseases and other health problems. Usually calculated as body mass index (BMI).

product technologies—The actual tools developed to make idea technologies a reality (e.g., the conveyor belt, workstations).

social networking—An idea technology that focuses on building communities of people who share interests and activities and are interested in exploring the interests and activities of others. One product technology stemming from social networking is online social networking sites.

technology—Application of current knowledge for some useful purpose; tool developed for some practical purpose.

transport technologies—Tools or vehicles that move people or goods from one place to another. Such technology seeks to increase efficiency and speed of transport.

virtual communities—A group of people who interact via communication media such as listservs, newsletters, telephone, e-mail, online social networks, or instant messages rather than face to face, for professional, social, personal, or educational reasons.

virtual reality—A simulated environment that is created with computer software and presented to the user so that he suspends belief and accepts what is presented as a real environment.

References

Anderson, C.A., Sakamoto, A., Gentile, D.A., Ihori, N., Shibuya, A., Yukawa, S., et al. (2008). Longitudinal effects of violent video games on aggression in Japan and the United States. *Pediatrics, 122*(5), e1067-1072.

Blair, S. (1993). Physical activity, physical fitness, and health. *Research Quarterly for Exercise and Sport, 64,* 365-376.

Bryce, J. (2001). The technological transformation of leisure. *Social Science Computer Review, 19*(1), 7-16.

Buffardi, L.E., & Campbell, W.K. (2008). Narcissism and social networking Web sites. *Personality and Social Psychology Bulletin, 34*(10), 1303-1314.

Chandra, A., Martino, S.C., Collins, R.L., Elliott, M.N., Berry, S.H., Kanouse, D.E., et al. (2008). Does watching sex on television predict teen pregnancy? Findings from a national longitudinal survey of youth. *Pediatrics, 122*(5), 1047-1054.

Fitzgerald, J.D., & Mayer, M. (1967). *The great brain.* New York: Dial Press.

Godbey, G. (2003). *Leisure in your life: An exploration* (6th ed.). State College, PA: Venture.

Hooper, S., & Rieber, L.P. (1995). Teaching with technology. In A.C. Ornstein (Ed.), *Teaching: Theory into practice* (pp. 154-170). Needham Heights, MA: Allyn & Bacon.

Kleiber, D.A. (1999). *Leisure experience and human development: A dialectical interpretation.* New York: Basic Books.

Kohut, A., Wike, R., & Speulda, N. (2006). *Truly a World Wide Web: Globe going digital.* Washington, DC: Pew Global Attitudes Project.

National Geographic News. (2003). New Internet tech 153,000 times faster than modem. *National Geographic.* http://news.nationalgeographic.com/news/2003/03/0318_030318_internet.html

Moore, T. (1965). Cramming more components onto integrated circuits. *Electronics, 38*(8), 114-117.

Palmer, G.K. (2007, September). The power of laughter. *Ensign,* pp. 32-35.

Rojek, C. (2000). *Leisure and culture.* London: Macmillan.

Russell, R.V. (1996). *Pastimes: The context of contemporary leisure.* Madison, WI: Brown & Benchmark.

Salaway, G., Caruso, J.B., & Nelson, M. (2008). *The ECAR Study of Undergraduate Students and Information Technology, 2008* (No. Research Study, Vol. 8). Boulder, CO: EDUCAUSE Center for Applied Research.

Skinner, B.F. (1969). *Contingencies of reinforcement: A theoretical analysis.* New York: Appleton-Century-Crofts.

Uys, J. (Writer). (1981). *The Gods Must Be Crazy.* J. Uys (Producer). Norway: Fox Films.

Walsh, D., & Gentile, D. (2008). *13th annual MediaWise video game report card.* Minneapolis: National Institute on Media.

Wojick, D. (1979). The structure of technological revolutions. In G. Bugliarello & D.B. Doner (Eds.), *The history and philosophy of technology* (pp. 238-261). Urbana: University of Illinois Press.

Leisure, the Environment, and Sustainability

Kelly Bricker • Dan Dustin • Nathan Bricker
University of Utah

Learning Outcomes

After reading this chapter, you will

- ▶ understand the historical foundations of leisure landscapes,
- ▶ understand the impacts of leisure pursuits on leisure landscapes,
- ▶ understand the ways in which leisure landscapes are managed for quality experiences, and
- ▶ understand the importance of sustainability as a guiding principle in managing leisure landscapes.

Vocabulary Terms

Antiquities Act of 1906

Bureau of Land Management

Civilian Conservation Corps

climate change

global positioning systems

Leave No Trace

leisure

manifest destiny

National Outdoor Leadership School

nongovernmental organizations

Organic Act of 1916

Outdoor Industry Foundation

Proposition 13

sustainability

Tennessee Valley Authority

Tourism Sustainability Council

U.S. Department of the Interior

U.S. Forest Service

U.S. National Park Service

wilderness

Works Progress Administration

Photo courtesy of N.K. Bricker

Natural beauty inspires inner reflection. Humans are merely a part of nature.

Imagine you are driving down a lonely highway late at night. Suddenly, in the road in front of you, is a small animal, frozen by your headlights. What do you do? Do you barge ahead in some sort of Darwinian fit? Do you brake your car out of a sense of altruism, endangering yourself for the sake of the other? Or do you stop because you really believe that if you destroy that creature you will be destroying a part of yourself? Therein lies the crux of this chapter. How do we see ourselves in relation to the larger living world?

Nature is the wellspring of our existence, a place for testing our mettle in the name of **leisure**, a place that gives increased meaning to our lives. Nature also provides us with the opportunity to extend ethical consideration to other people, to other creatures, and to the earth in its entirety through the leisure choices we make. In the end, leisure is a critical context for demonstrating our ethical progress as a species as well as a pleasant reminder of our essential grounding in the natural world.

This chapter begins with the assumption that leisure pursuits, at their best, contribute to the growth and development of socially and environmentally responsible citizens. Leisure provides a context within which we participate in personally and socially rewarding activities that help us better understand our place in the world and our obligations to other people and other living things. Leisure is fundamentally about human aspiration and quest.

The chapter focuses on the interactions between human beings and the environment within a leisure context. From our pioneer beginnings to our gradual awakening to the possibility of seeing ourselves as ordinary members and citizens of a larger community of life, we examine the evolution of North Americans' relationship with the natural world. In the end, informed by ecology, we characterize the need for personal, social, economic, political, and environmental relationships that will benefit and sustain generations to come.

AN ADVANCING CIVILIZATION

When the first western Europeans emigrated to the North American continent, they brought with them a Judeo-Christian tradition that viewed nature as a storehouse of raw materials that became valuable only when opened up for human use. These settlers saw no intrinsic value in wild lands, and they set about cutting back and taming nature to tap its instrumental value.

Reinforced in their pioneering spirit by the logic in Adam Smith's *The Wealth of Nations* (1776), the settlers plowed westward, fortified by the belief that if they looked out for their own individual best interests they would be led by an "invisible hand" to promote the public interest. This perspective gave them license to slash and burn and otherwise convert the **wilderness** into domesticated farmland, and they went about their business imbued with the self-confidence that they were doing the right thing for themselves and their nation.

There were so few people scattered about North America that little thought was given to the possibility of exhausting the country's natural resources. Almost anything in the path of the rapidly expanding population was eradicated, including native peoples. As the pattern of westward conquest unfolded (Limerick, 1987), trees were cut down, forests were destroyed, and much of the landscape was denuded of its primeval character. This was carried out in the name of **manifest destiny**, and the young nation was proud of its efforts to subdue the wilderness to meet the needs of an advancing civilization.

> Everybody needs beauty as well as bread, places to play in and pray in, where Nature may heal and cheer and give strength to body and soul alike.
>
> *John Muir*

It was not until the middle of the 19th century that attitudes toward the American landscape began to change. Three forces, in particular, accounted for this turn of events (Nash, 1967). First, Romanticism as a way of thought worked its way into the hearts and minds of America's East coast literati. Romanticists believed that pristine nature was God's best handiwork and humankind could not improve on it. Wild lands were to be revered in their own right, and people could learn much from observing them in quiet contemplation. Henry David Thoreau, Ralph Waldo Emerson, John James Audubon, and George Perkins Marsh were of this tradition, as was John Muir in the twilight of the 19th century.

SELF-DISCOVERY

John Muir once said, "I only went out for a walk, and finally concluded to stay out till sundown, for going out, I found, was really going in" (Wolfe, 1938). What do you think Muir meant by this statement? In what ways does nature serve as a mirror unto us? Why does a walk in the woods, or along the shore, or in the mountains, lend itself to introspection and self-reflection?

Second, nationalism emerged as a powerful influence. The fledgling United States of America suffered a cultural inferiority complex and needed something to distinguish itself from its Old World roots. Although Europe had its share of mountains, they were not wilderness. Indeed, the Alps had been developed for centuries. An idea began to take form that America should cherish its wild lands and protect and preserve parts of them as parks in perpetuity. The establishment of Yellowstone National Park in 1872 was the first manifestation of the federal government's commitment to this ideal.

Third, and perhaps most important, by the end of the 19th century the United States had been transformed into an urban society. In the early 1800s, only 20 percent of the populace resided in towns and cities, whereas 80 percent resided in rural areas. By the turn of the century the percentages were reversed. Now 80 percent of the citizenry lived in towns and cities and only 20 percent lived in rural areas. The most famous expression of this reversal was an essay published by historian Frederick Jackson Turner in 1893 in which he pronounced the end of the frontier (Turner, 1921). North America was settled from the Atlantic coast to the Pacific coast. There was no more undiscovered territory. There were no more blank spots on the map.

Progressive Movement

The collective effect of these three 19th-century forces resulted in a new appeal to safeguard wild lands that heretofore had been thought to have little intrinsic value. The 20th century was ushered in by what was termed *progressive thinking,* led by President Theodore Roosevelt. The country's leaders championed setting aside the nation's "crown jewels" as national parks, whereas other large tracts of wild land were set aside as national forests. The former were managed as "museums" (look but don't touch) by the **U.S. National Park Service** (NPS), established in 1916 and housed in the **U.S. Department of the Interior**. The latter were managed for multiple uses (timber, watershed, mining, grazing) by the **U.S. Forest Service** (USFS), established in 1891 and housed in the Department of Agriculture. Large parcels of less desirable land west of the 100th meridian were turned over to the Interior Department's **Bureau of Land Management** (BLM) for custodianship. Still other public lands were assigned to the U.S. Fish and Wildlife Service (USFWS), also housed in the Department of the Interior, to care for wildlife habitats. Together, these four federal agencies were entrusted with the stewardship of the lion's share of the United States' public domain.

Throughout the first half of the 20th century, recreation lands at the federal, state, and local levels were expanded dramatically and the roles of large land-managing agencies solidified. The USFS, under the early leadership of Gifford Pinchot, adopted a utilitarian philosophy toward land management, whereas the NPS, under the early leadership of Stephen Mather, adopted a preservationist philosophy. To this day the differences in land management practices between these two federal agencies can be explained by those philosophical differences. The USFS' emphasis is on using nature. The NPS' emphasis is on appreciating nature.

Other forces of progressive thinking were equally hard at work. The American **Antiquities Act of 1906** made it possible for presidents to single-handedly protect pockets of the public domain from exploitation by private interests by designating these areas as national monuments. Every president of the United States since 1906—Republican and Democrat alike—has used the Antiquities Act to his advantage (Dustin et al., 2005). During the Great Depression, many of President Franklin Roosevelt's New Deal initiatives were devoted to recreational development. The **Civilian Conservation Corps**, the **Tennessee Valley Authority**, and the **Works Progress Administration** all contributed to growing the public recreation estate. Still, there was little demand for these public pleasuring grounds in the first half of the 20th century because the American public was largely homebound.

"See the USA in Your Chevrolet"

World War II changed everything. Prior to the Second World War, few Americans had the wherewithal to travel about their country. But when the engines of industry resumed operation at full throttle upon the war's conclusion, masses of Americans outfitted with more free time, more discretionary income, more knowledge about available opportunities, and more mobility set out to enjoy their public lands.

These factors resulted in an explosion of demand for outdoor recreation in the 1950s and 1960s. In the melodic voice of Dinah Shore, Americans were invited to "See the USA in your Chevrolet."

This upswell of interest in outdoor recreation was welcomed at first as a boon. Recreation was not viewed as inherently problematic: Everything about it was good. People were beginning to enjoy nature and each other in a leisure context. They were learning about their cultural and natural heritage in a way that led to countless individual, social, cultural, economic, and environmental benefits. Measures were taken to sustain this growing interest in the outdoors, and projects like the NPS' Mission 66 were undertaken to make sure a sufficient infrastructure was in place to accommodate the growing enthusiasm for exploring America's cultural, historic, and scenic treasures.

Recreational Limits

Skyrocketing demand for outdoor recreation eventually ushered in a variety of management problems. The problems were rooted in the limited nature of the nation's store of outdoor recreation resources in the face of seemingly unlimited demand for them (Dustin & McAvoy, 1980). Heavy recreational use resulted in unwelcome

©Kapu

Exploring scenic treasures can lead to artistic inspiration.

impacts on the quality of recreation experiences as well as the quality of the environment itself. Recreation congestion, crowding, conflict, and constraints became part of the managerial lexicon. How best to manage for outdoor recreation? How best to manage recreation settings that were now in danger of being loved to death?

These issues, occurring in the late 1960s and during all of the 1970s, led to the development of a variety of management strategies, such as attempts to determine "recreation carrying capacity," assess "limits of acceptable change," and develop elaborate organizational frameworks like the "recreation opportunity spectrum," within which to accommodate the public's wide-ranging recreational tastes (Manning, 1999). Essentially, the management challenge was how best to satisfy those tastes while safeguarding the quality of the recreation settings themselves. The inherent contradiction in this challenge—making all kinds of recreation available to all kinds of people while simultaneously protecting the environment—has been at the center of the recreation debate since the **Organic Act of 1916** charged the NPS with meeting that challenge. Serving these two masters has been daunting.

Financial Limits

Exacerbating the managerial challenge has been a fundamental change in the way outdoor recreation is funded. For much of the 20th century, the nation's parks and open spaces were treated as public goods. Their existence was subsidized through taxes, and admission was otherwise free of charge. Then, in 1979, a taxpayer revolt in California culminated in **Proposition 13**, a referendum that put a lid on property taxes. Because public parks and recreation, museums, libraries, and other public goods relied on property taxes for their lifeblood, they had to look elsewhere for financial support. The thinking behind Proposition 13 spread like wildfire across the country, and the last quarter century saw an uphill battle for money to support what used to be paid for by taxes. What formerly was treated as a public good (tax supported) is now treated as a merit good (a combination of tax and private support) and soon may be treated merely as a private good (fees and charges). This could eventually result in public parks and recreation being available only to those who are willing and able to pay for them. This raises serious questions about fairness and equity as well as what ought to be the role of public parks and recreation in a democracy. In the meantime, the stewards of access and custodians of choice do what they must do to sustain the services and settings for which they are responsible.

WHAT DO YOU THINK?

Do you think the provision of parks and recreation should be treated as a public good and be paid for entirely through taxes? Or do you think parks and recreation should be treated as a merit good, paid for partially through taxes and partially through fees assessed directly to those who use them? Or do you think parks and recreation should be treated as a private good, paid for solely by those who benefit directly from their enjoyment? What are the implications of your thinking for issues of access, fairness, and social justice?

The decline in tax support for public parks and recreation also has forced the profession to become more creative and innovative in its service delivery. Before Proposition 13, little thought was given to marketing leisure services, and little thought was given to leisure services outside the traditional public parks and recreation mainstream. Marketing is now a cornerstone of professional preparation, and the field has broadened its focus dramatically. Specializations in therapeutic recreation, commercial recreation, hospitality management, event planning, convention and visitors bureaus, festivals, sport management, outdoor adventure, outdoor leadership, organized camping, tourism, ecotourism, and sustainable tourism are all now considered to be important parts of the service delivery mix. This has opened up new career opportunities for students interested in parks and recreation and has expanded the potential impact of the field as a whole. At the same time, subdividing parks and recreation into myriad specialties has made it difficult for its parent organization, the National Recreation and Park Association, to speak on everyone's behalf with one voice.

Widening the Circle of Ethical Consideration

Adding to the complexity is a slowly evolving idea that there is more to parks and recreation than looking out for human interests. Proponents of this line of thought argue that nature is much more than a backdrop for the unfolding of our human drama. They speak of the "rights" of nature. They advocate for extending ethical consideration outward from people to other species to the earth in its entirety. They urge us to become less anthropocentric, be less human-centered, and consider the possibility that the earth was made for more than human beings alone.

This is a difficult idea to wrap our brains around because it is not easy to escape our human-centeredness. It is hard to step outside ourselves to consider other perspectives. Yet this is precisely the challenge presented to us by Aldo Leopold, who introduced the idea of environmental ethics more than 60 years ago. He implored us to step off our anthropocentric pedestal and become plain members and citizens of a larger community of life. He reasoned further that the best measure of our progress as a species is in the extent to which we offer ethical consideration outward. In *A Sand County Almanac* (1966), Leopold built a moral compass for guiding our human aspirations rooted in ecological wisdom.

There are many obstacles to finding our way to Leopold's preferred future. Chief among them is our increasing separation from nature, our increasing detachment from our biological moorings. We have become city dwellers through and through, and our connections to nature are increasingly tattered. Visits to national parks are on the decline, and we seem to be more and more likely to stay inside and live highly technological, sedentary, urban lives. We are ensconced in our homes and workplaces, spending most of our time in front of televisions, computers, and video games (Pergams & Zaradic, 2006). We behave this way even as we comprehend our fundamental reliance on nature as the ground of our being. It is our emotional distancing, the living of our lives as if we are apart from rather than a part of nature, that presents the major roadblock to realizing Leopold's dream of a "land ethic."

Our gradual withdrawal from nature uncovers yet another obstacle to building a more harmonious relationship with the world around us. We humans are uncanny in our ability to adjust to changing circumstances. Indeed, our highly adaptable human nature has been touted as one of the keys to our evolutionary success. Yet there is a downside to human adaptability that is seldom talked about—our skill at conforming to bad as well as good situations. In a leisure context, this means we are still able to find joy in recreation environments that are slowly deteriorating. We

PERSONAL LEISURE

Consider your own existence on this planet. Where do you live? What is the air quality in the area you currently call home? Do you have easy access to fresh water? Consider this—almost one fifth of the world's population (about 1.2 billion people) live in areas where the water is scarce. One quarter of the global population also live in developing countries that face water shortages due to a lack of infrastructure to fetch water from rivers and aquifers (World Health Organization, 2009). How much water do you use daily? Could you adapt to one third of your use today? How would this affect your life?

adapt to poorer air and water quality as well as declining recreation opportunities and environments (Dustin & McAvoy, 1982). In sum, our adaptable human nature makes it possible for the world around us to change for the worse without our even being aware of it (think about **climate change**). Therein lies a much more nuanced, but perhaps more dangerous, by-product of our increasing separation from the natural world: We may well adapt to living without close association to it. We may not miss what we do not know.

The 21st Century

The gargantuan task before us is to figure out how to live, and how to recreate, in ways that recognize and honor our embeddedness in a larger community of life. Our charge is to learn how to enjoy ourselves in a manner that does not harm other people, other living things, or the earth in its biological wholeness. This requires a basic understanding of ecology. It also requires a willingness to conduct our lives with a conscious appreciation of the condition of the rest of the world. This is not an easy thing to do. It demands the will to restrain ourselves when restraint is called for out of a concern for others. More than anything else, it requires understanding the consequences of our actions before we act and then conducting our lives accordingly.

Ultimately, what we are talking about is sustaining health—the health of people and the health of the larger world of which we humans are but a small part. Health, in turn, is a function of living in the light of ecologic interrelationships and interdependencies. In Leopold's words, "a thing is right when it tends to preserve the stability, integrity, and beauty of the biotic community. It is wrong when it tends otherwise" (Leopold, 1966, p. 262). Our quest is to find the right path, the path that preserves the stability, integrity, and beauty of us all.

Photo courtesy of N.K. Bricker

The human-nature connection is always evolving.

In 1930, T.K. Whipple said, "All America lies at the end of the wilderness road, and our past is not a dead past, but still lives in us. Our forefathers had civilization inside themselves, the wild outside. We live in the civilization they created, but within us the wilderness still lingers. What they dreamed, we live, and what they lived, we dream" (p. 65). Whipple's insight captures the essence of the times in which we live. We inhabit a civilized world that was carved out of the wilderness. But within us the wilderness flame still flickers. Getting back in touch with that part of ourselves is what draws us to outdoor recreation. When we recreate in the out of doors, we are going back home to that place where our psyches were formed, where we grew into self-aware people. Through outdoor recreation we are able to get in touch with our inner selves again, with our evolutionary history, with our sense of who we were, who we are, and who we may yet become. Wild lands act as a mirror unto ourselves. This is what John Muir meant when he said, "I only went out for a walk and finally concluded to stay out till sundown, for going out, I found, was really going in" (Wolfe, 1938, p. 439).

CONQUERING MANAGERIAL CHALLENGES

The leisure landscape has changed significantly since the founders of our nation exercised their wisdom in setting aside large tracts of the public domain for the common good. Through the influence of political giants like Teddy Roosevelt; the educational writings of Gifford Pinchot, Aldo Leopold, and Rachel Carson; the eloquent prose and philosophical insights of Henry David Thoreau, Walt Whitman, and John Muir; and the artistic influence of Thomas Moran, George Catlin, and Ansel Adams, voices from the past have shaped much of the philosophical discussion surrounding humankind's relationship with the natural world. But these voices are now in danger of being muted by a host of new forces influencing our leisure choices. Characterized by a growing population and increasing pressure on public lands, today's management challenges are daunting. They can be sorted into three categories: volume, diversity, and access. Now more than ever before, the sheer volume of interest, diversity of use and perspective, and unprecedented and unequal access confront and confound recreation planners, resource managers, and the recreating public.

Volume

In 1900, the population of the United States was 76 million. By 2000 the population had climbed to 281 million, more than tripling in size (U.S. Census Bureau, 2010). By 2100 the population is expected to more than double again to 571 million (U.S. Census Bureau, 2010). The impact of this exponential population growth on the public recreation estate is amplified when we consider the urbanization of America and the burgeoning number of communities now located adjacent to our public lands. The buffer zones that once protected outdoor recreation settings now have the additional burden of large numbers of people living in close proximity to them. Where once no roads existed, there are now roads and trails made passable by the latest off-road vehicles and mountain bikes. Isolation is no longer the frugal land manager's insurance policy, and new ways of thinking about the volume and type of use are required to address the evolving challenges associated with massive access to outdoor recreation.

To grasp fully the complex relationships between people and outdoor recreation settings, it is important to understand the different kinds of pressure that affect those settings. When we speak of volume, it is helpful to consider both the economics of visitor use and the numbers of visitors themselves. From an economic standpoint, access to disposable income and the willingness to apply it to outdoor recreation interests are alive and well. This is demonstrated clearly by annual reports of the **Outdoor Industry Foundation** (OIF), which help us quantify volume of use in dollars and cents. OIF research shows that more than three in every four adults, or better than three fourths of all Americans, seek the benefits of, and participate

© vigorin/fotolia.com

Roads and trails offer easier access to public lands than was once possible, so land managers face the challenge of increased traffic.

in, active outdoor recreation each year (OIF, 2006). Furthermore, those adults contribute in excess of $730 billion annually to the economy, which in turn provides 6.5 million jobs and is responsible for 1 in every 20 workers (OIF, 2006). On average, the outdoor recreation industry is estimated to generate $88 billion in state and national tax revenue annually (OIF, 2006). Furthermore, three of every four adults are generating roughly $289 billion a year in retail sales relative to outdoor recreation, which means that the industry influences more than $1 in every $12 spent on personal consumption expenditures (OIF, 2006). As an industry, outdoor recreation ranks as one of the economic and political heavyweights of our time.

Outdoor recreation is big business, and the resulting political clout has been demonstrated across the country where environmentalists and recreationists regularly join forces in disputes over how public lands are managed for leisure. The political power of the outdoor industry was recently demonstrated in Utah, for example, when the state ignored concerns over how oil leases were being managed by the BLM. The Outdoor Industry Association (n.d.) threatened to withdraw its endorsement of the Outdoor Retailer Show in Salt Lake City, which is responsible for generating an estimated $24 million annually. With the support of all those who benefit from the Outdoor Retailer Show (e.g., restaurants, hoteliers, tour providers), the state eventually recognized the positive economic impact of outdoor recreation and now affords a significant voice to outdoor recreation in decision-making processes. This advocacy process helped establish a task force on the environment that included representatives from the outdoor industry and added 175,000 square feet to the Salt Palace Convention Center to accommodate the show and the industry's projected growth.

Rates of participation in outdoor recreation are strong indicators of a vibrant outdoor recreation industry. In terms of human-powered outdoor recreation alone, people engage in bicycling (an estimated 60 million participants), camping (an estimated 45 million participants), fishing (an estimated 33 million participants), hunting (an estimated 13 million participants), paddling (an estimated 24 million participants), snow sports (an estimated 16 million participants), hiking and trail use (an estimated 56 million participants), and wildlife viewing (an estimated 66 million participants) (OIF, 2006). Consider the following as well:

- More Americans camp than play basketball and more paddle than play soccer.
- The number of Americans who bicycle is double the population of Canada.
- The number of New Englanders who participate in trail-based recreation annually is greater than the combined attendance for all 81 Boston Red Sox home games.
- The number of annual participants in snow-based recreation is more than double the combined annual attendance for NASCAR's two premier series.
- The number of Americans who recreate in the snow each year is greater than the combined populations of Ireland, Costa Rica, New Zealand, and Mongolia. (OIF, 2006, p. 9)

In sum, the sheer numbers of outdoor recreationists and the economic benefits they generate have a tremendous effect on the environment. They influence how our public lands are managed, and, for better or worse, they shape the nature of outdoor recreation experiences. If managing volume were the only issue, we might be inclined to think that the custodial challenge is not that complex. However, several other issues affect our public lands.

Diversity

Because of the multiple use missions of many large public land–managing agencies (e.g., the USFS and BLM), space is commonly allocated for a vast array of recreational activities. The diversity of these activities, and the unique management challenges they present, complicate our love affair with outdoor recreation in manifold ways. For example, accommodations are typically made for mountain biking, dog sledding, rafting, kayaking, hot air ballooning, snowmobiling, hang gliding, heli-skiing, scuba diving, and an assortment of off-road motorized, water-based motorized, and nonmotorized leisure pursuits. Accommodation is also made for a cornucopia of "extreme sports," wherein adventure loving, thrill-seeking participants tumble down hillsides in inflated, see-through bouncing balls (called *zorbing*); jump from bridges, natural arches, and overhangs on what amounts to nothing more than industrialized rubber bands (bungee jumping); ski and rollerblade using a kite wing (called *skimbating*); or wear wetsuits, body armor, and flippers while boogie boarding (called *river sledging*). Other adventure sports include paragliding, "shark diving," ski paragliding, kiteboarding, and BASE jumping. Then there are all the iterations of motorized use, including cross-country flying in ultralights called "aero-trekking" and rock crawling in machines that defy gravity as they claw at the rock and earth in an effort to go where no man, woman, or machine has gone before.

Stretching the imagination even more are organized events like Burning Man, where several thousand scantily clad event goers, hippies, goths, and members of every other imaginable subculture converge on Nevada's Black Rock country to burn a 40-foot stick figure (which, coincidently, is the tamest part of the event). It has been said that "Burning Man enables all the black sheep of the world to graze

Photo courtesy of N.K. Bricker

Nature offers a range of opportunities to push yourself beyond your comfort zone.

together" (Rough Guides, 2007, p. 184). There is also the annual convergence of college students who flock from all over the country to spend their spring break on beaches, lakes, and other public lands conducive to seasonal congregation.

Rocket launching, pumpkin tossing, and continent crossing (people engaged in some form of extreme race using the natural environment as their base) are other emerging activities making their demands on leisure landscapes. Crossing the continent, states, or regions are extreme racing events like the Eco Challenge and the Iditarod sled dog race and many motorized events such as the Rubicon Jeep Race in the Sierra Nevada region of northern California and the Iron Dog, a 2,000-mile snowmobile race across Alaska.

Another emerging use of the public lands is treasure stashing or geocaching, an outdoor pursuit where treasure hunters and seekers post and obtain coordinates via the Internet and strike out on satellite-facilitated treasure hunts that take players to some of the most unusual, beautiful, and fragile places on earth. To date, there is only one Web site dedicated to this activity (www.geocaching.com), and there are more than 700,000 active cache locations globally. This is an activity that has integrated technology, the environment, and leisure into a global phenomenon.

Mix together the volume of use, the economics of the industry, the diversity of activities, and increasing multiculturalism, and you can see why managing leisure landscapes becomes even more daunting. Understanding changing demographics and how to manage to ensure quality leisure experiences is no mean feat. Different values drive different recreational choices, including how, when, and where recreationists will interact with the outdoor recreation environment. What historically may have been a one-dimensional, traditional-use landscape has quickly become a multidimensional, non-traditional-use landscape.

Adding to this managerial task is the changing face of America's populace. The Pew Research Center estimates large changes within various ethnic groups over the next 45 years (table 9.1) (Passel & Cohn, 2008, p. 1). As table 9.1 demonstrates, the largest changes may be within the Hispanic and white communities. How might these changes affect the management of leisure landscapes? Research has shown that Hispanics primarily recreate in large family groups, and they place high value on the social qualities of participating in outdoor recreation that promotes family cohesiveness (Chavez, 2000; Gobster, 2002; Shaull & Gramann, 1998; Virden & Walker, 1999). Hispanic Americans are more likely to recreate with immediate and extended family than with friends, and they often travel in groups of three or more (Sasidharan et al., 2005; Virden & Walker, 1999). Because of these cultural differences, recreation land managers need to plan for diversity in outdoor recreation opportunities, for example, accommodating a range of group sizes (Gobster, 2002), providing for a greater variety of activities, and creating facilities to accommodate divergent interests (Sasidharan et al., 2005). Enjoyment of the outdoors by an increasingly diverse population heightens the complexity of the managerial challenge. There is every indication that these demographic profiles will become increasingly varied, requiring more creativity and innovation from those charged with managing public lands for all citizens. But once again, it is not only increasing volume and diversity that shape recreationists' choices and associated management challenges. The next factor we discuss is access to leisure landscapes.

Access

Today there is unprecedented access to public lands created through increased population, road access, creative technology, urban sprawl, and the combined effects they have on leisure landscapes. Access plays a critical role in the types and volume of use taking place. Lands once protected by their remoteness or difficult terrain are now being affected by the growth in mechanized outdoor recreation. From snowmobiles to rock crawlers, ultralight aircrafts to hovercrafts, the outdoors is being accessed in ways once unimagined. Rock crawlers and motorcyclists are exploring the "frontcountry" and backcountry like never before, whereas aero-trekkers and hovercrafts are going places once thought impossible. In just 10 years, the total number of off-road vehicles and all-terrain vehicles in the United States exploded from 2,920,000 in 1993 to more than 8 million

TABLE 9.1 Changing Populations in the United States Over the Next 45 Years	
2005	**2050**
5% Asian	9% Asian
14% Hispanic	29% Hispanic
13% black	13% black
67% white	47% white

©Chris Mautz

Outdoor environments support a variety of health and personal benefits.

in 2003 (Cordell et al., 2005). Furthermore, motorized recreation, which was not taken into account by the Outdoor Industry Foundation economic figures, contributes an additional $14 billion in total economic impacts (OIF, 2006).

This type of unprecedented access is complicated not only by advances in transportation but also by the technological birth of cell and satellite phones and **global positioning systems**, which now empower recreationists to go farther afield than ever before. Perhaps with the reassurance of help being only a phone call away and the mystery of direction and location virtually eliminated, outdoor spaces have become more broadly accessible to an expanded population of outdoor users. Access to the outdoors is also influenced by the growth of population centers, creating a wildland–urban interface. As more and more Americans find their way out of cities, the resulting sprawl affects lands once considered more backcountry than frontcountry. This has increased human–wildlife interactions, increased threats to neighborhoods from wildland fires, and decreased buffer zones between frontcountry and backcountry access.

Another consideration is that all Americans have fair and equitable access to parks in their communities. Because many physiological and psychological health benefits are associated with outdoor recreation (Kaplan, 2001; Kaplan, 1995; Ulrich, 1981), community parks that are accessible to the citizenry have numerous benefits. Unlike the buildings we work and live in, the natural environment is a place where we have learned to recover, to feel refreshed, and to feel restored from the everyday stressors of life (Hartig & Evans, 1993; Hartig et al., 1991; Ulrich, 1981). These and other qualities provide the basis for our continued relationship with the natural world. For many, the natural environment provides the roots of our very existence, testing our mettle in the pursuit of leisure and giving meaning to life. Unfortunately, not all citizens have safe and equal access to outdoor places for recreation (Garcia, 2006; Neighbors et al., 2007; Parks et al., 2003). Access to parks is unevenly distributed throughout the United States, and important reasons for this disparity include socioeconomic influences such as race, income level, and urban or rural status (Garcia, 2006; Neighbors et al., 2007; Parks et al., 2003).

The average life expectancy of Americans is likely to exceed 80 years in the near future (U.S. Census Bureau, 2008). As baby boomers search for retirement communities featuring outdoor recreation

Everyone deserves fair and equitable access to parks, but the challenge is to overcome socioeconomic obstacles like race or income level.

Photo courtesy of N.K. Bricker

amenities, the types of demands placed on leisure landscapes are likely to change because users have decreased physical ability. The desire to explore, commune with nature, and enjoy outdoor recreation is not likely to subside with age. Rather, the nature of involvement will likely gravitate toward types of recreation more suitable to an aging power train. This could mean increased use of off-road and all-terrain vehicles and an increased dependency on other forms of technologically assisted recreation.

Our love affair with the outdoors has evolved in ways we could never have imagined and will continue to do so as technology advances and the demographics of our society change. Perhaps the good and bad news is that human desire to engage in outdoor recreation activities may be on a grander scale than any other time in history, which requires recreationists and resource managers alike to seriously consider their relationship to, impact on, and sustainable use of the natural environment. This may indeed be an indication of good news simply because engagement in, and dependence on, outdoor recreation by the masses may increase our interest in protecting and conserving our natural resources for future generations. The bad news may be that we will be constantly in danger of "loving the environment to death." With greater diversity of demand, we may also see increased user conflicts and negative impacts, increasing the debate over what is and what is not appropriate use of our public lands.

PROMISE OF TOURISM

Tourism is another form of leisure pursuit that has a long history and codependent relationship with the environment. Tourism has grown significantly in the past 50 years; it is now recognized as the world's largest industry and carries sizeable economic benefits, generating upward of $7 billion annually (World Travel and Tourism Council, 2007). Tourism is the world's largest employer, generating 231 million jobs, or nearly 1 out of every 12 jobs globally (World Travel and Tourism Council, 2007). Although tourism originally was promoted as a "smokeless" industry, the impact of more than 800 million travelers (World Travel and Tourism Council, 2007) roaming the globe at the start of the new millennium has forced governments, **nongovernmental organizations**, communities, and the tourism industry to recognize the importance of sustaining the environments upon which tourism, especially nature-based tourism, depends (Honey, 1999). Sustainable tourism development "meets the needs of the present without compromising the ability of future generations to meet their own needs" (United Nations World Commission on the Environment and Development, 1987).

To support biodiversity conservation, which can affect community health and quality of life, tourism should provide benefits. Where nature-based tourism is concerned, the money collected from tourists can support parks and conservation efforts (Brandon, 1996). This typically happens through taxes, tourist entry fees, and funds to support conservation research donated by the tourism industry.

Because tourism happens within some of the most biologically diverse areas of the world, it can provide an economic justification for park protection. When tourism revenues flow into a country, the host government may realize that nature is good for tourism, which is good for the economy, and eventually begin to protect the "natural capital" desired by those who spend money to visit. All tourism that depends on a healthy ecosystem can provide local people with economic alternatives

Photo courtesy of N.K. Bricker

Sustainable tourism supports local communities and conservation. Rivers Fiji protects the environment through tourism and partnerships with local communities.

to encroachment into conservation and protected areas (Brandon, 1996). In many countries, protected areas and surrounding lands are often both geographically remote and agriculturally marginal. Nature-based lodge or tourism operations can help avert environmental degradation by providing employment, income-generating opportunities, and financing for community projects (Curzon, 1993).

Tourism can assist in building constituencies who promote conservation. Because of the interdependence of healthy economies with healthy ecosystems, tourism has the economic clout to build constituencies for conservation at local, national, and international levels. At various lodges around the world associated with national parks and protected areas, interpretive programs and naturalist guides help educate visitors about biodiversity and resources (Koeppel, 2000). In Costa Rica and Ecuador, interpretive programs include guided walks and brochures explaining low-impact strategies such as use of composting toilets, use of renewable energy sources such as solar and hydroelectric, and ways to minimize negative impacts on local communities (e.g., problems caused by photographing local people or giving money or presents to individuals, and the need to respect the area's traditions) (Koeppel, 2000; Rodriguez, 1999).

Tourism can provide an impetus for additional private conservation efforts (Brandon, 1996). Worldwide, private nature reserves, operated by either commercial or nonprofit organizations, have been established to generate income and preserve habitats. Many of these private reserves contain lodges and offer tourism activities. Such reserves supplement public protected areas, help to broaden the range of habitats, and serve as wildlife corridors. Private conservation areas are frequently designed for multiple uses, combining areas for consumptive resource use (e.g., grazing, forestry, and fishing) with areas for wilderness and recreation (such as wildlife viewing, birding, or sport hunting or fishing). Many of these areas serve as catalysts for sustainable development, whereby a lodge provides a successful example of conservation, creating a stimulus to establish lodges and private reserves elsewhere (Ceaser, 1998; Dallen & White, 1999; Hviding & Bayliss-Smith, 2000). One example of this type of tourism benefit can be found in the country of Fiji, where Rivers Fiji, a whitewater rafting and sea kayaking company, worked with tribal landowners called *matqali* to set up a conservation corridor on the upper Navua River. In this case, tourism has provided direct economic gain to local landowners in trade for conserving the river corridor from destructive land uses such as gravel extraction and unsustainable logging practices. See www.RiversFiji.com for more information on this unique partnership and conservation strategy.

Some studies have shown that environmental degradation has resulted from mismanagement of lodges and tourism enterprises, including waste disposal, energy, and resources at sites that can lead to pollution of fragile habitats (Curzon, 1993); the consumption of enormous amounts of energy, water, and other scarce resources; pollution caused by guests (noise, air, and sewage); and erosion and depletion of some species of plants through the building of trails (Bookbinder et al., 1998; Jeffreys, 1998; Mwalyosi & Sosovele, 2001; Wallace & Pierce, 1996). It appears that for every positive impact of tourism, a negative impact can occur as well, thus emphasizing the need for a commitment to best practices and sustainable principles.

Many lodges and tourism operations around the world, including guide and tour services, are making efforts to implement a number of sustainable tourism practices that reflect social and environmental responsibility. These efforts will be helped by the development of voluntary and perhaps eventually mandatory tools aimed at measuring environmental and social impacts. For example, with respect to indigenous populations' quality of life, nature-based tourism has significant potential to be a positive influence on host communities and the surrounding environment. Not only can tourism provide much-needed economic development, it can also improve the quality of the environment for residents through improved infrastructure, protection of natural habitat, and improved access to recreation and leisure opportunities.

The park, recreation, and tourism profession is thus challenged to leadership in shaping a more sustainable way of life, one that brings real benefit to biodiversity conservation and protection of ecosystems at all levels. To that end, several initiatives are underway to help ensure sustainable parks, recreation, and tourism for generations to come.

MOVING TOWARD A SUSTAINABLE FUTURE

Several initiatives support concepts of **sustainability** and promotion of responsible use of the outdoors and related areas. More and more programs are being implemented to help our current and future generations adopt a responsible use ethic, which will assist in conserving the natural capital we all depend upon. Some of these programs and initiatives are described next.

Leave No Trace

To address the challenges associated with the sheer number of recreationists, the diversity of their pastimes, and types of access they use when visiting their public lands, the NPS, USFS, BLM, and other federal and state land managing agencies have implemented an educational approach to visitor management known as **Leave No Trace** (LNT). LNT is founded on the principle that education can help reduce the impacts of recreational use to create a more sustainable relationship with the outdoors we depend on for quality experiences. LNT's mission is "to promote and inspire responsible outdoor recreation through education, research and partnership." The fundamental goal is to instill responsibility in outdoor recreationists by providing them with the knowledge to make informed decisions about their outdoor recreation choices and practice the skills necessary to reduce their impacts.

©John Keith/fotolia

We must learn to live in harmony with nature by minimizing our impact on the environment.

The ideas underpinning LNT grew out of Paul Petzoldt's work with the **National Outdoor Leadership School** (NOLS) in the mid-1960s (Marion & Reid, 2001). Petzoldt had witnessed firsthand the negative impacts outdoor recreation programs were having on the natural environment, and he began exploring and experimenting with new techniques and teaching approaches to reduce those impacts. By the 1970s and 1980s, reducing impacts on wild lands from recreational use was gaining popular support within the USFS as well (Marion & Reid, 2001).

The phrase "leave no trace" was first used by the Forest Service in an effort to reduce visitor impacts on popular recreation sites located in Utah's Uinta Mountains to the east of Salt Lake City (Tilton, 2003). The concept spread gradually through other Forest Service districts and other outdoor education programs across the United States, including NOLS, Outward Bound, and the Wilderness Education Association. However, it was not until 1990 that a veteran forester named Bill Thompson was asked to serve as the first Leave No Trace coordinator for the Forest Service. Thompson realized that to promote the principles of Leave No Trace, he had to find an effective way of reaching the masses. To accomplish this task, he chose NOLS to implement Leave No Trace. In 1993, the Forest Service, Bureau of Land Management, National Park Service, Fish and Wildlife Service, and NOLS signed a memorandum of understanding establishing Leave No Trace as the officially recognized national outdoor ethics education program in the United States. In 1994, the Leave No Trace Center for Outdoor Ethics was established as a nonprofit organization, funded and supported by the Sporting Goods Manufacturers Association, the Outdoor Recreation Coalition of America, NOLS, and a collection of other corporate sponsors who embraced the wisdom of establishing the program. This was a defining moment in the history of outdoor recreation. It was an open collaboration between business, government (public land managers), and recreationists themselves. The guiding principles LNT instills through its training programs and materials include these:

- Plan ahead and prepare
- Travel and camp on durable surfaces
- Dispose of waste properly
- Leave what you find
- Minimize campfire impacts
- Respect wildlife
- Be considerate of other visitors

From Leave No Trace. Available: www.lnt.org.

Other organizations are attempting to reach the general public with similar conservation-minded educational approaches. The mission of Tread Lightly (TL), for example, is "to help arm recreationists and the industries that serve them with essential outdoor ethics. Our mission is to proactively protect recreation access and opportunities in the outdoors through education and stewardship initiatives" (Tread Lightly, 2009, p. 1). TL promotes outdoor recreation ethics similar to LNT's with a unique twist. As its name implies, TL was originally developed with a strong focus on mechanized recreation. Over time the organization has adapted its literature and messages to meet the needs of a number of other outdoor recreation user groups that include fishing enthusiasts, hunters, snow sport participants, hikers, geocachers, and campers. TL asks all outdoor recreationists to

Travel responsibly,

Respect the rights of others,

Educate yourself,

Avoid sensitive areas, and

Do your part.

For more information on Tread Lightly, see www.treadlightly.org.

Many other organizations, including schools, university outing clubs, and recreation providers (commercial and nonprofit), are addressing environmental issues through information, voluntary certification, and educational programs. In fact, it is hard to find outdoor organizations, schools, and clubs that don't promote a reduced-impact message or provide training to educate their constituents. Considering the many benefits of leisure participation in the outdoors and the many threats to the environment that come with those benefits, "striving for a more harmonious

©Maridav

Tread lightly and leave no trace to ensure enjoyable outdoor recreation experiences for all.

relationship between the environment and individuals, families, communities and nations is imperative" (Dustin et al., 2010).

Partnership for Global Sustainable Tourism Criteria

The tourism industry is also engaged in a global effort to address the meaning of sustainable tourism and find common ground in measuring its effectiveness. To that end, the Global Sustainable Tourism Criteria (GSTC) initiative is underway. One of the primary objectives of this initiative is to "build consumer confidence, promote efficiency, and fight green-washing (tourism businesses making claims at being 'green' without merit)" (Partnership for Global Sustainable Tourism Criteria, 2009, p. 1).

The GSTC partnership has developed baseline criteria organized around the four pillars of sustainable tourism:

* Effective sustainability planning
* Maximization of social and economic benefits to the local community
* Reduction of negative impacts to cultural heritage
* Reduction of negative impacts to environmental heritage

These criteria were developed through an expansive consultation process within the tourism industry, including review of more than 60 certification and voluntary sets of criteria already being implemented around the globe. More than 4,500 criteria have been analyzed, with the resulting criteria receiving comments from more than 1,500 stakeholders. Hence, the initiative has significant tourism industry buy-in and support. The expected uses of the criteria include the following (Partnership for Global Sustainable Tourism Criteria, 2009):

* Serve as basic guidelines for businesses of all sizes to become more sustainable, and help businesses choose sustainable tourism programs that fulfill these global criteria
* Serve as guidance for travel agencies in choosing suppliers and sustainable tourism programs
* Help consumers identify sound sustainable tourism programs and businesses
* Help certification and other voluntary programs ensure that their standards meet a broadly accepted baseline
* Offer governmental, nongovernmental, and private sector programs a starting point for developing sustainable tourism requirements
* Serve as baseline guidelines for education and training bodies such as schools of hotel management and universities

Tourism Sustainability Council (TSC) (Certification Accreditation)

In addition to the development of a common language relative to sustainable tourism, a growing need for evaluation of certification programs is recognized. The impetus for the **Tourism Sustainability Council** (TSC) resulted from marketing, communication, and international credibility concerns. For marketing purposes, many organizations make false claims of being "green," creating confusion between tourism certification and other tourism awards and endorsements. There is also confusion among consumers and the industry about the number and variety of certification seals in the marketplace. Several local certification schemes with no international recognition have crept into being. Much of the communication to date is fragmented and isolated, and many efforts have been duplicated. Given the global marketplace, information travels across borders with unprecedented speed, and some certification programs labeled as "eco" are in reality "eco-greenwashing." Consequently, there is a need for an international mechanism to help coordinate efforts and enhance credibility of certification through accreditation (Rainforest Alliance, 2009).

The TSC provides industry support through volunteer collaborative efforts, education, and information on baseline criteria for the tourism industry to embrace. The TSC also works with the baseline criteria to develop standards for credible certification programs around the world. Both efforts under the guidance of the TSC operate with the common goal of protecting the planet and unique worldwide travel experiences.

ISLANDS OF HOPE

Now, more than ever before in history, sustainability is a critical consideration. From the impacts of climate change to the impacts of millions of travelers exploring the globe, the health of the natural world is threatened by human conduct. Encouraging people to recreate in the outdoors—to romp the far reaches of the earth in pursuit of new experiences, cultures, and ecosystems—must be undertaken responsibly and sustainably, so that when we write about leisure and the environment in the future we can extol their same qualities that we do today.

More than a century ago, Theodore Roosevelt defined the importance of our conduct when he said, "Conservation of natural resources is the fundamental problem. Unless we solve that problem it will avail us little to solve all others" (Theodore Roosevelt Association, 2009, p. 1). Roosevelt's statement was prophetic. The value of wild places is incalculable. They provide inspiration to a nation of dreamers, artists, inventors, politicians, engineers, musicians, and citizens who make our country great. These places are storehouses of baseline biological data, providing insight into a natural world that is deteriorating at an alarming rate. They are religious sanctuaries, homes, and burial grounds to native peoples. They are retreats from the trappings of modern technology. They are "islands of hope" (Brown, 1971), where we can slow down and take time off from the hustle and bustle of our fast-paced lives, giving us cause and opportunity to reflect on our place in the world.

SELF-DISCOVERY

Consider where you are today and your dreams for tomorrow. How will you make a difference in the world you live in? What will you contribute? How should you contribute? What are you passionate about? What motivates or inspires you to action or inaction in your life?

Don't simply enjoy the land; work to protect it for future generations.

Our future lies not only in what we create but in what we can preserve of value from the past. Our future lies not only in technological advancement but in how we use those advances to safeguard nature. The greatness of the United States is sung not only in our songs but in the echoes of our canyons and in the whisperings of our pristine wilderness. Our achievements are not merely measured against those of other men and women but against the grandeur of our nation's mountains and deserts. If we cannot see our future, we should at least strive to protect the giant trees from which we hope to gain a better perspective on it, the clear lakes from which we attempt to glimpse a reflection of it, the deep canyons in which we strain to hear its echoes, the wild rivers upon which we pursue it, and the mountain meadows from which we contemplate it.

Wild lands are not something we can create or re-create. Once these lands are altered, once changed, the impacts run through every thread of our existence, and how different we all become. We may never be able to experience the same places and walk the same trails that helped inspire our country's founders to give identity to our nation. Still, the burden to conserve our natural environment rests not solely on the shoulders of the NPS, USFS, BLM, and other governmental agencies but on our own individual shoulders as well. Our obligation is not simply to enjoy the land but to protect it for those who follow us, including nonhuman inhabitants. If we are to remember where we came from and how we got here, protecting wild places that inspired generations before us is crucial. These landscapes helped develop our character and the greatness of our country. What will inspire future generations, and what will they build upon, if we allow these natural treasures to disappear?

SUMMARY

Many people who came before you have changed the way we think about wild places, the out of doors, and responsible use of our planet's natural resources. We understand that through nature, we can learn a lot about ourselves, and the way in which we as human beings fit in the larger picture of life. We also note the importance and challenges of a large outdoor industry and how decisions we make today in managing wild places will ultimately affect future generations. As a society, we use our environmental landscapes in many ways, and one important use is for renewal, recreation, and the health of all beings who inhabit these places. A sustainable future rests on the shoulders of today's generations, and as we have learned from our historical roots, decisions made today affect tomorrow. Many programs and initiatives support conservation of these landscapes, yet how we individually decide to live on the planet affects not only these decisions but also decisions of policy makers and those who take the responsibility to value these places. Will you be a changemaker? How will you contribute to the future? What will your impact be on future generations?

Learning Activities

1. Test your knowledge on treading lightly. Managing agencies, private users, commercial operators, and outdoor retailers are reaching out more than ever to the general public in an attempt to educate outdoor recreationists in the reduction of their impacts and preservation of the experiences they seek to enjoy. One of the more widely known programs is Leave No Trace. Go to www.lnt.org. Click on "Training" at the top of the page. In the drop-down menu click on "Educational and Training Resources." Scroll toward the bottom of the page and click on "Evaluation of Leave No Trace Knowledge Quiz". Print it out and take the quiz.

2. Go to www.lnt.org. Click on "Training" at the top of the page. In the drop-down menu click on "Educational and Training Resources." Under Leave No Trace Presentation Materials, click on "Leave No Trace Slideshow (PowerPoint Format)" and answer the questions provided with this exercise.

For additional assignments, Web links, and more, visit the online student resource at www.HumanKinetics.com/DimensionsOfLeisureForLife.

Review Questions

1. What key events shaped our current use of the outdoors?

2. What challenges are present in managing leisure landscapes for future generations?

3. Why is sustainability important, and how does it affect our leisure environmental landscapes?

4. Considering the present-day use of our leisure landscapes. What influences will shape how these places are managed 25 years from now?

Leisure Reading

Duncan, D., & Burns, K. (2009). *The national parks: America's best idea*. New York: Alfred A. Knopf.

Dustin, D. (2006). *The wilderness within* (3rd ed.). Champaign, IL: Sagamore.

Dustin, D.L., McAvoy, L.H., & Schultz, J.H. (2002). *Stewards of access/custodians of choice*. Champaign, IL: Sagamore.

Esty, D.C., & Winston, A.S. (2006). *Green to gold*. New Haven, CT: Yale University Press.

Mowat, F. (1963). *Never cry wolf*. Boston: Little, Brown.

Schendler, A. (2009). *Getting green done*. New York: Public Affairs.

Glossary

Antiquities Act of 1906—Act that resulted from concerns about protecting mostly prehistoric Indian ruins and artifacts—collectively termed *antiquities*—on U.S. federal lands in the West. This act authorized permits for legitimate archeological investigations and penalties for persons taking or destroying antiquities without permission. It also authorized presidents to proclaim "historic landmarks, historic and prehistoric structures, and other objects of historic or scientific interest" as national monuments, "the limits of which in all cases shall be confined to the smallest area compatible with the proper care and management of the objects to be protected" (www.nps.gov/history/history/hisnps/npshistory/antiq.htm).

Bureau of Land Management—U.S. agency that manages 253 million acres of surface acres of public lands located primarily in the 12 western states, including Alaska. The agency manages an additional 700 million acres of below-ground mineral deposits located throughout the country. Originally, these lands were valued principally for the commodities extracted from them; today, the public also prizes these lands for their recreational opportunities and their natural, historical, and cultural resources (www.blm.gov/wo/st/en/info/About_BLM.html).

Civilian Conservation Corps—Depression-era U.S. government program for unemployed men who performed projects that improved our forests and parks (www.uwsp.edu/natres/nres743/Definitions/CCC.htm).

climate change—A statistically significant variation in the mean state of the climate or its variability, persisting for an extended time (typically decades or longer). Climate change, as defined here, may be caused by natural internal processes or external forcings or by persistent anthropogenic changes in the composition of the atmosphere or land use (www.ipcc.ch/ipccreports/tar/wg2/index.php?idp=663).

global positioning systems—Devices used to geographically identify your position on the earth.

Leave No Trace—Leave No Trace is a national and international program designed to assist outdoor enthusiasts with their decisions about how to reduce their impacts when they hike, camp, picnic, snowshoe, run, bike, hunt, paddle, ride horses, fish, ski, or climb. The program strives to educate all those who enjoy the outdoors about the nature of their recreational impacts as well as techniques to prevent and minimize such impacts. Leave No Trace is best understood as an educational and ethical program, not as a set of rules and regulations (www.lnt.org/programs/index.php).

leisure—Freedom from time-consuming duties, responsibilities, or activities.

manifest destiny—Concept that heavily influenced American policy in the 1800s. The idea that the United States was destined to expand across the continent was the driving force behind the rapid expansion of America from the East Coast to the West, and it was heavily promoted in newspapers, posters, and through other media. Although manifest destiny was not itself an official government policy, it led to the passage of legislation such as the Homestead Act, which encouraged westward colonization and territorial acquisition. This concept also played an important role in American thought (www.wisegeek. com/what-is-manifest-destiny.htm).

National Outdoor Leadership School—Founded in 1965 by legendary mountaineer Paul Petzoldt, NOLS—a 501(c)(3) not-for-profit educational institution—takes people of all ages on remote wilderness expeditions, teaching technical outdoor skills, leadership, and environmental ethics in some of the world's wildest and most awe-inspiring classrooms. What NOLS teaches cannot be learned in a classroom or on a city street. It takes practice to learn outdoor skills and time to develop leadership. The wilderness provides the ideal setting for this unique education (www.nols.edu/about/).

nongovernmental organizations—Nonprofit organizations that work to promote human good while operating separately from any national government. The definition of a nongovernmental organization varies slightly from nation to nation, but most nongovernmental organizations fall within this framework. Because of the somewhat nebulous definition, the total number of nongovernmental organizations worldwide is unknown, with a wide range of estimates available.

Organic Act of 1916—Act by U.S. Congress to establish the U.S. National Park Service (www.yellowstone-online.com/history/NPS1916.html).

Outdoor Industry Foundation—A not-for-profit foundation established by Outdoor Industry Association to inspire future generations of outdoor enthusiasts. Its vision is to be a driving force behind a massive increase in active outdoor recreation in America (www.outdoorfoundation.org/about.html).

Proposition 13—Initiative that added Article XIII A to the California Constitution. This initiative limits property tax rates to no more than 1 percent of full cash value. Increases in assessed value per year are capped at 2 percent or the percentage growth in the Consumer Price Index, whichever is less. In 2002-2003, the increase was 1.87 percent. It has been less than the 2 percent cap only five times since 1977. New construction and the sale of property, with some exceptions, also increase assessed values (www.ed-data.k12.ca.us/Articles/Article.asp?title=Proposition%2013).

sustainability—Meeting the needs of the present without compromising the ability of future generations to meet their own needs (www.afsc.org/TradeMatters/ht/d/sp/i/13425/pid/13425).

Tennessee Valley Authority—A U.S. federal corporation organized in 1933 to provide cheap electric power, flood control, and irrigation by developing the entire basin of the Tennessee River, especially by building dams and reservoirs (www.yourdictionary.com/tennessee-valley-authority).

Tourism Sustainability Council—A global membership council that will offer a common understanding of sustainable tourism and the adoption of universal sustainable tourism principles and criteria. The TSC will bring together tourism businesses presently operating to various degrees of sustainability performance, governments, U.N. bodies, research and academic institutions, social and environmental nongovernmental organizations, certification programs, and others from distinct regions of the world (www. sustainabletourismcriteria.org).

U.S. Department of the Interior—The federal executive department of the U.S. government responsible for the management and conservation of most federal land and the administration of programs relating to Native Americans, Alaska Natives, and Native Hawaiians and to insular areas of the United States. The department is administered by the U.S. Secretary of the Interior, who is a member of the Cabinet of the President. The DOI includes several bureaus: The National Park Service, Bureau of Land Management, U.S. Geological Survey, U.S. Fish and Wildlife Service, Office of Surface Mining, U.S. Minerals Management Service, Bureau of Indian Affairs, and U.S. Bureau of Reclamation (www.doi.gov).

U.S. Forest Service—Agency of the U.S. Department of Agriculture established in 1905. The Forest Service manages public lands in national forests and grasslands. Gifford Pinchot, the first chief of the Forest Service, summed up the mission of the Forest Service: "to provide the greatest amount of good for the greatest amount of people in the long run." National forests and grasslands encompass 193 million acres of land, which is an area equivalent to the size of Texas. With a national headquarters in Washington, DC, the Forest Service operates through nine geographical regions around the United States (www.fs.fed.us/aboutus/).

U.S. National Park Service—A bureau of the Department of the Interior. Directly overseeing its operation is the department's assistant secretary for fish and wildlife and parks. The National Park Service was created by an act signed by President Woodrow Wilson on August 25, 1916. Yellowstone National Park was established by an act signed by President Ulysses S. Grant on March 1, 1872, as the nation's first national park. The National Park System comprises 391 areas covering more than 84 million acres in every state (except Delaware), the District of Columbia, American Samoa, Guam, Puerto Rico, and the Virgin Islands. These areas include national parks, monuments, battlefields, military parks, historical parks, historic sites, lakeshores, seashores, recreation areas, scenic rivers and trails, and the White House (www.nps.gov/faqs.htm).

wilderness—A wild and uncultivated region, as a forest or desert, uninhabited or inhabited only by wild animals.

Works Progress Administration—U.S. work program for the unemployed. Created in 1935 under the New Deal, it aimed to stimulate the economy during the Great Depression and preserve the skills and self-respect of unemployed persons by providing them useful work. During its existence, it employed 8.5 million people in the construction of 650,000 miles (1,046,000 km) of roads, 125,000 public buildings, 75,000 bridges, 8,000 parks, and 800 airports. The WPA also administered the WPA Federal Art Project, the Theater Project, and the Writers' Project, which provided jobs for unemployed artists, actors, and writers. In 1943, with the virtual elimination of unemployment by the wartime economy, the WPA was terminated (www.answers.com/topic/works-progress-administration).

References

Bookbinder, M., Dinerstein, E., Rijal, A., Cauley, H., & Rajouria, A. (1998). Ecotourism's support of biodiversity conservation. *Conservation Biology, 12*(6), 1399-1404.

Brandon, K. (1996). *Ecotourism and conservation: A review of key issues, environmental department papers* (No. 033). Washington, DC: The World Bank.

Brown, W. (1971). *Islands of hope: Parks and recreation in environmental crisis.* Arlington, VA: National Recreation and Park Association.

Ceaser, M. (1998). Wildlife news: Phinda wins tourism award. *African Wildlife, 52,* 37.

Chavez, D. (2000). Wilderness visitors in the 21st century: Diversity, day use, perceptions and preferences. *International Journal of Wilderness, 6*(2), 10-11.

Cordell, H., Betz, C., Green, G., & Owens, M. (2005). *Off-highway vehicle recreation in the United States, regions and states: A national report from the National Survey on Recreation and the Environment (NSRE).* Asheville, NC: USDA Forest Service Southern Research Station.

Curzon, C. (1993). Ecotourism—Conservation ethics—Profit: Getting it right in the eastern Transvaal. *Africa—Environment and Wildlife, 1*(2), 36-42.

Dallen, T., & White, K. (1999). Community-based ecotourism development on the periphery of Belize. *Current Issues in Tourism, 2*(2&3), 226-242.

Dustin, D., Bricker, K., & Schwab, K. (2010). People and nature: Toward an ecological model of health promotion. *Leisure Sciences, 32*(1), 3-14.

Dustin, D., & McAvoy, L. (1980). "Hardining" national parks. *Environmental Ethics, 2*(1), 39-44.

Dustin, D., & McAvoy, L. (1982). The decline and fall of quality recreation opportunities and environments? *Environmental Ethics, 4*(1), 49-57.

Dustin, D., McAvoy, L., & Ogden, L. (2005). Land as legacy. *Parks & Recreation, 40*(5), 60-65.

Garcia, R. (2006). *Equal justice, democracy, and livability: Lessons from the urban park movement.* FLAC Public Interest Law Seminar Series, PILL Roundtable, 30 June 2006. Center for Law in the Public Interest, Los Angeles, CA. www.flac.ie/download/pdf/pil11_rgarcia_urbanpark_rndtbl_30jun06.pdf

Gobster, P. (2002). Managing urban parks for a racially and ethnically diverse clientele. *Leisure Sciences, 24,* 143-159.

Hartig, T., & Evans, G. (1993). Psychological foundation of nature experience. In T. Garling & R. Golledge (Eds.), *Behavior and environment: Psychological and geographical approaches* (pp. 427-457). Bridgewater, NJ: Elsevier Science.

Hartig, T., Mang, M., & Evans, G. (1991). Restorative effects of natural environment experiences. *Environment and Behavior, 23*(1), 3-26.

Honey, M. (1999). *Ecotourism and sustainable development: Who owns paradise?* Washington, DC: Island Press.

Hviding, E., & Bayliss-Smith, T. (2000). Rumors of Utopia: Conservation and eco-tourism. In *Islands of Rainforest: Agroforestry, logging and eco-tourism in Solomon Islands* (pp. 291-320). Burlington, VT: Ashgate.

Jeffreys, A. (1998). Ecotourism in northwest Ecuador. *Geography Review, 11*(3), 26-29.

Kaplan, R. (2001). The nature of the view from home: Psychological benefits. *Environment and Behavior, 33*(4), 507-542.

Kaplan, S. (1995). The restorative benefits of nature: Toward an integrative framework. *Journal of Environmental Psychology, 15,* 169-182.

Koeppel, D. (2000). Costa Rica: Me rainforest, you Jane. *Travel Holiday, 183,* 94-101.

Leopold, A. (1966). *A Sand County almanac: With essays on conservation from Round River.* New York: Ballantine Books.

Limerick, P. (1987). *The legacy of conquest: The unbroken past of the American West.* New York: Norton.

Manning, R. (1999). *Studies in outdoor recreation: Search and research for satisfaction* (2nd ed.). Corvallis: Oregon State University Press.

Marion, J., & Reid, S. (2001). Development of the United States Leave No Trace programme: A historical perspective. In M.B. Usher (Ed.), *Enjoyment and understanding of the natural heritage* (pp. 81-92). Edinburgh: Scottish Natural Heritage, The Stationery Office.

Mwalyosi, R., & Sosovele, H. (2001). *The integration of biodiversity into national environmental assessment procedures—National case studies—Tanzania.* Copenhagen: Biodiversity Planning Support Programme UNDP/UNEP/GEF.

Nash, R. (1967). *Wilderness and the American mind.* New Haven, CT: Yale University Press.

Neighbors, C., Marquez, D., & Marcus, B. (2007). Leisure-time physical activity disparities among Hispanic subgroups in the United States. *American Journal of Public Health First Look, 98*(8), 1460-1464.

Outdoor Industry Association. (n.d.) www.outdoorindustry.org

Outdoor Industry Foundation (OIF). (2006). *The active outdoor recreation economy: A $730 billion annual contribution to the U.S. economy.* Boulder, CO: Outdoor Industry Foundation.

Parks, S., Housemann, R., & Brownson, R. (2003). Differential correlates of physical activity in urban and rural adults of various socioeconomic backgrounds in the United States. *Journal of Epidemiology and Community Health, 57,* 29-35.

Partnership for Global Sustainable Tourism Criteria. (2009). www.sustainabletourismcriteria.org

Passel, J., & Cohn, D. (2008). *U.S. population projections: 2005-2050.* Washington, DC: Pew Research Center: Social and Demographic Trends & Pew Hispanic Center. http://pewhispanic.org/files/reports/85.pdf

Pergams, O., & Zaradic, P. (2006). Is love of nature in the US becoming love of electronic media? 16-year downtrend in national park visits explained by watching movies, playing video games, internet use, and oil prices. *Journal of Environmental Management, 80*(4), 287-293.

Rainforest Alliance. (2009). *Sustainable tourism: Sustainable tourism stewardship council.* www.rainforest-alliance.org/tourism.cfm?id=council

Rodriguez, A. (1999). Kapawi: A model of sustainable development in Equadorean Amazonia. *Cultural Survival Quarterly, 23*(2), 43-44.

Rough Guides. (2007). *World party: The rough guide to the world's best festivals.* New York: Rough Guides.

Sasidharan, V., Willits, F., & Godbey, G. (2005). Cultural differences in urban recreation patterns: An examination of park usage and activity participation across six population subgroups. *Managing Leisure, 10,* 19-38.

Shaull, S., & Gramann, J. (1998). The effect of cultural assimilation on the importance of family-related and nature-related recreation among Hispanic Americans. *Journal of Leisure Research, 30*(1), 47-63.

Smith, A. (1776). *The wealth of nations.* London: Strahan and Cadell.

Theodore Roosevelt Association. (2009). *The address to the Deep Water Way Convention, Memphis, Tennessee, October 4, 1907.* www.theodoreroosevelt.org/life/conservation.htm

Tilton, B. (2003). *Master educator handbook: Leave No Trace outdoor ethics.* Boulder, CO: The Leave No Trace Center for Outdoor Ethics; Lander, WY: The National Outdoor Leadership School.

Tread Lightly. (2009). www.treadlightly.org

Turner, F. (1921). *The frontier in American history.* New York: Holt.

Ulrich, R. (1981). Natural versus urban scenes: Some psychophysiological effects. *Environment and Behavior, 13*(5), 523-556.

United Nations World Commission on the Environment and Development. (1987). *Our common future.* Oxford, UK: Oxford University Press.

U.S. Census Bureau. (2008). *Expectation of life at birth, 1970 to 2005, and projections, 2010 to 2020.* www.census.gov/population/www/projections/2008projections.html

U.S. Census Bureau. (2010). *Global population 2002 and beyond.* www.census.gov/prod/www/abs/popula.html

Virden, R., & Walker, G. (1999). Ethnic/racial and gender variations among meanings given to, and preferences for, the natural environment. *Leisure Sciences, 21,* 219-239.

Wallace, G., & Pierce, S. (1996). An evaluation of ecotourism in Amazonas, Brazil. *Annals of Tourism Research, 23*(4), 848-873.

Whipple, T. (1930). *Study out the land.* Berkeley: University of California Press.

Wolfe, L. (1938). *John of the Mountains: The unpublished journals of John Muir.* Madison: University of Wisconsin Press.

World Health Organization. (2009). *Fact file: Water scarcity.* www.who.int/features/factfiles/water/water_facts/en/index2.html

World Travel and Tourism Council. (2007). *Key facts at a glance.* www.wttc.org/eng/Tourism_Research/Economic_Research/Country_Reports/United_States_of_America/index.php

10

Economics of Leisure

Brent Beggs

Illinois State University

Learning Outcomes

After reading this chapter, you will be able to

▶ explain the role that economic status once played in determining leisure,

▶ demonstrate an understanding of the relationship between economics and leisure,

▶ describe the significant economic impact that different sectors of the leisure service industry have on society, and

▶ know key economic terms related to leisure services, such as *discretionary income, direct expenditure, indirect expenditure,* and *economic multiplier.*

Vocabulary Terms

direct expenditure   economic multiplier   leakage

discretionary income   indirect expenditure

©Stephen Mally/Icon SMI

Just hanging out with friends during leisure time typically has an economic impact.

It is a typical Friday afternoon on campus and Brendan is making plans for the weekend. He and some friends decide to cook some hamburgers on the grill. Brendan makes a run to the grocery store and spends $20 on ground beef, buns, chips, and beverages. Upon returning home, he fires up the grill, and he and his friends play a game of bags while consuming beverages. After they eat, they decide to go to the local pub to meet some other friends and hang out for the evening. At the end of the evening, after spending $20 at the pub, Brendan stops at the all-night taco joint for a snack where he spends another $5. After sleeping in on Saturday morning, Brendan calls his girlfriend and makes plans with her to rent a movie and order a pizza that night, which will cost him another $20. By the time Sunday rolls around, Brendan decides to do his homework and then download some music. He purchases $15 worth of music.

Brendan has spent $80 on the weekend and really hasn't had any large expenditures or done anything special. If there are 20,000 students at Brendan's college and each spends $80 over the weekend, the total amount of expenditures by college students in that community over one weekend is $1.6 million. If there are four weekends in a month, that translates into $6.4 million in expenditures. If college students are on campus for 9 months of the year, that results in $57.6 million in expenditures per year. That figure only accounts for college students' weekend expenses and does not consider weekday expenses. Also, consider that college students aren't known for having lots of discretionary income. This figure doesn't account for other expenditures by residents in the community who have much higher levels of income and more likely to have more discretionary expenses.

The economic impact that college students have on society is surprising. The average college student spends about $324 a month on discretionary activities (State University, 2009). Consider that there are more than 4,000 colleges in the United States (U.S. Department of Education, National Center for Education Statistics, 2005) and approximately 13.6 million college students (Alloy Media and Marketing, 2008). This translates into $53 billion of discretionary income for college students (Alloy Media and Marketing, 2008). Some of this spending may be for clothing or electronics, but it is estimated that college students spend nearly $3 billion a year on movies, DVDs, and video games and $11 billion a year on snacks and beverages (State University, 2009). The economic impact of college student expenditures during leisure time is staggering when you consider that we typically don't consider college students to have high levels of income. The leisure service industry is often regarded as an industry of service. However, the economic impact of leisure services cannot be ignored. All people participate in some type of leisure activity, and we have to pay for many of those activities.

This chapter looks at the relationship of economics and leisure and the impact that the leisure service industry has on the economy. The relationship of economics to leisure is discussed by examining the role that economic status once played in determining one's leisure and social status. Although the role that economics plays in determining one's leisure can be debated, it cannot be debated that leisure has a significant economic impact on society. The chapter introduces some key economic terms and also demonstrates the significant economic impact that different sectors of the leisure service industry have on society.

RELATIONSHIP OF ECONOMICS AND LEISURE

Leisure services are designed to provide quality experiences for all people. However, leisure service agencies also operate as businesses. Being such, the agencies typically incur costs by providing services and products. Because of this, consumers must pay to participate in activities or obtain products from leisure service agencies. In some instances, these costs may be minimal; however, costs associated with leisure activities and products can be significant. These costs frequently create barriers to participation in leisure activities. If people do not have the money to participate in an activity, they will probably find something else to do.

It has long been argued that leisure participation is designed for those who can afford it, and, in fact, having leisure is a symbol of status (memberships in country clubs, eating at ritzy restaurants, or owning an expensive car or boat are examples of social status being defined by leisure). The theory of the leisure class (a theory as well as a book by the same title; Veblen, 1899), although economic in nature, had strong social implications for the United States and suggested that only the wealthy could afford and were entitled to leisure. This idea is based on the principle that people spend their discretionary income on leisure services. **Discretionary income** is money that you have after paying taxes and paying for necessities such as food and shelter. Discretionary income is usually higher for people who make more money. So, the argument is that if you make more money, then you have more money to spend on leisure. The theory of the leisure class suggested that if you were in a high social class and had a high income, then you could afford leisure. The theory also stated that those who only had enough money for the necessities of life and were in a low social and economic class could not afford leisure and that this was reflected in their status in society.

> Conspicuous consumption of valuable goods is a means of reputability to the gentleman of leisure.
>
> *Thorsten Veblen, 1899*

We have come a long way in understanding leisure since the theory of the leisure class was proposed in 1899. We now understand that leisure isn't only about money but is more about time for leisure and meaning of activities that take place during leisure time. In fact, you could argue that those who have high incomes and work many hours during the week do not have as much leisure as those who make less money, because the people with high incomes have less time for leisure. This is a paradox of leisure: Money allows us the opportunity for leisure, but the time required to earn that money limits opportunities for leisure.

©Eyewire/Getty Images

Skiing is not always just for the wealthy, but is it still a sign of social class?

Whether you agree with the theory of the leisure class, you cannot ignore the fact that participation in leisure services can be limited by money. A typical college student cannot afford to travel every weekend or purchase high-end leisure products. In fact, lack of money is a significant barrier to leisure participation (Crawford & Godbey, 1987). However, if our activities are limited because of money, we still find other leisure outlets. Regardless of how much discretionary income we have, we still manage to spend money on leisure services.

PERSONAL LEISURE

Think about what you spend your money on. If you were to write it down, would it surprise you?

SPENDING MONEY ON LEISURE

The money spent on leisure services is extraordinary. According to the 2007 U.S. Economic Census, we spent $190.5 billion on recreation that year. This number seems astounding, and it only takes into account the direct impact that recreation has on the economy. Many leisure service activities also have an indirect impact. Take, for instance, someone who travels out of town for the weekend to attend a concert. The direct expense is the concert ticket. There are also considerable indirect expenses such as travel (air travel or gas for car travel), dining, clothing, souvenirs, and accommodations such as a hotel. To estimate the economic impact of leisure services, we must consider both **direct expenditure** and **indirect expenditure**. Another consideration in understanding economic impact is the degree that money spent on leisure services is "re-spent" in the community. For instance, you eat at a nice restaurant with friends and have a $100 tab. Part of that $100 goes to staff wages. The staff may spend some of that money on rent or groceries. In that instance, the grocer may spend some of that money on dry cleaning or the landlord may spend some of that money hiring a plumber. The dry cleaner or plumber will spend some of that money as well, and so on and so on. The idea is that some of the money that is spent on leisure services is spent again within the community and may be spent over and over again. The concept is called the **economic multiplier**, and every community has one. In a community that has many businesses and in which money keeps turning over within the community, the economic multiplier is high. In a community where products are purchased outside a community, the economic multiplier is lower. Money spent outside the local economy is called **leakage**.

©Bananastock

Part of the money spent on this meal will be used to pay wages. In turn, the restaurant staff will spend some of that money on their own leisure.

Economic impact occurs in all sectors of leisure services. Typically, the commercial recreation sector is the first that comes to mind when we discuss economic impact. However, municipal and not-for-profit leisure service agencies significantly affect the economy as well. The following section provides a sample of the economic impact of different sectors of leisure services. Some of the numbers in the upcoming snippets are staggering, and these are only some of the types of leisure service organizations; there are many others.

COMMERCIAL RECREATION

Commercial recreation agencies are primarily funded through money collected by the resale of their products or services. Because it is rare for commercial recreation agencies to have other sources of revenue and because their intent is to make a profit, they typically charge more money for their programs and services than do municipal and not-for-profit agencies. Thus, the impact of the many different types of commercial recreation agencies on the economy is significant. Commercial recreation can include things such as travel and tourism, sporting events, health clubs, golf courses, special events and festivals, food services, retail products, amusement and aquatic parks, and gambling. Following is a glimpse of the economic impact of these commercial recreation industries.

Travel and Tourism

Travel and tourism include the movement of people to leisure destinations around the world. This industry has grown considerably as modes of travel have improved. According to the World Tourism Organization (2009), from 1950 to 2007, international tourist arrivals grew from 25 million to 903 million. These tourism numbers translate into $3 billion in receipts per day and more than $1 trillion a year! Even more astounding is that tourist arrivals have been increasing between 5 and 7 percent each year, and it is estimated that there will be more than 1 billion international arrivals by the year 2010 and 1.6 billion by the year 2020. In addition to generating revenue from tourist travel, the tourism industry employs more than 200 million people internationally (World Travel and Tourism Council, 2009).

PERSONAL LEISURE

Think about your last family vacation. How much money did your family spend on travel? How much was spent on lodging? How much was spent on food and beverage? How much was spent on souvenirs, shopping, or attending an event? Estimate the total cost for the trip.

Sporting Events

Another leisure service industry that makes a significant contribution to the economy is sporting events. Sporting events that take place before a paying audience generate direct and indirect revenue that can have a major impact on a local or regional economy. There are more than 4,000 professional or semiprofessional sport teams in the United States (U.S. Census, 2009). The sporting event industry employs more than 100,000 people and generates more than $22 billion in revenue (U.S. Census, 2009).

The National Football League (NFL) is one of the most well-known leagues of professional sports in the United States. Although attendance varies from city to city, the impact that the NFL has on the economy is worth noting. NFL teams, over a season, can have an economic impact of more than $100 million in their host cities (Fans, Taxpayers and Business Alliance, 2009). The culminating event of the NFL, the Super Bowl, has an even greater impact. It is estimated that the 2009 Super Bowl had a $300 to $400 million economic impact on the Tampa Bay area (National Football League, 2009). Most of the Super Bowl attendees (85 percent) are from another state and travel by plane (Touchdown Experiences, 2009). In addition to travel expenses, visitors spend an average of four nights in a hotel in the host city (Touchdown Experiences, 2009). More than 50 million people in the United States attend a local Super Bowl party and nearly 10 million will go to a bar or restaurant to watch the game (Big Research, 2005). During the week of the Super Bowl, consumers purchase 1.4 million televisions and more than 500,000 pieces of furniture to use when watching the game (Big Research, 2005).

Watching a big game with friends is a popular leisure activity that can affect the economy.

Another major sport league in the United States is Major League Baseball (MLB). The MLB (2008) reports that between major league and minor league baseball, more than 122 million spectators attended a professional baseball game in 2008. Like the NFL, MLB has a culminating event, in this case the World Series. The World Series consists of multiple games in two host cities. It is estimated that each game of the World Series has an economic impact of $6.8 million on the host city (Matheson and Baade, 2005).

Health Clubs

The health club industry includes agencies that typically require memberships and offer a variety of fitness opportunities. Some health clubs may also offer various aquatic, sport, child care, food, and entertainment options for members. About half of health clubs are commercial facilities, according to the International Health, Racquet and Sportsclub Association (2009). More than 41 million people have health club memberships in the United States and Canada and more than 105 million internationally. There are more than 92,000 health club facilities worldwide, most of whose members are adults. The majority of health club members are age 35 to 54; however, the fastest-growing segment is adults over the age of 55, which has grown more than 400 percent since 1990. Health club memberships for an individual can be as little as $25 per month, but most are much more expensive. Many clubs have membership categories for families, older adults, or other specialty groups. Revenue generated by the health club industry has increased by more than 100 percent since 1995. This may be attributed to an increase in the number of health club facilities during that time and an increase in the number of memberships. The health club industry generates more than $16 billion in revenue annually, and that number also continues to grow (International Health, Racquet and Sportsclub Association, 2009).

Golf Courses

Golf is an industry that has seen considerable growth over the last 25 years. According to statistics from the National Golf Foundation (2008), more than 29.5 million people play golf in the United States, an increase of 50 percent since 1985. Approximately 16,000 golf courses exist in the United States and 32,000 worldwide (Golf Research Group, 2008). Consumer spending on golf equipment and green fees has increased from $7.8 billion in 1982 to $24.3 billion in 2007 (National Golf Foundation, 2008). The golf industry generated a total economic impact of $195 billion in 2005 and employed approximately 2 million people (SRI International, 2005). Golf may have reached its peak in growth, as more than 1,000 golf courses shut down between 2002 and 2007 and the number of golfers in the United States decreased 6.2 percent between 2005 and 2007 (Golf Research Group, 2008). Regardless, the golf industry makes a significant contribution to the economy.

Special Events and Festivals

Special events and festivals take place in all communities, regardless of size or accessibility. Special events and festivals take the form of large-scale events that last many days or small events that occur in one afternoon; they take place in large metropolitan areas or small rural communities. These types of events can be hosted by municipalities, state departments of tourism and commerce, theme parks, convention and visitors bureaus, chambers of commerce, independent event planners and consultants, media, sponsors, industry suppliers, and educational institutions (International Festival and Events Association, 2009). Events include local cultural celebrations, conference expositions, parades, corporate gatherings, and Olympics opening ceremonies. The International Festival and Events Associa-

RESEARCH TO REALITY

Identify a festival in your home town and do some research. How long has the event been in existence? How many people attend? How much money do you spend when you attend the festival? Does this event have an economic impact on the community?

tion (2009) estimates that between 5 and 6 million regularly occurring festivals and events are held throughout the world annually. There are numerous one-time events as well, less-than-annual major events, and smaller informal events every year. The festivals and events industry is estimated to have economic impact that reaches more than $1 trillion (International Festival and Events Association, 2009).

Food Services

The food service industry is a large part of the recreation industry. Many recreation facilities provide vending and concession services to patrons. Facilities that host special events and sporting events rely heavily on concessions as a major source of revenue. However, the main source of revenue from food services is generated through the restaurant industry. Visiting a restaurant for a meal is a popular leisure activity and has a major impact on the economy. In the United States, on an average day, 133 million people go to a restaurant. The restaurant industry generates more than $1.5 billion in sales in 1 day and $566 billion in sales in a year! There are approximately 945,000 restaurants in the United States, and the restaurant industry employs more than 13 million people (National Restaurant Association, 2008).

Retail Products

Products purchased for use during leisure activities affect the economy significantly. Americans spend $4 billion on golf equipment and $5.5 billion on exercise equipment annually. It is estimated that more than $25 billion is spent annually on sporting goods equipment (National Sporting Goods Association, 2008). More than $17 billion is spent annually on sporting goods footwear and nearly $11 billion on sporting goods clothing. In 2007, recreational transportation, such as bicycles, snowmobiles, boats, and recreational vehicles, generated more than $37 billion in sales (National Sporting Goods Association, 2008). Retail product purchases are not limited to sporting goods. It is estimated that Americans spent $9.66 billion purchasing music in 2007 and $18.85 billion on video games (International Federation of the Phonographic Industry, 2008). The video gaming business continues to grow at a rapid rate. The video game industry is expected to generate $65.9 billion in sales by 2011 (ABI Research, 2008).

Amusement and Aquatic Parks

Amusement parks attracted more than 341 million visitors in 2007 in the United States and generated $12 billion in revenue. The amusement park industry includes more than 450 parks in the United States and employs approximately 500,000 people (International Association of Amusement Parks and Attractions, 2008). Amusement parks can be a regional attraction, such as Six Flags, which is the largest regional amusement park system. In 2007, Six Flags generated $972 million in revenue (Six Flags, 2008). Other amusement parks are also much larger in scope and serve as an international attraction. The most well-known and most visited amusement park is Walt Disney World's Magic Kingdom (Themed Entertainment Association, 2008). In 2007, 17.06 million people visited Walt Disney World's Magic Kingdom and 14.87 million people visited Disneyland Park in California; these parks generated more than $35 billion in revenue (Mouse Planet, 2008). Aquatic parks attract many users. There are more than 1,000 water parks in North America,

We spend lots of money to get into an amusement park and even more once we are inside.

which attract more than 73 million visitors annually (World Waterpark Association, 2005). This industry continues to grow at a rapid rate, with an 11 percent increase in visitors from 2006 to 2007 (Themed Entertainment Association, 2008).

Gambling

The gambling industry includes various forms of gambling. Despite the many legal restrictions on gaming in the United States, the gambling industry is growing rapidly. In 2007, 54.5 million people visited casinos in the United States and spent $93.8 billion. That was a 184 percent increase in revenue generation over a 10-year period (American Gaming Association, 2008). Most of that revenue was generated through gambling; however, the gambling industry also generates revenue by providing casino visitors with amenities such as hotels, restaurants, and retail shopping. The casino experience is more than just gambling for many guests. According to the American Gaming Association (2008), 72 percent of casino visitors reported eating at a fine-dining restaurant in 2007 as part of their visit to the casino.

MUNICIPAL RECREATION

Municipal recreation agencies exist at local, state, and federal levels in the United States. These agencies receive most of their revenue from taxes. Because people support these agencies by paying taxes, municipal agencies typically charge low fees for programs and services. However, municipal recreation still has a significant impact on the economy.

The National Park Service consists of approximately 400 parks and recreational sites across the United States. In 2007, more than 272 million people visited a national park, generating a total of $308 million in revenue. There are 8,500 campgrounds located in-route or near national parks and tourist attractions (Go Camping America, 2008). Indirect expenses associated with visiting national parks generated $10 billion of economic impact for local economies (National Park Service, 2008).

There are more than 5,800 state park areas in the United States, which host more than 700 million visitors annually. Many state park areas are free to visit, although fees are charged to visit some areas and for camping. Nearly half of those who visited a state park in 2007 visited an area that charged a fee (National Association of State Park Directors, 2008). National parks employ more than 20,000 people in full-time and part-time capacities (National Association of State Park Directors, 2008).

NOT-FOR-PROFIT RECREATION

Despite the term *not-for-profit*, that sector of leisure services has a significant impact on the economy. Not-for-profit organizations create considerable economic activity; however, unlike agencies in the commercial sector, not-for-profit organizations put their revenue back into the organization and its programs. In the commercial sector, revenue generated often goes toward employee bonuses or dividends to stockholders.

The majority of not-for-profit organizations in the United States are in the fields of health care (42 percent) and education (22 percent) (Independent Sector, 2008). The not-for-profit sector in leisure services includes many organizations that are advocates for the environment, such as Greenpeace, Rainforest Action Network, Sierra Club, Nature Conservancy, and Rainforest Alliance. Most not-for-profit organizations operate with a mission to serve a cause.

Not-for-profit organizations employ more than 12 million people in the United States (Independent Sector, 2008). Two of the most well-known not-for-profit organizations in leisure services are the YMCA and the Boys & Girls Clubs of America. The 2,686 YMCAs in the United States serve more than 21 million people (YMCA, 2009). The YMCA generates $5.96 billion in revenue annually. Most of that money comes from program fees and memberships, but the Y also receives more than $900 million in donations and nearly $700 million in grants annually (YMCA, 2009). The Boys & Girls Clubs of America serve 4.8 million boys and girls and have 4,300 locations. These clubs employ more than 50,000 people and in 2007 generated approximately $195 million in revenue (Boys & Girls Clubs of America, 2008).

The not-for-profit sector of leisure services serves many people. It also employs a considerable number of leisure services professionals and generates billions of dollars in economic activity.

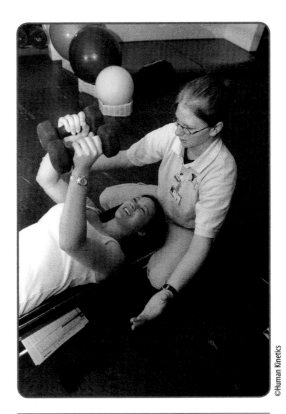

©Human Kinetics

The YMCA is a not-for-profit leisure services organization that generates almost $6 billion in revenue annually.

SUMMARY

All sectors of leisure services have a significant impact on the economy. However, for years, commercial recreation has been the sector that has followed a business model with its focus on revenue generation. Not-for-profit and municipal leisure service agencies have operated on a service model, focusing on the customer and providing the best experience possible. In an effort to do this, not-for-profit agencies and municipal agencies have worked to keep costs down. With the battle for tax and grant money in society today, these agencies are not supported by government, as they once were. The call to action for future leaders in the field is to embrace the quality of the service model and to incorporate the concepts of the business model. Revenue generation in all sectors of leisure services will only become more important over the years, and administrators and professionals in these areas must develop agencies that can be self-sustaining, as are commercial agencies. If this happens, you can expect the economic impact of leisure services to be even greater than it is today.

Regardless of our economic situation, we will spend money on leisure activities. Society has moved beyond the idea that leisure is a status symbol. Leisure is for everyone, and everyone spends money on leisure services and products. The economic impact of leisure is tremendous and continues to grow in all sectors of leisure services.

Learning Activities

1. **U.S. Economic Census:** Select a type of leisure service that is present in your community. Go to the U.S. 2007 Economic Census Web site (http://factfinder.census.gov/servlet/IBQTable?_bm=y&-geo_id=D&-ds_name=EC0271A1&-_lang=en) and determine how that type of leisure service is categorized. Then, identify the number of establishments in the United States and the amount of revenue generated from that type of business.

2. **Leisure inventory:** Identify all of the leisure products that you own. Place a monetary value on each item and total all of the values. What is the overall value of your leisure inventory? Is it more or less than you thought it would be?

For additional assignments, Web links, and more, visit the online student resource at www.HumanKinetics.com/DimensionsOfLeisureForLife.

Review Questions

1. What role did economic status once play in leisure?

2. Explain the relationship between economics and leisure.

3. Describe the significant economic impact that different sectors of the leisure service industry have on society.

4. What is discretionary income, and why is it important to leisure?

5. What is a direct expenditure? An indirect expenditure?

6. Explain the concept of the economic multiplier.

Leisure Reading

Schor, J. (1998). *The overspent American*. New York: HarperCollins.

Tribe, J. (2004). *The economics of recreation, leisure and tourism* (3rd ed.). Burlington, MA: Elsevier.

Veblen, T. (1899). *The theory of the leisure class*. Whitefish, MT: Kessinger.

Glossary

direct expenditure—Money spent to purchase the primary leisure service or product.

discretionary income—Money that is made after taxes have been taken out and necessities such as food and shelter have been accounted for.

economic multiplier—The degree that money spent on leisure services in a community is re-spent in the same community.

indirect expenditure—Money spent on leisure services or products that support the primary leisure service or product.

leakage—Money spent in a community that is re-spent outside the community.

References

ABI Research. (2008). *Video game business to double by 2011, driven by online and mobile gaming.* www.abiresearch.com/press/600-Video+Game+Business+to+Double+by+2011,+Driven+by+Online+and+Mobile+Gaming

Alloy Media and Marketing. (2008). *The class of 2012 grows up green: College students back on campus in record numbers, with more green in their pockets and greener practices on their minds.* Available at: www.alloymarketing.com/investor_relations/news_releases/index.html

American Gaming Association. (2008). *2008 state of the states, the AGA survey of casino entertainment.* www.americangaming.org/survey/index.cfm

Big Research. (2005). *Super Bowl Sunday becoming big business for retailers, advertisers.* www.bigresearch.com/news/bignrf012705.htm

Boys & Girls Clubs of America. (2008). *Who we are: The facts.* www.bgca.org/whoweare/facts.asp

Crawford, D.W., & Godbey, G. (1987). Reconceptualizing barriers to family leisure. *Leisure Sciences, 9,* 119-127.

Fans, Taxpayers and Business Alliance. (2009). *Economic impact of NFL teams.* http://ftballiance.org/stadiums/impact.php

Go Camping America. (2008). www.gocampingamerica.com

Golf Research Group. (2008). www.golf-research-group.com/start.html

Independent Sector. (2008). *Nonprofit almanac: Facts and findings.* www.independentsector.org/economic_role

International Association of Amusement Parks and Attractions. (2008). *Amusement park and attractions industry statistics.* www.iaapa.org/pressroom/Amusement_Park_Industry_Statistics.asp

International Federation of the Phonographic Industry. (2008). *Music market statistics.* www.ifpi.org/content/section_statistics/index.html

International Festival and Events Association. (2009). www.ifea.com/joomla1_5/

International Health, Racquet and Sportsclub Association. (2009). *Consumer research.* http://cms.ihrsa.org/index.cfm?fuseaction=Page.viewPage&pageId=19549&nodeID=15

Major League Baseball. (2008). *National League, seven clubs set all-time attendance records.* http://mlb.mlb.com/news/press_releases/press_release.jsp?ymd=20081001&content_id=3578727&vkey=pr_mlb&fext=.jsp&c_id=mlb

Matheson, V., & Baade, R. (2005). *A fall classic? Assessing the economic impact of the World Series.* College of the Holy Cross, Department of Economics Faculty Research Series, Working Paper No. 05-01. http://academics.holycross.edu/files/econ_accounting/Matheson_WorldSeries.pdf

Mouse Planet. (2008). *Walt Disney world park update.* www.mouseplanet.com/8271/Walt_Disney_World_Park_Update

National Association of State Park Directors. (2008). www.naspd.org

National Football League. (2009). *Super Bowl XLIII quick facts.* http://tampabaysuperbowl.com/sponsor_sb43.htm

National Golf Foundation. (2008). www.ngf.org

National Park Service. (2008). *Quick facts.* www.nps.gov/aboutus/quickfacts.htm

National Restaurant Association. (2008). *2008 national restaurant industry pocket factbook.* www.restaurant.org/pdfs/research/2008forecast_factbook.pdf

National Sporting Goods Association. (2008). www.nsga.org/i4a/pages/index.cfm?pageid=1

Six Flags. (2008). *Financial release.* http://investors.sixflags.com/phoenix.zhtml?c=61629&p=irol-newsArticle&ID=1116721

SRI International. (2005). *The 2005 golf economy report.* Menlo Park, CA: SRI International. www.golf2020.com/reports/2005GolfEconomy%20Report.pdf

State University. (2009). *A look at the spending habits of college students.* www.stateuniversity.com/blog/permalink/The-Spending-Habits-of-College-Students.html

Themed Entertainment Association. (2008). www.themeit.com

Touchdown Experiences. (2009). www.touchdownhotels.com/super-bowl-xliii-hotels.html

U.S. Census. (2009). http://factfinder.census.gov

U.S. Department of Education, National Center for Education Statistics. (2005). *2003-04 National Postsecondary Student Aid Study (NPSAS:04) undergraduate financial aid estimates for 2003-04 by type of institution (NCES 2005-163).* Washington, DC: U.S. Department of Education.

U.S. Economic Census. (2007). http://factfinder.census.gov/servlet/IBQTable?_bm=y&-geo_id=D&-ds_name=EC0271A1&-_lang=en

Veblen, T. (1899). *The theory of the leisure class.* Whitefish, MT: Kessinger.

World Tourism Organization. (2009). *Facts and figures.* http://unwto.org/facts/menu.html

World Travel and Tourism Council. (2009). www.wttc.org

World Waterpark Association. (2005). www.waterparks.org

YMCA. (2009). www.ymca.net

11

Leisure, Politics, and Public Policy

Robert Barcelona
Clemson University

Learning Outcomes

After reading this chapter, you will

- ▶ understand the concept of politics and its connection with leisure behavior,
- ▶ understand the government's role in leisure services provision,
- ▶ understand how politics influences the development of public policy, and
- ▶ become familiar with key public policy areas affecting leisure behavior.

Vocabulary Terms

blue laws	life politics	public policy
city manager–council	morale, welfare, and recreation	separation of powers
commons		special district
efficiency	parliamentary system	strong mayor–council
enabling legislation	pluralist politics	Supremacy Clause
federalism	public goods	

©Katrina Brown/fotolia

Publicly accessible leisure spaces such as national parks provide benefits to both individuals and society.

Have you ever been to a local, state, or national park or recreation area? How did the experience affect you? Maybe you had the chance to learn something about the history of your country, or perhaps you had the chance to renew yourself physically, emotionally, or spiritually. Maybe you had the opportunity to marvel at a unique natural wonder, like the geysers in Yellowstone, the waterfalls in Yosemite, or the swamps in the Everglades. As you reflect on these experiences, have you ever considered what would happen if these places weren't protected or available to the public to visit? Think about recreation opportunities closer to home, perhaps even those offered at your college or university. What if there were no leisure spaces, places, activities, or opportunities available to you? Or what if the opportunities that were available didn't meet your needs or you believed that you had no say in what was available to you? These questions highlight the political nature of leisure services delivery, and in this chapter we examine its implications for our leisure lifestyles as well as for the management of leisure programs and resources.

You don't often put *politics* and *leisure* in the same sentence. When thinking about leisure, you tend to think about personal preferences, developmental experiences, and positive effect. Generally, the terms *power, control, influence, policy, stakeholders,* or *government bureaucracies* seem to run counter to the very idea of leisure as freely chosen activities done for their own sake.

However, leisure is experienced socially as well as individually, and much of our leisure takes place in or on public spaces, such as parks, playgrounds, schools, recreation centers, athletic fields, arts centers, museums, and concert halls. Being public spaces, all of these venues have been developed and are managed by some external body with the authority to make decisions that influence the way leisure is experienced in these places. For example, someone must decide where to locate a new playground, how much public money will be spent to build it, who will be eligible to use it, how it will be used, and who will be responsible for management and upkeep. The same is true with any number of public spaces used for leisure and recreation activity.

All of these decisions are political—they involve issues of power, control, and influence. All of these decisions affect the way you experience leisure, including what you do and when, where, and how you do it. Because of this, it is important to view leisure through a political lens to better understand how these decisions are made, how they affect your life, and how you might be able to influence their outcomes. This chapter focuses on the political aspect of leisure, including the concept of politics, the government's role in leisure, how public policy is formed, and how it affects leisure behavior.

GOVERNMENTAL ROLE IN LEISURE

When you think about politics, you tend to think about the governing of society. Government is a good starting point in thinking about the political process. Thinking about the formal levels of the U.S. government's power—the executive, legislature, and judiciary—is useful, because it is through these mechanisms that priorities are set, compromises are brokered, and decisions are made that affect the citizenry.

> There can be nothing in the world more beautiful than the Yosemite, the groves of giant sequoias and redwoods, the Canyon of the Colorado, the Canyon of the Yellowstone, the Three Tetons; and our people should see to it that they are preserved for their children and their children's children forever, with their majestic beauty all unmarred.
>
> *Theodore Roosevelt, 1908*

Western democracies, such as the United States and Canada, most often have three branches of government—the executive, legislative, and judicial branches. Although the actual form of these branches of government differ from system to system, the basic framework holds true. In the classic sense, the legislative branch makes and debates laws and other forms of legislation, the executive branch helps to set policy and carry out the work of the legislature, and the judiciary ensures that laws and policies created by the other branches meet constitutional muster.

Legislative Branch

In the United States, the legislature is truly a law-making body (Grant, 2004). The major function of the U.S. Congress—the House of Representatives and the Senate—is to introduce bills and make laws. This is similar at the state level. Although it is true that law and public policy are often formulated elsewhere, both inside and outside of government, by a variety of executive agencies and public interest and advocacy groups, it usually

©Human Kinetics

What are some of the political decisions that need to be made prior to and following the development of public recreation areas, like this community sports complex?

Ever wonder how politicians affect your leisure experiences? Do some research on one of the following acts: National Park Service Organic Act of 1916, Multiple Use-Sustained Yield Act of 1960, Wilderness Act, Federal Water Project Recreation Act, Wild and Scenic Rivers Act, or National Trails Systems Act. What was the legislation about? What effect did it have on leisure in general? How did it affect your leisure experiences specifically? What do you think about more recent legislation that is working its way through Congress, such as the No Child Left Inside Act (2008) or the Paid Vacation Act (2009)? Do you think these are good ideas? Why or why not?

takes an active and supportive member of the legislative branch to help turn public policy ideas into law (Peters, 1996).

Hundreds of laws have been passed by federal and state legislatures dealing with parks and recreation provision and leisure behavior. Every time you visit a national park, you experience the influence of the legislative branch. For example, the National Park Service Organic Act of 1916 is the law passed by Congress that created the National Park Service. Other laws such as the Multiple Use-Sustained Yield Act, Wilderness Act, Federal Water Project Recreation Act, Wild and Scenic Rivers Act, and National Trails Systems Act help provide opportunities for recreation delivery and regulate visitor behavior and land use. At the federal and state level, legislatures pass **enabling legislation** that provides the authority for appropriate administrative bodies or officials to carry out mandates or enforce the laws. Enabling legislation at the federal level is used to provide guidance in managing specific national parks and provides authority to manage aspects of armed forces **morale, welfare, and recreation** (MWR) programs. At the state level, enabling legislation might create special parks and recreation districts or empower county and municipal governments to provide parks and recreation services or create conservation commissions.

Federal and state legislatures also make laws that regulate and control certain types of leisure behavior. For example, federal drug laws establish the legal status of controlled substances. Some drugs, such as codeine, are legal to possess with a valid prescription, whereas others such as heroin

The United States Capitol is the home of the legislative branch of the U.S. government and is the place where federal legislation is debated and passed.

©Christopher Howey/fotolia

are illegal in all circumstances. Federal and state laws limit or prohibit prostitution, pornography, and sex trafficking. Even alcohol and tobacco use is regulated by state laws, including the legal age of purchase and possession. In some states, laws restrict alcohol purchases to special state-run liquor stores. Local legislatures sometimes pass laws prohibiting the sale of alcohol at certain times and days, such as prohibitions on the sale of alcohol on Sundays. Laws that are enacted to protect the Sabbath, traditionally defined as Sunday, from commercial or other forms of activity are sometimes referred to as **blue laws**. These laws are sometimes broadened to restrict other types of activities primarily because of concerns with moral or ethical standards. For example, there may be laws dictating where adult-only clubs can be located or where places that sell adult media or products (e.g., magazines, videos, paraphernalia) can be purchased.

In addition to making laws, the legislature serves as an important check on the executive branch through its oversight function, represents the interests of the American people, and, perhaps most important for leisure services provision, controls the budget and allocates scarce tax dollars. In fact, most of the National Recreation and Park Association's major legislative priorities deal with funding and resource allocation (see figure 11.1).

The legislative branch in the United States is a separate and independent branch of government. This idea of a **separation of powers** was developed by the founders of the United States to avoid an accumulation of power within one branch of government. The U.S. Congress may coordinate with the president on legislative matters, but the responsibility for making and passing laws rests primarily with the members of Congress. This often makes for a slow and deliberate legislative process that has been described as an "obstacle race" (Grant, 2004). The legislative process in other Western democracies with strong parliamentary forms of government, such as Great Britain or Canada, is different. Governments under the **parliamentary system** have the ability to both make and execute laws. The executive in a

---

FIGURE 11.1

Legislative Priorities: National Recreation and Park Association (2009)

1. Appropriate $125 million in funding for the Land and Water Conservation Fund Stateside Assistance program.

2. Appropriate $50 million to specifically fund urban parks through programs such as the Urban Park and Recreation Recovery program (UPARR) or other federal programs.

3. Fund the Community Development Block Grant program at $4.6 billion.

4. Increase funding in the reauthorization of the Surface Transportation Program for bike and pedestrian trails; the recreational trails program; boating safety and fishing education; Safe Routes to School; and other transportation-related programs that improve community health and livability.

5. Ensure that legislation that expands environmental education identifies park and recreation agencies as entities that are eligible for direct funding. This will allow agencies to partner with state and local education agencies and nonprofit organizations to actively engage children in nature and expand environmental education.

parliamentary system is the head of the government. The "government" is the political party with the most members or largest coalition in the legislature. The primary function of the parliamentary legislature in these countries is to debate and pass laws introduced by the government. This makes for a less cumbersome legislative process but one that is less responsive to checks and balances.

Executive Branch

The executive branch in the United States consists of the president, vice president, Executive Office of the President (EOP), and the cabinet (see figure 11.2). Although the president, and, to some extent, the vice president, are the most visible members of the executive branch, more than 1.7 million civilians are employed in positions representing 15 executive departments as well as the EOP. The number of civilians employed by the executive branch swells to more than 4 million when including active-duty personnel in the U.S. Armed Forces and the National Guard and Reserve (The White House, 2009).

At first glance, it might appear that leisure and recreation services are absent from the executive branch and agenda. However, many of the public policy priorities related to recreation and leisure can be found in the executive branch. For example, the Office of Management and Budget is where the president forms his budget priorities that are then sent to Congress for debate and approval. In President Barack Obama's fiscal year 2010 budget, for example, the president proposed to increase the National Park Service's budget for park operations by $100 million to better maintain facilities and natural resources (Office of Management and Budget, 2009). This proposed increase in the NPS budget is in addition to the $750 million allocated to the NPS by Congress in the American Recovery and Reinvestment Act of 2009 (Recovery.gov, 2009). Other executive-level priorities related to leisure and recreation can be found in the various executive departments, including the Departments of Agriculture, Defense, Education, Health and Human Services, Housing and Urban Development, and Interior, among others. Although the priorities of the executive branch with respect to leisure and recreation (as well as other areas) are subject to frequent changes and revisions, selected leisure and recreation priorities that are covered within executive branch agencies at the time of this writing are listed in Figure 11.3. In addition to these priorities, the day-to-day administrative functions related to leisure services provision are carried out in the executive branch. Although the legislature makes the laws that provide legal authority and mandates, approves the budget, and allocates funding, executive branch agencies carry out the actual duties of service provision.

There is no single, coordinated national policy related to leisure, recreation, or sport in the United States. Laws and policies related to recreation and leisure are set at the federal, state, and local levels of government, depending on the priorities of the citizenry. In other Western democracies such as Great Britain, Canada, and Australia, leisure policy is formulated and coordinated at the highest level of government and implemented at the local levels. In Great Britain, the government consists of a Secretary of State for Culture, Media and Sport, who is responsible for championing the tourism, creative, and leisure industries (Culture.gov, 2009). The Department of Culture, Media and Sport elevates issues concerning arts, libraries, sports, museums, physical activity, tourism, and parks to the cabinet level of government in Great Britain.

FIGURE 11.2

U.S. Executive Branch

President
Vice President

Executive Office of the President

Council of Economic Advisors

Council on Environmental Quality

Council on Women and Girls

Domestic Policy Council

National Economic Council

National Security Council

Office of Administration

Office of Management and Budget

Office of National AIDS Policy

Office of National Drug Control Policy

Office of Science and Technology Policy

Office of the U.S. Trade Representative

President's Intelligence Advisory Board and Intelligence Oversight Board

Privacy and Civil Liberties Oversight Board

White House Military Office

The Cabinet

In order of succession to the presidency:

Vice President of the United States

Department of State (www.state.gov)

Department of the Treasury (www.treasury.gov)

Department of Defense (www.defenselink.mil)

Department of Justice (www.justice.gov)

Department of the Interior (www.doi.gov)

Department of Agriculture (www.usda.gov)

Department of Commerce (www.commerce.gov)

Department of Labor (www.dol.gov)

Department of Health and Human Services (www.hhs.gov)

Department of Housing and Urban Development (www.hud.gov)

Department of Transportation (www.dot.gov)

Department of Energy (www.energy.gov)

Department of Education (www.ed.gov)

Department of Veterans Affairs (www.va.gov)

Department of Homeland Security (www.dhs.gov)

Cabinet-Rank Positions

Council of Economic Advisers (www.whitehouse.gov/administration/eop/cea/)

Environmental Protection Agency (www.epa.gov)

Office of Management and Budget (www.whitehouse.gov/omb/)

U.S. Trade Representative (www.ustr.gov)

U.S. Ambassador to the United Nations

White House Chief of Staff

FIGURE 11.3
2010 Executive Budget

Department of Agriculture
- Activities of the U.S. Forest Service
- Conservation easements
- Nutrition assistance
- 4-H and extension services at land grant institutions
- Rural broadband infrastructure
- Wildfire management

Department of Defense
- Morale, welfare, and recreation (MWR) programs
- Base funding for family support initiatives

Department of Education
- Early childhood education programs
- After-school programs and activities

Department of Health and Human Services
- Research funding for health promotion and disease prevention
- Expansion of Head Start programs

Department of Housing and Urban Development
- Funding for the Community Development Block Grant (CDBG) program
- Community improvement funding for concentrated poverty neighborhoods

Department of the Interior
- Funding activities of the National Park Service
- Conservation of federal and state land through the Land and Water Conservation Fund (LWCF)
- Environmental education initiatives for youth
- Wildfire management on NPS lands

Corps of Engineers/Civil Works
- Maintenance of infrastructure supporting land- and water-based recreation

Environmental Protection Agency
- Restoration of the Great Lakes

Corporation for National and Community Service
- Expand funding and opportunities for AmeriCorps volunteers
- Expand opportunities for service learning opportunities in schools, higher education, and community-based organizations

Judicial Branch

The judicial branch in the United States consists of two separate systems—the state system and the federal system—set up to try both civil and criminal cases. In cases where state and federal laws come into conflict, the federal system takes precedence based on the **Supremacy Clause** in the U.S. Constitution (Grant, 2004). In the United States, the federal judiciary consists of three tiers—district courts, circuit courts of appeals, and the Supreme Court. District courts make up the first tier. They are primarily trial courts and hear federal cases that arise within the states themselves. There are 94 federal district courts operating in the United States and its territories. The second tier consists of 12 circuit courts that span the boundaries of several states. The 12 circuit courts of appeals hear cases that are appealed from the district courts in their circuit or appeals of decisions made by federal administrative agencies. The vast majority of federal cases are heard in either district courts or circuit courts of appeals. In matters of extreme importance to federal law or on serious constitutional questions, the U.S. Supreme Court may elect to hear a few select cases each year from the state or federal court system (U.S. Courts, 2009).

©Junial Enterprises/fotolia

Most federal cases involving parks and recreation are likely to be heard in district courts or circuit courts of appeal.

Most federal cases involving parks and recreation are likely to be heard in the district courts or circuit courts of appeal. For example, the District Court of the District of Columbia has been involved in the ongoing snowmobile ban controversy in Yellowstone National Park, and the District Court of the Northern District of California has adjudicated a case involving restricted access of off-road vehicles in the Bureau of Land Management's California Imperial Sand Dunes. Other high-profile cases heard by federal courts involving parks and recreation issues include the rights of boaters using the Colorado River in Grand Canyon National Park and recreation uses of the White River National Forest (Haas, 2003).

FEDERALISM

Many Western democracies, most notably Australia, Canada, and the United States, have federal political systems. **Federalism** refers to the constitutional arrangement of balancing and sharing rights and powers between different levels of government. Federal systems in general have five main characteristics (Smith, 2004):

- The combination of shared rule (central government) and local self-rule
- The constitutionally protected autonomy of each unit of government
- A written constitution and courts that are empowered to settle disputes

- A constitution amendment process designed to prevent any unit of government from changing the constitution on its own
- A central government that in part, represents the various units of government of the federation

Although most federal systems share these five characteristics, not all federal systems are the same in practice. Closer examination of federalism in Canada and the United States, for example, reveals differences both in structure and practice. Examples include the structural differences in the nature of both countries' constitutional governments, including Canada's historical ties to the British Crown and its parliamentary system, which differs substantially from the U.S. system of checks and balances and strong separation of powers (Thomas, 2008).

Government has a significant responsibility in managing recreation resources and in the delivery of leisure services and programs. Because of this, students of recreation and leisure behavior should understand the basic concepts of federalism, because the nature of political units such as the federal government, state and provincial governments, and local governments dictates the type of services offered through public-sector leisure services provision. Particularly in the United States, where there is no coordinated national policy for leisure services provision, knowing the differences between federal, state, and local levels of government is important in understanding the nature and scope of leisure services delivery.

Federal Government

Federal agencies provide a range of functions related to leisure services provision and delivery. Perhaps one of the largest federal functions is land and natural resources management for recreation and conservation purposes. Dozens of federal agencies, including the National Park Service, National Forest Service, Bureau of Land Management, U.S. Fish and Wildlife Service, and Army Corps of Engineers, are responsible for managing thousands of acres of land available to the public for recreation and leisure uses. Outdoor recreation spaces such as the properties managed by the National Park Service provide opportunities for millions of Americans and non-Americans to engage in numerous recreation activities. In addition to the benefits to individual users of these outdoor recreation areas, significant economic benefits accrue to the larger community as well. For example, money that tourists spend while vacationing on land managed by federal agencies can help to create business and stimulate local economies. The sale of timber and other natural resources from federal land such as national forests provides an important funding source for the federal government.

The federal government leverages its financial resources to support local priorities by distributing funding to the states for projects that are often related to leisure and recreation services provision. Programs such as the Land and Water Conservation Fund (LWCF), the Community Development Block Grant Program, and the 21st Century Community Learning Centers Program are important funding mechanisms for state and local recreation provision. For example, the LWCF provides funding to state and local governments through the provision of matching grants—grants that are given contingent on the recipient's raising money for the project from other sources. The goal of the LWCF is to "create and maintain a nationwide legacy of high quality recreation areas and facilities and to stimulate non-federal investments in the protection and maintenance of recreation resources across the United States" (National Park Service, 2009). One of the advantageous features of LWCF projects is the requirement that they be developed for use by the public for recreation purposes in perpetuity—that is, that they always be available for public recreation with no definitive end.

Although the main responsibility of the federal government in recreation and leisure services provision is land and resource management and development, program delivery can also be found in federal agencies. For example, each of the five branches of the U.S. Armed Forces—the Air Force, Army, Coast Guard, Marine Corps, and Navy—provides recreation programs and services for military personnel and their families. Referred to as morale, welfare (or well-being), and recreation programs (MWRs), these services provide a comprehensive set of recreational, social, and community support services, including sports, physical fitness, youth and child development programs, entertainment, and food and beverage services. Other recreation programs offered through the federal government include therapeutic recreation services offered through the U.S. Department of Veterans Affairs.

State Government

In many ways, the system of recreation delivery at the state government level parallels that of the federal government. State governments often manage large outdoor recreation areas, such as state parks, forests, nature areas, historical sites, and trail systems, among other

State parks, forests, historical sites, and trail systems help to make outdoor recreation opportunities accessible to local populations.

recreation resources. In most states, these recreation areas are funded through some combination of taxes and user fees, supplemented by other public and private funding sources. As mentioned above, the federal government often assists states in the acquisition and development of outdoor recreation resources through matching grant programs like the Land and Water Conservation Fund.

States are often in a position to influence recreation and leisure services through regulation and oversight functions. States provide environmental oversight and regulation, enforce safety codes, regulate private recreation and leisure services providers, and in some states, oversee the licensing of certain recreation professionals, such as recreational therapists (McLean et al., 2008). States also provide support for the marketing of recreation resources and amenities as a way of promoting tourism and economic development. For example, the state of South Carolina spent $464 million in support of tourism in 2007, resulting in $17.2 billion in tourist spending in the state that year. Tourism in South Carolina contributes almost a quarter of a million jobs to the state's economy and provides more than $1.2 billion in state and local tax revenues (South Carolina Department of Parks, Recreation, and Tourism, 2009).

Federal and State Cooperation in Tilton, New Hampshire

Some states work with local communities as a liaison with the federal government to ensure that needed funds and support are provided for environmental cleanup or other public works projects that affect recreation provision. For example, the New Hampshire Department of Environmental Services (DES) and the United States Environmental Protection Agency (EPA), along with other public and private funders (including the LWCF), helped to create a $1.3 million riverfront park on the 2-acre (8,000-square meter) site of a former mill in downtown Tilton, New Hampshire. Site assessment and cleanup of the contaminated property were funded by the EPA, and an additional $100,000 grant from the LWCF will provide additional resources to develop the area into a public-use downtown park, including boat ramps, fishing piers, picnic areas, and a main pavilion (National Park Service, 2009).

Local Government

Local government represents the level of government closest to the citizenry. Local government generally encompasses municipalities (cities, towns, villages), counties, and special districts. Municipalities are the smallest unit of government and are typically governed by a democratically elected mayor and city council. In some municipalities, the mayor plays a strong administrative role in municipal governance. In this **strong mayor–council** model of governance, the mayor has broad administrative duties, including hiring and firing, budgeting, and setting the strategic direction of the city. In other municipalities, a professional public administrator or city manager is hired to carry out the day-to-day governance of the municipality. The public administrator or city manager often works with the elected city council and, in many cases, an elected mayor to provide governance, hire employees, approve budgets, and make administrative decisions. This form of municipal governance is referred to as the **city manager–council** model (Hurd et al., 2008).

Municipal governments often provide a broad range of services for their citizens. Many municipalities have police and fire departments, maintain local roads, provide schools, manage public housing units, enforce planning and zoning rules, assess and collect taxes, handle judicial cases, engage in environmental conservation and protection, and promote economic development. Municipalities often have responsibility for providing parks and recreation services to their community. In particular, municipal parks and recreation agencies are responsible for developing and maintaining a diverse range of public recreation facilities that meet the leisure needs in their community. These facilities may include parks, playgrounds, athletic fields, community centers, aquatics facilities, beaches, pet or dog parks, community gardens, fitness facilities, golf courses, boat launches, multiple-use trail systems, skateboard parks, ice arenas, and even downhill ski hills! Municipal parks and recreation agencies are generally responsible for providing recreation programs as well. Like facilities, recreation programs vary from community to community,

© Human Kinetics

Municipal and city agencies provide a wide range of leisure services, including sports, parks, youth services, and cultural and performing arts programs.

depending on the need of the citizenry. Programs offered by the municipal parks and recreation agency may include youth and adult sport leagues, instructional lessons, fitness classes, camps, after-school programs, historical and cultural activities, therapeutic recreation services, senior activities, and performing arts. Parks and recreation departments are often funded by some combination of appropriated tax money from the municipal government as well as user fees and other forms of public and nonpublic financing.

Many county governments offer parks and recreation services, generally focused on rural or unincorporated areas within their jurisdiction. Many of the services found in municipal parks and recreation agencies can be found at the county level as well. This reflects a shift in the original mandate for county services, because counties were traditionally seen as administrative arms of state government, helping to provide state level services locally (Todd, 1996). Today, many county governments are involved in a vast range of service provision, including parks and recreation, and often work with local municipalities to coordinate services and to avoid duplication.

Another form of local government that has applicability to parks and recreation is the **special district**. Special districts are created by enabling legislation. Special districts are separate, independent forms of government that have the authority to tax and administer specific services (Hurd et al., 2008). Not all special districts are set up to administer parks and recreation services, although many special districts are set up specifically for this purpose. For example, the Greenville County Recreation District was created by enabling legislation passed by the South Carolina legislature in 1968 (see the Leisure Awareness sidebar on the next page).

LEISURE AWARENESS

The Greenville County Recreation District is responsible for providing residents of the district with parks and recreation services, which are defined in the enabling legislation. Residents in the district pay taxes that are specifically designed to support parks and recreation services, and the residents are represented by seven appointed electors. Based on the enabling legislation, the Greenville County Recreation District has the following powers:

- To develop plans for recreation services and facilities for the district and a financial program to implement the plans
- To work with civic groups and school officials to provide supervised recreation in areas not already served
- To seek land acquisition and development funds through federal and state agencies and acquire land and facilities by gift or purchase
- To prescribe rules and regulations governing the use of the facilities
- To fix rates and charges for the use of any facility
- To make contracts and execute instruments for the discharge of its functions, including contracts for constructions and other services

---

PLURALISM AND PUBLIC POLICY

Focusing on just the formal branches of government is an incomplete view of the political system. In liberal democracies like the United States and Canada, political activity can be found working outside the boundaries of formal government structures. Individuals and groups organize to build support for their interests and then use this support to influence the political decision making process.

These individuals and groups can be as diverse as a mother who starts a petition drive to get a playground built in her neighborhood, a group of youth development organizations who band together to advocate on behalf of the needs of youth, or a formal organization that lobbies members of Congress on behalf of parks and recreation priorities. The pluralist nature of political life in liberal democracies takes into account the vast array of interest groups and the opportunities that they have to influence the political system and, ultimately, public policy (Peters, 1996).

Politics in liberal democracies happens at multiple levels, by multiple factions—both inside and outside the formal structures of government. As such, any definition of politics needs to focus on the pluralistic nature of the United States and Canada and must take into account the role that the citizen plays in the political process. **Pluralist politics** can be seen as the process of various interest groups working, and sometimes competing, to influence the institutions of government to advance ideas and policies that reflect their goals (Grant, 2004). The importance of citizen action in influencing the political process is described in the research literature related to leisure, politics, and public policy as published in the major research journals in this field. Politics, as the research literature has come to define it within the leisure sciences literature, is both formal and informal—occurring at the highest levels of government and at the most basic level of individuals, families, and communities.

A discussion of leisure and its relationship with the political process will necessarily focus on the role of the formal institutions of government as well as the body politic and its various factions and interest groups that work to influence these formal institutions. Sometimes you may be tempted to think of the political process as a frustrating and dirty game, rife with corruption and focused on greed. Or you may view politics from a partisan perspective, viewing policy decisions through the framework of a particular political party's agenda. The political process is a social construction and as such reflects the individuals who work within it. The process may at times be overly partisan and influenced by corruption, and other times it may lead to outcomes that result in the greatest good for the greatest number. The pluralistic and competitive nature of politics in liberal democracies will almost always lead to winners and losers. As such, it is virtually impossible to find unanimous agreement on any particular political decision. Yet in the end, politics should be seen as a means to an end—a tool that is used to advocate for the issues and policies that are most important to a particular interest group.

Political influence is not directed only toward government institutions. Interest groups might organize to advocate for specific causes and to influence policy outcomes associated with nongovernmental organizations as well. Some scholars have noted that the traditional political system is not the center of political action any longer. Citizens are no longer as dependent on the political party apparatus to organize and advocate for a particular cause. This is due to a general feeling of alienation from political parties and political life as well as to new forms of political organization, such as online communities. This new political activism has been termed "life politics" (Rojek, 2001). **Life politics** is defined as "a nonparty form of social and cultural orientation focusing on issues of lifestyle, environment, and

Citizen advocacy is at the center of life politics and focuses on the role that citizens play in drawing attention to the issues and causes that are most important to them and their communities.

globalization" (Rojek, 2001, p. 115). Leisure is, in many ways, at the center of this new kind of politics, as citizens begin to define the kind of world that they want to live in and organize to draw attention to the issues and causes that are most important to them and their communities.

As a citizen, you might put politics into practice through the formal political process, such as voting or working on a political campaign. You might get involved by volunteering on behalf of a moral cause that is important to you outside of the formal political process, or you can volunteer for service projects focused solely on the betterment of your community. One way to understand this more expansive view of the political landscape in communities is to see a civic engagement continuum, with formal political involvement on the one side, political or moral advocacy at the center, and community service involvement on the other side (see figure 11.4). Oftentimes, formal participation in the political process will emerge from basic participation in the life of a community (Youniss et al., 2002).

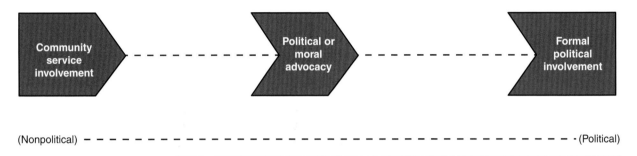

Community service involvement

Political or moral advocacy

Formal political involvement

(Nonpolitical)  (Political)

Figure 11.4 Civic engagement continuum.

Consider this: A group of young adults become involved in a community service project to help build a system of walking trails within the community. As they begin to research community issues, they might become more aware of the need for public places to be physically active, the need to preserve land for public use instead of commercial development, or the need to encourage nonmotorized transportation to reduce carbon emissions. In the process, the group might organize to advocate for a more livable, walkable community, raising funds and awareness for their cause. Perhaps at some point, some of the members might align with a political party or candidate that supports their active living agenda. Through the process, the participants begin to develop a common identity as they share ideologies and values (Youniss et al., 2002). This simple example draws attention to the civic engagement process and how involvement in one particular community issue may spur a more deepened sense of political involvement along the way.

Public policy, much like the politics that helps to shape it, is a complex process. A basic definition of **public policy** is the activities of government, working directly or through its agents, that influence the lives of citizens. Three levels of policy affect citizens: policy choices, policy outputs, and policy impacts (Peters, 1996). To demonstrate these levels as they relate to leisure and recreation, consider the following quotation regarding the political position of parks and recreation:

It has been noted that the provision of park, recreation opportunities for their own sake still lacks political clout. They have to be shown to solve community problems before politicians see them as being worthy of additional funding. The present position of parks and recreation services that has existed in the minds of most stakeholders for several decades is that they are relatively discretionary, non-essential services. They are nice to have if they can be afforded after the important, essential services have been funded. (Crompton, 2000, p. 68)

Consider how each of the following levels of public policy is reflected in the quotation.

Policy Choices

Policy choices refer to the decisions made by people who have an influence over the formation of public policy. Oftentimes, these are elected officials at the local, county, state, or national level, or they may be political appointees serving in administrative roles. The people who wield the power and authority to make public policy must choose among a variety of competing priorities. According to the preceding quotation, those with the power to make policy choices include elected officials as well as stakeholders—those individuals or groups who have a vested interest in the decisions of government because of the effect the decisions have (or might have) on them. Stakeholders may influence policy choices through their votes for elected officials, votes on public ballot measures, or political organization and advocacy.

Read the quotation again. What policy choices must be made? Although the details are vague, the basic policy choice is whether to pursue the public (i.e., government supported) provision of parks and recreation opportunities for the citizenry, presumably at the expense of other forms of public services such as education, health services, police, and fire protection. This is fundamentally a policy choice—the process of prioritizing one set of policy options over another. How political choices are made is part of the political process as described here. Sometimes these choices reflect the collective will of the people, sometimes they reflect the preferences and platform of a particular political party or government agency, and sometimes they represent the influence of a powerful group of stakeholders working on behalf of a particular constituency. In any case, policy choices are the result of the political process.

Policy Outputs

Although policy choices refer to the key policy priorities of a particular government, the outputs of policy refer to what governments actually do. In the previous example, the policy output refers specifically to funding—how much money should be allocated to the provision of parks and recreation opportunities within the community. Political decision makers may give lip service to a particular set of policy choices. But to really see where their priorities lie, it is important to examine how the policy choices are put into action. Most of the time, this refers to the money that is appropriated for particular programs and services. Other types of policy outputs could be the people who are hired or the infrastructure that needs to be provided for the policy to be enacted.

Policy Impacts

The policy impact refers to how public policy actually affects people. How do the support and funding of parks and recreation programs, facilities, and services affect the broader population? Recreation professionals need to do a better job articulating and demonstrating that parks and recreation services positively affect society beyond just providing a place for fun and games. To gain political (and policy) clout, parks and recreation must show that they have a significant impact on other broad public policy agendas in order to be worthy of additional funding (Crompton, 2000). These agendas will differ depending on the local community. For example, depending on the community, alleviating juvenile crime, stimulating economic activity, preserving scarce land resources, or improving health and physical well-being of citizens may be more or less important. This means that for parks and recreation agencies to be seen as viable public priorities worthy of funding and public support, they need to be seen as contributing in some way to these broader policy impacts. Otherwise, public resources may be allocated to other community services, like police departments (juvenile crime), chambers of commerce (economic stimulation), conservation commissions (preservation of natural resources), or local hospitals and public health facilities (health and well-being). In the eyes of stakeholders, these organizations may be more worthy of public support because they are more easily associated with the desired ends of public policy.

JUSTIFICATION FOR PUBLIC RECREATION AND LEISURE

Historically, the justification for public involvement in parks and recreation services came about as a means of social reform in response to the social conditions that were created in the mid- to late-19th century as a result of the growing industrialization and urbanization of the United States. Separate but parallel social movements such as the creation of urban and national parks, settlement houses, and playgrounds began to merge in the early 20th century with the development of professional groups and associations, such as the Playground Association of America. These early associations brought together leaders of the various parallel movements and began to advocate for public funding for parks and recreation services to address the growing social concerns largely occurring in America's cities. Whereas many of the early social movements were supported by voluntary and private efforts, the emerging recreation movement required public support to meet the growing needs for recreation and leisure services (Russell, 2005).

The movement toward public funding and resource support for parks and recreation was exemplified at the federal level by the conservation and setting aside of land by the federal government that would eventually be used to form the National Park Service; the creation of public spaces within cities, such as Central Park in New York and Golden Gate Park in San Francisco; and the public funding of neighborhood playgrounds in cities such as Boston and Chicago. Public infrastructure support for parks and recreation was accelerated through the "make work" programs associated with Franklin Delano Roosevelt's New Deal. In fact, much of the state park infrastructure was built through the efforts of Depression-era organizations such as the Civilian Conservation Corps.

Historically, support for public recreation was rooted in the notion that such services helped to alleviate many of the distressed social conditions that arose from the industrialization and urbanization of America. The general philosophy underlying public (government) support of parks and recreation is that they are considered to be a public good—that there is broad public value that accrues for both users and nonusers of these services. As with any public good, such as fire protection, police, education, and transportation, the service is assumed to have value regardless of whether a citizen is using it, and it also is assumed that the ser-

> ## WHAT DO YOU THINK?
>
> Can you imagine what our communities would look like if everyone were required to pay for their own private security services to protect their homes and property? Think about a more extreme example—what if everyone were required to build their own private roads to get to and from their houses or were forced to pay others a full market rate for the use of their road? These examples may sound extreme, but they can be useful when thinking about the public nature of certain goods and services as well as how these services are delivered and distributed and who has primary responsibility for paying for them.

vice should be available to the public regardless of their ability to pay full market value for its use.

We can think about these same questions or examples when considering the role of government in the provision of parks and recreation services. There are at least three major justifications for public recreation (Kelly, 1995):

1. Efficiency
2. Equity
3. Preservation

All three of these justifications are explained in further detail next.

Efficiency

Consider how much it might cost an individual property owner to install a private, backyard swimming pool. Although the price of equipment and installation will vary from place to place, let's assume that it will cost the homeowners $20,000 to install their swimming pool. Of course, this price does not include accessories, chemicals, energy to operate the pool, and yearly maintenance, which increase the financial burden on the individual consumer. However, by paying 100 percent of the price for the swimming pool, the homeowner gets to enjoy 100 percent of its benefits—convenience, privacy, and unlimited use. To determine whether this is the most efficient use of a homeowner's financial resources, one needs to do a cost–benefit analysis related to the purchase. How often does the family use the pool? How important is the pool to the family's quality of life? Can the family afford the expense, given its other needs? If the family is not using the pool frequently enough to justify its annual cost and impact on the household budget, then the purchase of the pool might be an inefficient use of the family's financial resources. In addition, think of the potential waste of scarce resources (e.g., water, energy, raw materials, human effort) that are needed to build, install, and maintain the pool. Multiply these factors by all of the private swimming pools in the community, and you can see how this system of service delivery is inefficient.

Imagine another community—one with a municipal parks and recreation department. In this community, the average household pays approximately $25 per year as part of its property taxes to support a full range of parks and recreation services, including a public swimming pool. In addition, the average household pays $25 per year in fees to the city for a pool membership, which includes a bundle of other services such as swimming lessons and water aerobics classes. In this case, the

Public recreation facilities that are accessible to the public, such as swimming pools, provide opportunities for communities to share recreation costs and use.

©Linda Mattson/fotolia

household is only paying for a fraction of the total cost of the swimming pool and reaps many of the other benefits of a full-service parks and recreation department (e.g., parks, athletic facilities, playgrounds, community centers). Given the physical, human, and fiscal resources involved with installing an outdoor swimming pool, it makes sense to spread the resource burden, especially if there is an expressed need for the service and it has value to the broader community (a "public good").

This example refers to what is known as a **commons**—an opportunity for the entire community to share recreation costs and use (Kelly & Freysinger, 1999). This allows community members to pool their collective resources to develop and preserve recreation spaces that everyone in the community can use. If we define **efficiency** as the effective allocation of scarce resources to produce the most benefit for the most people, then there is another efficiency argument for government involvement in parks and recreation (More, 1999). Government agencies are generally thought of as being responsible for the common good, and as such they play a pivotal role in planning and ensuring that scarce space is allocated to promote that public good. For example, government entities can ensure through effective planning and zoning processes that there is enough space for public recreation as well as commercial interests.

Equity

One of the major roles of government in public recreation is to provide equity in the distribution of leisure services and programs. Some have argued that given their mandate, government provision of parks and recreation services should be primarily concerned with issues of equity before considering other issues such as effectiveness and efficiency (Crompton & Lamb, 1986). Returning to our swimming pool example, if access to a swimming pool is truly considered to be a public good, then some provision must be made to ensure that everyone in a community, regardless of his or her background, has access to the resource. For example, cities don't, as a rule, have income requirements for the use of city parks. In general terms, and as we see in our swimming pool example, the cost of many public recreation resources is subsidized through some system of taxation or differential pricing method that spreads the cost burden throughout the community as a whole. This allows access to the park for a diverse range of users from different financial means.

However, the issues about what constitutes a public good, who should pay, and how much should be paid are rife for debate in public policy circles. In the 1970s and 1980s, a number of state and municipal governments began to respond to the political shifts against government provision of public services by passing legislation to reduce the tax burdens on citizens. California led the way with Proposition 13 in 1978, which placed a limit on state property taxes, reducing property tax rates and at the same affecting the public services that could be provided to citizens. By 1980, approximately 13 other states followed California's lead. The debate about whether parks and recreation services are **public goods** is still active today.

Since the tax revolts of the 1970s and 1980s, government agencies have been asked to continue to provide the same (or increased) levels of service with less appropriated (tax) funds. One financial response has been to charge user fees for the use of certain parks and recreation services, as is evidenced in the swimming pool example. Some argue that charging fees for certain parks and recreation services creates equity in that these fees place a greater proportion of the financial burden on the citizens who use the service directly. Others argue that fees lead to greater efficiency as well, because they allow administrators to direct user behavior through various pricing schemes. For example, the fee for access to a popular public park during peak demand times might be higher than the fee for access to a less popular park during the same time period. In this case, efficiency may be created by shifting demand and spreading out use. This could also have a positive impact on resource preservation as well (discussed subsequently) by controlling the overuse of a particular natural resource (More, 1999).

Although there may be good reasons for user fees, public recreation managers must take issues of equitable access into account. Who owns public lands? Should only those with the ability to pay be allowed access to places like Yellowstone National Park or the Grand Canyon? Should only those who have the ability to pay be able to access the swimming lessons offered at the local community pool? Should only those who have the ability to pay have access to an after-school playground program? Questions about resource allocation and equity—who gets what and who pays—are political questions that public recreation managers must contend with.

Preservation of Resources

Theodore Roosevelt, the 26th President of the United States, is widely considered to be one of the great conservationist presidents and an important figure in the development of public outdoor recreation in America. In his book, *Outdoor Pastimes of an American Hunter,* Roosevelt summed up his conservation ethic: "There can be nothing in the world more beautiful than the Yosemite, the groves of giant sequoias and redwoods, the Canyon of the Colorado, the Canyon of the Yellowstone, the Three Tetons; and our people should see to it that they are preserved for their children and their children's children forever, with their majestic beauty all unmarred" (Roosevelt, 1908, p. 317). This statement reveals another justification for government involvement in leisure provision—the conservation, preservation, and management of natural resources for the public good.

This principle goes beyond efficiency and equity arguments. It speaks to the government's role as a protector or steward of public treasures that need to be preserved for both the good of the citizenry today and for future generations. The idea here is that government is in the best position to manage historical, cultural, and sensitive natural resources for the long term and to avoid making decisions that sacrifice long-term preservation for short-term benefits. This speaks to the understanding that such resources are not infinite. We have only one Old Faithful, one Grand Canyon, and one Washington Monument. Federal, state, and local government agencies are tasked with the responsibility of balancing present use of

©AP Photo/Laura Rauch

Policy decisions on balancing recreation use and resource preservation are heavily debated, such as the ongoing issue of whether to allow snowmobiles in Yellowstone National Park.

these sensitive natural, historical, and cultural resources with the need to preserve them for future generations and protect the interests of local stakeholders.

The balancing act is not always easy, and decisions are often influenced by the political process. Consider the ongoing debate about whether snowmobiles should be allowed in Yellowstone National Park. Proponents argue that banning snowmobiles reduces air and noise pollution and protects wildlife. Opponents argue that snowmobile bans place limits on citizens' enjoyment of the park, limit personal freedom, and hurt the region's economy by causing job losses and an overall negative economic impact (Pawelski, 2000). This debate has spanned the terms of at least two U.S. presidents, has involved state and federal legislators, and has reached various levels of the judiciary. The politics on this issue have taken a number of twists and turns, from outright bans to limits on the number of snowmobiles allowed in the park at one time. The latest decision by Federal Judge Emmet Sullivan has been to reinstate a total ban on snowmobiles within Yellowstone Park on the grounds that snowmobile use violates "the fundamental purpose of the national system . . . to conserve park resources and values" (Cart, 2008). At the time of this writing, Yellowstone National Park officials were crafting a new proposal to allow limited snowmobile use within the park.

SUMMARY

Leisure is political. Because leisure is experienced socially, as well as individually, decisions will always need to be made related to leisure services delivery. These decisions are made both within and outside the formal political process. The formal political process includes the major structures of government, particularly the executive, legislative, and judicial branches. The government's role in leisure services provision is to ensure efficiency, equity, and preservation of resources. Politics and public policy formation in a federal system takes place at various levels of government. In the United States and Canada, public policy related to leisure behavior and service delivery takes place at the federal, state or provincial, and local levels of government. Public policy is also influenced by the pluralist nature of liberal democracies, giving voice to people through organized advocacy and special interest groups. Leisure policy is often driven directly by the expressed needs, desires, and interests of the citizenry through organized political action.

Learning Activities

1. **Outsourcing the parks:** Consider the following fictional scenario: Imagine that a legislative proposal to reform the federal government of the United States would have the government sell off its 88 million acres (more than 3.5 million square kilometers) of land to private entrepreneurs at fair market value, allowing them to manage sensitive, historical, or cultural areas as private enterprises by charging users and keeping profits. All nonsensitive areas or areas that do not have historical or cultural significance could be developed as the private entrepreneurs see fit. The federal government would save $1.7 billion annually, would gain the revenue from the sales of the real estate, and would be out of the business of land and recreation program management.

   - What do you think about this proposal?
   - Would this solution work?
   - Is there anything you like about the proposal?
   - Is there anything that you don't like about it?

2. **Is leisure a public good?** Consider the following questions about the potential benefits and drawbacks of leisure for both individuals and society.

   - Leisure and recreation activities have the potential to play a role of fundamental importance for both individuals and society at large. In groups, brainstorm and discuss the potential benefits of leisure experiences and recreation activities on our lives from both an individual and a social perspective.

   - Leisure experiences and recreation activities can produce negative impacts for individuals, societies, and the environment. Can you think of some of the potential negative impacts of leisure and recreation?

   - What role should government play (if any) in the promotion and delivery of leisure services or in the regulation of leisure behavior? What is your justification for this position?

3. **Civic and political engagement:** Consider this scenario: Citizens concerned with traffic congestion and the physical and environmental health of Anytown, USA, propose that the downtown business district be closed to all automobile traffic in order to create a walkable community. This group says that walkable downtowns increase business for shops, restaurants, and entertainment businesses in the downtown district. The business community vehemently disagrees, claiming that people do not want to walk and that they will instead drive to, park, and shop in the suburban megamall

outside of town. What arguments could you make to the mayor, city council, and planning department that might support walkable downtowns? Take a look at your argument. Is it persuasive? Is it more persuasive than the argument from the downtown business community? What evidence might you cite to support your position?

4. **Public Recreation Philosophy:**

  • If you were given the responsibility to draft a philosophy statement for a public recreation department in your home town, what key points would you include?

  • Look at your philosophy statement. Does it resonate politically? Do you think politicians and community leaders would see public recreation as worthy of receiving additional public funds (i.e., money from taxes) based on what you believe the emphasis should be? Think about this from both sides of the issue.

For additional assignments, Web links, and more, visit the online student resource at www.HumanKinetics.com/DimensionsOfLeisureForLife.

Review Questions

1. Why is leisure political?
2. How does the political process influence leisure?
3. What is the justification for government involvement in leisure?
4. What role does the government play in leisure services provision?
5. How can citizens become involved in the political process to influence policies affecting leisure behavior?

Leisure Reading

de Graaf, J. (2003). *Take back your time: Fighting overwork and time poverty in America.* San Francisco: Berrett-Koehler.

Hochschild, A. (2001). *Time bind: When work becomes home and home becomes work.* New York: Owl Books.

Putnam, R. (2004). *Better together: Restoring the American community.* New York: Simon & Schuster.

Glossary

blue laws—Laws that are enacted to protect the Sabbath, traditionally defined as Sunday, from commercial or other forms of activity.

city manager–council—A system of local governance where a professional public administrator or city manager works with the elected city council and, in many cases, an elected mayor to provide governance, hire employees, approve budgets, and make administrative decisions.

commons—Resources that are collectively owned, or opportunities for all members of a community to share in the costs, use, and benefits of public goods.

efficiency—The effective allocation of scarce leisure resources to produce the most benefit for the most people.

enabling legislation—Legislation that provides the authority for appropriate administrative bodies or officials to carry out mandates or enforce the laws.

federalism—The constitutional arrangement of balancing and sharing rights and powers between different levels of government.

life politics—A "nonparty form of social and cultural orientation focusing on issues of lifestyle, environment, and globalization" (Rojek, 2001, p. 115).

morale, welfare, and recreation—Programs offered to military personnel and their families, often including a comprehensive set of recreational, social, and community support services, including sports, physical fitness, youth and child development programs, entertainment, and food and beverage services.

parliamentary system—A type of governmental system, such as that found in Great Britain, in which the legislature has the power to both make and execute laws.

pluralist politics—Process of various and multiple interest groups working, and sometimes competing, to influence the institutions of government to advance ideas and policies that reflect their goals (Grant, 2004).

public goods—Services provided through the public sector that produce and accrue value for both users and nonusers.

public policy—Activities of government, working directly or through its agents, that have an influence on the lives of citizens.

separation of powers—A system where each branch of government is considered separate and independent in order to avoid an accumulation of power within any one branch of government.

special district—A separate, independent form of government that has the authority to tax and administer specific services, such as parks and recreation.

strong mayor–council—A system of local governance where the elected mayor has a strong administrative role in government, including hiring and firing, budgeting, and setting the strategic direction of the city.

Supremacy Clause—A U.S. constitutional provision that establishes the federal system's precedence in cases where federal and state laws come into conflict.

References

Cart, J. (2008, October). *Yellowstone is speeding up action on snowmobile use.* http://articles.latimes.com/2008/oct/02/nation/na-snowmobiles2

Crompton, J.L. (2000). Repositioning leisure services. *Managing Leisure, 5*(2), 65-75.

Crompton, J., & Lamb, C. (1986). *Marketing government and social services.* New York: Wiley.

Culture.gov. (2009). *Great Britain Department of Culture, Media, and Sport.* www.culture.gov.uk/

Grant, A. (2004). *The American political process* (7th ed.). New York: Routledge.

Haas, G. (2003). Applying judicial doctrine to visitor decision making capacity. *Society and Natural Resources, 16,* 741-750.

Hurd, A.R., Barcelona, R.J., & Meldrum, J.T. (2008). *Leisure services management.* Champaign, IL: Human Kinetics.

Kelly, J.R. (1995). *Leisure* (3rd ed.). Needham Heights, MA: Allyn & Bacon.

Kelly, J.R., & Freysinger, V.J. (1999). *Twenty-first century leisure: Current issues.* Needham Heights, MA: Allyn & Bacon.

McLean, D.D., Hurd, A.R., & Brattain Rogers, N. (2008). *Krause's leisure in modern society* (8th ed.). Boston: Jones & Bartlett.

More, T.A. (1999). A functionalist approach to user fees. *Journal of Leisure Research, 31*(3), 227-244.

National Park Service. (2009). *National Park Service Land and Water Conservation Fund.* www.nps.gov/ncrc/programs/lwcf/

Office of Management and Budget. (2009). *A new era of responsibility: Renewing America's promise.* Washington, DC: U.S. Government Printing Office.

Pawelski, N. (2000, March). *Smog-choked Yellowstone mulls snowmobile ban.* http://archives.cnn.com/2000/NATURE/03/06/yellowstone.snow.fight/index.html

Peters, B.G. (1996). *American public policy: Promise and performance.* Chatham, NJ: Chatham House.

Recovery.gov. (2009). *American Recovery and Reinvestment Act of 2009.* www.recovery.gov/Pages/home.aspx

Rojek, C. (2001). Leisure and life politics. *Leisure Sciences, 23,* 115-125.

Roosevelt, T. (1908). *Outdoor pastimes of an American hunter.* New York: Scribner's.

Russell, R. (2005). *Pastimes: The context of contemporary leisure* (3rd ed.). Champaign, IL: Sagamore.

Smith, J. (2004). *Federalism.* Vancouver: University of British Columbia Press.

South Carolina Department of Parks, Recreation, and Tourism. (2009). *The economic contribution of tourism in South Carolina—2007 tourism satellite account results.* www.scprt.com/our-partners/tourismstatistics/researchreports.aspx

Thomas, D.M. (2008). Past futures: The development and evolution of American and Canadian federalism. In D.M. Thomas & B.B. Torrey (Eds.), *Canada and the United States: Differences that count* (pp. 295-316). Buffalo, NY: Broadview Press.

Todd, B.S. (1996). *The implications of changing federalism: The county view.* www.farmfoundation.org/news/articlefiles/73-fedcount.pdf

U.S. Courts. (2009). *United States courts.* www.uscourts.gov

The White House. (2009). *The executive branch.* www.whitehouse.gov/our-government/executive-branch

Youniss, J., Bales, S., Christmas-Best, V., Diversi, M., McLaughlin, M., Silbereisen, R. (2002). Youth civic engagement in the 21st century. *Journal of Research on Adolescence, 12*(1), 121-148.

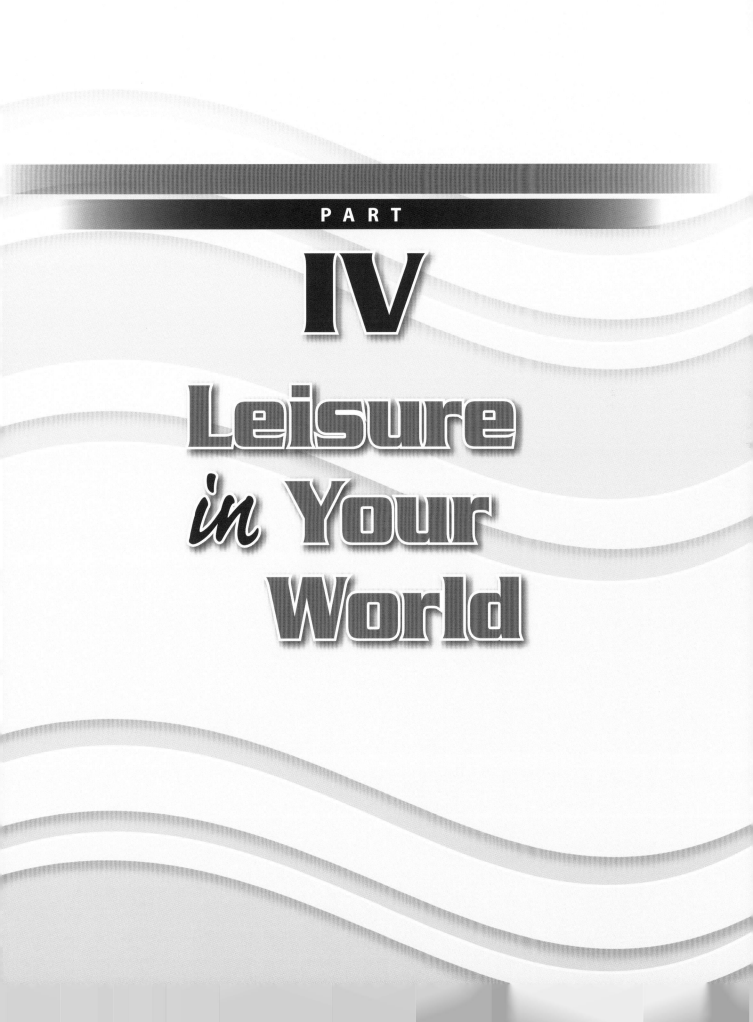

PART

IV

Leisure *in* Your World

12

Campus and Community

H. Joey Gray

Middle Tennessee State University

Learning Outcomes

After reading this chapter, you will

- ▶ be able to define and identify microcosms within the campus and community settings,
- ▶ better understand recreational activities and associations offered in campus and community settings,
- ▶ know the benefits associated with leisure participation,
- ▶ understand the importance of getting involved in campus and community activities, and
- ▶ be familiar with some of the leisure theories associated with microcosms, campus recreation, and community recreation.

Vocabulary Terms

campus community	community recreation	serious leisure
campus recreation	microcosm	theory of student involvement
casual leisure	recreational sport	
community		

Supporting a particular school or team means you are part of that microcosm.

If someone on the street stopped you to ask what a Hoosier was, would you know what she meant? If you attended or were a fan of Indiana University you certainly would! The mascot for Indiana University is a Hoosier, and those who attend the university identify closely with their mascot. Ironically, there is much debate what the word *Hoosier* means. But just say the word *Hoosier* and Indiana students, faculty, and fans alike fill with pride because of their association with Indiana University; they have made themselves a part of the Hoosier community, a microcosm. Can you think of a microcosm that you belong to? Most college students are loyal fans of their sports teams. Perhaps you are one of the legendary Cubs fans who are well known for their loyalty despite the scoreboard (Woolsey, 2008). Or maybe you have discovered a new world of friends through geocaching, by frequenting your local Jewish Community Center, or by using Facebook.

What makes people have pride for an organization? Often it is a sense of belonging or community. Community can be created in a variety of ways such as through shared enjoyment from time spent in leisure activities. Various organizations offer a variety of recreation opportunities. Do you know all of the recreation opportunities offered on your campus? What recreational activities are available within your community? Do you have a say in what is offered? In this chapter we explore the facets of microcosms within campus and community recreation. We discuss the leisure opportunities and benefits associated with participation in the campus and community settings. Last, we examine leisure theories as they relate to our topics.

College campuses and one's residential communities are filled with microcosms, small worlds within one or more larger worlds. For instance, a family is a microcosm living within a neighborhood microcosm within a community microcosm, and so on. A sense of belonging is an important aspect of defining a microcosm and an integral part of campus and community recreation. Like those who are a part of the Hoosier community, we all share a sense of value, individualism, and acceptance within our campus and community recreational activities. These affiliations allow us to develop unique relationships that form into microcosms.

WHAT IS A MICROCOSM?

Did you know you live in a community microcosm? A **microcosm** is often referred to as a miniature world; therefore, a community microcosm refers to the little worlds in which we live our daily lives. This tiny world might consist of our friends, social groups, clubs, and recreational groups. Who do you choose to spend time with? Your answer reveals your own community microcosm. You may be a part of several community microcosms (sorority or fraternity, club sports, religious groups, circle of close friends). The theory of serious leisure is closely related to the concept of microcosms. **Serious leisure** is the methodical pursuit of an amateur, a hobbyist, or a volunteer activity so substantial and interesting that the participant centers her life on special skills, knowledge, and experience associated with the leisure pursuit (Stebbins, 1997). Those who participate in serious leisure gain a sense of belonging within their community, which becomes a microcosm. An example would be marathon runners, and those on campus might train together for marathon events, thus forming their own circle of friends and running community. At times, serious leisure joins people together from various backgrounds and ages based on a common leisure interest, resulting in a microcosm.

©Photodisc

People come together based on their common recreational interests. What microcosms do you belong to?

W H A T   D O   Y O U   T H I N K ?

Your community microcosm will probably change over time as you develop and grow. Think about the time before you started college: Who were your friends? Are they the same people now or have you added new affiliations? Other changes in your community microcosms may include starting a new job, beginning a new romantic relationship, or moving to a new place. Give some thought to your life: What small worlds do you participate in?

How Is Your Campus Community a Microcosm?

Consider the meaning of *microcosm*. How might a campus community be considered a microcosm? Sports teams, club sports, special interest groups, fraternities, sororities, and individual colleges are examples of campus community microcosms. Each has its own formal and informal rules in addition to identity and values.

Student life is more than just going to class and learning from a textbook; an important part of the collegiate experience is learning life lessons and being a part of community. One's sense of **campus community** is associated with being valued as an individual, gaining acceptance within the community, and improving individual quality of campus social life (Cheng, 2004). Fraternities and sororities are prime examples of

In our leisure we reveal what kind of people we are.

Ovid, Metamorphoses

community microcosms, because students affiliated with these organizations some-times spend a great deal of their collegiate life participating in events or socializing with their fellow members in the organization. A key component of Greek life is to establish its own miniature world with unique rituals, rules, and social activities. The **theory of student involvement** refers to "the quantity and quality of the physical and psychological energy that students invest in the college experience" (Astin, 1984, p. 307). The theory proposes that the more involved students are in extracurricular and academic activities, the more they will experience enhanced socioemotional development, particularly through sport. An early longitudinal study found that students involved in Greek life were less likely to drop out of college (Astin, 1975). The most important aspect of the theory of student involvement is that the more involved students are, the more likely they are to have positive devel-opmental experiences. One could conclude that increased involvement in chosen microcosms increases feelings of cohesion to the campus community, increasing the likelihood that students will want to stay long enough to graduate.

Collegiate campuses are full of opportunities to become involved in microcosms. Are you a member of a social group, sports club, academic club, or fitness class? Do you attend scheduled campus events like movies, concerts, and plays? Do you have classmates and friends whom you hang out with frequently who also attend your university? All of these groups establish their own community relationships with rules, social norms, and expectations. Think about the little world that only you and your close college friends experience. Consider all the inside jokes, spring break vacations, social situations, and recreational activities that you and your cohorts have shared together. Within your own little world, you share good times, recreate, and enjoy your time together. You are a part of your own campus

©AP Photo/Mike Roemer

Fraternities and sororities are well known for building their own unique microcosmic (community) affiliations.

community, a microcosm, and these community ties are likely to help you have a better college experience than people who are less socially engaged. Recreational activities enrich life in so many ways.

How Is Community Recreation a Microcosm?

As previously mentioned, microcosms are worlds that fit within larger worlds. The campus microcosm exists as a world unto itself, but it also exists within a larger community, city, and state. Each of the larger systems is capable of exerting pressures on the smaller systems; thus, the systems can never be fully separated. Similar to the campus community, community recreation consists of microcosms. Sports clubs, social groups, family, neighbors, friends, and other recreational groups all consist of microcosms. Have you ever seen those soccer ball stickers on windows of minivans or cars that say things like "Go Rockets" or "Seth, #16, is #1"? Youth sport microcosms are common within communities. Parents, youth, families, and neighbors all join in and participate in their own worlds of soccer, baseball, basketball, gymnastics, and other sports. Of course, community microcosms are not limited to sport. One can find microcosms in all aspects of community recreation and activities. For instance, Nashville, Tennessee, is well known for its musical endeavors. Musically inclined people often want to be a part of the music community in Nashville. They form bands, play music, and listen to other musicians almost every weekend. Other activities from gardening clubs to religious organizations are also part of community recreation: All have their own individual microcosms.

Have you ever moved to a new place and wondered how to make new friends who shared your interests and values? A great way to make new friends is to explore and join recreational opportunities offered in your area. Community recreation helps us find microcosms to which we may comfortably belong.

PERSONAL LEISURE

What does this discussion mean for you? Be aware of your surroundings and the microcosms you join. Are these activities you enjoy? Do the people you recreate with share your beliefs and values? Do you enjoy the time you spend with your friends? Is there some activity or a group you have always wanted to learn about or be a part of? Explore your campus and community recreational opportunities now. Seize the opportunities that you have. Explore opportunities you might find interesting. Take chances and join activities you always wanted to attempt. You never know what doors campus and community involvement might open for you in the future.

EXPLORE YOUR CAMPUS AND CAMPUS RECREATION

A large number of students graduate from college without fully exploring the recreation opportunities available on campus. Are you aware of the numerous recreational opportunities and student organizations that are offered on your campus? Did you know that many campus recreation centers offer low-cost massages and personal training sessions? What other unique opportunities are offered on your college campus? If you do not know, you must explore your campus! It is unlikely that you will ever have unrestricted access to as many free recreation opportunities ever again.

How can you find out all that your campus recreation center has to offer? The most efficient way to explore your campus is by using the Internet. The key to useful exploration is knowing where to look. Most students are aware of the campus recreation center. Campus recreation centers usually disseminate their activities on a Web site, through flyers, and posting schedules around campus. Facebook is another way to capitalize on activities. But do not stop there! The student affairs department often has a list of activities as well; these offerings may be listed under "student life" or "student programs" on your college's Web site. Check with the student government association and with individual academic departments for clubs that you might be interested in joining. Explore all interesting opportunities, because many academic clubs are not restricted to majors. For example, the Recreation Opportunities Club at Middle Tennessee State University (MTSU) is open to all students who attend MTSU. You may need to keep your eyes open to find all the opportunities campus recreation has to offer. In fact, some feel that campus recreation centers need to do a better job of publicizing program information to students (Schneider et al., 2007). Research has shown that some of the top reasons students do not participate in campus recreation programs are lack of awareness, lack of time, lack of a partner, and beliefs that their skills are inadequate (Young et al., 2003). In an effort to better understand why students do not participate in campus recreation activities more, one researcher found that freshman believed they had less access to campus recreation facilities than did students in upper classes (Reed, 2007). Do not let any of these obstacles stand in your way. Campus recreation is a great way to meet people who share similar interests and to try new activities. At no other time in your life will you have this many recreational opportunities for such little cost. Do not make the mistake and think you will have time later—do not wait. Carpe diem (seize the day)! When exploring your campus, look for five major opportunities for involvement: campus recreation, student programs, student organizations and clubs, Greek life, and learning environments.

LEISURE AWARENESS

Campus Recreation

Words of Wisdom from Dr. Ray Wiley, associate director of campus recreation at Middle Tennessee State University: "Campus recreation offers students a positive, safe environment where they feel welcome and at home. Campus recreation programs and facilities are designed to help students relieve stress, make friends, participate in competitive and recreational programs, experience learning both in and out of the classroom in an environment that values diversity. Campus recreation programs strive to create an atmosphere that encourages everyone to live healthy lifestyles while having fun. Do not miss out; take advantage of every program your campus recreation facility offers today."

Dr. Ray Wiley is a recreation professional with more than 30 years of experience in both community and university recreation settings. Dr. Wiley serves as the associate director of campus recreation, where he is responsible for a 160,000 square foot (15,000 square meter) university recreation facility.

DISCOVER OPPORTUNITIES: COMPONENTS OF CAMPUS RECREATION

The purpose of **campus recreation** is to provide a wide variety of recreational experiences and opportunities for students, faculty, and staff. According to Dr. Ray Wiley, the most popular activities offered by the campus recreation centers he directs are (1) intramurals; (2) fitness programs (weight room, fitness classes); (3) club sports; (4) outdoor trips, often referred to as outdoor pursuits; and (5) aquatics, similar to results at other universities. With all of these activities, one might think that all college students would use their campus recreation centers several times per week. However, research shows that not all students are aware of activity choices, and students participate at differing rates. One study found that males tend participate in campus recreation activities more than do females (Zizzi et al., 2004). Another study revealed that freshmen were less aware of recreational offerings on campus and that men and women had different understandings of their campus choices (Reed, 2007). These results suggest that students participate more in campus recreation activities as they learn about their options.

Campus recreation's primary goal is to serve students; thus, a great deal of the activities and programming revolves around student interests. Students, faculty,

LEISURE AWARENESS

NIRSA 2009 Award Descriptions

Creative Excellence Awards

The Creative Excellence Awards focus on outstanding marketing and advertising materials published by NIRSA members. Previous winners of the Creative Excellence Award include these:

- University of Illinois—comprehensive brochure
- University of Missouri—facility publication
- Virginia Tech—audiovisual material

Outstanding Sports Facilities Award

The OSF Awards recognize excellence in newly constructed, renovated, or expanded recreational facilities at NIRSA member institutions.

- Springfield College
- University of Texas San Antonio
- Colorado School of Mines
- University of Wisconsin Oshkosh

Check out the NIRSA Web site (www.nirsa.org) to see whether your institution has received one of these prestigious awards and to explore scholarship opportunities!

and staff participate in campus recreation activates to have fun, maintain healthy lifestyles, and socialize. Leisure activities assist with life stress, enhancing both mental and physical health (Iwasaki & Mannell, 2000). Now a major marketing and recruiting tool for many universities, campus recreation has become a vital component to universities and their students, faculty, and staff. In fact, the National Intramural–Recreational Sports Association (NIRSA) provides several awards to campus recreation programs and professionals for outstanding programs and innovations. Among the most prestigious are the Creative Excellence Award for innovation and creativity in marketing programs and the Outstanding Sports Facilities Award.

The benefits associated with participation in campus recreation activities are endless and range from stress management to social engagement. Areas that many campus recreation centers address are recreational sport, fitness and aquatics, outdoor opportunities, and student program opportunities.

Recreational Sport

The term **recreational sport** was coined because of the popularity of informal sports programs: It is an umbrella term that refers to intramurals, extramurals, club sports, informal sports, and instructional sports (Mull et al., 2005). Numerous benefits are associated with recreational sports involvement, including decreased stress, improved social integration, enhancement of self-esteem, improved grades, and student development (Belch et al., 2001; Bryant et al., 1994; Haines, 2001; Kanters, 2000; Nesbitt, 1998). The most popular of all recreation sports activities are intramurals (Artinger et al., 2006). Intramurals are structured sports programs within the campus. They offer a wide range of sport opportunities with various levels of competition (beginner, intermediate, advanced). Typical examples of intramurals include softball, basketball, rugby, disc golf, hockey, badminton, volleyball, Wiffle ball, and flag football.

©Human Kinetics

Many recreational sport opportunities build lifelong friendships, skills, and love for the sport.

Fitness

Although sports are a large part of campus recreation, there are numerous recreational opportunities in addition to recreational sports. Most universities offer fitness programs, often in state-of-the-art fitness centers. Universities began incorporating fitness programs around the 1970s, although at the time such programs were considered a passing fad. Fitness programs are one of the top recreational activities on college campuses today, and it is predicted that fitness programming will remain essential as our country continues to struggle with obesity. Programs of interest tend to be group fitness classes such as tai chi, swim classes, water aerobics, Spinning classes, yoga, kick boxing, Pilates, and zumba (a type of dance fitness). Research has revealed a significant decrease in depression and anxiety in those who exercise regularly (Goodwin, 2003). Fitness activities also offer a stress-free way to meet people who share the common interest of fitness. The benefits from fitness opportunities, such as regular exercise and stress management, are key components to a healthy life.

Outdoor Trips

Outdoor trips are another unique opportunity offered by campus recreation programs. The trips range from short day hikes to longer international trips. Students can also learn skills such as canoeing, rock climbing, and scuba, and campus recreation often incorporates these skills into outdoor trips. One such example might be a spring break trip to Hawaii for scuba diving. Equipment for personal or major-related camping or kayaking trips is often available for rent through the campus recreation center. You are unlikely to ever find equipment rental as inexpensive as that offered by the campus recreation center: Rental can be as little as $5 a day! Whether students are skilled outdoor enthusiasts or simply would like to learn to kayak, the campus recreation center offers a variety of outdoor recreation opportunities.

©Irmina Mamot/fotolia

When your life depends on those with whom you dive, engaging in the activity often fosters deep respect and kinship with fellow divers.

Student Programs

Recreational opportunities also exist outside of campus recreation facilities. Some are called student programs or student activities, and some are sponsored by the office of student affairs. Regardless of the name, universities are filled with various microcosms outside of campus recreation. Perhaps somewhat unique from campus recreation, most outside activities are created, programmed, and delivered by students. Examples include inexpensive movies, concerts, comedians, lectures, variety shows, and fine arts. Student fees usually cover the majority of the expenses for these events, and therefore they are provided for students either free of charge or a minimal cost. A variety of leisure pursuits have been classified as **casual leisure**, intrinsically rewarding activities requiring little skill or training to enjoy (Stebbins, 1997). Some believe that casual leisure activities are just as important as serious leisure because people highly value casual leisure opportunities. Everyone participates in casual leisure, and most appreciate the opportunity to relax and emotionally recharge (Stebbins, 1997). Examples of casual leisure within campus recreation include going to movies or hanging out with friends. Campus recreation activities can also require specialized skills and time commitment, considered as serious leisure. Student programs for serious leisure activities include concert or theater productions or active participation in committee work. More than just an opportunity to participate in inexpensive, fun social activities, student programs offer great leadership and experiential opportunities.

PERSONAL LEISURE

Take a moment to reflect on your own casual leisure. What simple leisure activities give you the most enjoyment? How about a quick on-line game of Bejeweled or solitaire as a reward for finishing a paper? Or perhaps spending quality time with your dog at the park on a nice sunny day?

Clubs and Student Organizations

Your campus offers a host of other student program opportunities such as student organizations and clubs, Greek life, religious organizations, and cultural opportunities. Additionally, student unions and other venues on campus are filled with social learning environments such as cyber cafes, study spaces, and open green spaces. One can never overlook the importance of informal collegiate experiences that occur as people gather to study or simply to hang out.

Clubs and student organizations are a major part of campus recreation and can range from the Rock Paper Scissors Club, like the one at The University of Florida, to the Young Republicans club, such as that at Wellesley College in Massachusetts. The Rock Paper Scissors Club has grown nationally and even has a college tournament, which is broadcast on ESPN. Of course, there are the typical clubs; for example, each major on campus usually has a club (math club, theater club, Spanish club). Notably, the recreation major's club should be having the most fun! Special interest clubs and organizations are plentiful on campus. Every collegiate campus has student government organizations and most have Greek organizations. Other clubs or organizations may range from the 24-hour movie club to a gardening club. If you are not in at least two clubs, it may be fair to say you are missing out. There are collegiate clubs for just about every leisure interest one could imagine. And if one does not exist on your campus, you could start one tomorrow. On second thought, why wait until tomorrow? You could start a Mustache Club just like the one at Carlton College in Minnesota. (This Carlton College club does include women, as long as they agree to shave everything except their upper lip!) Club and student organizations are derived from common leisure interests and frequently include philanthropic pursuits: The Carlton College Mustache Club raises money for a domestic abuse shelter. However, some clubs are purely for casual leisure experiences, like the Harvard Tiddlywinks Society or the University of Minnesota Campus People Watchers. According to the People Watchers' Web site, it is a "noncreepy organization" of people who enjoy the "social, psychological, and analytical aspects of people watching." Do not wait: Join or start a club or student organization today!

HAVE A VOICE AND GET INVOLVED: VOLUNTEER AND JOB OPPORTUNITIES ON CAMPUS

There is no need to wait until after graduation to seek experience. Let your voice be heard and get involved in both planning and providing feedback regarding campus programs. Volunteer for committees. Serve on student boards. Participate in service learning, and seek employment opportunities in campus recreation and on campus. Some available positions include trip leader, referee or official, student director, program chair, events coordinator, fitness instructor, and student program specialist. Internships, practicum learning, and field experiences are also excellent ways to gain valuable life skills that will serve you in both your personal and professional careers. Another way to make your voice heard is through evaluations. Comprehensive evaluations of campus recreation programs are vital for their success (Cooper & Faircloth, 2006). When you have the opportunity, make

LEISURE HEALTH

Carpe Diem (Seize the Day)!

What do all these opportunities mean for you? Get involved! There are numerous reasons students should get involved in campus activities:

- You may never again in your life have as many recreational opportunities at such little cost.
- The mental health and physical benefits of frequent recreation are invaluable necessities to staying healthy while in college.
- Important life skills and lessons are obtained through the opportunities offered on campus: new leisure pursuits, leadership skills, social skills, professional contacts, and practical experiences.
- You are constantly building the habits you will carry forward, including in your fitness and leisure practices.
- You have a voice! Get involved in planning the activities offered on your campus.

Most student programs (movies, concerts, variety shows, guest lecture series, and other special events) are student driven. Students decide, plan, and deliver many of the activities offered on campus. You can be a part of fun activities, which will benefit your life in many ways. Take advantage of your campus microcosm's recreational opportunities now!

sure to provide feedback. Directors, program managers, and instructors really do care about what you have to say, and they want to hear from you! If leisure constraints are interfering with your ability to participate (e.g., hours of operations) or if you would like to see changes in campus activities, providing feedback is an important place to start.

EXPLORE YOUR COMMUNITY

Students hear the word *community* almost daily while participating in college life, but what does the term really mean? Most agree that **community** can refer to a group of people living in close proximity to one another; a group of people sharing common interests, like the scientific community; people comprising a distinct segment of the population, like the gay community; or people sharing a common identity, like the Irish community. Given these definitions, it is easy to see how a university can be considered a community containing many smaller communities, such as dorms, fraternities, majors, and campus organizations. But beyond the borders of the university is a larger community, city, township, neighborhood, or area.

Community recreation providers and centers strive to provide recreation and leisure opportunities to people living nearby (much like the opportunities offered by the campus recreation center), but community recreation organizers must cater their offerings to a larger range of age groups. Activities are likely to vary widely, such as holiday events for toddlers, league sports for youth and teens, tournaments for adults, and water aerobics targeted for senior citizens. With the diverse selection of age groups, ability levels, and interests that community recreation centers seek to serve, building a sense of community is a task that must be carefully managed. Recreation professionals want participants not only to participate but also to feel connected, which increases the likelihood that community members will return and benefit from other leisure offerings as well.

Community is created in many ways. Living physically near others is one way community is built and might be the most easily recognized meaning of community. However, simply being near others is not enough for people to call themselves a community: We do not normally consider ourselves the community of moviegoers as we wait in line! A sense of community also requires a level of shared identity. Sometimes a sense of community is gained through being near others and participating in activities together, as in being teammates or classmates. Community may

©Photodisc

Some people may feel isolated until they find others who share similar lifestyles or recreational interests.

be gained even when people are not near one another, as with online organizations: People may be separated by continents but may be connected through their shared commitment to a task or belief system. People may be committed to beliefs such as fighting global warming, supporting adoption, or seeking equal rights. People may become a community through participating in adult and youth athletics, special interest clubs, online gaming, and cultural events. These shared desires and beliefs can unite people, helping virtual strangers feel like next-door neighbors.

So what is this sense of community we have been discussing? Cohesiveness is fundamental. People bond through a shared purpose or shared interests. As people feel emotionally connected, this creates a shared sense of identity, which reduces feelings of isolation. **Community recreation** is "a means for improving and maintaining societal cohesion and the quality of life; its development is dependent on social participation" (Torkildsen, 2005). Thus, community recreation activities facilitate opportunities for community members to participate and create emotional attachments to the activity, to the recreation facility, and to one another, which builds a shared sense of community. Both serious and casual leisure can be found in community recreation activities. Serious leisure may take the form of avid motorcycle riders, NASCAR race fans, or members of local community theater. Casual leisure examples include attending movies, watching television, surfing the Internet, or having dinner with friends.

DISCOVER OPPORTUNITIES IN COMMUNITY RECREATION

Community recreation provides numerous opportunities for participation. Activities may be organized by local recreation departments, which usually maintain facilities, plan, organize, and deliver programs. Some of the most common community activities include adult and youth sports, cultural arts, senior centers, educational and instructional courses, aquatics facilities, wellness programs, and special events. Amenities include pavilions, parks, playgrounds, lakes, walking trails, greenways, bike paths, dog parks, and skate parks. Although many of the activities offered by parks and recreation departments are organized, free play opportunities are an important component of parks and recreation as well. Lakes, greenways, bike paths, walking trails, and open access to facilities and spaces are an integral part of the services offered and an important part of building community.

Community centers may be owned and operated by the local parks and recreation department or they may be

©Richard Schultz/Taxi/Getty Images

Visiting a dog park is a great way to meet and recreate with people who share your love for animals! Members of the dog park community (usually) follow common rules of play such as recreation combined with social responsibility: "Leave no trace (wink)!"

privately owned. Local YMCA centers, Jewish community centers, Boys and Girls Clubs, and fitness centers are examples of privately owned community centers. Although not government funded or operated, these centers play a valuable role in community recreation. Private community centers sometimes offer a wider variety of opportunities, and a competitive market tends to work in favor of the participant.

Many communities and even small towns offer unique activities for their populations. For example, Nashville, Tennessee, holds a variety of musical festivals, concerts, and programs given the resources and common interests of the people within the community. In a much smaller area, Smithfield, North Carolina, the annual Ham & Yam Festival attracts hundreds of community members. Many community activities are not hosted by or even affiliated with the local parks and recreation department but are spearheaded by community members themselves. In rural communities, common Halloween events are haunted forests, hay rides, and corn mazes. Many farmers will organize hay rides and transform their cornfields with great detail for the community. Often those who share a common interest organize activities. Other examples of activities created around shared interests include quilting, knitting, and garden clubs and block parties. Still other community members may open horseback trail rides for members of the public.

GET INVOLVED NOW AND IN THE FUTURE

There are many ways to take part in community recreation. People can become active voices in the community for leisure pursuits, volunteer to serve on advisory boards, assist with programs, and act as activists for the community. The National Recreation and Park Association (NRPA) is active in legislative efforts. RecreAC-TION Online is NRPA's free policy and advocacy listserv tool: It is designed to empower community advocacy efforts. Volunteers can play a vital role in community recreation by providing experience, expertise, and labor. People volunteer based on their relationships, community context, and personal characteristics (Wilson, 2000). Volunteering builds relationships and brings communities together (Henderson & Silverberg, 2002), creating and nurturing a sense of cohesion among community members. There are numerous volunteer opportunities in community recreation, such as senior centers, youth sports (coaching and refereeing), and event management; in fact, many activities are planned, organized, and implemented solely by volunteers. Serving as a volunteer can be a valuable way to gain experience and skills for future employment. Taking part in community recreation planning not only provides volunteer opportunities but is also a good way to have a voice regarding which local programs are offered, who should be served, and how money is allocated.

Other people choose to create a career in community recreation. Jobs include recreation director, athletics coordinator, facilities coordinator, aquatics director, events coordinator, marketing director, official or referee, groundskeeper, skills instructor, day camp counselor, and entrepreneur or owner. Some of these positions are full-fledged career paths, whereas others are excellent sources of secondary income. For instance, officials often make as much as $55 dollars for a regular season game and may earn more for refereeing tournament play.

SUMMARY

Campus recreation activities (recreational sport programs, fitness programs, outdoor trips, and aquatics) play a major role in student leisure, and numerous campus recreation opportunities are available on campus: student programs, student organizations and clubs, Greek life, religious organizations, cultural arts opportunities, cyber cafes, and student unions. Serious leisure and casual leisure can be found in all aspects of campus activities and community recreation, although leisure constraints can impede participation in either arena. An important task for college students is to become aware of the leisure opportunities and get involved! Capitalize on the benefits that your campus and community recreation opportunities offer. Getting involved allows participants to stay healthy, reduce stress, meet new people who share common leisure interests, learn new skills, gain new experiences, and rejuvenate. After having experienced campus and community recreation offerings, participants are able to use their knowledge to improve service delivery. Use your voice: Volunteer to serve on advisory boards, committees, and event delivery. Understanding how communities fit one inside the other to create a sense of belongingness, experiencing campus and community recreation activities, and then using lessons learned to become an activist will give you a fuller appreciation for the time you spend in leisure activities.

Learning Activities

1. **Scavenger hunt exercise:** Explore your campus: Your mission is to find and provide details (costs, dates, instructions) for the following:
   - An individual class that you could take alone to become more physically fit
   - A team sport that is offered this semester that everyone in class could register for
   - A club sport developed in the past 5 years
   - A new leisure activity you have never participated in
   - An aquatics program offered in the mornings
   - A spring break trip
   - Hours of operation for the recreation center

- The name of the recreation center's director
- The recreation center schedule of events
- Web address for the recreation center
- Web address for student programs
- Schedule of events from student programs
- Contact information for becoming a member of student programs
- Name of the movie playing next Friday at the student union
- One student organization you could join
- Two clubs you could join
- The next concert on campus
- Two sororities or fraternities you could join
- Six different pieces of equipment you can rent from campus recreation
- Other programs or events specific to your campus

Add any details, restrictions, time constraints, and parameters specific to your campus.

2. **New leisure activity:** Select a leisure activity that you have never done before (but perhaps always wanted to) and try it! Write a summary of your experience. Include a description of the activity, and explain what you liked or did not like about it. Will you continue to participate? Why or why not? What did you learn about yourself through this experience?

For additional assignments, Web links, and more, visit the online student resource at www.HumanKinetics.com/DimensionsOfLeisureForLife.

Review Questions

1. What are the ways you can get involved in your campus activities? Community activities?
2. What is a microcosm?
3. What are three community microcosms on your campus, in your hometown community, and in the world?
4. What are the major categories of campus recreation?
5. What is the purpose of campus recreation?
6. What are some of the common activities on your campus that are provided by campus recreation and by student programs?
7. What are some of the top reasons students do not participate in campus recreation programs?
8. How does a sense of community bring people together?
9. How can you learn about campus recreation programs?
10. How can you find out about student programs, clubs, or organizations?
11. What are some ways to learn about programs offered in the community?
12. What are some of the benefits of participating in campus activities? Community activities?
13. How can you become more active and effective on campus? In the community?

14. How can you become an activist on campus? In your community?

15. How can leisure constraints (interpersonal, intrapersonal, structural) hinder a person's participation in campus or community activities?

Leisure Reading

Canfield, J., Hansen, M.V., Newmark, A., & Clapps, M. (2009). *Chicken soup for the soul: Campus chronicles: 101 real college stories from real college students.* Deerfield Beach, FL: Health Communications.

Canfield, J., Hansen, M.V., Newmark, A., & Heim, S. (2009). *Chicken soup for the soul: All in the family: 10 incredible stories about our funny, quirky, lovable & "dysfunctional" families.* Deerfield Beach, FL: Health Communications.

Dalgarn, M.K. (2001). The role of the campus recreation center in creating a community. *Recreational Sports Journal, 25*(1), 66-72.

Faircloth, S., & Cooper, N. (2007). *Communities of practice in campus recreation: A framework for developing student intramural officials.* Champaign, IL: Human Kinetics.

Glossary

campus community—Associated with valuing people as individuals, accepting people within the community, and improving individual quality of campus social life.

campus recreation—Campus agency that provides a wide variety of recreational experiences and opportunities for students, faculty, and staff.

casual leisure—Intrinsically rewarding activities requiring little skill or training to enjoy.

community—A group of people living in close proximity to one another; a group of people sharing common interests, like the scientific community; a group of people comprising a distinct segment of the population, like the gay community; or a group of people sharing a common identity, like the Irish community.

community recreation—A means for improving and maintaining societal cohesion and the quality of life; its development is dependent on social participation.

microcosm—A world within a world; a miniature world.

recreational sport—An umbrella term that refers to intramurals, extramurals, club sports, informal sports, and instructional sports.

serious leisure—The methodical pursuit of an amateur, a hobbyist, or a volunteer activity so substantial and interesting that the participant centers his life on special skills, knowledge, and experiences associated with the leisure pursuit.

theory of student involvement—The quantity and quality of the physical and psychological energy that students invest in the college experience.

References

Artinger, L., Clapham, L., Meigs, C.H.M., Sampson, N.M.B., & Forrester, S.A. (2006). The social benefits of intramural sports. *NASPA Journal, 43*(1), 69-86.

Astin, A.W. (1975). *Preventing students from dropping out.* San Francisco: Jossey-Bass.

Astin, A.W. (1984). Student involvement: A development theory for higher education. *Journal of College Student Personnel, 25*(4), 297-308.

Belch, H.A., Gebel, M., & Mass, G.M. (2001). Relationship between student recreation complex use, academic performance, and persistence of first-time freshmen. *NASPA Journal, 38*(2), 254-268.

Bryant, J., Bradley, J., & Milborne, C. (1994). Comparing student participation in campus recreation to other aspects of campus life. *NIRSA Annual Conference Review, 45,* 144-168.

Cheng, D.X. (2004). Students' sense of campus community: What it means, and what to do about it. *NASPA Journal, 41*(2), 216-234.

Cooper, N., & Faircloth, C. (2006). Repositioning campus recreation: A case report on designing program evaluation procedures. *Recreational Sports Journal, 30,* 126-135.

Goodwin, R.D. (2003). Association between physical activity and mental disorders among adults in the United States. *Preventive Medicine, 36,* 698-703.

Haines, D.J. (2001). Undergraduate student benefits from university recreation. *NIRSA Journal, 25*(1), 25-33.

Henderson, K., & Silverberg, K. (2002). Good work, if you can get it. *Parks & Recreation, 37*(11), 25-35.

Iwasaki, Y., & Mannell, R.C. (2000). The effects of leisure beliefs and coping strategies on stress-health relationships: A field study. *Leisure/Loisir, 24*(1-2), 3-57.

Kanters, M.A. (2000). Recreational sport participation as a moderator of college stress. *Recreational Sports Journal, 24*(2), 11-24.

Mull, R.F., Bayless, K.G., & Jamieson, L.M. (2005). *Recreational sports management* (4th ed.). Champaign, IL: Human Kinetics.

Nesbitt, G.M. (1998). Social-emotional development and extracurricular involvement of sport club participants. *Recreational Sports Journal, 2*(22), 6-9.

Reed, J. (2007). Perceptions of the availability of recreational physical activity facilities on a university campus. *Journal of American College Health, 55*(4), 189-194.

Schneider, R.C., Stier, W.F. Jr., Kampf, S., Gregory, E., Wilding, G.E., & Haines, S.G. (2007). Perceived problems in campus recreation programs in North America. *Recreational Sports Journal, 31*(1), 51-60.

Stebbins, R.A. (1997). Casual leisure: A conceptual statement. *Leisure Studies, 16*(1), 17-25.

Torkildsen, G. (2005). *Leisure and recreation management* (5th ed.). London: Routledge.

Wilson, J. (2000). Volunteering. *Annual Review of Sociology, 26,* 215-240.

Woolsey, M. (2008, October 7). Worst losing streaks in sports. *Forbes Magazine.* www.forbes.com/2008/10/07/worst-losing-streaks-forbeslife-cx_mw_1007sports.html

Young, S.J., Ross, C.M., & Barcelona, R.J. (2003). Perceived constraints by college students to participation in campus recreational sports programs. *Recreational Sports Journal, 27*(2), 47-62.

Zizzi, S., Ayers, S.F., Watson, J.C. II, & Keeler, L. (2004). Assessing the impact of new student campus recreation centers. *NASPA Journal, 41*(4), 588-630.

13

Leisure for All

Nancy Nisbett • H. Joey Gray
With contributions by J. Michael Wallace

California State University, Fresno
Middle Tennessee State University • University of Illinois

Learning Outcomes

After reading this chapter, you will be able to

▶ Identify at least two constraints to recreation participation for the following:

  ▸ People with disabilities

  ▸ People in rural areas

  ▸ People in urban areas

  ▸ Men, women, gay and lesbian, and transgender groups

  ▸ Ethnic and racial groups

▶ Articulate how a person's socioeconomic status influences leisure choices.

▶ Articulate how a person's ethnic, cultural, religious, and sexual orientations influence leisure choices.

Vocabulary Terms

ethic of care	impairment	marginality hypothesis
ethnic hypothesis	inclusive recreation	normalization
ethnicity	interpersonal constraints	recreation therapy
homeless	intrapersonal constraints	socioeconomic status
homophobia	leisure constraints	structural constraints

Does everyone have equal opportunity for leisure?

Do the CEO of a Fortune 500 company, the 12-year-old living in the inner city, the couple living on their family farm in the rural Midwest, and the young man who uses a wheelchair for mobility all deserve the same opportunities to engage in leisure? If one assumes leisure is a basic human need that provides time to recuperate, learn, and grow, then the answer is yes. The question then becomes "Does everyone have the same access to leisure?" That's where it gets more complicated.

For many, societal rules and social roles limit their opportunities for leisure. The child in the inner city or the couple in the country might not have access to recreation services because of their geographical locations; others might be denied opportunities because of their race or membership in cultural groups. This chapter explores common constraints to leisure due to disability, age, sex, sexual orientation, race, ethnicity, religion, socioeconomic status, and location; it includes a discussion of the benefits that leisure provides for all of these people.

As you read this chapter, keep in mind that no one is a member of just one cultural group. We all exist in multiple cultural groups. One of the authors of this chapter, for instance, is a European-American middle-class Christian woman from a rural area of the Midwest and now living in the urban West; another author is a liberal athletic woman from the South. Within each of us, our varied cultural group memberships interact, each creating a different level of impact on our daily lives as well as on our leisure choices and opportunities.

Leisure for all is about how and to what extent diverse groups engage in leisure activities. This chapter has two sections. The first section focuses on leisure for people with disabilities, veterans, and older adults; location and income are also discussed. The second section concentrates on leisure in relation to men and women; lesbian, gay, bisexual, transgendered, and queer and questioning populations; and ethnicity, race, and culture.

PEOPLE WITH DISABILITIES

The U.S. Census Bureau (2007a) reports that just over 19% of the nation's citizens have a disabling condition. People of all ages, ethnicities, and socioeconomic statuses have impairments related to their sight, hearing, physical abilities, cognitive abilities, and emotional functioning. An **impairment** is an organic or functional condition that may be temporary or permanent (Dattilo, 2002). Those impairments range from mild to severe and may or may not be visible to an observer.

Some people with disabilities are born with the conditions and others acquire their impairments through injury, disease, and age. Those who are born with impairments typically learn to adapt to barriers at an early age. Those who acquire impairments later in life may have more difficulty accepting their conditions and adjusting to resulting changes (Mackelprang & Salsgiver, 1999). People with disabilities, whether they are born with the conditions or the conditions are acquired, have a range of feelings about that part of themselves, just as various attitudes are connected to the physical, emotional, and cognitive features we are born with or acquire.

> Leisure is the exultation of the possible.
> *Martin Buber*

Only a small percentage of people with disabilities, even those with severe impairments, live in care facilities, institutions, or group homes. According to Nelis and Rizzolo (2005) and the Research Information for Independent Living (2009), the number is approximately two million. What that means is that people with disabilities, even with severe impairments, live, work, and play as our neighbors in every corner of the country.

W H A T   D O   Y O U   T H I N K ?

Consider the people in your life. Do you know someone with a disability? If so, in what ways do that person's leisure interests differ from your own? Are those differences based on personal preferences, or are they influenced by the person's impairment? Does the person modify leisure activities in any way as a result of the impairment? If you don't know the answer, now is a great time to ask.

In 1990, the Americans with Disabilities Act (ADA) was signed into law by President George H.W. Bush. This civil rights act was passed to ensure equal opportunities in employment, housing, and access to goods and services (including recreation) for individuals with disabilities. In the decades before the passing of the ADA, people with disabilities were often relegated to recreation programs for special populations, separate from the services provided to those without disabilities. Program choice and availability were often sparse. The passing of the ADA, however, spurred a growing trend toward inclusive recreation programming. In **inclusive recreation** programs everyone, regardless of ability, participates together in the same programs. Adaptations, if needed, are provided so that the person with a disability is an equal participant. The concept of inclusion enables people the freedom to choose programs and services based on their interests and to engage in activities with friends and family.

The benefits of recreation for people with disabilities are the same as the benefits for those without disabilities (American Academy of Pediatrics, 2008). Whether it's a child gaining social skills from participating in a team sport or an adult joining a tennis league to meet people, the benefits are the same for all. For someone with a disability, however, recreation can do even more. Recreation provides opportunities for **normalization**, to be in an environment and engaged in activities that are as normal as possible for someone of a given age, sex, or location.

©Radu Razvan

Don't be afraid to get in there and play, no matter what your abilities or skill level.

Some people with disabilities may also benefit from recreation as part of a prescribed treatment program by receiving **recreation therapy** services, an allied health field that uses recreation as a tool to treat individuals with physical, emotional, or cognitive impairments. Recreation therapists work with clients to identify specific goals to enhance their clients' quality of life. Clients participate in individual or group treatment to achieve their goals under the guidance of the recreation therapist. People with disabilities may encounter a recreation therapist in various settings, depending on their impairment. A child with a learning disability may work with a recreation therapist at her school, while an adult who has had a stroke may receive recreation therapy services while in a rehabilitation hospital.

VETERANS

Within the broad scope of individuals with disabilities, specific focus is now being given to military veterans. More than 3.3 million U.S. veterans of all ages, not including those from the most recent wars in Iraq and Afghanistan, are identified as having a service-related disability (National Center for Veterans Analysis and Statistics, 2009). To date, in the wars in Iraq and Afghanistan, over 35,000 soldiers have been wounded (Defense Manpower Data Center, 2009). Although body armor has reduced the number of deaths, the number of survivors with severe injuries is high. Additionally, according to the Center for American Progress (2008), up to 40% of troops returning from Iraq and Afghanistan will face the psychological effects of war, including depression, anxiety, and posttraumatic stress disorder (PTSD). A 2008 Iraq and Afghanistan Veterans of America (IAVA) report contends that one out of every three veterans of the Iraq and Afghanistan wars will face a serious psychological injury; multiple tours of duty and inadequate breaks between deployments significantly increase the potential for psychological disorders. Since the average age of discharge from the service is currently 25.3 years (U.S. Department of Veterans Affairs, 2006),

WHAT DO YOU THINK?

Why might veterans have difficulty when returning from war? In addition to potential physical injuries, what types of injuries or conditions might they have that would make it difficult to adjust to civilian life? Are there students on your campus who are veterans of recent wars? What services does your campus provide? What services does your community provide?

the result is thousands of young active men and women reentering civilian life, a high percentage of those dealing with physical and emotional impairments. Marital stress and substance abuse are increasingly being reported, as are rising suicide rates (IAVA, 2008).

OLDER ADULTS

The nation's older adult population is growing. The U.S. Census Bureau (2007b) estimates there are just over 50 million people over the age of 60 in the United States. As this population continues to increase in numbers, it also increases in age as the average life span increases. For the 2000 Census, the largest increase among older adults was in the 85-and-over age range (U.S. Census Bureau, 2001). While most older adults do have health problems related to their advancing years, medical advances and health education have allowed many older adults to remain active well into their retirement. And as noted by Epstein (1994), the conditions that are often accepted as signs of aging are "now understood to be hypokinesia, a disease of *disuse*, the degeneration and functional loss of muscle and bone tissue" (p. 65). As a result, through activity, older adults can prevent much of the degeneration that results from sedentary lifestyles.

The notion of older adults and their recreation interests has changed in recent decades. Traditional programming for older adults at community or senior centers often consisted of activities such as bingo and card clubs and other sedentary activities. Programmers recognized this group's need for socialization and focused on large-group activities that required little mobility. Over the years, the need for socialization has not changed. Leisure still serves as the primary social outlet for many older adults, especially those who are retired, single, or widowed. What has changed are the types of programs people in this age group desire. A lifestyle survey (Kluge, 2005) published in the *Journal of Physical Education, Recreation and Dance* reports active recreation as the leading leisure interest for older adults. Older adults are now engaged in activities such as casino trips, hikes, biking tours, and wine clubs.

Although the legislation is now in place to ensure equal access to recreation programs and services, and lawmakers and the public are beginning to recognize the need to improve services to groups such as older adults and veterans, not all problems are solved. The numbers of inclusive recreation programs and services have increased, but people with disabilities continue to report difficulty in accessing services. In a Harris survey, 69% of adults with disabilities reported their disability

Age should never be a limitation. You're never too old to get involved and have some fun.

©Human Kinetics

prevented them in some way from attending cultural or sporting events, participating in recreation, or socializing with friends outside their home (Taylor, 1998). Barriers include negative attitudes of staff and participants, refusal to provide services, and lack of physical access. Recreation professionals need to continue their efforts to increase awareness, train staff, and retrofit facilities as we strive to meet the spirit of inclusive recreation.

SPORTS

People with disabilities, veterans, and older adults benefit from all areas of recreation, including outdoor adventure, art, and volunteering. One particular area of recreation warranting notice is sport participation. Depending on the level of impairment, a person with a disability may participate in regular league sports along with others in their age group, whether it is the over-35 softball league or the senior chair volleyball league. Another option is participating in one of several sport leagues or associations developed for people with specific disorders.

The United Cerebral Palsy Athletic Association, the Dwarf Athletic Association of America, the Veterans Golden Age Games, and Special Olympics International are all examples of associations that sponsor various sport leagues or events for individuals with those disorders. Other associations, such as the National Wheelchair Basketball Association and the International Wheelchair Rugby Federation, provide opportunities in particular sports for individuals with various disabling conditions (in these cases, for those who use wheelchairs).

Most of these associations create competitions on local, state, national, and sometimes international levels; requisite skill levels increase as the level of competition increases. Players range from weekend warriors (those who play for fun on the weekends) to those who compete nationally and internationally at a very high level of competition.

At the highest level of sport for people with disabilities is the Paralympics. What originated as a way to help World War II veterans rehabilitate in 1948 has now become the international Paralympic movement, hosting the world's elite disabled athletes. The Paralympic Games are held during the same years as the Olympics, and since the Seoul games in 1988, both Games have been held at the same venues. The International Olympic Committee and the International Paralympic Committee now work together to host both Games (Paralympic Movement, 2009).

LOCATION AND INCOME

Where a person lives has a strong influence on his or her leisure choices. Easy access is one reason why a person who lives in a rural area may be more likely to engage in fishing, whereas a person who lives in a city may be more likely to attend an art hop (an open house of several nearby art galleries or other businesses displaying local artists' work; attendees socialize as they enjoy an evening viewing art). Of course, the person in the rural area may enjoy art hops as well, but he does not have the same access as the person in the city.

Both rural areas and large urban areas create constraints to leisure involvement. Lack of organized programs, facilities, and transportation are common constraints in rural communities in addition to constraints related to family roles and motivation (Perry & Kendall, 2008). Without an official recreation department, schools, not-for-profit organizations, and other community organizations fill in the gaps

©Photodisc/Getty Images

Recreation is wherever you make it happen.

of recreation service by sponsoring sport leagues and craft clubs and organizing social events. Rural recreation initiatives, such as the Illinois Rural Recreation Development Project, are focused on developing sustainable recreation opportunities through the promotion of partnerships among community organizations. Nonprofit organizations, churches, schools, and county and state agencies work together to maximize offerings and minimize duplication of services.

Those living in an inner city face many of the same constraints as those encountered in rural areas. Lack of facilities, organized programming, and transportation are just as prevalent in these areas. In addition, inner cities lack green space and parks are often not well maintained, creating unsafe environments for play. Gang activity, run-down facilities, and lack of trained staff have all been cited as reasons for limited availability. The need for recreation in these areas, however, continues to grow. Especially for inner-city youth, recreation provides opportunities to learn prosocial skills, stay off the streets, and develop interests outside of their immediate neighborhoods. Through initiatives like Austin's roving leaders programs, recreation leaders go to the inner-city neighborhoods, develop rapport with the youth, keep them engaged in positive activities, and expose them to a wide variety of recreation skills, stimulating their interest in the organized programs the city offers.

Closely connected to where a person lives is his or her **socioeconomic status** (SES), which refers to "the status one retains in society as a consequence of three individual attributes: income, occupation, and education" (Dawson, 2000, p. 100). If recreation programs are indeed to be available to all, then public recreation facilities should provide programs at little or no cost. This was the case in the late 1900s as public and not-for-profit recreation agencies provided programs aimed at improving quality of life for those of lower SES. Budget cuts over the past several decades, however, have reversed those efforts. Currently, most recreation opportunities are fee based, and even those offered by municipal recreation departments require ever-increasing registration fees as other funding sources are reduced. Since leisure funds are typically pulled from citizens' expendable income, those with lower SES have limited funds to dedicate to leisure interests, limiting their leisure opportunities.

Of special note for recreation professionals are those who are homeless. Nickasch and Marnocha (2009, p. 40) define a **homeless** person as one "who lacks a fixed, regular, and adequate nighttime residence." People who are homeless may be living with friends, in shelters, in their cars, or on the streets. Estimates for the number of homeless in the United States vary based on the definition used but range from 500,000 to 2.5 million. While white males make up the largest number of homeless, a growing number of families, especially single-mother families, fall into this category. Recreation providers are in a unique position to provide services for this population through drop-in centers or outreach services at shelters; they can collaborate with other community service agencies, becoming part of a referral network. Recreation programs provide opportunities to decrease social isolation, increase self-awareness, and offer a sense of community to those who are homeless.

LEISURE AND SEGMENTS OF SOCIETY

Like other important elements of American culture, access to resources for leisure and recreation is regarded as one of the cherished rights of citizenship. However, not all segments of society participate equally, as has been demonstrated for various activities in relation to socioeconomic background (Burch, 2009). All those who sail boats are not considered yachtsmen. Those who are considered yachtsmen are usually affiliated with a particular social class. There are various dimensions that may be viewed as a constraint to leisure. **Leisure constraints** theory explains that leisure impediments may interfere with participation; these are referred to as interpersonal, intrapersonal, and structural constraints (Crawford & Jackson, 2005). **Interpersonal constraints** are barriers to participation that deal with social relationships with others. For instance, a student may not eat lunch at a particular table at school because she is not in the popular clique at school. If she dares to socialize with the popular group, she will be ridiculed by the group. **Intrapersonal constraints** are individual psychological factors that get in the way of leisure participation. These may be ability level, personality needs, prior experiences, or supposed attitudes of peer groups. For instance, a woman may believe that mostly men use the fitness center; therefore, she might not go. Alternatively, a young adolescent male might avoid taking a ballet class because of the fear of teasing from his male peers. **Structural constraints** are factors that interfere with leisure preference and participation. Amish people do not travel as far as those who use automobiles due to their religious and cultural beliefs. These

LEISURE AWARENESS

Have you ever wanted to participate in a leisure activity, but did not? Think about why you did not participate. Can you identify what type of leisure constraint might have prevented your participation? Was it an interpersonal, intrapersonal, or structural constraint?

findings illustrate how time and proximity issues can act as structural constraints. Dimensions such as sex and gender, race and ethnicity, culture, and religion are examined more closely in this section.

Women and Men

You or someone you know might have been left out of an activity or chosen last just for being a girl. Or you might know a girl who was teased and called a tomboy because she liked to play sports. Or perhaps you know a boy who was teased because he liked to play with Barbie dolls. Gender has been shown to substantially affect quantity and quality of leisure practices, opportunities, and experiences (Shaw & Henderson, 2005). Girls often stop playing sports because the stigma is intimidating if playing sports is viewed as contradicting their gender role (Guillet et al., 2000). Despite advances in equality such as Title IX and the corporate and societal sense of equality of the sexes, questions still remain regarding diversity in background, marital conditions, and degrees of power (Henderson & Shaw, 2006). Research on gender and leisure has adopted a gender relations approach, in which the connections are explored between women's disadvantaged position in terms of access to leisure and their lack of power in society in general (Aitchison, 2001). Until recently, most of this research has been concerned with the gendered nature of women's leisure, with relatively little attention to men's leisure from a gendered perspective (Shaw & Henderson, 2005). Issues surrounding gender constraints should be given equal attention to both women and men. Today, boys face as much discrimination for certain leisure pursuits as girls do, which can result in significant damage to self-esteem. However, it is important to note that societal roles are often supported by peer groups (Leaper & Friedman, 2006), and an "athletic" girl could be a good or bad label depending on the peer group.

The **ethic of care**, or obligation to care for one's family, has been identified as a major constraint to women's leisure. In the past, women's societal roles have been confined to the home and family, making them the primary caregiver. Women, regardless of ethnicity, maintain that family obligations are the main constraint on their leisure (Miller & Brown, 2005). Traditional power relationships in society have proscribed women's leisure activities and emphasized that women should be at home to take care of their children. Therefore, women typically provided for the needs of others first, thus neglecting their own leisure needs (Miller & Brown, 2005). Economics have also been reported by both men and women as a constraint to

©Franz Pfluegl - Fotolia

What is your perception of female athletes?

leisure participation. Women's lack of economic power and their lower earning power compared to that of men have been shown to be particularly constraining on their leisure time as well (Bryson, 2008). Lack of opportunities, or lack of facilities or programs, may also constrain leisure. The availability of recreational opportunities (Henderson & Hickerson, 2007), particularly sport opportunities, is reflected in the continued unequal funding and unequal provisions of programs, teams, and sport leagues for men and women. Other constraints to women's leisure include stress and lack of time (Shaw & Henderson, 2005). Overall, research has documented constraints on women's leisure, and much of this research links their constraints to specific positions within a patriarchal society. While recognizing and addressing leisure constraints for women are still an important agenda, women are beginning to negotiate constraints as they cast aside social barriers (Shaw & Henderson, 2005). Once women can identify the benefits of a leisure activity, they are more apt to overcome the constraint. Men are less constrained by fear than women; however, women are more likely than men to take more precautions and preparations to overcome the fear (Coble et al., 2003). Participation is the key. Whether policy changes are needed, constraints are overcome, or women ignore social pressures to conform to a stereotype, leisure benefits can be recognized only through participation.

The lack of research on men, leisure, and gender means relatively little is known about the gendered nature of men's leisure constraints. Although much of the research on leisure has been about men, this research has rarely used gender or masculinity as an analytic concept (Shaw & Henderson, 2005). Is it possible that gender is viewed as an enabling factor for men rather than a constraint? At times, yes, it is possible because men frequently have a higher level of participation and a stronger sense of entitlement to leisure compared to most women. However, males do face problems in leisure activities. Men may feel that they do not fit the ideal image of masculinity; they might not feel competitive, tough, successful, or heterosexual. Males participating in feminine-classified sports, such as figure skating, face homophobic ridicule, which can be considered a constraint to participation (Schmalz et al., 2008). Thus, males may reject leisure activities and possibilities they otherwise might enjoy because of the desire to appear masculine (Henderson & Shaw, 2006) to conform to social pressures. So, how do males overcome this societal or cultural constraint? They have a strong sense of inner self, and the desire to participate supersedes what their peer group thinks. Or perhaps other extrinsic motivational factors come into play; more specifically, they may take ballet to meet women!

Indeed, both men and women face leisure constraints. As society becomes more liberal with promotion and acceptance of differences, these leisure constraints

SELF-DISCOVERY

Are you gender biased, or do you hold gender constraints? You might have said to a man, "You throw like a girl." Do you think that some activities are for boys only or girls only? If so, you have gender biases or constraints. Most people do have gender biases; it is our culture and human nature. However, it is important to recognize these biases and constraints and determine for ourselves if this is right or wrong. Think about your bias or constraint again. Should you think about changing your views? Why or why not?

should fade. However, it is vital that individuals, communities, and government officials continue to strive for equality in leisure opportunities for everyone.

Lesbian, Gay, Bisexual, Transgendered, and Queer and Questioning (LGBTQQ)

The label LGBT has changed to LGBTQQ: lesbian, gay, bisexual, transgendered, and queer and questioning. One of the most endearing qualities of LGBTQQ is the ongoing desire to be inclusive rather than to be exclusive; hence the name change. The needs of LGBTQQ are no different from the needs of heterosexuals: acceptance and equality. Thus far we have discussed leisure constraints as they relate to women and men, socioeconomic status, and age. LGBTQQ are no different; this community experiences interpersonal, intrapersonal, and structural constraints just as any other group does. The most common constraint for the LGBTQQ community may be in the form of homophobia, which could take the form of both an interpersonal and an intrapersonal constraint. A boy might not try out for the football team because members of the team have caused physical harm to other boys who were suspected of being gay. An intrapersonal constraint for someone in the LGBTQQ community might involve not attending church because she worries that she will not be accepted by the congregation. The LGBTQQ community advocates for equal participation in their leisure pursuits. In fact, some consider the LGBTQQ a cultural community all its own and in this way remove constraints to leisure participation for those in the LGBTQQ community.

Homophobia is "societal discrimination and stigma of individuals who do not conform to traditional norms of sex and gender" (Sugano et al., 2006, p. 217). Homophobia is pervasive in American society and is taught implicitly and explicitly by parents, family members, teachers, coaches, professors, clergy, friends, and even leisure service professionals. This does not mean that all parents, teachers, coaches, and others promote homophobia; however, its prevalence in society confirms that its promotion remains an active practice. Ask yourself whether you have ever been ridiculed or bullied because of the way you dressed or your choice of friends. Perhaps you felt isolated because of whom you chose to date. Did that form of discrimination affect where you went or the activities you chose to participate in? This is how homophobia can constrain the leisure pursuits of the LGBTQQ community. People will often avoid places or activities where they know they are not wanted or accepted. That is why it is important for communities to have places and activities that are accepting of LGBTQQ members. Those who do not wish to interact with LGBTQQ persons simply do not have to attend or participate in LGBTQQ activities. But, rest assured that LGBTQQ persons pay their community taxes and are valuable employees, parents, and community members just like everyone else; they deserve equal respect and consideration.

Some communities have responded to the unique needs of LGBTQQ persons. LGBTQQ recreation centers; Neil Christie Living Centers; Billy DeFrank Center in San Jose, California; recreation, support, and partnerships with other agencies; Gay Games; and Gay Olympics all cater to the recreational needs of the LGBTQQ. Most university campuses today have one or more LGBTQQ organizations or support groups. Many of these centers and organizations are dedicated to assisting LGBTQQ youth and adults who have difficulties relating to their sexuality and fostering social connections. Particularly in a school setting, dealing with sexual thoughts and feelings that are atypical of social and societal norms can be

©AFP/Getty Images

According to the *Same-Sex Couples and the Gay, Lesbian, Bisexual Population: New Estimates from the American Community Survey,* there are about 8.8 million LGBTQQ persons in the United States (Gates, 2006).

difficult. Those who are perceived as or identify as LGBTQQ are often teased, bullied, sexually harassed, and discriminated against more than their heterosexual peers (Williams et al., 2005). Often the senses of true self, safety, and acceptance for those who identify as LGBTQQ are found only at centers such as the Billy DeFrank Center.

Underlying themes in all recent research related to gay and lesbian issues are that homosexuality is deeply stigmatized in American society and that this stigmatization, rather than sexual orientation per se, is the cause of severe stress factors for gays and lesbians, especially youth. Studies show that suicide attempts and rates are higher among LGBTQQ than among those who identify as heterosexual (Ryan et al., 2009). More specifically, those who are rejected by their family are 8.4% more likely to attempt suicide than peers who had low levels of family rejection. The founding of LGBTQQ centers and organizations is the first step in improving the delivery of leisure services to individuals who have been denied essential parts of their personalities and their basic human rights as citizens. More important, these outlets for LGBTQQ youth and adults help combat these staggering statistics. The leisure service professional's attitude toward homosexuality is critical to providing meaningful services to gay and lesbian participants. Positive attitudes can assist in the recovery of the damage of negative stigmatization that has and continues to occur (Graybill et al., 2009). Positive attitudes can be expressed by ensuring that "sexual orientation" is added to the agency's nondiscrimination, recruitment, and program policies; providing opportunities for building professional competencies on issues facing gay and lesbian participants; working to avoid stereotyping; and integrating needs of gay and lesbian participants into the planning and delivery of services.

On a more positive side, the LGBTQQ community has made great strides regarding community acceptance and leisure pursuits. Today, the LGBTQQ community often determines what is trendy or chic. Today's market holds the common view that the LGBTQQ community (particularly gay men) maintain a higher level of discretionary income and are more frequent recreational travelers than heterosexuals (Hughes, 2005). As LGBTQQ has become more accepted, tourism and travel industries have catered to the community's needs. American Airlines and the Olivia cruise line provide exclusive travel destinations for LGBTQQ persons. However, the discrimination issues still exist, which can cause significant leisure constraints, particularly for youth and young adults. Accepting and building on the successes of today while continuing to fight for equality are essential for the LGBTQQ members and supporters.

Ethnicity, Race, and Culture

By the year 2020, the population of the United States is projected to increase from 284 million to 325 million. In anticipation of changes in racial and ethnic composition, leisure professionals will need to consider demographic-driven programming factors when deciding what leisure activities to provide in their communities. Professionals will need to examine the cultural values among ethnic and racial groups since these values influence perceptions and behaviors of participants (Li et al., 2008). To address the changing demographics, leisure service providers should have an understanding of past research dealing with leisure participation among minority groups and the constraints to participation by these groups (Bell & Hurd, 2006).

Despite strides in societal acceptance regarding ethnic and cultural differences, these differences can often foster discriminatory behavior. For several decades social scientists have been exploring participation patterns involving race, ethnicity, and cultural diversity. **Ethnicity** refers to large groups of people classed according to common racial, national, tribal, religious, linguistic, or cultural origin or backgrounds. Historically, there are two explanations for the divergence between ethnic minorities and whites: the ethnic hypothesis and the marginality hypothesis (Floyd et al., 1994). The **ethnic hypothesis** maintains that minorities' underparticipation or intergroup variation results from differences between racial or ethnic groups. Ethnicity attributes differences in recreation behavior to value differences based on subcultural norms. The theory suggests that subcultures of ethnic minorities have unique cultural value systems that influence their recreation behavior (Johnson et al., 1998). The **marginality hypothesis** emphasizes minority status as a causal factor of underparticipation among minorities. That is, based on cultural practices, some activities would be out of the norm for minority groups, such as sunbathing (white people flock to beaches and pools for the sole purpose of tanning their skin). But just as some sports or recreational activities are considered

---

W H A T   D O   Y O U   T H I N K ?

Guilty of ethnic or cultural discrimination? Have you ever been at a night club, social gathering, or recreational activity and thought, What are *they* doing here? Not that you had ill intentions with the thought, but perhaps you did notice someone was culturally out of place.

feminine or masculine, some recreational activities are still culturally defined by race or ethnicity: sunbathing at the beach, outdoor recreational activities, wearing the FUBU clothing line, or recording "real" hip-hop music. There are exceptions to the rule, but for the most part we can identify numerous recreational activities that are solely depicted by ethnicity or culture. However, as a society we have to educate and expose ourselves and our children to a variety of leisure pursuits to break down the cultural constraints and discrimination barriers.

In the past, research tended to view ethnic groups as culturally homogeneous despite significant cultural, educational, and socioeconomic differences that exist within the ethnic group. The fact that groups participate in similar activities does not indicate that the meaning of their participation is the same. What might be considered leisure by one cultural group may not be defined as leisure by members of a different cultural group. For example, in the United States getting a tattoo is usually considered a recreational activity. However, if you are a member of the Maori tribe, the tattooing of your face (an elaborate design called a moko) is part of your cultural heritage and ancestry. Within a group, differences could also be observed due to microcultural (subcultural) differences (e.g., social class, education, values, beliefs, and ancestral background). Membership in an ethnic group (e.g., Hispanic) may be determined by commonality in language, religion, or ancestral country, but differences will result from association with a specific microculture. These microcultural differences are found in social class, education, music, food, and residential location. While language might be a commonality among cultures, slang and pronunciations can vary among microcultures. The most dominant language in the United States is English; yet, someone from rural North Carolina might have a hard time understanding someone from Boston, and vice versa. Hopefully, most people will embrace racial, ethnic, and cultural differences, and there are several ways to assist in this effort. Education is the key to success. Festivals and awareness programs that celebrate ethnic and cultural differences are a great way to expose and educate members of a community. Almost all universities hold cultural activities on campus and support off-campus activities in an effort to increase cultural awareness. The next steps are to be a participant of such activities and to be an advocate.

SUMMARY

This chapter explored the true meaning of leisure for all by examining the leisure of diverse groups. Recreation therapy services use recreation as a tool to treat individuals with physical, emotional, or cognitive impairments. This service is frequently used with military veterans and older adults. Leisure for persons with disability reaches far beyond ADA accommodations. We must recognize that leisure pursuits provide opportunity, skills, and inclusion for persons with disabilities just as they do for those without a disability. Motives for participation resonate with most people. One key benefit that leisure offers is normalization, the ability to fit in and be like everyone else.

Location and income can have a major impact on leisure activities. Those who live in rural areas might be drawn to fishing or gardening because of the landscape and where they live. Socioeconomic level also plays a role in our leisure choices. Those with higher incomes can participate in more expensive leisure pursuits like hopping on a jet and traveling to Paris for dinner, whereas those from lower socioeconomic levels might choose leisure opportunities that are less expensive like a family movie night at home.

Leisure constraints play a role in all walks of life. Those who are homeless often face a lack of opportunity, while others face location and economic constraints. Specifically, we can categorize leisure constraints into three basic areas: interpersonal, intrapersonal, and structural. Women and men; LGBTQQ; and those of different racial, ethnic, and cultural backgrounds all face unique challenges and opportunities in their leisure endeavors. Leisure service providers must be aware of the constraints that affect all groups—particularly diverse groups—and ensure that they plan recreational opportunities to alleviate barriers. Leisure should be available to everyone, regardless of group affiliation, gender, socioeconomic status, or general differences. Thus, the most important role for any recreation professional is to ensure leisure for all by having a thorough understanding of the populations they serve.

Learning Activities

1. Visit a local homeless shelter. Find out what services are provided. As a class, develop and implement a recreation program for the shelter.

2. Research cultural activities both on campus and within the community. Pick two activities and attend them. Write a summary paper and reflection on what you learned about the culture. Address whether you would return and how your perspectives about the culture have changed.

3. What cultural program is *not* offered on your campus but should be? Do some research and plan your own cultural festival. You should determine a schedule of activities. Remember that the festival should be both educational and fun.

4. Reflect on a time when you experienced or witnessed recreation discrimination. How did it make you feel at the time? Now do you have a different perspective about the situation? After reading this chapter, how might you approach the situation today?

For additional assignments, Web links, and more, visit the online student resource at www.HumanKinetics.com/DimensionsOfLeisureForLife.

Review Questions

1. Identify the constraints to recreation for a person with a disability.

2. How are recreation interests of older adults changing?

3. What can recreation providers do to increase opportunities for people with disabilities?

4. Why do rural areas pose constraints to recreation?

5. What constraints to recreation are present in inner cities?

6. How does a person's SES affect recreation choices?

7. Does everyone deserve equal access to recreation?

8. What are leisure constraints? Explain and define the various types of leisure constraints.

9. Are women still experiencing discrimination regarding recreational activities?

10. How might men experience constraints in leisure pursuits?

11. Define LGBTQQ.

12. What can recreation providers do to increase recreation opportunities for LGBTQQ persons?

13. What are the characteristics of a microculture?

14. Why do leisure professionals need to examine cultural differences and values?

15. What can leisure professionals do to promote cultural diversity and acceptance?

Leisure Reading

Bissinger, H.G. (1990). *Friday night lights.* Reading, MA: Addison-Wesley.

Blumenthal, K. (2005). *Let me play: The story of Title IX: The law that changed the future of girls in America.* New York: Atheneum.

Emmons, C., & Anger, S. (2002). *Sammy wakes his dad.* New York: Star Bright Books.

Engh, F. (2002). *Why Johnny hates sports.* Garden City Park, NY: Square One.

Grossman, A.H. (1993). Providing leisure services for gays and lesbians. *Parks and Recreation, 28*(4), 26-29, 90-91.

Jones, R. (1976). *The acorn people.* New York: Bantam Doubleday.

Longmore, P.K. (2003). *Why I burned my book and other essays on disability.* Philadelphia: Temple University Press.

Weihenmayer, E. (2002). *Touch the top of the world: A blind man's journey to climb farther than the eye can see.* New York: Plume.

Glossary

ethic of care—Obligation to care for one's family.

ethnic hypothesis—Maintains that minority underparticipation or intergroup variation results from differences between racial or ethnic groups. Ethnicity attributes differences in recreation behavior to value differences based on subcultural norms.

ethnicity—Refers to large groups of people classed according to common racial, national, tribal, religious, linguistic, or cultural origin or backgrounds.

homeless—A state of lacking a fixed, regular, and adequate nighttime residence.

homophobia—Societal discrimination and stigma of individuals who do not conform to traditional norms of sex and gender.

impairment—An organic or functional condition that may be temporary or permanent.

inclusive recreation—Everyone, regardless of ability, participates together in the same programs.

interpersonal constraints—Barriers to participation that deal with social relationships with others.

intrapersonal constraints—Individual psychological factors that interfere with leisure participation. These may be ability level, personality needs, prior experiences, or supposed attitudes of peer groups.

leisure constraints—Impediments to participation; referred to as interpersonal, intrapersonal, and structural constraints.

marginality hypothesis—Emphasizes minority status as a causal factor of underparticipation among minorities.

normalization—To be in an environment and engaged in activities that are as normal as possible for someone of a given age, sex, or location.

recreation therapy—An allied health field that uses recreation as a tool to treat individuals with physical, emotional, or cognitive impairments.

socioeconomic status—The status one retains in society as a consequence of three distinct attributes: income, occupation, and education.

structural constraints—Factors that interfere with leisure preference and participation.

References

Aitchison, C. (2001). Gender and leisure research: The "codification of knowledge." *Leisure Sciences, 23*(1), 1-19.

American Academy of Pediatrics. (2008). *Recreation.* www.medicalhomeinfo.org/health/Recreation.html

Bell, C.M., & Hurd, A.R. (2006). Research update: Recreation across ethnicity: People of different races often seek contrasting recreation opportunities. *Parks & Recreation,* October, 28-34.

Bryson, V. (2008). Time-use studies. *International Feminist Journal of Politics, 10*(2), 135-153.

Burch, W. Jr. (2009). The social circles of leisure: Competing explanations. *Journal of Leisure, 41*(3), 313-335.

Center for American Progress. (2008). *Veterans' mental health by the numbers.* www.americanprogress.org/issues/2008/04/veterans_mental_health.html

Coble, T.G., Selin, S.W., & Erickson, B.B. (2003). Hiking alone: Understanding fear, negotiation strategies and leisure experience. *Journal of Leisure Research, 35,* 1-21.

Crawford, D.W., & Jackson, E.L. (2005). Leisure constraints theory: Dimensions, directions, and dilemmas. In E.L. Jackson (Ed.), *Constraints to leisure* (pp. 153-167). State College, PA: Venture.

Dattilo, J. (2002). *Inclusive leisure services: Responding to the rights of people with disabilities.* State College, PA: Venture.

Dawson, D. (2000). Social class and leisure provision. In M.T. Allison & I.E. Schneider (Eds.), *Diversity and the recreation profession: Organizational perspectives* (pp. 99-114). State College, PA: Venture.

Defense Manpower Data Center. (2009). *Global war on terrorism casualties by military service component: Active, guard and reserve October 2, 2001-October 10, 2009.* http://siadapp.dmdc.osd.mil/personnel/CASUALTY/gwot_component.pdf

Epstein, R. (1994). How much do you know about recreation for older adults? *Parks & Recreation, 29*(3), 65-69.

Floyd, M.F., McGuire, F.A., Noe, F.P., & Shinew, K.J. (1994). Race, class, and leisure activity preferences: Marginality and ethnicity revisited. *Journal of Leisure Research, 26*(2), 158-173.

Gates, G.J. (2006). *Same-sex couples and the gay, lesbian, bisexual population: New estimates from the American Community Survey.* Los Angeles: Williams Institute.

Graybill, E.C., Varjas, K., Meyers, J., & Watson, L.B. (2009). Content-specific strategies to advocate for lesbian, gay, bisexual, and transgender youth: An exploratory study. *School Psychology Review, 38*(4), 570-584.

Guillet, E., Sarrazin, P., & Fontayne, P. (2000). "If it contradicts my gender role, I'll stop": Introducing survival analysis to study the effects of gender typing on the time of withdrawal from sport practice—A 3-year study. *European Review of Applied Psychology, 50,* 417-421.

Henderson, K.A., & Hickerson, B. (2007). Women and leisure: Premises and performances uncovered in an integrative review. *Journal of Leisure Research, 39*(4), 591-610.

Henderson, K.A., & Shaw, S.M. (2006). Leisure and gender: Challenges and opportunities for feminist research. In C. Rojek, S.M. Shaw, & A.J. Veal (Eds.), *A handbook of leisure studies* (pp. 216-230). London: Palgrave.

Hughes, H. (2005). A gay tourism market: Reality or illusion, benefit or burden? *Journal of Quality Assurance in Hospitality & Tourism, 5*(2), 57-74.

Iraq and Afghanistan Veterans of America (IAVA). (2008, January). Mental health injuries: The invisible wounds of war. *Issue Report,* 1-15.

Johnson, C.Y., Bowker, J.M., English, D.B.K., & Worthen, D. (1998). Wildland recreation in the rural south: An examination of marginality and ethnicity theory. *Journal of Leisure Research, 30*(1), 101-120.

Kluge, M.A. (2005). Active recreation grows among older adults. *Journal of Physical Education, Recreation and Dance, 76*(5), 39-46.

Leaper, C., & Friedman, C.K. (2006). The socialization of gender. In J. Grusec & P. Hastings (Eds.), *The handbook of socialization: Theory and research* (pp. 561-587). New York: Guilford.

Li, C., Absher, J., Graefe, A., & Hsu, Y. (2008). Services for culturally diverse customers in parks and recreation. *Leisure Sciences, 30*(1), 87-92.

Mackelprang, R.W., & Salsgiver, R.O. (1999). *Disability: A diversity model approach.* Pacific Grove, CA: Brooks/Cole.

Miller, Y.D., & Brown, W.J. (2005). Determinants of active leisure for women with young children—an "ethic of care" prevails. *Leisure Sciences, 27,* 405-420.

National Center for Veterans Analysis and Statistics. (2009). *Analysis of unique veterans utilization of VA benefits and services.* www1.va.gov/vetdata/docs/SpecialReports/uniqueveteransMay.pdf

Nelis, T., & Rizzolo, M.C. (2005). *Use of state institutions for people with intellectual disabilities in the United States.* University of Colorado: Coleman Institute.

Nickasch, B., & Marnocha, S. (2009). Healthcare experiences of the homeless. *Journal of the American Academy of Nurse Practitioners, 21*(1), 39-46.

Paralympic Movement. (2009). *Paralympic Games.* www.paralympic.org/Paralympic_Games

Perry, C., & Kendall, J. (2008). Rural women walking for health. *Western Journal of Nursing Research, 30*(3), 295-316.

Research Information for Independent Living. (2009). *Disability statistics.* Author.

Ryan, C., Huebner, D., Diaz, R.M., & Sanchez, G. (2009). Family rejection as a predictor of negative health outcomes in white and Latino lesbian, gay, and bisexual young adults. *Pediatrics, 123*(1), 346-352.

Schmalz, D., Kerstetter, D., & Anderson, D. (2008). Stigma consciousness as a predictor of children's participation in recreational vs. competitive sports. *Journal of Sport Behavior, 31*(3), 276-297.

Shaw, S.M., & Henderson, K.A. (2005). Gender analysis and leisure: An uneasy alliance. In E.L. Jackson (Ed.), *Constraints to leisure* (pp. 23-34). State College, PA: Venture.

Sugano, E., Nemoto, T., & Operario, D. (2006). The impact of exposure to transphobia on HIV risk behavior in a sample of transgendered women of color in San Franscisco. *AIDS and Behavior, 10,* 217-225.

Taylor, H. (1998). *Americans with disabilities still pervasively disadvantaged on a broad range of key indicators.* [Harris Poll 56]. www.harrisinteractive.com/vault/Harris-Interactive-Poll-Research-AMERICANS-WITH-DISABILITIES-S-TILL-PERVASIVELY-DIS-1998-10.pdf

U.S. Census Bureau. (2001). *Census 2000 brief: 65 years and older population 2000.* Washington, DC: U.S. Department of Commerce.

U.S. Census Bureau. (2007a). *Census 2000 brief: Disability status 2000.* Washington, DC: U.S. Department of Commerce.

U.S. Census Bureau. (2007b). *Population 60 years and over in the United States.* www.census.gov/prod/2001pubs/c2kbr01-10.pdf

U.S. Department of Veterans Affairs. (2006). *Memorandum of understanding veterans. California education opportunities partnership.* Washington, DC: Author.

Williams, T., Connolly, J., Pepler, D., & Craig, W. (2005). Peer victimization, social support, and psychosocial adjustment of sexual minority adolescents. *Journal of Youth and Adolescence, 34,* 471-482.

Leisure and Geography

Minsun Doh
Western Illinois University

Learning Outcomes

After reading this chapter, you will be able to

▶ discuss patterns in the spatial distribution and development of leisure places,

▶ understand people's movement pattern for leisure,

▶ discuss the influence of development of transportation on leisure, and

▶ understand various aspects of influences of leisure on places.

Vocabulary Terms

carrying capacity	greenhouse effect	recreation business districts
cultural distance	places	spaces
distance decay	pleasure periphery	staycation
environmental justice	pull factor	tourism destination
greenbelt		

Mina, a second-generation Asian American, is a first-year college student. Before the new semester on campus started, Mina traveled to her parents' home country with her sister. She met her grandparents and relatives and toured the surrounding Asian countries before returning to the United States. It was a great opportunity for her to get to know her family members and learn about other cultures. She came back refreshed to start her new life with a broadened view of the world.

Leisure happens in **places** through people's encounters with different places and consumption of places. As we relate human leisure experience with geography in this chapter, we explore the interactions among people, place, and the environment in the context of recreation and tourism. Specifically, we will investigate how leisure **spaces** are distributed in our contemporary society and the movement patterns of people to different places for leisure. Consuming spaces for leisure and sometimes exploiting them will inevitably affect these spaces. Therefore, we also examine the impacts that human leisure behavior has in places and what can be done to protect these places to preserve them for future generations.

Mina and her sister visiting their parents' home country to meet their relatives, and Mina and her sister visiting a calligraphy exhibition to learn their mother culture.

As seen in Mina's case, taking a trip is a way of spending leisure time and also a good way to learn about cultures. In the 17th century, a trip called the "grand tour" was popular among young English men. The grand tour was a long trip (taking 6 months to 3 years) to the European continent for educational purposes. The wealthy young English traveled to the "civilized world" to learn the cultural legacies and to study arts and literature. Popular destinations included France, Italy, Austria, Germany, and Belgium (Mill & Morrison, 2006). Later on, the popularity of this itinerary spread to other parts of Europe and the grand tour remained a trend until the late 18th century, coming to a halt with the French Revolution in 1789. Mina's trip was very similar to that of the European grand tourists. To travel to a place with a culture she was not accustomed to, Mina had to learn about each country's transportation system, culture, currency, and custom. She had to find information about which airport to use, how to greet people, and how to pay for and use the local transportation (many of these tasks were done

---

PERSONAL LEISURE

Be a Grand Tourist!

- If you were to take a 3-month grand tour abroad for educational purposes, which tourism destination would you choose and why?
- What can you get out of taking this trip? What is your goal for taking this trip?
- Because you don't have any servants or guides to accompany you, you have to plan your own trip. What information do you need to plan for this long trip?
- Discuss some of the geographical and cultural characteristics you might find in the destination that differ from your native land.

---

by servants and guides for the European grand tourists). Mina also had to locate the must-see attractions and decide which routes to take for the most effective use of her resources, in this case time and money. Without noticing, she could have influenced each place in many ways during her trip, such as by participating in recreational activities, buying things, or talking to residents. These are the topics discussed in this chapter. We explore how leisure places, especially tourism-related destinations and attractions, are distributed and developed and how tourism and tourists affect the destination. In this context, the World Tourism Organization's (2002) definition of a **tourism destination**, a physical space containing tourism products and services, is used throughout the chapter.

SPATIAL DISTRIBUTION OF LEISURE PLACES

How do you spend your leisure time? Some of you might enjoy going to the movies or playing flag football. Others entertain themselves by staying at home watching TV or surfing the Internet. A more active person will find things to do outside or take a trip. Whatever activities you choose, all leisure activities occur in places; you watch TV or talk on the phone with friends at home, play basketball at the court near your residence, watch a movie at a theater, or fish on a riverbank. All leisure activities occur in places, and leisure time is spent in spaces that are built or managed for specific reasons. Let's look at an example of leisure travel.

The early geographical research on leisure was mostly focused on classifying scenic quality of the places and investigating people's land use patterns (Aitchison, 1999). By the late 1930s and early 1940s, the emphasis of geographic research on leisure shifted from recreation to tourism, and by the 1970s a line of research on leisure geography began to focus on how leisure places, mostly tourism attractions such as resorts, were distributed spatially. These researchers explained the concentration of a leisure space in terms of the resources it held and the capacity of the space.

Ever since the American leisure service provision system was organized, meeting the demands of domestic leisure has been an important function of local government.

> The use of traveling is to regulate imagination by reality, and instead of thinking how things may be, to see them as they are.
>
> *Samuel Johnson (1709-1784)*

However, as we look at how leisure places are distributed around us, we can easily see differences and specific patterns in the distribution of leisure attractions. In some parts of a city a variety of leisure facilities are clustered close to residences, whereas residents in another area of the city do not have easy access to these leisure facilities. In fact, it is difficult to balance the provision of leisure services in different parts of a region in a highly diversified and free competitive market. Providers tend to locate their services close to large population centers that are capable of maximizing profit. Therefore, urban destinations are the center of leisure services because they offer a wide variety of culture-based leisure activities and can support tourists and residents alike.

A variety of cultural and entertainment opportunities are present in urban areas and their peripheries, such as shopping, art displays, performances, sports, night life, meetings and conventions, and exhibitions. It is said that more than 50 percent of the international tourists to the United States during the year 2000 visited the top 10 U.S. city destinations (Hwang et al., 2006). According to the study, many small cities don't have sufficient **pull factor** as centers of leisure to attract visitors and compete with large metropolitan areas (Butler, 2004). Small, isolated towns, even those with rich historical backgrounds and cultural resources, are restricted from becoming tourism centers because of their distance from potential visitors. Therefore, there are more recreation facilities in suburban areas and in small towns that are easily accessed, including linear trails, parks and open spaces, and youth recreation facilities. On the other hand, rural leisure is characterized as outdoor activities taking place in natural settings, because access to these environments is easier in rural regions. This is evidenced by the statistics generated by U.S. Department of Commerce. According to 2007 statistics, the top 10 U.S. cities visited by foreigners are all located in highly urban metropolitan areas with large populations (see table 14.1) (U.S. Department of Commerce, Office of Travel and Tourism Industries, 2007).

In addition to being affected by cost and distance to the destination, travel decisions are influenced by the traveler's personality, available resources at the origin, the characteristics of the destination, and **cultural distance** (Lew & McKercher, 2006). One of the motives of people traveling is to seek novelty, and therefore travelers who are eager to learn and see new things will visit culturally distant places (places that are different than their local area in many aspects)

PERSONAL LEISURE

Think about how the distribution pattern shown in table 14.1 applies to you. Think about the most recent trip you took for pleasure, and then answer the following questions.

- What was your primary destination? Was it an urban, a rural, or a suburban destination?
- What attractions did you visit during the trip? What type of attractions were they? Are they the ones that are easily found in such a destination? In your local area?

If you had to choose a tourism destination for your upcoming summer vacation, how would you decide? What factors would affect your decision?

TABLE 14.1 Top U.S. Tourism Destinations

	Inbound tourist arrivals[a]		Internal tourist visits[b]		
Rank	U.S. city	Number of arrivals (millions)	Place	Location	Number of visitors (millions)
1	New York	7.6	Times Square	New York	35
2	Los Angeles	2.7	Las Vegas Strip	Las Vegas	31
3	Miami	2.3	National Mall and Memorial Parks	Washington, DC	24
4	San Francisco	2.2	Faneuil Hall Marketplace	Boston	20
5	Orlando	2.1	Disney World's Magic Kingdom	Lake Buena Vista, FL	17.1
6	Las Vegas	1.7	Disneyland Park	Anaheim, CA	14.9
7	Oahu/Honolulu	1.6	Fisherman's Wharf and Golden Gate Area	San Francisco	14
8	Metro DC area	1.2	Niagara Falls	Buffalo, NY	12
9	Chicago	1.1	Great Smoky Mountains National Park	Cherokee, NC, and Knoxville, TN	9.4
10	Boston	1.0	Navy Pier	Chicago	8.6
Total		23.5			186

[a]Number of travelers to the United States from other countries (U.S. Department of Commerce, Office of Travel and Tourism Industries, 2007).

[b]Internal tourists include both domestic tourists (people traveling within their own country, in this case U.S. residents traveling within the United States) and inbound tourists (Baedeker, 2008).

From U.S. Dept. of Commerce.

rather than culturally proximate places. Other travelers might choose to visit places because of cultural similarities, familiarity with the place, proximity, and lower travel costs (Hwang et al., 2006). That is, the more familiar the tourist is with the location and its culture, the more she knows about local activities and attractions and the easier to fill an entire trip schedule. Language barriers, health risks, or risks of crime and terrorist activity at the destination, as well as the spatial configuration of the destination, may affect travelers' movement patterns (Hwang et al., 2006; Lew & McKercher, 2006). Depending on his personality, a traveler might visit places that use the same language as his; have low risks in terms of health, safety, and security; and have well-developed transportation links. These factors all affect how tourism attractions are distributed and the pattern of people's movement to these places. This concept is further discussed later in this chapter.

Even though many factors influence a traveler's movement for leisure purposes, some places are more popular and frequently visited than other places. At an international level, movement of some types of leisure travelers is characterized by a flow of tourists from developed areas to peripheral or developing countries with lower socioeconomic status (Backman & Morais, 2001; Lin et al., 2003), and tourism is typically concentrated in the **pleasure periphery**, defined as regions with lower socioeconomic status away from developed centers of production and consumption (Brown & Hall, 2000). In addition, one study that examined 6 million international pleasure trips to the United States confirmed that the popularity of American city destinations differed substantially among visitors from three different continents (Hwang et al., 2006). According to the researchers, Latin American travelers to the United States favored Orlando, Florida, with 40 percent of the visitors visiting the city, followed by New York, Miami, and Tampa, Florida. European tourists also favored Orlando (26 percent) as a leisure travel destination. Only about 7 percent of trips made by Asians included Orlando. The most popular city for Asian tourists was Los Angeles (36 percent), followed by Las Vegas (17 percent), San Francisco (15 percent), and Seattle. Do you notice a particular trend from this result? The result of this study can be related to geographical proximity in choosing a destination. Asian travelers to the United States preferred cities located near the West Coast, which are closer to the Asian continent, whereas Europeans favored destinations, such as Miami, which are located in the eastern United States, showing that travelers generally choose leisure places located closer to their homes for reasons of time and cost. Tourism companies such as Disney use this concept in marketing their tourism products. Disney's advertisement efforts are diversified depending on where their products are located. For example, Tokyo Disney Resort and Hong Kong Disneyland focus on marketing primarily to the Asian population, whereas Disneyland Resort Paris tries to attract European visitors. In the United States, Disneyland in Anaheim, California, focuses its marketing efforts on Asians, whereas promotional efforts for Disney World in Lake Buena Vista, Florida, are focused on Europeans and Latin Americans.

A recent trend in leisure geography research uses GIS (geographic information systems) to analyze spatial data to track the distribution of leisure spaces, development process, and people's travel and use patterns (Butler, 1980; Hwang et al., 2006; Lew & McKercher, 2006; Tarrant & Cordell, 1999; Vogel, 2005; Wu & Cai, 2006). Some of these researchers report that leisure often occurs in close proximity to the traveler's primary residing town or city, which includes activities such as walking in the local parks or eating out at a local restaurant (Mitchell & Smith, 1989). Think about how many times you visit a local park compared to visiting a state park or a national park that are farther from your primary residence. This can be explained through the concept of distance decay (Fotheringham, 1983). **Distance decay**, applied to leisure geography, explains the effect of distance on people's interaction with places: Demand varies inversely with the distance traveled. That is, the farther a place is located from the traveler's home, the lower the tendency for her to travel to the place; thus, she tends to travel to

RESEARCH TO REALITY

- Create an inventory of leisure attractions that are less than 50 miles (80 kilometers) from your town.
- Create a 1-day travel itinerary for your neighbors, who have two school-age children.
- Create a 1-day travel itinerary for a couple in their 50s who live on your street.
- Are there differences in the two types of travel itinerary? If yes, why?

To gain a firm understanding of the distance decay concept, complete the following exercise.

First, count the number of trips you made in the last 5 years. How many were informal day trips within your resident city or town? (These may be countless.) How many were within your state? Within neighboring states? Within America? How about international trips? How many times were you out of country? As you count the numbers, you will realize that the numbers for each category decrease, explaining the distance decay concept. The farther from your residence, the less you tend to visit.

places closer to her residence more often. It is common for people to frequently visit easily accessible (in terms of time and cost) neighborhood parks rather than a national park that may be located 100 miles (160 kilometers) or more from their residence. People are rational consumers and will choose to use their time and resources (travel cost) most efficiently. As such, they are unlikely to travel long distances for something of equal reward that is available close to them (Lew & McKercher, 2006).

Distance decay also involves people's tendency to visit more places within the destination as they travel father, especially while taking pleasure trips (Oppermann, 1995). This is done to use resources most effectively. Instead of traveling from the United States to Korea on one occasion and later traveling from the United States to other Asian countries, Mina and her sister had combined two trips to save money on plane tickets and time on the plane. Together, distance and the number of intervening opportunities influence tourism decision making. This is demonstrated by many research findings, including a study by Chinese scholars who found that Shanghai urban residents traveled to the series of belt-shaped suburban destinations for leisure (Wu & Cai, 2006). Another study found that city residents participated more in recreation activities and day trips in or near their home city than in visiting remote destinations involving overnight trips (Jansen-Verbeke, 1986). The popularity of short-term, short-distance leisure increased as a consequence of the September 11 terrorist attacks and related safety issues, changes in individual time use patterns, difficulty in coordinating leisure activities among family members, and increased gasoline prices (Vogel, 2005). This led to the decline of domestic, long-stay holiday tourism and the birth of the term **staycation**. A staycation is a vacation spent at home enjoying what one's home environment has to offer. Usually, staycation involves multiple short-term, short-distance leisure trips to suburbs and adjacent hinterlands, so travelers use less money and time for travel and enjoy more outdoor opportunities.

Many studies that look at the spatial distribution of leisure spaces and movement of people for leisure purposes are conducted in Europe and Asia. One of these studies reported that convenient access enables urban residents to easily visit suburban areas for leisure purposes. The authors noticed that leisure spaces such as public and private recreational facilities and tourism attractions were distributed in a circular pattern around cities, and the movement of urban residents to the suburbs for leisure purposes was distributed along the series of belt shapes (figure 14.1). This pattern of leisure space distribution is termed *recreational belt around metropolis* (ReBAM) (Wu & Cai, 2006). The formation of a ReBAM is driven by three factors: demand for weekend recreation, suppliers' development activities associated with land use, and spatial links attributed to transportation networks. Cities, especially those with large populations, are great sources of local visitors as well as international tourists (Pearce, 1981). The potential to feed a substantial number of recreationalists along with the trend toward short-term, short-distance travel has a significant implication for the future growth of ReBAMs in the cities with this pattern. In Shanghai, the largest city in China, with a population of more than 19 million, three recreational belts surround the metropolitan city. All three are located within a radius of 45 miles (72 kilometers) from the city core, and the recreational facilities located within these ReBAMs provide great leisure opportunities for those who look for places to visit as a part of staycation. With the physical growth of metropolitan areas along with increased disposable income, the significance of ReBAMs is expected to grow in Shanghai (see figure 14.1).

Some scholars criticize the uneven development of leisure places and argue this is due to certain demographic factors (Lin et al., 2003; Nicholls & Shafer, 2001; Tarrant & Cordell, 1999). Many studies have found evidence of possible inequities with regard to household income for some types of outdoor recreation sites. According to these studies, census block groups (CBGs, the smallest geographical unit used by U.S. Census Bureau) with lower household incomes were likely to

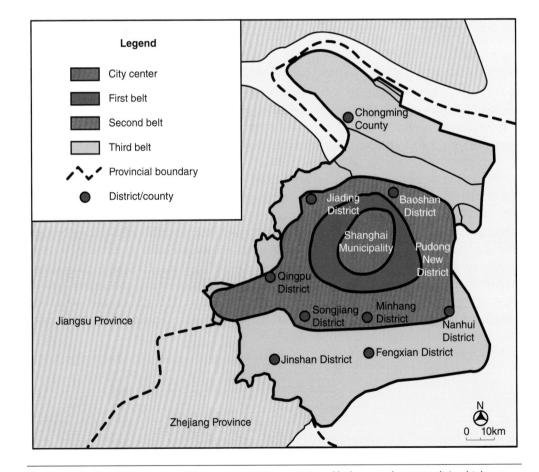

Figure 14.1   Spatial structure of Shanghai ReBAM (recreational belt around metropolis), which consists of the central city and three recreational belts.

Reprinted from *Shanghai Annals of Tourism Research*, Vol 33, B. Wu and L.A. Cai, "Spatial modeling: Suburban leisure," pgs. 179-198, Copyright 2006, with permission from Elsevier.

have a greater number of tourists near their residences than CBGs with higher household incomes (Lin et al., 2003; Porter & Tarrant, 2001). These studies also supported that the distribution of neighborhood parks in urban areas was inequitable with respect to income. CBGs with a higher proportion of low-income households were significantly more likely to be situated within 1,500 meters of wilderness areas, campgrounds, or good fisheries habitats than were CBGs with higher incomes (Tarrant & Cordell, 1999). Because low-income areas are more likely to receive tourists than are higher income areas, it is important to ensure that tourism improves socioeconomic conditions.

Following President Clinton's Executive Order 12898, all federal land management agencies have been required to address environmental justice for all communities regardless of their racial and economic composition. **Environmental justice** refers to rules, regulations, and decisions that "deliberately target certain communities for least desirable land uses . . . [and] support sustainable communities where people can interact with confidence that their environment is safe, nurturing and productive" (Bryant, 1995, p. 9). Many research studies, including those previously mentioned, report evidence of a relationship between race or income and the siting of LULUs (locally unwanted land uses), including commercial hazardous waste facilities, low-income housing, homeless shelters, landfills, and recycling centers, which tend to be more frequently located in areas with predominantly nonwhite populations (Tarrant & Cordell, 1999). In some communities, certain outdoor recreation sites may be considered LULUs by virtue of the negative impacts connected to their use. Tourism development in a local area, for example, may bring increased economic revenue and job opportunities but is also associated with environmental and social costs such as increased traffic, air and noise pollution, and crime.

We can consider leisure places from two perspectives. Some scholars consider outdoor recreation sites as locally desirable land use (LDLU) on the belief that these sites enhance community satisfaction, improve quality of life, increase property values, and provide leisure opportunities such as hiking and fishing (Allen, 1990; Jeffres & Dobos, 1993; Nelson, 1986). In 1986 it was reported that urban land 1,000 feet (300 meters) from a **greenbelt** was worth $1,200 less per acre than land immediately adjacent to the greenbelt boundary (Nelson, 1986). Similar findings have been reported by many scholars, claiming that houses in golf course communities that face the fairway were worth 8 percent more on average than other houses in those communities and that property values increased with the amount of open space that provided recreational access and opportunities (Corwell, 1986; Gee, 1996). Some recreational facilities are considered LULUs mainly because of perceived or actual negative impacts and poor condition associated with mismanagement and lack of resources (Tarrant & Cordell, 1999).

DEVELOPMENT OF LEISURE PLACES

Since the early 1960s, many geographic models have been developed to describe the process of tourism destination development (Butler, 1980, 2004). One of the concepts that attracted the most attention is the life cycle model, developed by Richard W. Butler, which explained the evolutionary process of a tourist area or a resort town development (Agarwal, 2002; Butler, 1980). According to Butler, a tourism geographer, tourism destinations or resort towns go through six stages

(Butler, 1980; Getz, 1992) (figure 14.2). The first is the exploration stage, the stage when the areas are not artificially developed and are visited by only a small number of tourists. Usually the attractiveness of these destinations is based on natural beauty or cultural uniqueness. A small number of adventurous tourists and active recreation participants are the major clientele of the destinations in this stage. Examples of these destinations include Antarctica and rural or peripheral regions of developing countries. Next is the involvement stage, when the number of visitors begins to increase and local residents begin to be involved with tourism-related activities. In this stage, small tourism-related businesses are started that provide basic services to the tourists. Government also starts to develop infrastructure to support the increasing tourism volume. Nepal, a South Asian country known for its proximity to the Himalayas, experienced this stage in the 1970s accompanied by the development of an airstrip in a gateway community to the Himalayas. This allowed easy access to the mountainous regions of Nepal, which rapidly increased the number of visitors from the Western world. The third stage is development, when the destination is settled as a tourist area and substantial number of tourists are attracted to destinations, making the area a mass tourism destination. These mass tourists are typically less adventurous, and the area becomes highly commercialized with their leisure activities. Fabricated attractions such as theme parks, staged festivals, and entertainment facilities replace natural or ethnic tourism resources. Because of use conflict, some areas in this stage suffer tensions between local residents and tourists. The fourth stage is called consolidation. In this stage, tourism becomes a major part of the local

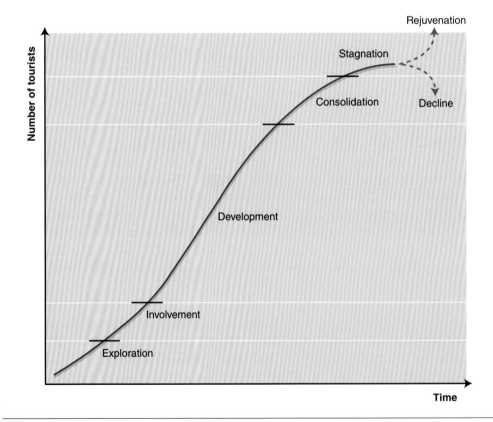

Figure 14.2   Destination life cycle. The number of tourists fluctuates depending on the destination's stage of development.

Reprinted, by permission, from R.W. Butler and L.A. Waldbrook, 1991, "A new planning tool: The tourism opportunity spectrum," *Journal of Tourism Studies* 2 (1): 1-14.

economy but the area experiences slowed growth in the number of visits. Therefore, product and service providers focus on attracting new markets rather than catering to the existing market. Up to this point, destinations only experience growth, although the rate of growth may differ. The last two stages are stagnation and decline/rejuvenation (see figure 14.2).

The stagnation stage occurs when the peak number of visitors and **carrying capacity** (the number of visitors who can be accommodated in a given area without degrading the natural, sociocultural, and economic environment) are reached. In accommodation facilities, occupancy rates decrease and there are frequent changes in ownership. The number of visitors will decline if the destination starts to lose existing market share because it cannot compete with newer destinations (Butler, 1980). Gradually the destination may become a slum or lose its tourism function completely. Destinations in this stage need to restructure or reorganize products and services or use new resources to avoid further decline. If the destination succeeds in reforming its products and services, there is a chance that it can be rejuvenated as a tourism destination. Until the early 1930s, Las Vegas had been barren land with nothing but dust and dry air. With the massive development of casinos, hotels, and associated tourism superstructure, it has now become a recreation business district and one of the world's most popular tourism destinations (ranked 48th in the world's top city destinations by Euromonitor [2007]), with more than 30 million visitors per year (table 14.1). If we apply Butler's model, it seems that Las Vegas is in a constant stage of rejuvenation. With new shows and performances introduced often, accompanied by new hotel and convention development projects, Las Vegas will continue to maintain its popularity as an international tourism destination for some time. To what stage do you think the other major tourism destinations shown in table 14.1 belong in this model?

LEISURE TRAVEL AND TRANSPORTATION

Another aspect of leisure that is related to geography involves its association with transportation networks. The mass production of the Ford Model T and mass ownership of automobiles in the early 1900s significantly affected how tourism-related spaces are shaped in the United States. With the ownership of automobiles by the mass public, the government determined a need to construct roads. Acts such as the Federal Aid Road Act of 1916 and Federal Highway Act of 1921 promoted the general welfare of the citizens, and all states had their own road-related organization by 1920. Americans were able to travel for leisure purposes to farther destinations, more conveniently and faster. To serve the needs of these travelers, auto camps, tourist courts, and motor hotels (motels) were built along the American road system. These amenities show cluster or linear development patterns along highways and major access roads. Suburban areas became popular locations for recreational development given the physical growth of cities accompanied by the construction of highways around urban areas to meet increasing transportation needs and to ease traffic. Clusters of businesses offering recreational activities, dining, entertainment, and shopping (called **recreation business districts**) or regional, county, or state parks can be easily found along the streets in suburban areas that are connected to major cities. These spaces provide recreational opportunities not only for local residents but also for tourists.

Photo courtesy of Kelli Luchs

Las Vegas Strip in the 1930s. The initial development of Las Vegas was focused on the main strip, with a few casinos and accommodation facilities.

Photo courtesy of Minsun Doh

Las Vegas Strip in 2008, long since the Las Vegas Strip was expanded. Casino hotels with thousands of rooms and a variety of shows are easy to find these days.

©Omar Bárcena

America's first motor hotel, constructed in San Luis Obispo, California, in 1925.

IMPACTS OF LEISURE ON PLACES

Development has often been seen as a means of economic growth. In the United States and elsewhere around the world, local communities have been trying to find the right industry for their area. The public sector, especially at the local level, has turned to leisure, recreation, and tourism as its economic savior with downtown renovation schemes. Public-sector agencies have sought tourism development to satisfy their economic, social, and psychological needs and to enhance the local quality of life (Ap, 1992). Tourism is also considered to bring many more nonmonetary (social, cultural, and environmental) benefits than any other export industries. Within the rapidly changing economic environment, many public officials seek tourism as a way to success, thinking that it is cleaner and more sustainable than industries that consume and extract natural resources. Indeed, in some parts of the country, tourism has stimulated local economies, led to modified land use and economic structure, and made a positive contribution to the community. Rural tourism development has been the trend for about two decades in small U.S. communities whose leaders wish to revitalize their communities in an alternative form (i.e., small-scale development as opposed to mass-tourism development; alternative tourism tends to lead to fewer negative impacts compared to mass-tourism development) (Gartner, 2004). Although tourism carries some negative influences, many of these communities have experienced positive economic impacts such as increased job opportunities and income, a large multiplier effect, and increased standard of living (Richards & Hall, 2000). Scholars contend that as tourism development matures, the demand for infrastructure increases, which in turn increases the demand for labor. In this way tourism development can create jobs and improve an area's economic structure. In this sense, tourism offers considerable potential for economic growth in the destination area during the early phase of development. Tourism development becomes a way of upgrading a community's economy in many areas (Doh, 2006). Some rural towns, such as Branson, Missouri, have been transformed into an urbanlike destination based on the entertainment and music industry (Gartner, 2004). Another example is the Sturgis Motorcycle Rally, held every year in Sturgis, South Dakota. With only about 6,500 residents (U.S. Census Bureau, 2000), Sturgis hosts a large-scale motorcycle rally event that attracts more than 700,000 visitors. Imagine how much economic impact these visitors will have on the community each year!

The growth of participation in outdoor recreation and tourism has fueled global concern for the environment, because tourism is likely to alter the economic and social goals of the hosts and modify the physical environment. In many parts of the world, economic motivation as a dominant theme justified tourism development as a growth strategy at the cost of environmental degradation and social and cultural disruption. Although tourism has stimulated employment and the economy and has modified land use and economic structure, the growth of tourism has raised many questions concerning the environmental desirability of encouraging further expansion (Harrill, 2004). Tourism development, within environmental contexts, provides resources as well as creates problems for the local community. Tourism may provide an area with a variety of outdoor recreation resources but at the same time may result in environmental degradation such as trampling, erosion, loss of wildlife habitat, and land use change, to name a few. Because tourism development may result in unexpected or negative environmental changes in a community, the terms *tourism impact* and *tourism-induced change* have gained attention in the tourism literature. Tourism impacts are defined as the net changes within the host communities, resulting from a complex process of interactions among tourists, host communities, and destination environments. Research on many communities shows that tourism is accompanied by a multitude of impacts, both positive and negative, on people's lives and on the environment.

POSITIVE IMPACTS OF LEISURE DEVELOPMENT

Of course, new development or addition to existing tourism resources bring many advantages to the community. These include the following:

- Investment and growth
- Increased property values
- Local area improvement
- Environmental awareness

Investment and Growth

Tourism is considered to be a growth inducer (Mill & Morrison, 2006). Leisure facilities and programs attract other related businesses. World-renowned leisure destinations that demonstrate this phenomenon include Vail, Colorado; Las Vegas, Nevada; and Orlando, Florida. Vail was an unused mountainous region belonging to the U.S. Forest Service before the first ski resort was developed and opened in 1962. With deep snow cover and proximity to large population centers such as Denver, Vail soon became the most popular ski area in Colorado. Followed by this success, interstate highway construction began, and the Town of Vail was established at the base of the Vail Ski Resort in 1966, growing at an incredible rate (Colorado Ski History, 2008). The 1970s brought more construction to Vail, developing more trails and lifts. The town focused on infrastructure and tourism-related development, including a transit system, a library, an ice arena, parking structures, and other facilities to serve incoming skiers. With an increased supply of services due to infrastructure development (such as high-quality restaurants, cultural facilities, and shopping) in a destination, community service and facilities are improved (Brunt & Courtney, 1999; Liu & Var, 1986), as is the quality of life for residents (Coccossis, 1996; Milman & Pizam, 1988).

©AP Photo/Cody Downard, Vail Resorts

Ski resorts, such as the one shown here in Vail, Colorado, attract millions of visitors per year. Just like Las Vegas, this leisure setting was developed from scratch and served as a growth inducer for the area to become an internationally renowned recreation center.

Increased Property Values

As mentioned in the previous section, some researchers note that the value of land is affected by the presence of leisure-related development (Corwell, 1986; Gee, 1996; Nelson, 1986). According to this research, large and well-maintained parks increase the value of adjacent properties. Houses located in golf course communities (especially houses that face the fairway) and residential property adjoining lakes, reservoirs, wildlife refuges, resorts, and other leisure sites record high values. Increased property values are not always a positive outcome because they can negatively affect some people, so this topic is discussed again in the section on negative impacts.

Local Area Improvement

Tourism development improves a community's infrastructure and appearance and provides more and better leisure facilities and parks (Green et al., 1990; Lankford, 1994). In the process of development, abandoned buildings are remodeled and used as attractions such as museums, and dilapidated or unused areas and wharves are revitalized and reborn as recreational destinations: good examples are Kemah, Texas; Navy Pier in Chicago; and Pier 39 in San Francisco. In some towns, old railroads are saved and converted to hiking trails that can be used by local residents as well as tourists; other towns engage with urban or downtown revitalization programs. The Community Heritage Development Division of the Texas Historical Commission has been involved with Texas Main Street Program to help Texas cities revitalize their historic downtowns and neighborhood commercial districts. These regenerations may raise questions concerning undesirable impacts on the place, as discussed in the next section.

©Richard Mack/Workbook Stock/Getty Images

Navy Pier was originally a municipal pier for shipping and a recreational facility for pleasure in the early 19th century. Since the late 1970s, it has evolved into Chicago's lakefront entertainment center, and it attracts more than 8 million visitors per year (Metropolitan Pier and Exposition Authority, 2009).

Environmental Awareness

As an area becomes a tourism destination, concern over resource use becomes an issue. Local and nonprofit organizations are created to protect the area's resources, and specific ecosystems can be protected with research and proper management schemes. Local and nonprofit organizations also provide environmental education programs for the public so that residents and tourists understand the environmental issues at play.

NEGATIVE IMPACTS OF LEISURE DEVELOPMENT

With increasing environmental awareness, researchers have recognized the potential destructive influences of leisure development and have acknowledged the detrimental consequences. The consequences include these:

- Changes in traditional land use
- Alteration of the natural environment
- Impacts on local life
- Increased land values

Changes in Traditional Land Use

Construction of tourism attractions or leisure facilities requires space. Deforestation and loss of vegetation are associated with clearing of the area. Loss of vegetation has been a noted environmental impact due to the development of ski resorts and golf courses (Medio et al., 1997; Terman, 1997). Croplands are converted into a "forest" of buildings, and unplanned buildings and settlements are developed in some cases. Overdevelopment, commercialization, and loss of open space are other outcomes associated with leisure development.

Alteration of the Natural Environment

The growing literature on the environmental impact of tourism emphasizes significant negative environmental impacts that leisure activities can bring to the host areas. These include

Leisure activities such as riding horses can significantly impact the environment, including contributing to soil erosion and damaging vegetation.

soil erosion and damage to vegetation due to outdoor activities such as hiking and horse riding (Cole & Spildie, 1998). Overharvesting of native species, littering, air and water pollution, and disruption of wildlife habitats, natural sites, and entire ecological systems have been documented in a number of studies (Andereck, 1995; Brunt & Courtney, 1999; Gilbert & Clark, 1997; Rouphael & Inglis, 1997; Snaith & Haley, 1999).

Impacts on Local Life

Research on the impacts of tourism on the host population is concerned with the changes in residents' way of life brought about by tourism development and interaction with the tourists. *Social impacts of tourism* is defined as the ways in which tourism contributes to changes in social conditions. The growth of tourism and inflow of tourists inevitably modify the destination environment. Although tourism may improve the social structure of the host community and broaden cultural understanding, it also brings problems: congestion, noise, overcrowding and subsequent use conflict, degradation of air and water quality, loss of local town atmosphere, and alteration of community structure (Andereck, 1995; Brunt & Courtney, 1999; Mason & Cheyne, 2000; McCool & Martin, 1994; Snaith & Haley, 1999; Teye et al., 2002).

Tourism development can contribute to social conditions that lead to serious problems in the host society. The main impact is that the hosts modify their behavior to imitate tourists (Richards & Hall, 2000). One of the most significant and least desirable by-products of tourism development is its effects on the moral standards of the host population (Koegh, 1990).

The growth of crime and gambling has been mentioned frequently as another negative side of tourism development (Andereck, 1995; Lankford, 1994; Mason & Cheyne, 2000). Crime rates are suspected to increase with increasing tourism development. One study about gambling development of a town in Massachusetts mentioned that residents showed negative perception of the gambling development in their town in terms of loss of traditional image of town and community identity (Long, 1996). Other studies have found loss of cultural identity, changes in the size and the demographic characteristics of the host population, changes in daily rhythm of life, decline in cooperation and mutual aid between families, degradation of morality, breakdown of family, drug addiction and alcoholism, and vandalism (Andereck, 1995; Burns & Holden, 1995; Evans, 1994; Koegh, 1990; Purdue et al., 1991; Richards & Hall, 2000).

Research is often undertaken to monitor the social well-being of destination areas in the presence of tourism, as the viability of an area's tourism industry can be affected negatively if deterioration is perceived to occur in the natural or social environment. Such negative perceptions can diminish residents' support for tourism development, which in turn affects visitors' experiences.

Increased Land Values

Increased land and property value was referred to as a positive impact in the previous section. However, for those who are native to the area but do not own land or property, increased property value may be a negative impact. In fact, some local residents are relocated to the peripheral regions because they no longer can afford housing in the newly developed areas where they used to live.

Although tourism often is considered a clean industry, this is not always true. Tourism can cause significant environmental changes and damages because it is often developed in attractive but fragile environments (Andereck et al., 2005). In addition, local development policy may focus on meeting the needs of tourists rather than the needs of the local residents and the area as a whole. Thus, tourism development has the potential to undermine itself by being insensitive to its environmental impacts on local areas (Doggart & Doggart, 1996).

CLIMATE CHANGE AND LEISURE

Global climate change and global warming have been recognized for some time. The tourism industry is one of the entities blamed for these climate changes (especially the transportation sector) as well as one of the industries most affected by such changes. Tourism is not the only industry to feel the effects of global warming, but tourism is arguably more susceptible than other industries because its attractiveness relies on the environment in many destinations, especially coastal and mountain regions. In this section we discuss how tourism is affecting the global climate, how tourism is affected by climate, and the industry responses to these issues.

The share of tourism's carbon dioxide emissions is said to be 4 to 6 percent, and transportation is the sector that least contributes to carbon dioxide emission reduction targets. Roughly 9 percent of the overall climate change is considered to be related to air traffic, and around 80 percent of international air traffic is connected to private trips (Becken, 2002). According to the Bureau of Transportation Statistics (BTS, 2007), the total consumption of aviation fuel in the United States in 1960 was 1,954 million gallons (more than 7 billion liters), whereas in 2006 the commercial aviation industry consumed 16,578 million gallons (63 billion liters) of jet fuel (see table 14.2). Fuel consumption by private automobiles and motorcycles on highways increased more than 24 percent within 10 years; Americans consumed more than 112 billion gallons (425 billion liters) in 1995 and 139 billion gallons (525 billion liters) in 2005 (BTS, 2007). Despite the introduction of more fuel-efficient aircraft and automobiles, fuel consumption by the transportation industry is still increasing.

Researchers report that carbon dioxide emissions from vehicles and air traffic have a tremendous impact on global climate change by contributing to destruction of the ozone layer and by reinforcing the **greenhouse effect** (Egli, 1995; Lu et al., 2007). What effects do these have on leisure? The possible impacts include heat waves, droughts, rising sea levels, flash floods, forest fires, and changing amounts and patterns of precipitation. These impacts may differ country by country or

TABLE 14.2   Fuel Consumption by Scheduled-Service Planes From All Major Airlines

	Fuel consumption (millions of gallons)			% Change
	Domestic	**International**	**Total**	
2000	12,700	4,754	17,455	
2001	11,996	4,637	16,633	−4.7
2002	11,146	4,291	15,438	−7.2
2003	10,607	4,055	14,663	−5.0
2004	11,165	4,411	15,576	6.2
2005	11,314	4,729	16,042	3.0
2006	11,687	4,891	16,578	3.3
2007	11,990	5,065	17,054	2.9
2008	11,562	5,207	16,769	−1.7

1 gallon = 3.787 liters

Bureau of Transportation Statistics 2009.

region by region. In cold areas, the impacts are related to warmer temperature and melting of snow. In coastal areas, the problem lies with the rising sea level. In mountainous regions, increased temperature reduces the spatial extent, depth, and persistence of snow cover (Fukushima et al., 2002). It is said that the amount of snow fall decreased 18 percent from 1953 to 2004. Therefore, headlines such as "Ski Industry Heading Downhill" and "It's All Downhill From Here" are only a few you can find in the news. Direct impacts are especially severe to the ski industry located in the European Alps and the Rocky Mountains region in North America. Unfavorable snow conditions are blamed for shorter skiing seasons, greater demand for high-altitude resorts, and greater risk of avalanches (Abegg & Froesch, 1994). Poor snow conditions have decreased the overall demand for skiing and resulted in major declines in visits and membership, which in turn reduce the demand for accommodation, decrease income at resorts, and even lead to bankruptcies of resorts. Winter tourism is the most important source of income for countries like Switzerland, Austria, and Italy, and snow reliability is a key element of the tourist resource. It appears that many resorts in these countries, particularly the traditional lower-altitude resorts of Europe, will be unable to operate as a result of lack of snow or will face additional costs, including artificial snowmaking. It is reported that some resorts already have had problems getting bank loans (DeVries, 2003). This is also happening in North America. Ski resorts in Ontario, Vermont, and New Hampshire are experiencing shorter seasons (reduced by 30-40 percent compared with 1960) and hosting fewer skiers (an average of 700,000 fewer visits

©AP Photo/Sunday Alamba

Many parts of the world, especially small island countries in the South Pacific Ocean, are suffering from rising sea level. Researchers say sea level rise seems to be underestimated by many, but it is affecting the residents' life tremendously. Some residents have even had to relocate to inner lands or other islands.

in New England), and an upward shift in the snowline has been prevalent in the Rocky Mountains (Clean Air Cool Planet, 2007). Ski resorts located in the Rocky Mountains and Pacific Northwest have experienced 30- to 50-inch reductions (75-125 centimeters) in average winter snow depth. Therefore, resorts incur costs to run snowmaking technology to smooth out inconsistent winters. Attitash, New Hampshire, spends about $750,000 per year on snowmaking to cover 97 percent of its terrain: This means that approximately 20 percent of the resort's operating costs go into making artificial snow.

Melting of glaciers is raising sea levels, which causes coastal and beach erosion, destruction of the coastal ecosystem, and, in extreme cases, total submersion of islands or coastal plains (Radford & Bennett, 2004). These events result in evacuation and resettlement of the residents and destroy the tourism industry for areas whose economy is based on tourism. Tropical islands and coastal regions are the areas most affected by the melting of glaciers associated with global warming. South Pacific islands and islands in the Indian Ocean such as Maldives, Kiribati, Tuvalu, and Papua New Guinea are experiencing decreases in tourism resources such as loss of beaches and increasing numbers of untenable beach resorts (Agnew & Viner, 2001). Some areas already have short-term and long-term evacuation or resettlement plans for their residents, and relocation of residents is already happening. To date, two islands of Kiribati have been submerged, and the Marshall Islands are under threat.

The affected industries are trying hard to adapt to the changes. Ski resorts use snow-making technology or move to higher altitudes. Eroded beaches are replenished with sand. However, these adaptive strategies may not cure the negative impacts but rather treat symptoms as they appear or even result in more negative impacts (De Vries, 2003). Snow-making machines emit carbon dioxide, consume enormous amount of water and energy, and increase operating costs for the business. If the resort moves to a higher altitude, it will need to extend transport infrastructure higher up the mountain; the move could degrade the more fragile environment by human use, littering, and increased energy use. Importing sand to beaches to maintain their amenity value is costly and temporary and may damage the area from which the sand is drawn.

Rather than applying these short-term and symptomatic treatments, industries are now trying to adopt more comprehensive plans to address the issues related to global warming. For example, ski resorts are combining skiing with other summer and fall activities (such as alpine slides, mountain biking, water recreation, trekking, special events, scenic lift rides, and climbing walls) and developing new non-snow-related winter activity schemes to make the area a year-round tourism destination. New leisure activities, such as grass-skiing, and residential lodging options are considered to compensate for the income decreased because of snow deterioration (Fukushima et al., 2002). The ski industry itself is committed to addressing environmental issues by creating a variety of programs such as the Sustainable Slopes program and the Keep Winter Cool public education campaign. The industry has recognized the danger of climate change and is taking steps to limit its own emissions of greenhouse gases that are responsible for climate change. Since 1998, Aspen Skiing Company, for example, has established a program to conserve energy and water and reduce greenhouse gas emissions by using wind power to run ski lifts and heat water, incorporating energy-efficient green buildings, and using alternative fuels, such as biodiesel, in resort vehicles. In 2000, more than 160 resorts signed a Sustainable Slopes charter initiated by the National

Ski Areas Association (NSAA) that promises environmental responsibility on the issues of energy efficiency, water use, and waste production. The NSAA started this environmental program in June 2000 to voluntarily reduce the industry's environmental impacts. Of the 492 ski resorts in the United States, about 180 participate in the Sustainable Slopes program (Shaw, 2006), encouraging their guests to use mass transportation and offering free parking to guests with low-pollution hybrid vehicles. Sustainable Slopes participants achieved carbon dioxide reductions in 2005 (from energy savings, green-power purchases, waste reduction and recycling, and vehicle-miles avoided) that totaled the equivalent of 87,000 round-trip flights between New York and San Francisco (Shaw, 2006). That would be like shutting down 126,000 ski lifts for a day.

SUMMARY

How leisure places are shaped and developed, and how they respond to these changes, are major topics for the leisure professional. Leisure places are changing because of varied participation patterns and differences in participants' perceptions of resources. These changes are sometimes for the better, but in many cases they influence the area for the worse. Leisure development must be well managed so that it does not become a tool to exploit developing areas.

Learning Activities

1. Take an inventory of your local leisure resources:
   - Find places for leisure in your community and locate them on a local map. These can include recreation sites such as parks, football and baseball fields, hiking and walking trails, or mountains, rivers, or lakes that are open for public use. The places can be related to tourism, such as accommodation facilities (hotels, motels, inns, campgrounds), cultural facilities (galleries, museums, shopping), or historic sites.
   - Which parts of the community are these places located? Are they close to residences or commercial districts?
   - What kind of pattern do you see in the distribution of leisure places? Are they distributed in circular or linear patterns? Or are they distributed in clusters?
2. Find a magazine article about global warming and leisure or tourism. Read the article and make a list of potential positive and negative impacts of global warming on leisure. How is your leisure affected by overall climate change and global warming? Discuss with the entire class the issue of climate change and its impact on leisure.

OSR

For additional assignments, Web links, and more, visit the online student resource at www.HumanKinetics.com/DimensionsOfLeisureForLife.

Review Questions

1. How do you think place and space differ? How is leisure related to space?
2. How can you apply the concept of distance decay to your leisure lifestyle?
3. Do you think there is uneven distribution or development of leisure places? If yes, do you find this pattern in your local area?

4. Do you think the way you spend leisure affects the environment? If so, in what way?

5. How are your local area's natural and cultural resources affected by leisure activities and tourists?

6. How can you change your leisure lifestyle to sustain natural and cultural resources?

Leisure Reading

Bruner, E. (2004). *Culture on tour: Ethnographies of travel.* Chicago: University of Chicago Press.

Chambers, E. (2009). *Native tours: The anthropology of travel and tourism.* Prospect Heights, IL: Waveland Press.

Edwards, A. (2005). *The sustainability revolution: Portrait of a paradigm shift.* Gabriola Island, BC: New Society.

Gopnik, A. (2001). *Paris to the moon.* New York: Random House Trade Paperbacks.

Gore, A. (2006). *An inconvenient truth: The planetary emergency of global warming and what we can do about it.* New York: Rodale Books.

Kincaid, J. (2000). *A small place.* New York: Farrar, Straus and Giroux.

Kolbert, E. (2006). *Field notes from a catastrophe: Man, nature, and climate change.* New York: Bloomsbury USA.

Pattullo, P. (2005). *Last resorts: The cost of tourism in the Caribbean.* Danvers, MA: Monthly Review Press.

Steinbeck, J. (1961). *Travels with Charlie: In search of America.* New York: Penguin Press.

Thubron, C. (2007). *Shadow of the Silk Road.* New York: Harper Perennial.

Glossary

carrying capacity—The number of visitors who can be accommodated in a given area without degrading the natural, sociocultural, and economic environments.

cultural distance—Difference between two cultures.

distance decay—The effect of distance on people's interaction with places.

environmental justice—The fair treatment and meaningful involvement of all people regardless of race, color, national origin, or income with respect to the development, implementation, and enforcement of environmental laws, regulations, and policies (Environmental Protection Agency [EPA], 2009).

greenbelt—Land use designation to protect undeveloped, wild, or agricultural lands surrounding or neighboring urban areas from building or development.

greenhouse effect—The effect produced as greenhouse gases allow incoming solar radiation to pass through the earth's atmosphere but prevent part of the outgoing infrared radiation from the earth's surface and lower atmosphere from escaping into outer space (EPA, 2009).

places—Physical environments or locations that have special or value-added meaning (such as culture).

pleasure periphery—Regions with low socioeconomic status away from developed centers of production and consumption (Brown & Hall, 2000).

pull factor—Force that draws people from a place to another.

recreation business districts—Clusters of recreational businesses offering recreational activities, dining, entertainment, and shopping.

spaces—Boundless extents without special meaning that can be represented by distance, area, and volume.

staycation—Vacation spent at home enjoying what one's home environment has to offer.

tourism destination—A physical space containing tourism products and services such as attractions, activities, and infrastructure.

References

Abegg, B., & Froesch, R. (1994). Climate change and winter tourism. In M. Beniston (Ed.), *Mountain environments in changing climates* (pp. 328-340). London: Routledge.

Agarwal, S. (2002). Restructuring seaside tourism: The resort lifecycle. *Annals of Tourism Research, 29*(1), 25-55.

Agnew, M.D., & Viner, D. (2001). Potential impacts of climate change on international tourism. *Tourism and Hospitality Research, 3,* 37-60.

Aitchison, C. (1999). New cultural geographies: The spatiality of leisure, gender and sexuality. *Leisure Studies, 18,* 19-39.

Allen, L.R. (1990). Benefits of leisure attributes to community satisfaction. In B.L. Driver, P.J. Brown, & G.L. Peterson (Eds.), *Benefits of leisure* (pp. 331-350). State College, PA: Venture.

Andereck, K.L. (1995). Environmental consequences of tourism: A review of recent research. In S.F. McCool & A.E. Watson (Eds.), *Linking tourism, the environment, and sustainability* (pp. 77-81). Ogden, UT: U.S. Department of Agriculture, Forest Service, Intermountain Forest and Range Experiment Station.

Andereck, K., Valentine, K., Knopf, R., & Vogt, C. (2005). Residents' perceptions of community tourism impacts. *Annals of Tourism Research, 32,* 1056-1078.

Ap, J. (1992). Residents' perceptions on tourism's impacts. *Annals of Tourism Research, 19,* 665-690.

Backman, K.F., & Morais, D.B. (2001). Methodological approaches used in the literature. In D.B. Weaver (Ed.), *The encyclopedia of ecotourism* (pp. 597-609). Wallingford, UK: CAB International.

Baedeker, R. (2008). *America's 25 most visited tourist attractions.* www.msnbc.msn.com/id/24487410/

Becken, S. (2002). Analyzing international tourist flows to estimate energy use associated with air travel. *Journal of Sustainable Tourism, 10*(2), 114-131.

Brown, F., & Hall, D. (2000). Introduction: The paradox of periphery. In F. Brown & D. Hall (Eds.), *Tourism in peripheral areas* (pp. 1-6). Clevedon, UK: Channel View Publications.

Brunt, P., & Courtney, P. (1999). Host perceptions of sociocultural impacts. *Annals of Tourism Research, 26,* 493-515.

Bryant, B. (1995). *Environmental justice: Issues, policies, and solutions.* Washington, DC: Island Press.

Bureau of Transportation Statistics (BTS). (2007). *Fuel consumption by mode of transportation in physical units.* www.bts.gov/publications/national_transportation_statistics/html/table_04_05.html

Burns, P., & Holden, A. (1995). *Tourism: A new perspective.* London: Prentice Hall.

Butler, R. (1980). The concept of a tourist area cycle of evolution: Implications for management of resources. *Canadian Geographer, 24,* 5-12.

Butler, R. (2004). Geographical research on tourism, recreation and leisure: Origins, eras and directions. *Tourism Geographies, 6*(2), 143-162.

Butler, R.W., & Waldbrook, L.A. (1991). A new planning tool: The tourism opportunity spectrum. *Journal of Tourism Studies, 2*(1), 1-14.

Clean Air Cool Planet. (2007). *Global warming threatens New England's ski industry.* www.cleanaircoolplanet.org/information/pdf/ski-factsheet.pdf

Coccossis, H. (1996). Tourism and sustainability: Perspectives and implications. In G.K. Priestley, J.A. Edwards, & H. Coccossis (Eds.), *Sustainable tourism? European experiences* (pp. 1-21). Wallingford, UK: CAB International.

Cole, D.N., & Spildie, D.R. (1998). Hiker, horse, and llama trampling effects on native vegetation in Montana, USA. *Journal of Environmental Management, 53,* 61-71.

Colorado Ski History. (2008). *Vail.* www.coloradoskihistory.com/areahistory/vail.html

Corwell, P. (1986). Open space on real estate values. In *Proceedings of the Governor's Conference in the Economic Significance of Recreation in Illinois*. Springfield, IL: Office of the Governor.

De Vries, L. (2003). *Ski industry facing meltdown?* www.cbsnews.com/stories/2003/12/03/tech/main586554.shtml

Doggart, C., & Doggart, N. (1996). Occasional studies: Environmental impacts of tourism in developing countries. *Travel and Tourism Analyst, 2,* 71-86.

Doh, M. (2006). *Change through tourism: Resident perceptions toward tourism development in the Big Bend area, Texas.* Unpublished PhD dissertation, Texas A&M University, College Station.

Egli, R. (1995). Climatic effects of air traffic. *Environmental Conservation, 22,* 196-198.

Environmental Protection Agency (EPA). (2009). *Environmental justice home.* www.epa.gov/compliance/environmentaljustice/index.html

Euromonitor. (2007). *Top 150 city destinations: London leads the way.* www.euromonitor.com/Top_150_City_Destinations_London_Leads_the_Way

Evans, G. (1994). Whose culture is it anyway? Tourism in Greater Mexico and the Indigena. In A.V. Seaton, C.L. Jenkins, R.C. Wood, P.U.C. Dieke, M.M. Bennett, L.R. MacLellan, et al. (Eds.), *Tourism: State of the art* (pp. 836-847). Chichester, UK: Wiley.

Fotheringham, A.S. (1983). A new set of spatial-interaction models: The theory of competing destinations. *Environment and Planning A, 15*(1), 15-36.

Fukushima, T., Kureha, M., Ozaki, N., Fujimori, Y., & Harasawa, Y. (2002). Influences of air temperature change on leisure industries: Case study on ski activities. *Mitigation and Adaptation Strategies for Global Change, 7,* 173-189.

Gartner, W.C. (2004). Rural tourism development in the USA. *International Journal of Tourism Research, 6,* 151-164.

Gee, C.Y. (1996). *Resort: Development and management.* East Lansing, MI: Educational Institute of the American Hotel & Motel Association.

Getz, D. (1992). Tourism planning and destination lifecycle. *Annals of Tourism Research, 19,* 752-770.

Gilbert, D., & Clark, M. (1997). An exploratory examination of urban tourism impact, with reference to residents' attitudes, in the cities of Canterbury and Guildford. *Cities, 14*(6), 343-352.

Green, H., Hunter, C., & Moore, B. (1990). Assessing the environmental impact of tourism development: Use of the Delphi technique. *Tourism Management, 11,* 111-120.

Harrill, R. (2004). Residents' attitudes toward tourism development: A literature review with implications for tourism planning. *Journal of Planning Literature, 18*(3), 251-266.

Hwang, Y., Gretzel, U., & Fesenmaier, D.R. (2006). Multicity trip patterns: Tourists to the United States. *Annals of Tourism Research, 33*(4), 1057-1078.

Jansen-Verbeke, M. (1986). Inner-city tourism: Recourses, tourists and promoters. *Annals of Tourism Research, 13,* 79-100.

Jeffres, L.W., & Dobos, J. (1993). Perceptions of leisure opportunities and the quality of life in a metropolitan area. *Journal of Leisure Research, 25*(2), 203-217.

Koegh, B. (1990). Resident recreationists' perceptions and attitudes with respect to tourism development. *Journal of Applied Recreation Research, 15*(2), 71-83.

Lankford, S. (1994). Attitudes and perceptions toward tourism and rural regional development. *Journal of Travel Research, 32*(4), 35-43.

Lew, A., & McKercher, B. (2006). Modeling tourist movements: A local destination analysis. *Annals of Tourism Research, 33*(2), 403-423.

Lin, C., Morais, D.B., & Hou, J. (2003). Case study of the relationship between socio-economic equality and spatial distribution of tourist sites in Taiwan: An application of geographic information systems. *Proceedings of the 2003 Northeastern Recreation Research Symposium,* pp. 177-184.

Liu, J., & Var, T. (1986). Resident attitudes toward tourism impacts in Hawaii. *Annals of Tourism Research, 13,* 193-214.

Long, P.T. (1996). Early impacts of limited stakes casino gambling on rural community life. *Tourism Management, 17*(5), 341-353.

Lu, J., Vecchi, G.A., & Reichler, T. (2007). Expansion of the Hadley cell under global warming. *Geophysical Research Letters.* www.atmos.berkeley.edu/~jchiang/Class/Spr07/Geog257/Week10/Lu_Hadley06.pdf

Mason, P., & Cheyne, J. (2000). Residents' attitudes to proposed tourism development. *Annals of Tourism Research, 27*(2), 391-411.

McCool, S.F., & Martin, S.R. (1994). Community attachment and attitudes toward tourism development. *Journal of Travel Research, 32,* 29-34.

Medio, D., Ormond, R.F., & Pearson, M. (1997). Effect of briefings on rates of damage to crabs by scuba divers. *Biological Conservation, 79,* 91-95.

Metropolitan Pier and Exposition Authority. (2009). *About Navy Pier—history.* www.navypier.com/about/history.html

Mill, R.C., & Morrison, A.M. (2006). *The tourism system.* Dubuque, IA: Kendall/Hunt.

Milman, A., & Pizam, A. (1988). Social impacts of tourism on central Florida. *Annals of Tourism Research, 15,* 191-204.

Mitchell, L., & Smith, R. (1989). The geography of recreation, tourism and sport. In G. Gaile & W. Cor (Eds.), *Geography in America* (pp. 387-408). Columbus, OH: Merrill.

Nelson, A.C. (1986, Spring). Using land markets to evaluate urban containment programs. *American Planning Association,* pp. 156-171.

Nicholls, S., & Shafer, C.S. (2001). Measuring accessibility and equality in a local park systems: The utility of geospatial technologies to park and recreation professions. *Journal of Park and Recreation Administration, 19*(4), 102-124.

Oppermann, M. (1995). A model of travel itineraries. *Journal of Travel Research, 33*(4), 57-61.

Pearce, D.G. (1981). *Tourist development: Topics in applied geography.* New York: Longman.

Porter, R., & Tarrant, M.A. (2001). A case study of environmental justice and federal tourism sites in Southern Appalachia: A GIS application. *Journal of Travel Research, 40*(1), 27-40.

Purdue, R., Long, T., & Gustke, L. (1991). The effects of tourism development on objective indictors of local quality of life. In *Travel and Tourism Association 22nd Annual Proceedings* (pp. 191-201). Salt Lake City: TTRA.

Radford, J.Q., & Bennett, A.F. (2004). Thresholds in landscape parameters: Occurrence of the white-browed treecreeper *Climacteris affinis* in Victoria, Australia. *Biological Conservation, 117,* 375-391.

Richards, G., & Hall, D. (2000). *Tourism and sustainable community development.* London: Routledge.

Rouphael, A.B., & Inglis, G.J. (1997). Impacts of recreational scuba diving at sites with different reef topographies. *Biological Conservation, 82,* 329-336.

Shaw, D. (2006). Ski bummer. *Daily Grist.* www.grist.org/article/shaw/

Snaith, T., & Haley, A. (1999). Residents' opinions of tourism development in the historic city of York, England. *Tourism Management, 20,* 595-603.

Tarrant, M.A., & Cordell, H.K. (1999). Environmental justice and the spatial distribution of outdoor recreation sites: An application of geographic information systems. *Journal of Leisure Research, 31*(1), 18-34.

Terman, M.R. (1997). Natural links: Naturalistic golf courses as wildlife habitat. *Landscape and Urban Planning, 38,* 183-197.

Teye, V., Sonmez, S.F., & Sirakaya, E. (2002). Residents' attitudes toward tourism development. *Annals of Tourism Research, 29*(3), 668-688.

U.S. Census Bureau. (2000). *Fact sheet: Sturgis, South Dakota.* http://factfinder.census.gov/servlet/SAFFFacts?_event=Search&geo_id=&_geoContext=&_street=&_county=sturgis&_cityTown=sturgis&_state=04000US46&_zip=&_lang=en&_sse=on&pctxt=fph&pgsl=010&show_2003_tab=&redirect=Y.

U.S. Department of Commerce, Office of Travel and Tourism Industries. (2007). *Top states, cities, and regions visited.* http://tinet.ita.doc.gov/outreachpages/download_data_table/2008_States_and_Cities.pdf

Vogel, A. (2005). *Modeling leisure day trips between Berlin and its surrounding.* Paper presented at the 45th Congress of the European Regional Science Association. Vrije Universiteit Amsterdam.

World Tourism Organization. (2002). *WTO think tank enthusiastically reaches consensus on frameworks for tourism destination success.* Madrid, Spain: World Tourism Organization.

Wu, B., & Cai, L.A. (2006). Spatial modeling: Suburban leisure in Shanghai. *Annals of Tourism Research, 33,* 179-198.

15

Leisure Through the Life Span

Erik Rabinowitz • Stephanie West
Appalachian State University

Learning Outcomes

After reading this chapter, you will be able to

▶ explain the terms *development, maturation,* and *learning* and give examples of these from your own life;

▶ explain Piaget's theory of cognitive development and give examples of how this theory applies to leisure; and

▶ explain each life stage of development and give examples of how they apply to leisure engagement.

Vocabulary Terms

baby boomers	formal operational	object permanence
cognition	learning	preoperational
concrete operational	leisure education	rites of passage
deadline decade	maturation	sensorimotor
development	nature	sociology
empty nest syndrome	nurture	

At some point you have probably been curious about one or more aspects of your development or the development of others. Maybe you have wondered what the world looks like to an infant. Do babies actually think that when you play peekaboo you have really disappeared like a magician? Or maybe you have seen older adults in the park feeding the pigeons and have tried to imagine what the world was like when they were growing up. How was it different than yours? Did they have more time to play? Did they have more fun? These are just a few of the thoughts surrounding this chapter, which focuses on leisure through the life span.

LIFE SPAN CONCEPTS

To appreciate leisure through the life span, you must understand a few basic concepts. **Development** is a systematic change in a person that begins at conception and ends with death. The word *systematic* implies that the changes you go through are orderly and patterned and relatively similar to those experienced by the student sitting next you. In some cases, this is true, like the beginning of a heartbeat in a healthy embryo within a month of fertilization, or the ability to walk and utter meaningful words at 1 year of age. Most of these biological systematic changes unfold in a person because of **maturation**, sometimes referred to as **nature**. Another critical component is **learning**. For example, consider the ability of a 5-year-old who wants to learn to ride a bike. Although his maturation must be at a level that will allow him to balance a bicycle, he still needs to learn how to shift his weight to balance that bicycle. A natural progression is that a child learns to ride a bicycle with the assistance of training wheels, which allow the child to better understand balance without falling as often; then learns to ride without the training wheels; and eventually is able to ride without even using his hands. What people learn in their environment is often referred to as **nurture**. Perhaps you have seen the old movie *Trading Places* (1983): Two wealthy older men have a bet over which

Your body and your lifestyle will go through many changes during your life span. How will your choices in leisure be affected?

http://johnfenzel.typepad.com/john_fenzels_blog/images/2008/01/18/wheels.jpg

316

contributes more to the behavior of the characters played by Eddie Murphy and Dan Aykroyd—nature or nurture. Although the answer is not known, we do know that when we combine nature and nurture, or maturation and learning, we get development.

PIAGET'S FOUR STAGES OF DEVELOPMENT

Development is greatly affected by numerous other components, such as cognition. **Cognition** (Latin: *cognoscere*, "to know" or "to recognize") is the process of applying our knowledge and information to the surroundings and situations in which we find ourselves. One of the most important cognitive developmental theories comes from Jean Piaget, a Swiss philosopher (1896-1980) who studied childhood development (see figure 15.1). Drawing on his research, Piaget concluded that there are four main stages in how people come to understand the world.

> Every single one of us can do things that no one else can do, can love things that no one else can love. We are like violins. We can be used for doorstops, or we can make music.
>
> *Barbara Sher*

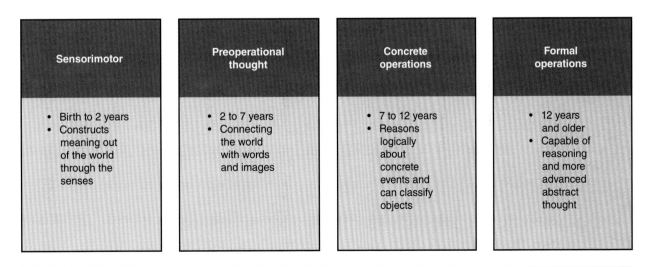

Sensorimotor	Preoperational thought	Concrete operations	Formal operations
• Birth to 2 years • Constructs meaning out of the world through the senses	• 2 to 7 years • Connecting the world with words and images	• 7 to 12 years • Reasons logically about concrete events and can classify objects	• 12 years and older • Capable of reasoning and more advanced abstract thought

Figure 15.1 Piaget's stages of cognitive development theory.

Stage 1: Sensorimotor Period and Leisure Development (Birth to 2 Years)

The period in Piaget's cognitive development theory is highlighted by the development of essential spatial abilities and learning through the senses, called the **sensorimotor** period (years 0-2). Newborn babies' main development in this stage occurs through their sense of touch, particularly through their mouths, because their vision, smell, and hearing are not completely developed at this time. For this reason, a newborn who is given a new toy will often place the toy immediately in her mouth. As their senses mature during infancy, infants begin to uncover new experiences with their other senses. For example, at 8 to 9 months of age, infants begin to develop **object permanence**, the awareness that objects continue to exist even when they are no longer visible, which may explain why the game peekaboo is so much fun for an infant (Santrock, 1995).

Stage 2: Preoperational Stage and Leisure Development (2-7 Years)

The second stage of Piaget's cognitive development theory is the **preoperational** stage (years 2-7). During this period the child learns to develop language and begins representing things with words and images. As such, young children have inventive minds and primarily learn through imitation and play (Santrock, 1995). Children in this age often pretend they are parents, doctors, teachers, cops, robbers, or pilots. Do you remember who you pretended to be at that age? If not, ask a parent or older relative who might remember. Participating in this type of play helps children learn the various roles they observe so that they can begin putting together the "big picture." For instance, someone who is 4 years old might understand who her father is, who her brother is, and who her aunt is but not that her aunt is her father's sister. That one might have even taken you a moment to decipher!

Stage 3: Concrete Operational Stage and Leisure Development (7-11 Years)

The **concrete operational** stage takes place when children are in elementary school. As children begin to transition from the preoperational stage into the concrete operational stage, they begin to understand high-order thinking and use logic. Thus, a child in this stage is interested in formulating strategies about an opponent (player or team) and anticipating an opponent's tactics. This can be seen on the Little League field when the players in the infield move forward to accommodate a batter in a situation with a high probability of bunting (Santrock, 1995).

Stage 4: Formal Operational Stage and Leisure Development (12+ Years)

The last of Piaget's stages is for children ages 12 and older who are now **formal operational** thinkers. At this period, a person can recognize and identify a problem, state numerous alternative hypotheses, carry out procedures to collect information about the problems to be studied, and test hypotheses. Children at this age are often very interested in collecting things (e.g., comic books, baseball cards, shells, postcards, stuffed animals, or dolls) (Santrock, 1995).

Let's consider each of the four stages of child development in a single example. Imagine a family of four children (ages 1, 4, 8, and 12) sitting at a table, each with two cookies. If the 4-year-old steals a cookie from the 1-year-old, the 1-year-old would not get upset unless she had touched the cookie (or placed the cookie in her mouth), because being at the sensorimotor stage, the 1-year-old did not understand that the cookie was really there until she connected to the cookie through touching it. Having stolen one of the 1-year-old's cookies, the 4-year-old brags to the 8-year-old that she now has three cookies. At this point, the 8-year-old, using concrete operational thinking, smashes the two cookies on his plate into numerous smaller pieces and offers a trade with the 4-year-old, who has three cookies. Seeing more cookie pieces on the 8-year-old's plate, the 4-year-old agrees to the trade because, as a preoperational thinker, she believes that she has gotten the better end of the deal. The 8-year-old then brags to the 12-year-old that he now has three cookies, at which point the oldest child then uses formal operational thinking and threatens to tell their mother if she is not given the extra cookie. The 12-year-old will then either eat the extra cookie or return the cookie to the 1-year-old.

SOCIAL DEVELOPMENT AND LEISURE DEVELOPMENT

Much like cognitive development, social development also has a significant role in understanding leisure throughout our life span. In **sociology**, scholars study the human interactions, rules, and processes that connect and divide people not only as individuals but also as members of associations, groups, and institutions. Understanding leisure through the life span is important because people believe

©Human Kinetics

Team sports provide kids with opportunities for social interactions, leading to benefits like improved self-esteem and discipline.

there are many benefits to leisure. For example, parents all over the world enroll their kids in numerous team sports activities, such as Little League baseball, to give their children the benefits of social interactions. These parents believe that these social experiences will likely improve the self-esteem and communication skills of the athletes, help them develop discipline and gain a respect for others, and assist them in building teamwork skills and learning to deal with adversity (Tischler, 2006).

Leisure is also influenced by many sociological factors. Where a person grows up and what opportunities he had in his community have a significant impact on the leisure activities that he participates in as an adult. For instance, people who are raised in warm climates are less likely to enjoy playing hockey than those raised in cold climates. Research has found that approximately one half of adults' current leisure activities are begun in childhood (Iso-Ahola et al., 1994). For example, many adults who enjoy camping were first exposed to camping when they were children.

One of the most important theories related to leisure and life span development comes from Erik Erickson, who created an eight-stage theory of psychosocial development, which combines psychology and social development. His theory presents two extremes (trust vs. mistrust) at each stage and postulates that each person must accommodate each extreme equally before moving onto the next life stage.

Leisure Development of Young Children (Ages 3-8)

Let's take stock of your development that brought you to where you are today and consider the role that leisure had on that development. At the age of 6 to 8 years, most of a person's physiological development is centered on the use of large muscles versus fine motor control. Energy levels at this age often run the gamut, going through moments of extreme activity to great needs for rest periods (Carlson et al., 2008). Additionally, because most people are cognitively transitioning from preoperational to concrete operational, attention spans are limited and there is a failure to truly understand risk, resulting in a peak of accidents for people in this age group. For example, did you know any kid who tied a cape around his neck and jumped from a place higher than he should have? Was it you?

Because this is a very exploratory time, learning and fun are interconnected. This is the age at which kids begin to seek the approval of others and look for opportunities to impress. The initial roles in a group (i.e., leader, follower, loner, athlete, or underachiever) are being established, and children in this stage view rules as edicts passed down from positions of authority. Many children at this age are looking for opportunities that provide a sense of autonomy and independence and are battling with balancing industry and inferiority. For example, kids at this age are beginning to be more competitive, but at the same time they can become easily frustrated.

From a leisure perspective, most kids this age are seeking opportunities to participate in activities that have gross motor components (hopscotch, jumping rope, skipping, and more challenging playground components like monkey bars), peer interaction (freeze tag, duck-duck-goose), problem solving (puzzles, building things, television tag), creativity (coloring, painting, building things with blocks, playing with puppets, dressing up, playing in fantasy worlds), and lots of socialization (dress-up, role playing: house, doctor, teacher). Because of this, playgrounds should not be built with a theme, such as a pirate ship, because it is difficult for kids to pretend that a pirate ship is a spaceship, whereas an unthemed playground can be a pirate ship or a space ship. One of the reasons that video games are so popular is that they allow children to solve problems at their own pace with increasingly difficult tasks to match their increasing skills, perhaps one of the reasons children are spending an increasing amount of time in front of the computer or television.

Group roles begin to take shape in young children. Here, the leader emerges.

Leisure Development of Children (Ages 9-10)

From 9 to 10 years of age is a time when the body is preparing for puberty. At the same time, kids begin to desire more independence. For example, kids can now get up in the morning and make their own breakfast. Unfortunately, they often do not have the maturity to make the best long-term choices so they may select a heavily sugar-based cereal rather than something more nutritious. As a result, this age is a very critical time for obesity-related issues. Luckily, the need for frequent rest periods is almost completely gone and stamina has increased enough to give these kids the energy to burn off any poor morning choices. At this time we begin to see slight gender differences in motor skills, with the girls beginning to mature faster than the boys. As such, girls this age at the playground may be faster or better athletes than boys.

Meanwhile, children at this age begin to separate and play within groups of their own genders. You may remember that this was when you contracted "cooties" on the playground. This is also when athletic girls were called "tomboys" for participating with the boys in typically male-dominated activities, such as tackling ball games. For most, the novelty of school and learning is beginning to wane, as perfecting skills becomes more difficult, homework responsibilities increase, and pressures to succeed from teachers and parents begin to rise. The automatic respect for these authority figures and the interest in following of rules are quickly diminishing, whereas the need to impress others, especially peers, is very high. Interestingly, "best friends" change often and beginnings of mob mentality and bullying can be found during this time.

Children from 9 to 10 years of age have improved stamina, which allows for longer, uninterrupted bouts of activity. Girls are beginning to mature faster than boys, which may make them better athletes.

Leisure Development of Tweens (Ages 10-14)

At ages 10 to 14 years, puberty starts, with the average onset for girls at ages 10 to 12 and the average onset for boys at ages 12 to 14. This is a period of rapid physical maturation, as kids' bodies go from those that resemble children to those that resemble adults. Although the physiological changes occurring at this time are too expansive for this text to cover in depth, they can be summarized by an increase in hormonal production that fuels extreme growth in the brain, bones, muscles, skin, breasts, and reproductive organs.

Emotional and intellectual changes are also strong during this time. Because of the significant increases in hormones, youth at this age are highlighted by extreme mood swings. Mentally, this is a time of transition from concrete operational thoughts to the beginning of formal operational thought and testing hypothesis and mental manipulations. In addition, a true sense of humor begins to form. Meanwhile, this is the time that people begin to create their identity—determine who they are. As such, they may be sexually confused or lacking in self-concept and self-respect. Recreation programs designed to incorporate and offer opportunities to explore these components are valuable, such as open mic nights (poetry slams, music, and comedy), video games like Rock Band, community service learning opportunities, scouts, lock-ins (sleepovers), opportunities for artistic expression, body image and satisfaction workshops, and leadership opportunities like counselor-in-training programs.

Tweens' appearance and clothing take on much greater importance, and best friends are often mirrors at this age. These kids begin to view gender roles as important components and they are often fickle about who they are "going out" with. The mall and music begin to take on new and significant roles, as opportunities for independence and "hanging out." Tweens need recreational hanging-out space (i.e., unprogrammed space that restricts access to this age group). For example, an ideal facility will include a safe place for tweens to hang out and will offer recreation activities that are highly sought after by this age group but do not necessarily require formal programs, such as skateboarding, climbing walls, BMX bike tracks, disc golf, and video games (preferably ones with "xergaming" components, i.e., video games that require physical activity, such as Dance Dance Revolution or Wii Sports). The beginnings of cliques and ascendance of leaders in peer groups is occurring. To capitalize on these occurrences, recreation agencies should consider offering peer leadership programs and providing youth with membership on recreation advisory boards to ensure that these kids have a voice and opportunities for leadership. Additionally, although tweens tend to look at authority figures and rules as mutual agreements, most will often test these rules. Examples of this can be seen in national data on risky behaviors (see figure 15.2).

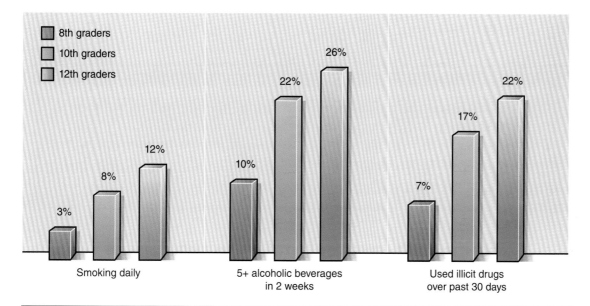

Figure 15.2 National data on risky behaviors among 8th, 10th, and 12th graders.

Leisure Development of Teenagers (Ages 15-18)

Although both genders have, for the most part, gone through puberty at this point, female teenagers are still ahead of their male counterpoints in almost every developmental area. These teenagers' behaviors and thoughts are typically consumed with gender roles, occupational testing, their place and roles in society, sexual identity, and a desire to please their peers. Identity and role confusion therefore remain critical to their psychosocial development. Cliques begin to form, such as jocks, nerds, hipsters, burnouts, and emos, and the desire to fit in is extremely high. This is especially evident when considering movies that target this age group. Examples of this include *High School Musical, Never Been Kissed, Mean Girls,* and the teen movie spoof *Not Another Teen Movie*. Even the popular teen singers Britney Spears and Mandy Moore have starred in their own teen movies, *Crossroads* and *A Walk to Remember*. Teenagers at this time are continually testing the rules of society (as in the classic movie *Breakfast Club*) and looking for opportunities, or

rites of passage, where they will be considered as adults rather than children. Cars take on an essential role because they allow for opportunities to participate in unsupervised activities. Along with this opportunity to make choices comes the potential for poor decision making and lifelong mistakes. This is perhaps compounded when teenagers have a great deal of time to fill and boredom becomes a significant problem (e.g., 46.8% have reported having had sexual intercourse and as many as 2.2% of 15- to 17-year-old females in the United States are having children).

In terms of screen time, the average child will watch 8,000 murders on TV before finishing elementary school, and by age 18 the average American has seen 200,000 acts of violence on TV, including 40,000 murders. Meanwhile, obesity among Americans has reached epidemic proportions, with approximately two thirds of Americans weighing in as overweight or obese. Teenagers, therefore, need a lot of **leisure education** to (1) inform them of opportunities to enhance the quality of their lives through leisure; (2) provide an understanding of opportunities, potentials, and challenges in their lives and leisure time; and (3) help them gain knowledge and skills so they can choose to make leisure a positive experience in their lives.

Leisure Development of Emerging Adults (Ages 18-25)

The typical college student is experiencing what is likely to be her first extended period away from home and initial taste of true independence, sometimes called "flying the coop." College is a very exciting, and ideally enlightening, experience for its students. You are completely an adult physically, using formal operational thinking and acting autonomously as an individual. Weighing heavily on the minds of most college students is what they are going to do when they "grow up." Thoughts of this nature focus not only on what occupation will be pursued but also on finding a life partner. Although you may not believe it at this time, college students have more free time and more disposable income than almost any other age, with the exception that due to the poor U.S. economy some college students are attending from home, and many more than previously are working their way through school. But for the most part opportunities for leisure exploration are numerous and college life has a significant influence on leisure behavior, particularly on the acquisition of new activities. One only has to open a school newspaper, click on a Web page, or look at campus billboards to see the numerous opportunities in the form of intramural sports, outdoor recreation trip outings, lectures on almost any available topic, fraternities and sororities, plays, spectator sports, and many more. Leisure participation in college has long-term consequences: It molds attitudes and

©Stockbyte

There are many kinds of leisure and recreation opportunities at college; try to find some that you like. Participation in these activities during your college years likely means continued participation later in life.

behaviors, likely leading to continued recreation participation in later life (Gordon & Catalbiano, 1996; Hultsman, 1993).

Unfortunately, data on the use of leisure time by college students suggest that not all of this time is used positively. For example, the Harvard School of Public Health has consistently found that the prevalence of "frequent binge drinking" is on the rise across college campuses. Alcohol remains the most popular substance of abuse on college campuses. According to the National Center on Addiction and Substance Abuse (CASA) at Columbia University, the abuse of prescription drugs and marijuana has increased dramatically since the mid-1990s. Casual sex has also increased across university campuses in the United States (CASA, 2007).

Leisure Development During Early Adulthood (Ages 25-35)

Once you have completed college, numerous changes and challenges await you. In most cases, your first real job and occupation take a front stage. Often, people at this time no longer see their positions as jobs but rather the first step in their

PERSONAL LEISURE

Many recreation behaviors and activities provide rich recreation experiences, ultimately enhancing your overall quality of life both today and in the future. What recreation behaviors and activities do you plan to pursue into mature adulthood and when you become an older adult? How do you think these behaviors and activities will differ from those of your parents and grandparents?

careers. However, all work and no play can make for a very dull life. For many, the bar scene and college life are now considered childish, and early adults begin to seek out their own social institutions (e.g., finding a place to worship, one of their own rather than their parents' place of worship). The development of long-term relationships and beginning a family are often typical goals. Time is often spent seeking new friends with common interests as well as similar social status, for instance, finding another couple looking to put down their roots or those with similarly aged young children. Common recreation activities include those related to work (corporate outings, golf, softball, or bowling with co-workers), developing family and friends ("couples" gatherings and family outings), finding a mate (dating, working out, playing co-ed sports, such as softball or rock climbing), developing lifelong interests (perfecting a sport or art, learning a new sport or hobby, attending music festivals), and shopping, which may take on a new, more recreational role rather than a role of necessity.

©Yellow Dog Productions/The Image Bank/Getty Images

Unfortunately, about 60% of American adults live sedentary lives, spending an average of 6 hours per day in front of the television and 90% of their time indoors and participating in little muscular activity (Godbey, 2009). Meanwhile, there is an increase in smoking, coffee and soda drinking, and candy nibbling. Research shows that people who exercise regularly at a younger age continue to do so in later life. In contrast, those who exercise only occasionally are more likely to stop exercising altogether as they get older. Health and lifestyle modifications are obviously necessary given the significant rates of obesity throughout the United States. These changes have to happen not only within the individual but also within local communities. These communities need to assess their opportunities for positive physical fitness, raise awareness of the importance of physical activity, and provide educational programs. Federal, state, and local governments should heavily support programs that promote increased physical activity. If governments fail to do so, the long-term effects of these poor behaviors are likely to place large burdens on the health care system of present and future generations.

People in the early adulthood stage often spend time developing friendships with people who have common interests, such as by tailgating before the big game with neighborhood friends.

Leisure Development During Middle Adulthood (Ages 36-45)

This is a time traditionally called the nesting period, because most leisure activities are based around the kids. Parents spend a majority of their time driving their kids from one location to another, attending their children's activities, and

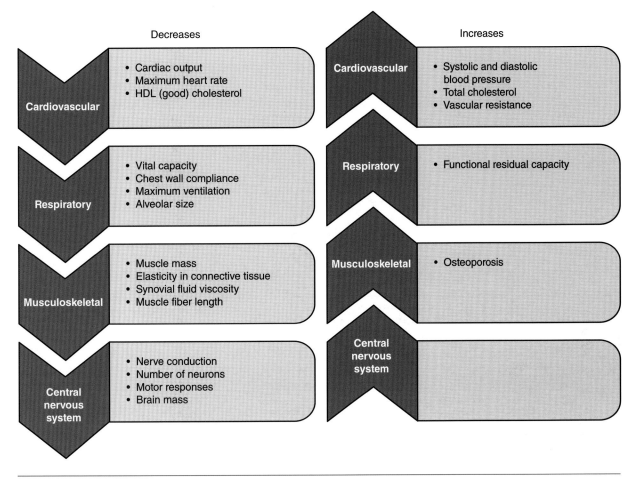

Decreases

Cardiovascular
- Cardiac output
- Maximum heart rate
- HDL (good) cholesterol

Respiratory
- Vital capacity
- Chest wall compliance
- Maximum ventilation
- Alveolar size

Musculoskeletal
- Muscle mass
- Elasticity in connective tissue
- Synovial fluid viscosity
- Muscle fiber length

Central nervous system
- Nerve conduction
- Number of neurons
- Motor responses
- Brain mass

Increases

Cardiovascular
- Systolic and diastolic blood pressure
- Total cholesterol
- Vascular resistance

Respiratory
- Functional residual capacity

Musculoskeletal
- Osteoporosis

Central nervous system

Figure 15.3 Physiological and functional changes associated with aging.

rarely engaging in egocentric activities for themselves. At this time, the physical abilities these parents had when they were in their 20s begin to slide and maintaining their body weight becomes much more difficult. Participation in physical activity by this age group is traditionally done for well-being or health rather than enjoyment. Figure 15.3 depicts the physiological and functional changes associated with aging.

Although participation in life-span sports continues during middle adulthood and gardening begins to increase, people with children often find their leisure interests taking a backseat to their children's sports. Home-based recreation is a major focus, and involvement in civic and community organizations increases, as does these adults' concern for the community in which their children are growing up. Some adults may find that their own parents' health is failing, whereas others find themselves financially supporting their parents. In addition, most middle-aged adults find themselves taking stock of their lives up to this point. Major life changes can happen when people begin to question their overall life quality; some go through an actual midlife crisis, whereas others decide to pick up a past recreational pursuit, try a new one, or even change careers. The term **deadline decade** has been used to describe this time when people's perceptions change; they recognize that their time is limited, and they begin to question how they would like to spend the remainder of their lives.

Leisure Development During Late Adulthood (Ages 46-65)

Late adulthood, on the other hand, is often signified by the **empty nest syndrome**. This is when children leave their parents' houses to attend college. This is the stage in which many of your parents are today. When all of their children leave home, these adults are left to deal with the newness of being alone again with their spouse. Because their lives had been centered around their children for so long, many adults in this stage have forgotten how to interact with one another without their children. As a result, divorce can be common for these adults. For many, however, the increasing free time and opportunity to regain independence lead to new leisure activities. Some adults (especially women) end up taking care of family in later life—responsibility for grandchildren or aging parents may be necessary and must delay the regained independence. Some adults do not have these additional responsibilities (which may account for higher sales of Harley Davidson motorcycles for this age group). For many of these people, leisure time is spent on house renovations to reflect their new interests or lifestyles. Perhaps some of you have found that your old bedroom has been converted into a yoga, exercise, or meditation room.

WHAT DO YOU THINK?

Think about how your parents' leisure and recreational activities have changed. Call you parents and ask them whether they perceive any such changes, and share your impressions with them.

This is also a time when beginning mentor roles are welcomed, especially at the workplace. As such, volunteerism and expertise sharing begin to increase and involvement in social organizations and institutions is high. At this age, some may reflect on whether their life goals have been achieved and may return to placing their recreational interests as priorities. For instance, they may visit travel destinations they previously longed to visit. Planning for retirement begins to receive greater consideration, including the financial ability to retire. Perhaps in preparation for their upcoming retirement, these adults begin to participate in leisure activities that they plan to pursue upon retiring, such as fishing, walking, gardening, adventure activities (paragliding and skydiving, for instance), RV groups, volunteer travel, riding bikes (either road bikes or motorcycles), and using Facebook. For many retirees, retirement provides the time necessary to maintain themselves physically at a more desirable level. This has never been true before for a cohort of seniors, and for some the idea that they may not be healthy enough to enjoy their future retirement years can be disconcerting.

Currently the largest age group of Americans, **baby boomers** were born between 1946 and 1964. According to census data in 2006, 4 million Americans turned 60 that year, at a rate of 7,918 each day or 330 every hour. With such a dramatic increase in the proportion of seniors within society, the entire concept of retirement has changed dramatically. The boomers' devotion to exercise and fitness is a prime example of their influence on society. These people grew up with an extensive amount of recreation and leisure opportunities. They were the first group to have

Little League baseball teams; the President's Council on Physical Fitness was created during their time; and as they matured, corporate fitness centers and private health clubs became numerous. The boomers' motto has been to "work hard, play hard, and spend hard," resulting in consistently overprogramming their days with very little down time. Because of this, many of these people see retirement as a "midlife" event; approximately half plan to launch into an entirely new job or career upon retirement. Likely due to their interests in exercise and fitness, they typically state that they feel 10 years younger than their chronological age. However, they fear aging and, as such, are health conscientious and want to live independently, out of "retirement homes," for as long as possible. Given that more people in this age group are married, they may just succeed in living independently for most of the remainder of their lives. In addition to having interests in health and exercise, these seniors are especially concerned with fall prevention, as many realize that a fall is often a precursor to loss of independence.

Baby boomers will likely avoid activities such as bingo, bridge, and shuffleboard, believing that these activities are for "old people." Similarly, terms such as *community center, adult center,* and *social center* are far preferable to *senior center.* This time might just be called The Golden Age of Aquarius, because these people are very nostalgic for the sights and sounds of their 1960s youth culture. As long as Mick Jagger, Bob Dylan, and Paul McCartney can crawl onto the stage, there will probably be boomers to fill the arena seats. Boomers love the outdoors and enjoy being active in it. Trails and greenways for walking, hiking, and biking are highly favored amenities for this age group. These people love to travel and make an effort to seek educational programming, technology, and opportunities for competition, both low-contact activities like tennis and golf and higher-risk recreation like in-line skating and rock climbing.

Leisure Development During the Senior Years (Ages 76 and Older)

Unfortunately, only 22% of adults at this age engage in at least 30 minutes of light to moderate physical activity five or more times per week and less than 10% exercise three or more times a week at the vigorous level, either of which is necessary to maintain cardiovascular fitness. Perhaps even more startling is that nearly 25% of adults participate in virtually no leisure-time physical activity (Centers for Disease Control and Prevention, 2002).

These figures are especially disconcerting given that research has shown that many chronic conditions facing this age group, such as arthritis, hypertension, hearing and visual loss, and heart problems, can be prevented through exercise, healthy diet, and early care (see figure 15.4). Interest in aquatic exercise activity increases for this age group as people discover that the benefits of exercise can be achieved in water without the accompanying joint pains associated with land-based exercises.

The senior years should be wonderful years; with a lifetime of experience and wisdom should come enjoyment and the freedom to start new hobbies, travel, and meet new people. For many people this is true. For others, however, these years of life are often associated with chronic illness, apathy, loss of friends and spouses, depression, fixed incomes, and, sometimes, bedside religion. As such, depression is estimated to be a significant issue among one third of the people at this age. Furthermore, scientists predict that by 2030, 20% of those ages 65 and over will

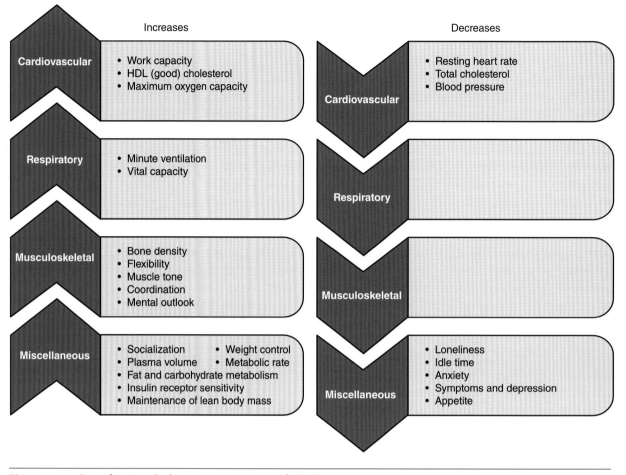

Figure 15.4   Some functional adaptations to exercise in frail elders.

have been diagnosed with Alzheimer's disease (American Association for Geriatric Psychiatry, 2009). Some of the best treatments for depression and memory loss are recreation, socialization, and exercise, especially mental exercises such as crossword puzzles. This may explain why public park and recreation agencies have traditionally taken the responsibility for coordinating and delivering recreation services to these adults, for whom recreation facilities are often a community focal point. Activities that are high in socialization, novelty, or familiarity, such as reading, socializing with friends, attending special events, or visiting historic or natural sites, are popular among this age group.

LEISURE AWARENESS

Locate the career development center, service learning center, or volunteer outreach program on your campus for opportunities to become involved with groups of people in various life stages. For example, mentor a young person in your community as a Big Brother or Big Sister, volunteer to spend time with senior citizens at a local retirement home, get a job as a summer camp counselor or youth sports official, or become certified as a personal trainer or fitness instructor and work with adults on their fitness goals.

Each generation is drawn to some of the same recreation activities at the same ages, for example, hula hooping and playing tag when we are children. Understanding human development is especially valuable for recreation providers.

SUMMARY

Leisure is an integral part of the systematic change in the person. As our cognitive, physiological, social, and psychosocial development occurs, we have choices and opportunities for leisure involvement. Leisure therefore requires attention throughout the life span. If a regimented lifestyle of activity is prescribed and adhered to beginning in early childhood, the long-term benefits into adulthood are apparent. Increases in discretionary time as one matures suggest that humans need positive leisure opportunities beyond childhood. To manage the rising numbers of older Americans and the need for leisure activities throughout the life span, steps should be taken to increase the number of qualified recreation professionals with long-term leisure education and training. This type of leadership will be necessary to ensure that appropriate leisure activities are available at every stage of one's life.

Learning Activities

1. List three of your favorite activities from each of the following life span categories: child, tween, teenager, and young adult. Now explain how each of the listed activities either does or does not fit into the description of typical activity types undertaken by that age group, as described in this chapter.

2. Using your local community or school newspaper, Web page, or activity calendar, identify the activities going on during any particular weekend. Now select an activity in which you would not normally participate (something brand new). Feel free to take a friend or two with you. After the activity, write a short reflection paper (one or two pages) on your new leisure experience.

3. Volunteer to work with a local youth or senior organization to host or assist with a recreation activity.

For additional assignments, Web links, and more, visit the online student resource at www.HumanKinetics.com/DimensionsOfLeisureForLife.

Review Questions

1. How do development and maturation work together and affect our leisure?

2. What are the four major stages of Piaget's theory of human development? Give examples of how leisure affects each.

3. Explain leisure through the eyes of each of the following major life stages:
   - Early childhood (ages 3-8)
   - Tweens (ages 10-14)
   - Teenagers (ages 15-18)
   - The college years (ages 18-25)
   - Early adulthood (ages 25-35)
   - Middle adulthood (ages 36-45)

- Late adulthood (ages 46-65)
- Elderly adulthood (ages 66-75)
- Seniors (ages 76 and older)

4. Research has shown that many chronic conditions, such as arthritis, hypertension, hearing and visual loss, and heart problems, can be prevented through what three things?

Leisure Reading

Brennert, A. (2003). *Molokai.* New York: St. Martin Press.

Cuadros, P. (2006). *A home on the field.* New York: HarperCollins.

Hosseini, K. (2003). *The kite runner.* New York: Berkley.

Krakauer, J. (1997). *Into thin air.* New York: Random House.

See, L. (2005). *Snowflower and the secret fan.* New York: Random House.

Walls, J. (2005). *The glass castle.* New York: Simon & Schuster.

Glossary

baby boomers—People born between 1946 and 1964.

cognition—Process of applying our knowledge and information to the surroundings and situations in which we find ourselves.

concrete operational—Stage when children begin to understand high-order thinking and use logic; usually occurs between ages 7 and 11.

deadline decade—Time when people's perceptions change, they recognize that their time may be limited, and they begin to question how they would like to spend the remainder of their lives.

development—Systematic change in a person that begins from conception and ends with death.

empty nest syndrome—Phenomenon that occurs in late adulthood, when people's children have left home.

formal operational—Stage when a person can recognize and identify a problem, state numerous alternative hypotheses, carry out procedures to collect information about the problems to be studied, and test hypotheses; usually begins at age 12.

learning—Obtaining new knowledge, behaviors, skills, values, or preferences.

leisure education—Teaching people about opportunities available for the use of their free time.

maturation—Systematic biological changes that occur in a person, sometimes referred to as *nature*.

nature—See *maturation*.

nurture—What people learn in their environment (i.e., the effect that people and experiences in your life have on you).

object permanence—Awareness that objects continue to exist even when they are no longer visible.

preoperational—Stage when a child learns to develop language and begins representing things with words and images; usually occurs between ages 2 and 7 years.

rites of passage—Rituals that mark a change to when a person is considered an adult rather than a child.

sensorimotor—Describing essential spatial abilities and learning through the senses; usually occurs between ages 0 and 2 years.

sociology—Study of human interactions, rules, and processes that connect and divide people not only as individuals but also as members of associations, groups, and institutions.

References

American Association for Geriatric Psychiatry. (2009). www.aagponline.org

Carlson, S.A., Fulton, J.E., Lee, S.M., Maynard, L.M., Brown, D.R., Kohl, H.W. III, et al. (2008). Physical education and academic achievement in elementary school: Data from the Early Childhood Longitudinal Study. *American Journal of Public Health, 98*(4), 721-727.

Center on Addiction and Substance Abuse (CASA). (2007). *Wasting the best and brightest: Substance abuse at America's colleges and universities.* Available at: www.casacolumbia.org

Centers for Disease Control and Prevention. (2002). Prevalence of health care providers asking older adults about their physical activity levels—United States, 1998. *Morbidity and Mortality Weekly Report, 51*(19), 412-414. www.cdc.gov/mmwr/preview/mmwrhtml/mm5119a2.htm

Godbey, G. (2009). *Outdoor recreation, health, and wellness: Understanding and enhancing the relationship.* www.rff.org/RFF/Documents/RFF-DP-09-21.pdf

Gordon, W.R., & Catalbiano, M.L. (1996). Urban and rural differences in adolescent self-esteem, leisure boredom, and sensation seeking as predictors of leisure time usage and satisfaction. *Adolescence, 31*, 883-901.

Hultsman, W.Z. (1993). The influence of others as a barrier to recreation participation among early adolescents. *Journal of Leisure Research, 25*(2), 150-164.

Iso-Ahola, S.E., Jackson, E., & Dunn, E. (1994). Starting, ceasing, and replacing leisure activities over the life-span. *Journal of Leisure Research, 26*(3), 227-249.

Santrock, J.W. (1995). *Children.* Dubuque, IA: Brown & Benchmark.

Tischler, H.L. (2006). *Introduction to sociology* (9th ed.). Belmont, CA: Wadsworth.

16

Charting Your Course

Linda Levine • Paul A. Schlag
San Jose State University • Western Illinois University

Learning Outcomes

After reading this chapter, you will be able to

- ▶ recognize and reflect on the physiological, sociocultural, spiritual, cognitive, and psychological influences on your development and well-being;

- ▶ recognize and challenge your perceived obstacles to intentional leisure engagement;

- ▶ learn about leisure resources that will help you make positive leisure lifestyle change;

- ▶ commit to an action plan of leisure that will meet your personal needs, enhance your growth, and help you achieve greater wellness and balance; and

- ▶ evaluate your leisure choices and experiences, celebrate your successes, and strategically modify your leisure plan where necessary.

Vocabulary Terms

balance	locus of control	social capital
gremlins	personal growth	wellness
identity		

©Brand X Pictures

Now is the time to celebrate leisure!

In this chapter we hope to ignite a fire in you to be a leisure explorer, to think about all the gifts of leisure exploration and enjoyment so that you can enjoy a leisure state of mind now and forever more! We're going to take inspiration from Nike's brilliant "Just Do It" campaign. We're going to show how we can all embark on our journey and silence our whining about why we can't do something or what "they" might think. Today is the day to locate and activate leisure.

WHOSE LIFE IS THIS, ANYWAY?

Why have free time if you are not acting freely to use it? The great thing about leisure is that it really is all about you. Unfortunately, far too many people do not realize what a privilege and responsibility this is.

Growing Into *You* at College

Young adults are typically engaged in **identity** development. The late teens and 20s is a time to look at oneself in a new and different way. At this time of life, leisure provides an important context for breaking with our personal identities associated with teen life as well as parental, family, and community expectations. College students are beginning to try out their new adult identity, which involves economic, social, cognitive, financial, spiritual, and physical independence. It's a time to reflect on and learn about yourself and decide what you want to happen in this lifetime and, more important, who you want to be. College is a time for setting priorities, making personal goals, and taking the responsibility to meet those life goals because you understand what you want to gain—physically, cognitively, socially, and emotionally. Campus life provides opportunities to help a young person develop an inner **locus of control**, meaning a perception that the self governs the source of control in one's life. Our leisure is a perfect arena in which to exhibit that we are not governed solely by external authorities. We have unique interests, dreams, and needs, and we can fill them through intentional leisure choices.

The Time for Action Is Now

This last chapter of this book prepares you for the next phases in your life. In this chapter we take all the leisure theory learned, reflect on personal relevance, and marry it to action. By now you should understand the importance of a healthy choice-driven leisure lifestyle. You will engage in self-assessment, leisure education, planning, commitment, and evaluation of your own leisure lifestyle. This book's ending is the beginning for you to launch your leisure ship and commit to perhaps new and different precious leisure that meets your current social, physical, cognitive, psychoemotional, spiritual, aesthetic, environmental, civic involvement, and other needs.

Meeting Your Developmental Needs

How are you doing in the following developmental areas? Are you satisfied with the quantity and quality of these experiences in current life? Following are some illustrations and action statements to illustrate the categories. Look at the following list and rank your level of interest in **personal growth** or progress needed in each of the categories. If you were to commit today to improving your leisure lifestyle, where would you begin?

Socially

- Meet new people
- Improve old relationships
- Spend time with family in new ways
- Enjoy dating in the hopes of meeting someone special

Physically

- Reengage again in a familiar fitness-related activity
- Try a new sport just for kicks, like fencing, BMX racing, snorkeling, or the RipStik
- Change your physical appearance by toning and tightening
- Take a dance class offered at the university

Cognitively

- Stretch your mind through civic engagement
- Read the newspaper
- Do mental gymnastics with old or new forms of word plays and puzzles (word searches, sudoku, multilevel Scrabble)

Psychoemotionally

- Actively chose to be with positive influences
- Participate in a 12-step program to avoid excesses (e.g., Alcoholics Anomynous)
- Read self-improvement books or join campus clubs
- Meditate or try yoga

Spiritually

- Take time to reflect
- Join a spiritual or religious community
- Show devotion through service to others
- Share an attitude of gratitude

> Develop interest in life as you see it; in people, things, literature, music—the world is so rich, simply throbbing with rich treasures, beautiful souls and interesting people. Forget yourself.
>
> *Henry Miller—American author (1891-1980)*

Aesthetically

- Renew interest in a craft
- Change the look of your dorm, apartment, or home
- Go to a museum
- Get a makeover at the cosmetic counter
- Have a friend dress you from your own wardrobe using his or her creative eye

Environmentally

- Sit in a park to study
- Ride a mountain bike
- Ski down a black diamond ski run
- Join a global warming action group
- Increase recycling in your neighborhood
- Go camping with new friends

Civic engagement

- Give back to the community by volunteering
- Get involved in nonprofit organizations
- Canvas for a political candidate or cause

Later in this chapter, you will be called upon to make an action plan for self-improvement and leisure goal attainment. Your top two prioritized areas will lend themselves beautifully to this activity. Some people like to assess their well-being visually in the form of a **wellness** wheel. Take a moment and fill out your wheel so you can get a visual of how balanced or out of balance you are today.

LEISURE HEALTH

A balanced life consists of focusing on important areas and needs in our lives. The wellness wheel shown here illustrates a balanced life where equal attention is given to many of the important needs of life. Take the time to fill out your own personal wellness wheel. Estimate the amount of time and effort you currently give to each of the following needs: social, physical, cognitive, psychoemotional, spiritual, aesthetic, environmental, and civic. Fill in a blank wellness wheel to illustrate how much time and energy you devote to each need. Does your life appear to be balanced? Which needs are receiving too much time? Which needs are you ignoring?

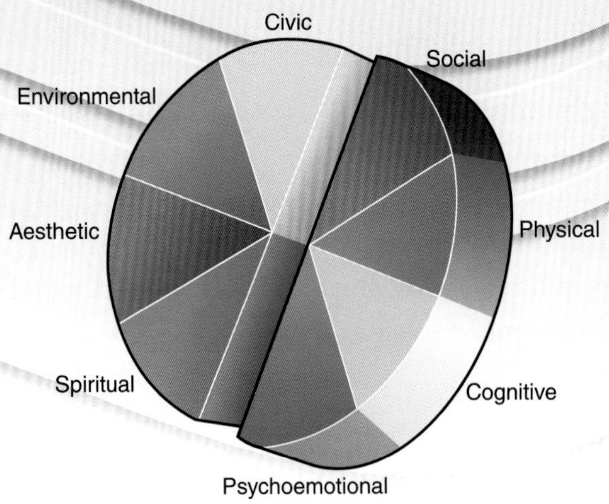

Core Values

Our core values are principles or qualities that are specific to us and intrinsically desirable. Your values represent what is most important to you. Ideally, in adulthood we know and believe our core values so completely that we are willing to speak of them and take stands for what we believe in. Most people feel best when their actions and core values are in alignment. For example, if you value fitness, you feel best when engaged in a plan of steady physical activity not only for the endorphins generated but also because we experience a positive psychological affect when we walk our talk.

What Is Missing in Your Life?

To feel satisfied, many people crave some or all of the elements that follow. Some people's needs are very different again. Does this list represent any of your current needs? What is relatable and what's missing for you?

- New experiences: competition, adventure, learning, travel, creative expression
- Safety and security: spiritual pursuits, religious community, home-based recreation, family time
- Connection: friendship, social groups, dating and experiencing the response of others
- Recognition: advocating a cause, political involvement, receiving praise for a job well done
- Aesthetics: exposure to natural or artistic beauty, cultural involvement, experience with the visual and performing arts

©Art Explosion

Are you feeling stagnant from too much concrete and not enough nature? Getting away from it all to enjoy natural beauty helps us connect with our inner spirit and with one another.

When you pause to assess your current life, what needs do you notice are not being met to your satisfaction? Do you feel happy? Leisure is an area where we can meet those needs.

Holistic Leisure and Balance

Although this chapter acts as a springboard to action, our ultimate goal in writing this text is to help you achieve greater **balance** and well-being. Balanced people tend to reflect, take a deep breath, and evaluate the way they juggle work, school, activities of daily life, and leisure. Such people are interested in leisure enjoyment and believe that doing too much can cause stress and doing too little causes boredom or apathy. They have learned to say no to things that could throw their timing out of whack and to say yes to things that are out of their comfort zone.

LEISURE HEALTH

Do you know when you are out of balance? Where in your body do you feel it? Are you more likely to do too much or too little? Are you more often frazzled and fried than calm, cool, and collected? Beginning with 15-minute changes daily can add up to big lifestyle changes in the end. These changes can be made in the workplace, school, or home and can affect any aspect of your life that could use improvement. Pick one leisure pursuit that would improve your life and devote 15 minutes to that pursuit for 1 week.

We feel balanced when we are achieving the following:

- Living in alignment with our core values
- Giving our developmental needs the attention they require
- Making time to be alone
- Making time for old and new friends
- Including a variety of experiences in our days
- Organizing our lives for efficiency
- Making time for daily recreation
- Choosing activities that promote health and wellness
- Allowing a leisure state of mind to make our chores and work more enjoyable
- Multitasking to save a bit of time
- Allowing ourselves to be singularly focused without outside distractions sometimes

CHANGING OBSTACLES INTO OPPORTUNITIES

Although we profess that we are on a quest for greater leisure satisfaction, most of us fight two kinds of obstacles on our journey to joy: external and internal obstacles. External obstacles are those circumstances that are imposed from the outside. We say we will meet our friends at an amusement park but external obstacles such as the weather, the price, nasty traffic, the boss's demands, and family obligations keep us from going. Internal obstacles are self-imposed deterrents that constrain us just as powerfully as if we wore shackles on our wrists and ankles. Guilt, perfectionism, fear, poor self-image, shyness, and many other internal obstacles can prevent leisure participation or distract us from enjoyment. We want to go to the aquarium but we should be doing homework, or our roommate can't afford the admission price so it doesn't seem fair to go without him. We are invited to a dance but we don't know all the people who are going so we are uncomfortable and unable to take the next step. Everyone is going to the beach but you see yourself as overweight and are too self-conscious to wear shorts or a bathing suit. Does any of this ring true for you? We all must acknowledge our internal and external leisure opportunity thieves and take action to create the leisure lifestyles we want.

W H A T   D O   Y O U   T H I N K ?

List 5 external obstacles and 5 internal obstacles that may prevent someone from pursuing a leisure activity. Now list 10 ways to overcome the obstacles listed. Do you face any of the obstacles you listed? Could any of the strategies you developed for overcoming obstacles be used in your life?

What Obstacles Hold You Back?

If you are like most people, there are many exciting leisure activities on your to-do list. These may be activities you once did and enjoyed but haven't gotten back to in a while. Perhaps there are activities you have not gotten to yet due to some perceived or real obstacles. Or maybe you have no idea what your leisure options are now. What would you do if you weren't doing what you habitually do?

Ideal Versus Habitual Leisure

Do these answers sound familiar or desirable to you? There are so many fun activities to imagine. Some cost a lot; some cost nothing in terms of money or time but they take a commitment to action. There are amazing places to travel and fascinating people to meet. What would you do if you had the chance to do whatever you wanted? Wouldn't it be sad if you never were able to do most of those things? If we don't have a plan, many ideal leisure activities go unrealized. One reason for this is that we are too busy participating in our ordinary patterned leisure to embark on the extraordinary ideal leisure pursuits we imagine.

When students discuss what they generally do for leisure, many typical answers are given:

- Hang out with friends
- Play computer games alone
- Hang out with family at home
- Work out
- Go to coffee shops

- Listen to music
- Communicate with friends using technology

What are your top five habitual leisure activities? What might you be doing if you were not doing the same old thing?

Live Like You Are Dying

A common theme in folklore, music, and literature is the idea of living today how you would live if you knew you were dying soon. The country singer Tim McGraw wrote a song by that very title—"Live Like You Are Dying"—which begs the question how you would live today if tomorrow was not guaranteed. In the song, the individual goes sky diving, mountain climbing, and lasts 2.07 seconds on a bull named Fu Manchu! The narrator also "became a friend a friend would like to have." Guess what? Tomorrow is a gift and not a guarantee, so how shall we live today with the knowledge that today may be our last? Do you find this idea sobering or invigorating? Some people enliven their time here by living from back to front. More simply, what do you want people to say about you at your funeral; how do you want to be remembered? This may inform your actions and the ways you choose to fill your leisure time.

SELF-DISCOVERY

In the movie *The Bucket List,* Jack Nicholson and Morgan Freeman are both diagnosed with terminal cancer. After their diagnoses they head out into the word with a "bucket list," things they want to do before they "kick the bucket." They skydive, race cars, climb a pyramid, and travel the world. If you only had 1 year to live, what would you do? What leisure pursuits would you like to do or master before you "kick the bucket"? These major activities are your ideal leisure pursuits. How can you make your ideal leisure a reality?

Common Obstacles

For most of us, there is a gap between our ideal and our real leisure. We say we are going skiing, to the movies, or even for a walk, but often we do not do what we say. What we notice about the difference between what we might do and what we actually do is a cavernous valley of risk, cost, knowledge, and routine. We get in a leisure rut because our regular leisure is familiar, easy, pleasurable, and comfortable, and we are confident doing it; however, sometimes it is boring! When we think about our routine, we know that it isn't meeting our current identity development requirements. We are aware that greater joy, meaning, and pleasure exist if we stir it up a bit! We hope that this realization will be a wake-up call to action, that you will realize that you have many areas of interest but have actually experienced few of them.

Gremlins

We all have gremlins in our minds—**gremlins** are little nasty creatures whose sole job it is to convince you that the path you are on is wrong, risky, selfish, or stupid. Gremlins are committed to squelching your fun and will do whatever it takes to

©AP Photo/Toby Talbot

Sometimes you need to shake up your usual leisure habits to get out of a rut. Try exploring other areas of interest, such as making clothing art—you may discover a new favorite leisure activity!

get you from taking good care of yourself. The nasty thoughts feed upon themselves and multiply if we do not conquer them with their great enemies: pleasure, optimism, joy, and an attitude of gratitude.

Cycle of the Blues

Another reason we sometimes do not engage in ideal leisure is we are just not feeling up to it emotionally. Pulling yourself up when you are down can be a difficult mountain to climb. Ironically, when you are emotionally and physically healthy and relaxed, you are more likely to make time for leisure. Conversely, making time for leisure promotes positive emotions, physical well-being, and balance, so it is a positive cycle. Martin Seligman, in his book *Authentic Happiness* (2002), describes happiness as consisting of both positive emotions (ecstasy and comfort) and positive activities (such as engagement in leisure activities or meaningful socialization time). So to get happy, we must feel good and do fun things, but to engage in leisure, we often think that we need a positive framework and a bit of joy to motivate us! Taking a walk, spending time with friends, and changing your environment can get your endorphins going to assist your mood. On your down days, is there something that you do in your leisure time that helps to bring you around? How do you get motivated to do something when you are just not in the mood? It is important to make yourself do something, or your blues may very well continue longer than necessary.

Leisure Ruts and Great Excuses

Why do we do the same leisure over and over? A long list of reasons explain our leisure paralysis. When students are asked why they do not change things up for the better, the answers can come in rapid succession. These are typical responses:

- No time
- Don't know what to try—too risky
- Unaware of local resources
- Boredom, which leads to repeated leisure
- Don't like change
- Sheer laziness
- Too much planning involved
- Too far out of my self-image
- Friends will think it is weird
- It costs too much
- I believe all of my lame excuses!

RESEARCH TO REALITY

Go to your university's Web site and locate the main calendar for the institution. Find activities that could help you to grow personally or enhance your life. What typically prevents you from participating in the events listed on this calendar? What excuses do you and your fellow students give for not participating in these events? How can you overcome the excuses or obstacles you mentioned? How else could you find out about activities on campus that could help you grow or enhance your life?

Overcoming Obstacles

The time is now to bridge the gap between leisure opportunities and pesky obstacles. Write yourself a prescription for vibrancy and joy by engaging in the following suggestions.

Prioritize Leisure and Personal Balance

Make time for leisure: "I have no time" is one of the most often spoken excuses for leisure nonparticipation. Juliet Schor, in her book *The Overworked American: The Unexpected Decline of Leisure* (1991), writes that as the value of and time for leisure declines, people feel more pressured and stressed. We thoughtlessly spend not only our time but also our money. Regrettably, we invest in the inanimate when investing in the animate—others, ourselves, culture, community, nature—would offer more meaningful and lasting rewards. Take time from habitual time thieves such as texting or computer play. Notice what leisure we do out of routine or obligation to others. Notice how much time we spend doing nonurgent, nonimportant things. It is time to put leisure on our daily, weekly, or even monthly to-do list!

Put Aside Money

Make a designated bank account just for fun expenses. As an experiment, put all your daily loose change in a huge jar and vow to use it for leisure when it is full. When the jar is filled, you may be shocked to find it contains hundreds of dollars, and with that money you can, for example, take a road trip on money that you will never even miss from your budget.

Invite a Friend or Join a Team

If getting up and going when the time arrives is challenging, invite a positive and adventuresome person to join you. Allow the commitment you have made to each other to keep you on track. Consider one man who rows crew and must be on the water at 6 a.m. For him, there is nothing like knowing that seven other guys are waiting for him to get out of his warm bed and onto the cold water so the team can practice.

Try Things That Will Likely Work Well for You

In elementary and high school you're expected to be equally good in all subject areas, straight A's across the board, but in adulthood that's not the case. As adults with free choice, we tend to move toward our preferences and strengths and engage in activities because we feel competent. Sometimes, we engage in something just for the fun of it, because life is short and we think "why not give it a try?" We also participate in activities just to share a memory with friends; whether you show skill or not, it may be a memorable experience.

Put Yourself on a Leisure Diet

Similar to replacing potato chips with carrots, we can replace a few of our habitual leisure activities with some new colorful healthy choices and then measure the results. Start with one or two changes and you are more likely to know success.

Silence Your Inner Critic

We need to trust ourselves to make safe forays into the unknown. Change the soundtrack that's always playing in your mind: instead of listening to negative tapes, give yourself pep talks again and again before your begin. Ask yourself what is the worst thing that could happen and then realistically assess the likelihood of that event. The best way to beat a gremlin is to engage in joy and positive experiences. You are a leisure explorer, and not the couch potato the gremlin would have you think that you are.

Plan Ahead for Unexpected Obstacles

A babysitter cancellation, the weather, or a friend's change of plans should not stop you from brightening your day. Plan for the unexpected and always have an alternate plan should the unexpected happen—because it often does. Obstacles do not need to be excuses: They can be challenges to successfully navigate toward a goal.

Recruit Leisure Cheerleaders

Only tell you plans to people who will support your new leisure choices. Leisure explorers need cheerleaders. Our gremlins are loud and active enough trying to convince us that our

Photo courtesy of Linda Levine

Be adventurous—you can scale a glacier and live to tell the tale!

plan is unworkable—invite your friends to support you in expanding your leisure. If you find that they are negative, then next time only tell friends who prove themselves as presidents of your leisure growth fan club!

Take a Risk

In leisure we generally use the term *high risk* in relation to leisure activities like bungee jumping and swimming with sharks. *Low risk* usually refers to passive leisure like watching a sporting or theatrical event or quiet leisure such as gardening and reading.

We encourage you to challenge this definition. To participate in new leisure, to go to an environment where you know no one or to try something new, is all high risk! And yet, without taking that risk, we are blindly repeating leisure patterns that are not meeting our current needs and expecting a different outcome! Doesn't that possibility of inviting greater joy and satisfaction make taking a risk sound desirable? As Nike says, just do it. Ask someone out on a date! Try a school opera! Go to the juggling club's beginner lessons. Life's short—what is on your list that you have not dared to do? Try participating in activities just to share a memory with friends, whether you show skill or not. It may be a memorable experience. Isn't friendship worth the risk? Commit to one "high risk" activity and share your success with the teacher and the class. Enjoy the pride you feel just for having done the deed!

Schedule Unscheduled Time

How can it be so difficult to find and hold onto unstructured time? We all need some down time to maintain balance and serenity, but sometimes, as crazy as it may sound, we need to block it out on our calendars to get it!

One study reported that among children 12 years of age and younger, unstructured time declined from 40% in 1981 to 25% in 1997 (O'Sullivan, 2000). Many hypothesize that adult leisure is facing the same trend as those children grow. How can you preserve opportunities for regeneration of your mind, body, and spirit through the opportunities of unstructured recreation? There is a different quality in the spontaneity of play than in structured recreation, and we need both. One possible solution could be to block out evenings or days and literally schedule unscheduled time, just letting the evening unfold as it may. If a friend calls to invite you to an activity that conflicts with your unscheduled time, you could decline it, saying you have "other plans on my calendar." The agenda is to do absolutely nothing, and you may find those times to be wonderful escapes for your overprogrammed life.

Take Yourself on a Date

Have you ever heard of an enlivening leisure date with yourself? You will love the company! You will go somewhere with your best self by your side. Ideally you are doing something special that is a relatively new or a long overdue activity. You can go anywhere and do anything—so long as you do it alone! We recommend spending at least 3 hours. Julia Cameron, in her popular book *The Artist's Way* (2002), suggests taking yourself on a creative date, which she calls an artist date, as a way to awaken your senses. It is a planned meeting with your creative self, guiding you to renewal, risk taking, confidence, idea gathering, rut-conquering, and authentic growth.

Invite Yourself in and Tag Along

Three is not always a crowd! When you overhear friends discussing a leisure opportunity that's new to you, ask whether you too can join them to be a leisure explorer. Invite yourself along to a friend's very different activity—a dulcimer club, a badminton tournament, a BMX race, or a yoga workshop. Go and enjoy it! Fake it until you make it: Be pleasant to all participants, including yourself. Only negativity on your part will make you a third wheel and undesirable future companion.

Unplug

Shut down all technology with an on–off switch. Pretend an entire evening is the first 15 minutes of an airplane ride. Consciously decide to trade a bit of technology time for time with people face to face. Get off the superhighway of modern leisure called the Internet and invest in **social capital** like a pet therapy program with your dog, a cultural group meeting, a hunger project, or political activism. You might be surprised how great it feels to put yourself out there with real people who are taking action for the common good.

Be a Lifelong Learner

Take a class just for fun; college campuses and communities are chock full of activities that may interest you. In college and in the community, you might take courses like ceramics, rock climbing, American Sign Language, digital photography, scuba diving, face painting, scrapbooking, karate, and many more. Some of those activities could become life-long leisure. Be sure to also consider informal learning—visit a museum, a library, or a performing or cultural event that gets you interested in new things and can lead to a new leisure pursuit.

Some of the preceding pursuits were something I did only once. Even though I found that they weren't for me, I was proud that I had taken a risk and tried something new.

Cultivate a Positive Attitude

The difference between those who live colorful, interesting lives and those who don't more often than not depends on the attitude they bring to every situation. People who choose a positive, open attitude are far more likely to enjoy their leisure, work, and home lives than those who meet life with a chip on their shoulder. Notice we said "choose a positive attitude." Beware of the nasty gremlins, whose sole job is to convince you that the path you are on is wrong, risky, selfish, or stupid. A gremlin's preferred leisure is to ruin yours. Gremlins are committed to squelching your fun and will do whatever it takes to get you from taking good care of yourself. The nasty thoughts feed upon themselves and multiply if we do not conquer them with their great enemies: pleasure, optimism, joy, and an attitude of gratitude really send the gremlins running.

LEISURE AWARENESS

List your top 10 leisure pursuits. Are these pursuits doing any harm to you and others, or are they enhancing your life and the lives of others? List your top 5 ideal leisure pursuits. How would these activities affect your life and the lives of others? If your pursuits and ideal pursuits could do harm, what is keeping you from replacing them with more healthy ones? What are the fruits of positive leisure choices? How does a positive leisure choice affect your life and the lives of others?

FINDING RESOURCES

If you don't know that a form of leisure exists, then for you, effectively—it does not. A person committed to a leisure lifestyle values discovery and does what it takes to educate herself about leisure. Earlier, you prioritized which of your developmental needs could use the most attention at present. Say you want to improve your social life: Where would you look for resources? Where would you go to work on your cognitive, physical, or spiritual development? Might there be overlap in where the leisure opportunities are found?

Finding Leisure That Meets Your Individual Needs

Sometimes leisure opportunities are right in front of us but we fail to see them. They await us quietly but we are wearing blinders, looking only for loud, boisterous, or expensive sports, entertainment, or special events. We are perhaps missing quieter leisure time such as enjoying a picnic in nature, auditioning for a play, throwing a Frisbee in the park, volunteering at a summer camp, or reading for pleasure. Speak with friends and leisure role models about how they find and commit to interesting leisure. There is wisdom all around waiting to be tapped.

©Comstock

If you only think of sports, entertainment, or special events when looking for leisure-time activities, you may be missing out on quieter but equally enjoyable activities.

College Opportunities

College is the great opportunity to explore. Whether your college has 4,000 or 40,000 students, there are countless opportunities, many for free, to meet your developmental needs and create a meaningful life. Naturally you are aware of some academic opportunities like a degree in nursing or business, but did you know there are degrees for people who want to take recreation so seriously they get a degree, or two or three, in it? Many of the authors of this textbook joyously took that route! On all campuses, there is plentiful intellectual, physical, social, and spiritual stimulation in traditional and nontraditional venues.

Campuses offer political lectures, art shows, cultural dance organizations, adventure leisure opportunities, health care, shops, restaurants, financial institutions, fitness facilities, vocational opportunities, and so much more. Some of these services are free, some cost money, and some you have already paid for with your student fees. Campus organizations provide opportunities to try out new experiences, rework old passions, and find what you are seeking as you leave your old life and step into this new one with an open mind. How can you locate campus activities that might be worth trying? Obviously the campus Web site, posters and flyers hanging around, the newspaper and resident advisors, and information desks may guide you. On campus it is very easy to start with your desires and then see whether this thing you want to try is on the menu. A sophomore named Sophie recently expressed a desire to try fencing, just for the heck of it. After 1 day of searching she learned that fencing was offered for credit as a semester course at the university, as a drop-in recreational sport in the student union, or as an 8-week class at the local community center. Matt, a frosh, wanted to join a longboarding club when he arrived on campus. On finding there wasn't a longboarding club on campus, he and a friend learned what it took to create an official club on campus and did so; now the club has a regular attendance of 15 participants. Matt has gotten a lot of exercise and made friends and is very much enjoying his first semester on and off his board.

Don't be afraid to band together to stand up for something you believe in.

Community Opportunities

On-campus activities are generally easy to locate, but some students yearn to get off of campus to mix with nonstudents, children, or seniors. Sometimes a political cause, service learning project, or environmental, civic, or cultural involvement can best be served off campus. Amusement parks, city, state, and national parks, restaurants, racket clubs, and more are available. To find recreational opportunities within walking distance from campus, or farther, widen your search by checking the Internet and Yellow Pages, asking a local resident, finding the visitors bureau, speaking to a travel agent, using a GPS unit, or consulting with a parks and recreation guide.

Creative Leisure Planning

What if you don't know what you want to try? Creativity and play experts suggest warming up the mind by brainstorming so that good ideas can flow. Brainstorming is a method of allowing all ideas to be validated and added to the written list without judgment from self or others. To make your own ABCs of leisure, simply free-associate with the alphabet whatever recreational activity comes to mind. A is for airplane (flying, models whatever), B is for boxing, and so on. A sample list follows—then it is your turn!

- African dance
- BMX racing
- CPR class
- Dominos
- Engage in civic activities
- Family time
- Grow a plant
- Hockey game
- Ice skating
- Journal article
- Karate
- Line dancing
- Marathon and then a massage
- Nap
- Oktoberfest
- Poetry night
- Quebec—practice French
- Raku pottery
- Social networking
- Text someone new who I am dying to talk to
- Use your brain
- Volunteer
- Water skiing and water rafting
- Xbox
- Yoga
- Zip line (bet you thought we would say zoo!)

PERSONAL LEISURE

Make an ABC of recreation activities that are appealing to you. Pull out five of the activities that interest you most. Are these activities something that can be done where you live? Would your friends and family support your pursuit of these activities? What planning would need to be done to participate in your list?

FORM AN ACTION PLAN

To create the life you want begins with reflection on your mission and goals. After reflection, you need to embark on a focused action plan. Creating a meaningful life does not happen accidentally. It requires thoughtful strategic planning and committed, faithful execution. Perhaps it sounds like a lot of work, but realizing that the internal locus of control allows for you to chart your future is one of the most satisfying of human experiences.

With reflection we know what leisure is calling to us. Through leisure education we have found resources to meet our leisure desires. We are also aware there will be obstacles but are willing to deal maturely with those obstacles to engage fully in our lives. Now we need a plan of action to help actualize our leisure and to keep us on the ship when the going gets rough.

Your Personal Life Mission

Meaning making begins with a personal mission statement. A personal mission statement includes central personal themes including your life philosophy, leisure philosophy, and core values.

A personal mission statement addresses the following questions:

- What actions are you taking to live out what you say your life is about and what you stand for?
- What character strengths do you wish to possess?
- Who do you want to be?

This personal mission statement should reflect what you want to accomplish within your lifetime. This is the general statement that governs the goals and objectives.

©Photodisc/Getty Images

Looking at beautiful scenery with your best friend can be an exhilarating experience. This sort of leisure materializes when one has created an action plan and painstakingly followed the steps through to dream fulfillment.

Some sample mission statements are these: I live a vibrant, abundant, and authentic life. My work makes a positive difference in the world. I live a healthy, balanced life full of leisure and love and positive people.

Sample sentences that may be included in a mission statement are these:

I travel to foreign lands and converse with the locals.

I am physically fit.

I give generously to my spiritual community in terms of my time and financial support.

I spend time regularly in the great outdoors.

Central to my life are my parents, partner, and children.

SMART Goals

Goals relate directly to the mission statement but are more specific and measurable. If you want to live a healthy life of fitness, some goals might be to work out three times per week for 45 minutes per workout. Goals state what behaviors are needed to achieve the lifestyle detailed in the mission statement. Vague goals are of little benefit. The mnemonic *SMART* is used to assist people in creating attainable "smart" goals.

S = Specific: detailed, particular, focused

M = Measurable: quantifiable; a standard of comparison

A = Attainable: can be performed and can produce results

R = Realistic: practical, achievable, accurate, possible

T = Time and resource constrained: scheduled, regulated by time, a definite duration of activity, extent of materials and supplies allowed, accounted for, a deadline

Here are examples of three SMART goal statements. As goals relate to the stated mission, these goals relate to the first mission statement above.

Mission statement: I travel to foreign lands and converse with the locals.

Goal 1: I will travel in Peru for a month during the summer after graduation.

Goal 2: I will communicate well enough in Spanish to perform all conversations with natives in Spanish while in Peru.

Goal 3: The cost for language classes and materials will not exceed $700.

Take a moment and assess these goals. Are they specific? Can you measure the results? Are they attainable and realistic? Is it clear in what time frame and with what resources the goals will be accomplished? How would you improve these goals so they are of the most benefit to the wannabe world traveler? She says that she wants to be a world traveler, so goals are of the utmost importance to get her to Peru right after graduation. If not, she may remain an armchair tourist, watching foreign lands on TV instead.

Action Plans

The next step in the leisure commitment process requires you to detail the activities and actions necessary to accomplish the goal. Revisit the prioritization you did of your developmental needs earlier in the chapter. Focus on your top two needed areas for improvement, and create a goal from that list that will bring you closer to your life mission. Written action plans can be done in a number of ways but we offer this sample and template for your use. It may seem tedious to give a leisure idea this much thought and attention, but well-thought-out, written goals and tactics to reach the goals are far more likely to be reached than those goals not written. Don't just think it—ink it!

Life mission statement: This statement should reflect what you want to accomplish within your life.

SMART goal: Writing SMART (specific, measurable, attainable, realistic, time and resource constrained) goals allows you to see clearly what it will take to make the dream a reality.

Rationale for goal: Note the importance of the goal to physical, cognitive, social, cultural, psychological, emotional, financial, and spiritual well-being.

SMART objectives: This is the most important aspect of the action plan because it outlines what must be done to reach the goal. Specific methods and tactics should be thought through with care.

Baby steps: Set small goals for change, procedures, and assignments to make sure the larger goal is met.

Deadlines: Allocate time for completion of the objectives to reach the goal.

Barriers to leisure: Note potential physical, psychological, or cognitive obstacles that could block progress.

Plan to overcome barriers: Make a contingency plan and list tactics to overcome obstacles.

Benefits to leisure goal: Note the positive results expected from goal success.

Cost (in money and time): State the allowable money and time for the goal to be achieved. A cost and resource constraint ensures that the return on investment is logical and acceptable.

Persons involved: Identify others involved in the plan. Others can assist with achieving the objectives, but only you are held responsible for goal achievement. Never intertwine and limit leisure goals such that your success is determined by anyone but you.

Resources and supports: List the resources or support that you need to be successful. Identify the exact resources available to you in terms of individuals, transportation, motivation, communities, skills, and money.

Success factors: Identify attitudes and behaviors that are crucial for success. These can correlate with specific tasks or may apply to the whole plan.

Goal completion date: Determine the exact time and date the goal will be achieved. Precise date and times encourage the activity.

Reward for success: Offer yourself a carrot that may help motivate you, besides the intrinsic joy of goal accomplishment.

Reflections: Note how you expect to feel after you accomplish your leisure goal.

Implement the plan: After planning your actions, start living them!

This is the fun part! Make a list and share your accomplishments with others around you. Introduce friends to your new pursuits to help them break out of their own leisure ruts. Note the elevated mood you have after following through on your commitments, even separate from the fun of engaging in the leisure itself. The written plan will help you transition into the person you want to be. You can use this action plan in your future as you adjust and readjust to life's many exciting opportunities. Imagine collaborating on leisure plans with a partner. How would you both feel about creating the most amazing weekend, which involved five first-time leisure pursuits for you both?

MONITOR, EVALUATE, AND MODIFY YOUR LEISURE EXPERIENCE

Now that you are in the leisure experience, it is important to monitor progress made at specific intervals. Monitoring confirms that the time and effort pay off in achieving the intended results. Midcourse evaluation allows for needed adjustments to ensure success. "How's it working for you?" asks the TV psychologist Dr. Phil. Are you going to the gym, saving for your trip, asking people on dates, or meditating 3 days a week as you stated in your plan? No? Then stay flexible. Revisit and revise the plan—it's your plan after all. Circumstances change, and so should your plans, objectives, and tactics; however, stay as true as possible to your mission and goals. If the goal is important it should not be easily changed just because something isn't working. Instead, revisit your tactics for achieving the goal. Your creative ideas can enhance your chances for success, so bask in the possibility of this leisure experience and figure out how to make it happen. Staying motivated is a common leisure challenge, but focusing on your mission, goals, action plan, and techniques for overcoming obstacles may be just what you need to get yourself in gear once again.

When you keep the commitment to goals and rework the tactic to actualize your plan, you are being honest and true to yourself. Research suggests that if you make your commitment known to yourself as well as to others, you are more likely to keep it. Being able to report success to those you shared your dream with adds to your feeling of self-worth and joy. Let's face it—the cheering crowd at the end of the marathon or the applause when the curtains fall after a performance are wonderful, even if they are not the primary motivators.

Beware of obstacles, and have a plan to manage them. Review the many tips in this chapter to help you think creatively about staying on track, and you will go far. If you are engaging in a new activity, you are more likely to stay committed if a friend signs up too. You are more likely to stay committed if an economic commitment is involved. By foreseeing challenges, you can solve the challenge before it begins.

SUMMARY

Balanced people reflect, affirm themselves, and celebrate their successes. You can become a leisure explorer and also serve as a leisure advocate and role model for others. Pat yourself on the back when you make positive changes. You can chart your course and live it at the helm. May your leisure journey surpass your greatest expectations.

Learning Activities

1. For each area of development (social, physical, cognitive, psychoemotional, spiritual, aesthetics, environmental, and civic engagement), list two recreational activities that would help you grow.

2. Using the list you created from question 1, discuss what obstacles might prevent you from participating in those activities. Develop strategies for overcoming those obstacles.

3. Locate five Web sites that list recreational opportunities in your area. Choose two events or activities from each Web site that interest you and list them. Rank the 10 events and activities you listed with your most desirable being

first. Commit to participating in at least two of the events or activities you listed. Be prepared to discuss during class which events and activities you participated in.

4. Develop a personal mission statement following the principles set forth in this chapter. Formulate six SMART goals related to your mission statement and leisure choices. Develop a leisure action plan to help you achieve those goals, and come to class prepared to share your plan.

For additional assignments, Web links, and more, visit the online student resource at www.HumanKinetics.com/DimensionsOfLeisureForLife.

Review Questions

1. What physiological, sociocultural, spiritual, cognitive, psychological, and additional factors influence your development and well-being?

2. What are some perceived obstacles that get in the way of intentional leisure engagement?

3. What have you learned about leisure resources that affect positive leisure lifestyle change?

4. What is your action plan of leisure that will meet personal needs and enhance growth while accessing greater wellness and balance?

Leisure Reading

Albom, M. (1997). *Tuesdays with Morrie: An old man, a young man, and life's greatest lesson.* New York: Doubleday.

Edgerton, C. (2003). *Lunch at the Piccadilly.* Chapel Hill, NC: Algonquin Books.

Fox Rogers, S. (2005). *Solo: On her own adventure* (2nd ed.). Berkeley, CA: Seal Press.

Gardner, C., Troupe, Q., & Rivas, M.E. (2006). *The pursuit of happiness.* New York: Amistad.

Hyde, C.R. (1999). *Pay it forward.* New York: Simon & Schuster.

Lewis, B.A., & Espeland, P. (1992). *Kids with courage: True stories about young people making a difference.* Minneapolis: Free Spirit.

Pausch, R., & Zaslow, J. (2008). *The last lecture.* New York: Hyperion.

Seligman, M.E.P. (2002). *Authentic happiness: Using the new positive psychology to realize your potential for lasting fulfillment.* New York: Free Press.

Stein, H. (2004). *The girl watchers club: Lessons from the battlefields of life.* New York: HarperCollins.

Glossary

balance—A stable, calm state of the emotions. A satisfying arrangement marked by even distribution of elements and characterized by the display of symmetry.

gremlins—Loud, vigilant, negative monsters in our minds that try to convince us that our plans are unworkable and that we are not adequate.

identity—Individuality, distinct personal uniqueness.

locus of control—The perception of the source of control in one's life.

personal growth—The process of increasing one's self knowledge.

social capital—Features of community life that include interpersonal networks, clubs for public good, and volunteering.

wellness—A state of health, balance, vigor, and energy.

References

Cameron, J. (2002). *The artist's way* (10th ann. ed.). Los Angeles: Tarcher.

O'Sullivan, E. (2000). Play . . . for life: Importance of leisure. *Park & Recreation*, October, 98-106.

Schor, J. (1991). *The overworked American: The unexpected decline of leisure*. New York: Basic Books.

Seligman, M.E.P. (2002). *Authentic happiness: Using the new positive psychology to realize your potential for lasting fulfillment*. New York: Free Press.

Index

Note: Page numbers followed by an italicized *f* or *t* indicate a figure or table on that page, respectively. Page numbers in **bold** show where the entry will be found in the glossary.

Robert Barcelona, PhD, is an assistant professor in the youth development leadership program and the department of parks, recreation, and tourism management at Clemson University. Barcelona received his doctorate from Indiana University after working professionally in the field of athletics and campus recreation. He has also worked with numerous recreation and sport organizations in both programming and research efforts and is a member of the board of directors for the Society of Park and Recreation Educators. His research on sport and recreation management has been published in refereed journals, trade magazines, and textbook chapters. Barcelona is also a coauthor of the textbook *Leisure Services Management.*

Brent Beggs, PhD, is an associate professor and the program director for recreation and park administration at Illinois State University, where he teaches undergraduate and graduate courses in entrepreneurial recreation, facility design, the management of sport and recreation, research methods, and trends. Dr. Beggs coauthored the textbooks *Recreation Facility Management* and *Mastering the Job Search Process in Recreation and Leisure Services* and has published scholarly papers and presented research findings at international, national, and regional conferences. Before teaching at Illinois State, he served as a lecturer and internship coordinator for the department of recreation, park, and tourism studies at Indiana University and worked for recreation agencies in the states of Illinois and Missouri. He is an active member of NRPA, NASSM, and NIRSA and serves on multiple editorial boards. Dr. Beggs earned his BS and MS in recreation from Southern Illinois University and completed his PhD in leisure behavior at Indiana University.

Jason N. Bocarro, PhD, is an associate professor at North Carolina State University in the department of parks, recreation and tourism management. He received his PhD from Texas A&M University. He was an assistant professor at the University of New Hampshire from 2001 to 2005. Bocarro has published book chapters and articles in several research journals. He has also conducted trainings and workshops at state and national conferences focusing on youth and adolescent issues and physical activity. Before working in academia, Dr. Bocarro was involved with the development and supervision of youth adventure and sport programs in a variety of places and settings, including London, England; Nova Scotia, Canada; Texas; and New Hampshire.

Kelly Bricker, PhD, is an associate professor at the University of Utah and chair of the International Ecotourism Society. She completed her PhD research at Pennsylvania State University where she specialized in outdoor recreation and nature-based tourism within the program of recreation, park, and tourism management. She has research and teaching interest in sustainable tourism development, natural resource management, and sense of place relative to ecotourism and sustainable tourism. She has conducted research on heritage tourism, social impacts of tourism, natural resource tourism environments, visitor management on public lands, sustainable tourism, and tourism certification programs. She has presented papers on issues in heritage tourism, sense of place, natural resource management, ecotourism, and sustainable tourism. Dr. Bricker has written about sense of place relative to whitewater recreationists and community tourism development, heritage tourism, incentive travel, sustainable tourism, and ecotourism management and issues. She has been a faculty member at the University of the South Pacific and West Virginia University; from 1999 to 2001 she served as president of the Fiji Ecotourism Association. With her husband, Nathan, she developed an ecotourism whitewater and sea kayaking operation called Rivers Fiji, located on the main island of Viti Levu, which established the Upper Navua Conservation Area and Fiji's first Ramsar site. Dr. Bricker also serves as chair of the Interim Advisory Committee of the Tourism Sustainability Council.

Nathan Bricker, MS, is the co-coordinator of the natural resources learning program in the University of Utah's department of parks, recreation, and tourism. Previously, he was the general manager for OARS Inc. Nathan completed his master's of science degree in parks, recreation, and tourism at West Virginia University in 2003, where his educational pursuits focused on management and geography of protected areas. His master's project focused on developing a lease for conservation, the Upper Navua Conservation Area (UNCA), and the Ramsar Wetland of International Importance designation in the Republic of Fiji. Together with George Wendt of OARS, Nathan and his wife, Kelly, started Rivers Fiji in 1998, and still run whitewater rafting and sea kayaking programs in the rural highlands. Nathan started his career in commercial guiding with OARS and Sobek Expeditions in 1984. From that time, he has guided extensively for World Heritage, Australian Himalayan Expeditions, and Sobek Expeditions, which provided firsthand experiences in the adventure and sustainable travel arenas as well as a solid background in the skills required for leading groups safely into a range of unique environments. Nathan has led groups in over 18 countries and holds instructor certifications with the Wilderness Education Association (WEA), Leave No Trace (LNT), Special Rescue Services (Swiftwater Rescue), Wilderness Medical Associates (WFR), and the American Canoe Association (ACA). Nathan has developed and led adventure travel programs to Tanzania, Kenya, Ecuador, Belize, Guatemala, Honduras, Portugal, Yugoslavia, Thailand, Bali, Sumatra, Borneo, China, Fiji, New Zealand, Australia, Nepal, Galapagos, India, and Tibet.

Cynthia Carruthers, PhD, is a professor in the department of recreation and sport management at the University of Nevada at Las Vegas. She received her bachelor's, master's, and doctoral degrees from the University of Illinois at Urbana-Champaign in the areas of leisure behavior and therapeutic recreation. Her research interests include leisure and well-being, mindfulness, recovery from addiction, and youth development.

Lee J. deLisle, PhD, is the chair of the health, physical education, and recreation department at Western Michigan University. He teaches courses in recreational management theory, festival and event management, and sociology of leisure, as well as graduate courses in sport management. He is currently a member of the Society of Park and Recreation Educators (SPRE) board of directors. He has served on the state board of directors for the Michigan Recreation and Parks Association, coordinates student activities for the Student Recreation Society on campus, and provides consultant services to municipal and private agencies. He previously worked as a recreation and parks director in Connecticut for 15 years. Dr. deLisle has contributed articles to *World Leisure Journal, Annals of Leisure Research, Journal of Park and Recreation Administration, Tourism Analysis, SCHOLE,* and *Adapted Physical Activity Quarterly*; he has also contributed to publications for the National Recreation and Park Association and the Michigan Recreation and Parks Association. Dr. deLisle coauthored the text *The Story of Leisure* in 1998 with Jay Shivers. His most recent book, *Designing Special Events,* was published in the summer of 2009. Dr. deLisle enjoys spending a leisurely portion of the summer at his home in Roccantica, Italy, with his wife, Rhonda Larson.

Virginia "Ginni" Dilworth, PhD, is an assistant professor in the health, physical education, and recreation department at Utah State University. She has a BS in recreation administration from California State University at Sacramento, an MBA from Bentley College, and a PhD in recreation, park, and tourism sciences at Texas A&M University. She has been involved in research on a variety of topics, including nature tourism, transportation in national parks, and the experience of flow. Her current research focuses on active aging in outdoor recreation.

Minsun Doh, PhD, works in the department of recreation, park, and tourism administration at Western Illinois University. She received a BA degree in geography education from Korea University in Seoul. Her master's and PhD degrees are from Texas A&M University in the field of tourism planning and development. Her academic interests are in community-based tourism development, geography of tourism, and special events management. She is interested in the balanced development of tourism in communities that involve all stakeholders, including the visitors, business owners, and the host community. She's also interested in how various geographical factors affect tourism destinations and how these places are shaped in regard to tourism-related changes. She teaches courses on concepts of leisure, introduction to tourism, international tourism, resort management, and special events planning and management.

Dan Dustin, PhD, is chair of the department of parks, recreation, and tourism at the University of Utah. His main academic interests center on environmental stewardship and the moral and ethical bases for leisure and recreation activity preferences and behaviors. A past president of the Society of Park and Recreation Educators and a recipient of the National Recreation and Park Association's National Literary Award, he was named an honorary lifetime member of the California Park Rangers Association in 1994 for his contributions to the literature of outdoor recreation resource management and planning. *Wilderness in America, Beyond Promotion and Tenure, For the Good of the Order, The Wilderness Within, Stewards of Access/Custodians of Choice, Nature and the Human Spirit* (coedited with B.L. Driver and George Peterson), *Making a Difference in Academic Life* (coedited with Tom Goodale), and *Service Living* (coauthored with Doug Wellman, Karla Henderson, and Roger Moore) are among his recent works as a contributing author and editor.

Dovie Gamble, PhD, is an assistant professor in tourism, recreation, and sport management at the University of Florida. She is a certified therapeutic recreation specialist and holds a BS degree in recreation from Grambling State University and master's and PhD degrees from New York University. Her teaching focuses on history and philosophy of recreation, leadership, and recreation programs. She has been a longtime member of NRPA, serving on numerous committees. At the University of Florida she has directed the Office of Graduate Minority Programs and served as chair and coordinator of the University Minority Mentor Program (UMMP). In these roles she addressed social functioning and quality of life issues related to the transition of graduate and undergraduate minority students into the university. She continues to address quality of life issues of minority graduate students in her work with the Florida Education Fund's McKnight doctoral fellows. Her research interests include quality for life issues of survivors of catastrophic health problems, with a focus of the role that leisure and social functioning play in long-term survivorship. As a longtime advocate and volunteer for the American Cancer Society, her involvement in efforts to develop and provide programs and services to address quality of life is ongoing.

H. Joey Gray, PhD, is an assistant professor and program manager of recreation and leisure studies at Middle Tennessee State University in Murfreesboro. She has worked and taught in the field of recreation and leisure since 1999 and has designed courses in youth development and programming, campus recreation, and marketing in recreation. Her research focuses on community recreation, youth development, and health and leisure. In addition to her teaching experience, Gray has several years of professional experience in recreation management and special event planning both in the public and private sectors. She has also served as the athletic director of the National Youth Sports Program. Gray has received the Future Leader Award from the Society of Park and Recreation Education (SPRE); the Recreation Professional of the Year Award from the Tennessee Association of Health, Physical Education, Recreation and Dance (TAHPERD); and the Trustee's Teaching Award from Indiana University.

Karla Henderson, PhD, is a professor in the department of parks, recreation, and tourism management at North Carolina State University. She has been on the faculty at the University of North Carolina at Chapel Hill, University of Wisconsin at Madison, and Texas Woman's University. She received her PhD from the University of Minnesota. She has given numerous presentations throughout North America, Europe, Asia, and Australia. Henderson publishes regularly in a variety of journals in the field and has authored or coauthored several books: *Both Gains and Gaps* (with Bialeschki, Shaw, and Freysinger), *Dimensions of Choice*, *Volunteers in Leisure* (with Tedrick), *Introduction to Leisure Services* (with Sessoms), and *Evaluation of Leisure Services* (with Bialeschki). She is currently coeditor of *Leisure Sciences*. Henderson has contributed to the profession in several ways by serving as president of SPRE, the AAHPERD Research Consortium, and the Academy of Leisure Sciences and on numerous state, national, and international boards and committees. She has received the J.B. Nash Scholar Award, the Julian Smith Award, the NCRPS Special Citation, the ACA Honor Award, the SPRE Distinguished Colleague Award, the North Carolina Recreation and Park Society Honor Award, and the NRPA Roosevelt Excellence in Research Award. When not working, Karla enjoys hiking in the Rocky Mountains, running, playing her trumpet, and reading and writing wherever she goes.

Colleen Hood, PhD, is a professor in the department of recreation and leisure studies at Brock University in St. Catharines, Ontario, Canada. She received her bachelor's degree in physical education from the University of Calgary and her master's and doctoral degrees in leisure behavior and therapeutic recreation from the University of Illinois at Urbana-Champaign. Her research interests include leisure and well-being, positive psychology and leisure, recovery from addiction, and professional practice in therapeutic recreation. She and Cynthia Carruthers recently developed the leisure and well-being service model for therapeutic recreation practice.

J. Joy James, PhD, is an assistant professor in recreation management at Appalachian State University. She received her doctorate in parks, recreation, and tourism management at Clemson University. She was a corecipient of the 2009 Society of Parks and Recreation Educators Innovation in Teaching Award. As a lifelong learner, Joy has a passion for innovation, best teaching practices, and scholarship in formal and nonformal learning environments.

Michael A. Kanters, PhD, is an associate professor at North Carolina State University. He received his PhD from Indiana University. Dr. Kanters has taught at Brock University in Canada and the University of Western Illinois. Dr. Kanters' research seeks to understand the role that sports play in the lives of children and adolescents. He is particularly interested in the impact of parental involvement and the association of sport participation with physical activity. His current sport and physical activity research is funded by the Robert Wood Johnson Foundation.

Linda "Rainbow" Levine, MEd, is an award-winning educator and facilitator. She has guided over 50,000 San Jose State University students and international workshop participants who rave about their experiences and personal successes. Linda's enthusiasm and engaging leadership style turn a learning experience into an exciting and enjoyable event. Professionally and personally, Linda lives creatively and abundantly. Her current pursuits include SJSU professor, professional clown, life coach, grief counselor, girls' empowerment camp director, and workshop presenter through her business Surprise Enterprise. Her areas of expertise include leadership, teamwork, life balance, diversity, grief and loss, and play and creativity. Linda received her bachelor's degree in recreation from Indiana University and a master's in education from the University of Cincinnati. For over 20 years Linda, her husband, and pet tortoises have lived in California, where she gets to teach courses with wonderful titles like Creating a Meaningful Life.

Nancy Nisbett, EdD, is an associate professor in the department of recreation administration at California State University, Fresno. She coordinates the community recreation and youth services specialization as well as the Serving At-Risk Youth certificate. Dr. Nisbett is certified at both the state and national levels as a recreation therapist and has been practicing for more than 15 years. Her past experiences include working at youth ranches, camps, and hospitals and as the inclusion director for a municipal recreation agency.

Erik Rabinowitz, PhD, is an assistant professor of recreation management at Appalachian State University. He taught previously at Oklahoma State University and Southern Illinois University. Erik received a PhD in educational psychology and an MS in recreation from Southern Illinois University and a bachelor's degree in social science from Colorado State University. Erik previously worked as assistant to the director of university assessment at SIUC and as manager of WDBX 91.1, a community radio station with over 100 volunteers. He also worked for Project Achieve and Brehm Preparatory School, both centers that assist individuals with learning disabilities. He is interested in research on the benefits of recreation, psychological constructs of leisure participation, and extreme sports. He spends his leisure time chasing around his two little girls. He enjoys skiing, soccer, canoeing, playing chess, playing his mandolin like David Grisman (he wishes), and going to a Dead show.

Ariel Rodríguez, PhD, is an assistant professor in the school of community resources and development at Arizona State University in Phoenix. His responsibilities include teaching undergraduate courses, conducting research, and generating externally funded projects. His teaching focuses on the management and evaluation of park, recreation, and leisure services with an emphasis on community and municipal services. His research focuses on safety behavior, obesity prevention, well-being, and life satisfaction primarily in younger populations. Moreover, he has been involved in numerous evaluation projects assessing the effectiveness of programs aimed at improving safety behavioral patterns, physical activity, and overall well-being of younger populations.

Paul A. Schlag, PhD, is an assistant professor at Western Illinois University in the recreation, parks, and tourism administration department. He has a bachelor's degree in recreation management and youth leadership from Brigham Young University, a master's of public administration from the University of Colorado at Colorado Springs, a master's of education in instructional technology from the University of Georgia, and a doctorate in recreation and leisure studies from the University of Georgia. He teaches courses in the philosophy of leisure, leadership in leisure services, youth and leisure services, leisure services for the elderly, and recreation facility management. His main interest is examining ways in which leisure may contribute to wellness through providing opportunities for dealing with developmental tasks throughout the life span. Paul and his family live in Macomb, Illinois.

Stephanie West, PhD, received a bachelor's degree from Auburn University and a master's degree from Georgia Southern University, both in recreation management. Her PhD is from Texas A&M University, where she worked with Dr. John Crompton. Before completing her PhD, Stephanie worked full-time in campus recreation for three years at the University of North Florida and for five years at Texas A&M University. Other noteworthy experiences include running a summer day camp in Blackville, South Carolina, as part of the Rural Recreation Development Project and completing an internship as a transportation hostess at Walt Disney World. She is currently an assistant professor at Appalachian State University, where she teaches in the recreation management program. She most enjoys teaching leisure promotions, program planning, and a course on the cruise line industry, in which she takes students aboard cruise ships for a behind-the-scenes look at their operations. Her research focuses on leisure-time physical activity. When she is not at work, she enjoys traveling, road cycling, running (very slowly), reading, watching television shows recorded on TiVo, and spending time with her cats.

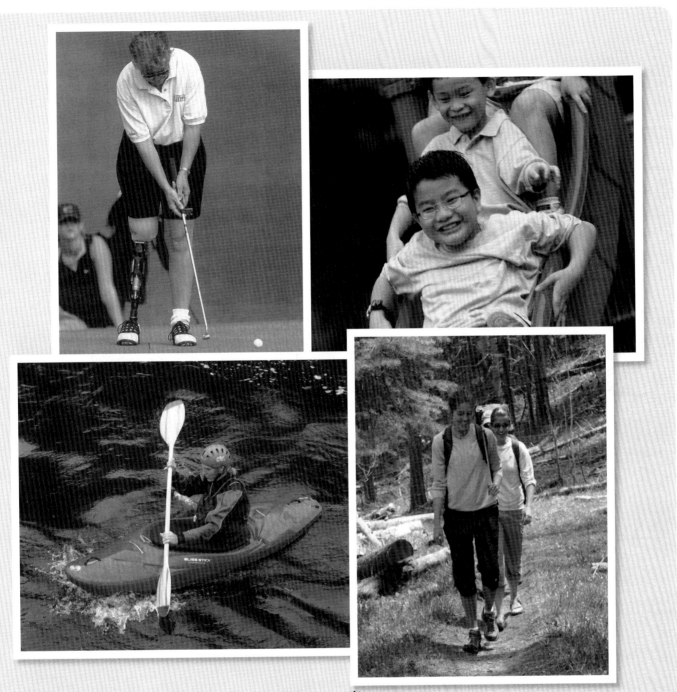

You'll find other outstanding
recreation resources at
www.HumanKinetics.com